SENTENCING—TOWARDS A COHERENT SYSTEM

SENTENCING—TOWARDS A COHERENT SYSTEM

Thomas O'Malley

ROUND HALL

THOMSON REUTERS

Published in 2011 by
Thomson Reuters (Professional) Ireland Limited
(Registered in Ireland, Company No. 80867.
Registered Office and address for service:
43 Fitzwilliam Place, Dublin 2)
trading as Round Hall

Typeset by
Carrigboy Typesetting Services

Printed in Dublin
by Gemini International

ISBN 978–1–85800–650–5

A catalogue record for this book
is available from the British Library

In memoriam

Professor Daniel J. Freed
(1927–2010)

Clinical Professor of Law and Its Administration
Yale Law School

FOREWORD

Once again Tom O'Malley has added to our legal literature in a magnificent publication. He addresses "Sentencing: Towards A Coherent System" from his profound store of knowledge on the topic. It is a book for everyone in the law or interested in it. However, it is not a primer on sentencing. It is an intellectual analysis of this difficult topic.

The various strands which should be brought together in any consideration of sentencing are analysed. Thus there is a reflection on sentencing policy by the legislature, in the sense of the debate that more serious offences should attract mandatory sentences, which leads to the legislature and not the judiciary exercising the sentencing discretion for those offences. The fact that murder is the only commonly prosecuted offence which carries a truly mandatory sentence in Ireland is noted, while it is pointed out that, for the vast majority of offences, the only formal limitations on judicial discretion are the maximum sentences prescribed by law. The author raises the question as to whether the current unstructured system is satisfactory or adequate to ensure that trial court sentencing practice meets the demands of legality, fairness and consistency of approach.

As the author states, the argument advanced in this book is that sentencing, in order to comply with the demands of justice, must remain discretionary and that the selection of sentence in a specific case must remain exclusively a judicial task. However, he argues, to comply with other important values including procedural fairness, equality and the rule of law, judicial sentencing must reform itself in order to produce consistency of approach, to reduce (if not eliminate) unwarranted disparity and to develop rational criteria for deciding on the nature and severity of appropriate sanctions.

This presents a challenge. The author admits it is a challenge to achieve consensus on acceptable methodologies for assessing offence gravity and other ethically relevant factors, on the weight to be attributed to those factors, and on the kind and quantum of punishment appropriate for various categories of offenders. To achieve these goals would result in what he refers to as *principled* discretion. While opposing strict guidelines, he supports the development of measures designed to make the exercise of discretion more structured and predictable. The fundamental justification offered for such structural reforms, it is argued, is that the current system lacks any formal and effective mechanism for generating consistency of approach. We are informed that the available data is insufficient to support any reliable conclusion on the existence or extent of sentence disparity in Ireland. However, he argues that some degree of disparity may be inferred. In addition, the lack of information, including statistics, to facilitate the analysis of the system, is referred to in several other aspects.

The author argues for a sentencing system that is just and which is perceived to be so. He points out that for it to retain public confidence it must be open to fair evaluation, which he argues requires three conditions. These conditions are: (a) sentencing practice must be governed by clearly established principles that trial courts, subject to the supervision of appeal courts, must routinely apply; (b) the principles should be sufficiently detailed to permit the hypothetical informed observer, appraised of all the relevant details, to predict, subject to a reasonable margin of error, the sentence likely to be imposed for a given offence; (c) the system must be accountable in the sense of allowing for public analysis of the sentences imposed and an assessment of their compatibility with governing norms and principles.

The author makes a suggestion to the judiciary in Chapter 3. His argument is for constructive discretion. It is pointed out that criminal appeal courts are particularly well placed to engage in this exercise. He points out that appeal judges are in a position to draw from the collective experience of many different trial judges in order to shape and refine general principles, which would create more consistency of approach on the part of trial judges in the future. He submits that the legitimacy and public acceptability of adjudication, as opposed to legislative direction, depends on the willingness of appeal and review courts to engage in elaborating and refining principles. He argues that when it becomes possible to set down benchmarks such courts should not shrink from doing so, provided they have the necessary empirical data and research findings. He suggests, however, that with or without benchmarks, the appellate courts can do much to transform a largely discretionary system into a more principled one. This suggestion should be given careful consideration by the judiciary.

The author analyses the controversial issue of mandatory penalties. He compares and contrasts statutory and judicial developed principles in other jurisdictions, and sentencing commissions and sentencing guidelines are considered. Sentencing information systems are also discussed. This is an area where the author and I have been involved in a pilot project. The Irish Sentencing Information System (ISIS) was established as a pilot project by the Courts Service Board to plan for and provide information on sentencing decisions. It developed a computerised information system that provides a snapshot portrayal on sentences and other penalties imposed for offences in criminal proceedings over a very limited time. The project was to explore the benefit of such an information database. The author refers to ISIS and he notes that once the preparatory work was complete, the collection of relevant data was very effective and the cost of developing the pilot project was small. The initial collection phase was nearly two years long and detailed information was gathered for 700 sentences from the Circuit Court. There is an information website: see *www.irishsentencing.ie*. It is to be hoped that there will be further funding in the future to develop the provision of information on sentencing through this or other relevant vehicles.

The choice of penalty is the subject of Chapter 8. This is an area where restorative justice may be developed, amongst other alternatives. The author discusses transforming the punishment environment. The success of the Drug

Court in Dublin illustrates the benefit of options wider than the traditional routes of imprisonment or fines.

Early release from prison, which is the task of the executive as distinct from the judiciary, is considered in Chapter 9. It is pointed out that early release and other executive reductions of punishment are motivated by a different ethic from that pursued by judicial sentencing authorities. The distinction between judicial word and executive deed is, the author states, a vitally important characteristic of the sentencing process. Mr O'Malley advocates a more objective and transparent system of early release. He states that the Irish parole system needs to be reformed in a number of aspects, and sets these out carefully.

Finally, the author concludes with a call for structured sentencing policies, principles and decisions and a system is suggested. He submits that the sentencing task is one more appropriately left to the judicial branch of government. He points out that obtaining a system of principled discretionary sentencing depends ultimately on the willingness of appeal courts to adopt a more dynamic approach towards the development of principles and benchmarks.

There is great merit in the call. However, the practical situation of our Supreme Court, with a such a heavy workload in both its own Court and in the Court of Appeal, may mean that it will be only when a Court of Appeal is established that judges will have the time to address fully in judgments the matters raised by Tom O'Malley.

I found this to be a most thoughtful publication and I have no hesitation in recommending it to all interested in the complex issue of sentencing. I congratulate the author on a magnificent publication.

Susan Denham
Chief Justice of Ireland,
Four Courts,
Dublin,
October 2011

PREFACE

The sentencing of criminal offenders, once described by Lord Kilbrandon as the most painful and unrewarding of judicial tasks, is a perennial source of interest and controversy. During the past 30 years or so, many countries have attempted to devise structures to regulate judicial sentencing discretion, without entirely abolishing it. Few, if any, can claim to have achieved an acceptable balance between consistency of outcome and the individualisation of punishment which justice will often seem to demand. Ireland retains a highly discretionary, largely unstructured sentencing system which has undoubted advantages, most notably the opportunity afforded to trial courts and appeal courts to fashion sentences which appear to reflect the particular circumstances of each case. Co-existing rather awkwardly with this extensive discretion are those statutory provisions, so far few in number, prescribing presumptive or mandatory minimum sentences for certain drug and firearms offences. The very existence of those provisions and their apparent constitutionality create an ongoing political temptation to extend their reach to other offences which happen to excite occasional public anxiety. Arguing against such restrictive measures, for all their conspicuous flaws, becomes fraught with difficulty when the only apparent alternative is virtually untrammelled judicial discretion. More detailed and directive principles developed at appeal court level would be much more effective in ensuring that serious offences attracted condign punishment while maintaining the flexibility needed to cater for exceptional cases. Other factors pointing to the need for more structured and principled sentencing include the spiralling prison population, the significant growth (when measured over a few decades) in the number of serious offences being processed by the courts, and the increased number of judges now exercising criminal jurisdiction. This book is not a treatise on sentencing law, but rather a sustained examination of sentencing as a decision-making process. Having surveyed the principal strategies employed here and elsewhere to regulate judicial sentencing, I suggest that the best way forward, for the foreseeable future at least, is to retain judicial discretion but only on condition that it is shaped and informed by more specific principles and benchmarks than currently apply.

Every sentence is the product of judgement. In the vast majority of cases, within our system at any rate, that judgement is exercised by judges who are subject to few constraints apart from the maximum sentence or other jurisdictional limit, and certain general principles derived from statute law and superior court jurisprudence. Mandatory sentences and strict guideline systems are often said to remove or significantly diminish the role of judgment in the sentencing process. It would be much more accurate to say that they merely transfer the adjudicatory function from the courts to the legislature or an administrative agency. When the legislature decides that a certain offence should invariably attract a specified term of imprisonment or a life sentence, it is making a judgement that this is always the appropriate punishment for the offence in question. Those responsible for drafting sentencing guidelines are essentially doing the same, though they may leave more room for manoeuvre by permitting upward or downward departures in exceptional cases. The key question in any sentencing reform exercise is where precisely judgement should be located or, at any rate, how it should be distributed. A commitment to the maintenance of judicial discretion need not entail the assumption that judges should be subject to no more than minimal constraints in the choice of sentence. Justice, after all, requires more than the opportunity to individualise penalties; it also demands a reasonable measure of distributional equity to ensure that similarly-situated offenders do not receive unjustifiably dissimilar punishments. Principles and precedents developed through appeal court case law are seldom adequate to answer both sets of demands. They must be supplemented and informed by broader research-based criteria and benchmarks designed to produce consistency of approach which is not to be confused with consistency of outcome. Variations in outcome are inevitable in any system which is committed to treating offenders as individuals rather than assigning them to actuarial categories without regard to their particular backgrounds, needs and circumstances.

Exactly a century ago, in 1911, the *Law Quarterly Review* published an article entitled "Discretion in Penalties" by R.S. de Vere who described himself as an Irish justice of the peace and a former colonial judge. His trenchant criticism of inconsistencies in the penalties imposed by courts of summary jurisdiction has a familiar ring even today. In fact, the entire article reads like a restrained version of Marvin Frankel's *Criminal Sentences: Law without Order*, published 60 years later in the United States and briefly described in Chapter 6 of this book. The solution then proposed by de Vere is equally interesting. He suggested establishing a "consistent and graduated scale of penalties" which would increase in severity for repeat offenders and which, rather ambitiously, would be drawn up by a specialist commission for application across the entire British Empire. He did admittedly concede that local modifications might be necessary because, to cite his own example, a penalty entirely reasonable in west London might be excessive in the west of Ireland and completely unsuitable to the conditions of West Africa. Thankfully, we no longer have to worry about creating a sentencing system for an empire spanning most of the globe, but we still face the same underlying challenge which is to develop a system characterised by a healthy balance between individualisation of punishment and consistency or coherence of approach.

What is proposed in this book falls well short of de Vere's ambition for a consistent and graduated system of penalties. A century on, we are in a position to evaluate systems of that kind, particularly the grid-based guidelines introduced in some American jurisdictions, and we can see how excessive uniformity may be as harmful as pervasive disparity. Perhaps what we have learned most is that there is no miracle cure, and this is scarcely surprising in the absence of a stable consensus on the precise nature of the illness. Eliminating perceived disparity has been a major concern of policy-makers and scholars in recent decades. A great deal of modern sentencing scholarship has been preoccupied with conceptual neatness and structural control. While it would be grossly unfair and over-simplistic to treat all recent scholarship, or even the greater part of it, as being motivated exclusively by these concerns, it is probably true to say that the ideal underpinning much of it is a sentencing system based on a philosophy of desert and governed by detailed benchmarks or guidelines. Such a system undoubtedly has ethical and practical advantages, but we are also witnessing a growing awareness of the importance of effectiveness. Desert-based sentencing certainly promotes important justice-based ideals, and few of us would advocate the abandonment of proportionality as the primary criterion for identifying an appropriate punishment range in any given case. But, subject to that limitation, we must remain open to the pursuit of sentencing strategies that will be effective in persuading or assisting offenders to refrain from further criminal conduct. The problem, in a nutshell, with a strict desert-based policy is that it may lead to vast numbers of prisoners serving just sentences without the sentences themselves serving any further useful or practical purpose.

Several chapters of this book have been test driven at various conferences and seminars, at home and abroad, during the past decade or so. I am most grateful to the organisers and participants, too numerous to mention, for the opportunities they offered to present ideas about sentencing reform and to benefit from the ensuing debate and discussion. It is always a particular pleasure to work with friends and colleagues from the Sentencing and Penal Decision-Making Working Group of the European Society of Criminology. On this occasion, I am especially grateful to the following who responded so quickly and enthusiastically to various enquiries as the book was coming to an end: Professor Kristel Beyens (Vrije Universiteit Brussels), Professor Miranda Boone (University of Utrecht), Professor Andreia de Castro-Rodrigues (Universidade Fernando Pessoa, Portugal), Professor Ioan Durnescu (University of Bucharest), Professor Martine Herzog-Evans (Université de Reims), Professor Grazia Mannozzi (University of Insubria), Professor Julian Roberts ((University of Oxford) and Dr Cyrus Tata (University of Strathclyde). Professor Stephan Terblanche, University of South Africa, kindly provided me with information on recent developments in South African sentencing law. My thanks also to the very helpful staff at the Yale Law School library where I spent a short time in October 2007 gathering material for this book. Perhaps it is a sign of the times that I must also express my indebtedness to a website, or a blog to be exact. The Sentencing Law and Policy blog (*http://sentencing.typepad.com*), authored by Professor Douglas A. Berman of Moritz College of Law at the Ohio State University, is justly regarded as one of the best of its kind in the English-speaking world, and has the awards to prove it. There can scarcely be anyone involved in sentencing research today who is not constantly indebted to Professor Berman for promptly drawing attention to recent case law and scholarship and for his ever-incisive commentary. Catherine Dolan, Martin McCann, Kristiina Kojamo and their colleagues at Round Hall shepherded the book through the editorial and production stages with their characteristic efficiency, generosity and encouragement. I am also most grateful to Chief Justice Denham for kindly agreeing to contribute a foreword.

Like many others who labour in this field, I had the great privilege of studying sentencing law and policy with Professor Dan Freed at Yale Law School in the mid-1980s. As well as being a wonderful teacher, he had a profound and transformative impact on American criminal justice policy over many decades, first as a senior government lawyer during the Kennedy and Johnson eras and, later, as a law professor at Yale. In 2009, the *Federal Sentencing Reporter* named him one of the three "giants" of modern American sentencing, the others being Norval Morris and the aforementioned Marvin Frankel. This was a richly deserved tribute, as all of Professor Freed's former colleagues and students will enthusiastically confirm. During a memorable visit to Galway in 2006, when he led some graduate seminars, we discussed this book and I am happy to say that he approved both the idea and the title. Sadly, he passed away in January 2010 and I would now like to dedicate the book to his memory.

April 2011

CONTENTS

Foreword vii

Preface xi

Contents xv

Table of cases xix

Table of legislation xxvii

CHAPTER 1 PRINCIPLED SENTENCING: WHY IT MATTERS 1
            Principled Discretion 5
            The Disparity Question 6
            Justifications for Reform 9
              Constitutional justice and the rule of law 9
              Instrumental value of procedural fairness 13
              Public accountability 15
              The European dimension 16
              The prison population 19
              Public opinion 24

CHAPTER 2 THE VALUE OF JUDICIAL SENTENCING 28

CHAPTER 3 DISCRETION AND RULES IN THE CRIMINAL
            PROCESS 42
            The Nature of Discretion 45
            Proper Exercise of Discretion 48
            Discretion in the Criminal Process 50
            Distribution of Discretion 54
            The Rediscovery of Discretion 57
            Influencing Discretionary Decisions 60
            Using Discretion Constructively 62

CHAPTER 4 MANDATORY PENALTIES 64
            The Lessons of History 67
            Mandatory Penalties Today 71
            Impact of Mandatory Penalties 78
              Conflict with fundamental principles of justice 80
              Displacement of discretion 81
              Disparity 83
              Impact on the criminal justice system 84

Constitutional Dimensions 86
   The safety valve 93
European Convention on Human Rights 94
The Sentence for Murder 98
Drug and Firearms Offences 101

CHAPTER 5 STATUTORY AND JUDICIALLY-DEVELOPED
   PRINCIPLES 106
Statutory Guidance 106
Judicially-Developed Principles 111
   Opportunity 116
   Co-ordination 118
   Transmission 120
Guideline Judgments 123
Assisted Appellate Review 129

CHAPTER 6 SENTENCING COMMISSIONS AND SENTENCING
   GUIDELINES 132
The Retreat from Indeterminate Sentencing 134
The Movement towards Determinate Sentencing 138
Sentencing Commissions and Guidelines 141
   The federal guidelines 145
Lessons from the American Experience 150

CHAPTER 7 SENTENCING INFORMATION SYSTEMS 156
Precedent and its Uses 156
Penal Purpose and System Design 164
Sentencing Information Systems: A Brief History 169
Content, Design and Maintenance 175
Data and Narrative 177
A Tentative Evaluation 180

CHAPTER 8 THE CHOICE OF PENALTY 185
The Custody Threshold 190
Short Prison Sentences 200
Alternatives to Immediate Imprisonment 204
Assistance and Desistance 206
The Amount of Punishment 209

CHAPTER 9 EARLY RELEASE FROM PRISON 211
Remission 212
Parole 214
A Right or a Privilege? 219
Animating Values 221

Models of Early Release 226
Steps Towards Reform 230

CHAPTER 10 STRUCTURED SENTENCING: POLICIES,
PRINCIPLES AND DECISIONS 236
Reconciling Penal Purposes 238
Allocation of Decision-Making Competence 241
Policy Formulation 245
Principles 248
The District Court 250
Decisions 253
Judicial Independence 255

Bibliography 259

Index 281

TABLE OF CASES

IRELAND

Anh v Browne [2009] IEHC 29 . . . . 158n
Art. 26 and the Regulation of Information (Services Outside the State for
    Termination of Pregnancies) Bill 1995, *Re* [1995] 1 I.R. 1,
    [1995] 2 I.L.R.M. 81 . . . . 107n
Attorney General v Doyle aka West [2010] IEHC 212 . . . . 18n
Attorney General v Ryan's Car Hire Ltd [1965] I.R. 642 . . . . 158n

Barry v Sentence Review Group [2001] 4 I.R. 167 . . . . 220n
Blake, *Re, ex tempore,* High Court, Nov. 16, 2006
    (*Irish Times,* November 17, 2006) 18n
Brennan v Minister for Justice [1995] 1 I.R. 612,
    [1995] 2 I.L.R.M. 206 . . . . 55n, 213n, 220n

Callan v Ireland [2011] IEHC 190 . . . . 212n
Cox v Ireland [1992] 2 I.R. 503 . . . . 88, 90, 107

D.H. v Groarke [2002] 3 I.R. 522 . . . . 158n
Dawson v Irish Brokers' Association, unreported, Supreme Court,
    November 6, 1998 . . . . 47n
Deaton v Attorney General and Revenue Commissioners
    [1963] I.R. 170 . . . . 87, 90, 92, 224n, 233, 241n, 253n, 257
Dennehy v Independent Star Ltd [2009] IEHC 458 . . . . 48n, 52n
De Rossa v Independent Newspapers plc [1999] 4 I.R. 432 . . . . 45n
Dowling v Minister for Justice, Equality and Law Reform [2003] 2 I.R. 535 . . . . 220n

Foley v Murphy [2005] 3 I.R. 574 . . . . 187n

G v DPP [1994] 1 I.R. 374 . . . . 10n
Grogan v Parole Board [2008] IEHC 204 . . . . 220n, 225n

H v DPP [1994] 2 I.R. 589, [1994] 2 I.L.R.M. 285 . . . . 82n
Harris v Delhunt [2008] IEHC 152 . . . . 214n
Heaney and McGuinness v Ireland [1994] 3 I.R. 593, [1994] 2 I.L.R.M. 420
    (High Court), [1996] 1 I.R. 580, [1997] 1 I.L.R.M. 117 (Supreme Court) 91
Hilliard v Penfield Enterprises Ltd [1990] 1 I.R. 138 . . . . 52n
Holland v Governor of Portlaoise Prison [2004] 2 I.R. 573 . . . . 10n

Irish Trust Bank Ltd v Central Bank of Ireland [1976–1977] I.L.R.M. 50 . . . . . . 158n

Kinahan v Minister for Justice and Law Reform [2001] 4 I.R. 454 . . . . 215n, 220n
Kinsella v Kenmare Resources Plc, *Irish Times*, November 18, 2010 . . . . 45n

Lynch and Whelan v Minister for Justice, Equality and Law Reform
    [2010] IESC 34 . . . . 56n, 87, 91, 92n, 98, 99n, 107n, 220n, 243n

McGee v Attorney General [1974] I.R. 284 . . . . 33n
Meadows v Minister for Justice, Equality and Law Reform [2010] IESC 3,
    [2010] 2 I.R. 701 . . . . 92n
Minister for Justice, Equality and Law Reform v Brennan [2007] 3 I.R. 732 . . . . . 19n
Minister for Justice, Equality and Law Reform v Stapleton [2008] 1 I.R. 669 . . . . 18n
Minister for Justice, Equality and Law Reform v Rettinger [2010] IESC 45 . . . . . 18n
Murray v Ireland [1985] I.R. 532 (HC), [1991] I.L.R.M. 465 (SC) 10n, 220n
Mogul of Ireland Ltd v Tipperary (N.R.) County Council [1976] I.R. 260 . . . . . . 158n

O'Brien v Mirror Group Newspapers Ltd [2001] 1 I.R. 1 . . . . 45n, 158n, 159n
O'Keeffe v An Bord Pleanála [1993] 1 I.R. 39 . . . . 92n
O'Neill v Governor of Castlerea Prison [2004] 1 I.R. 298 . . . . 56n
Oguekwe v Minister for Justice, Equality and Law Reform [2008] 3 I.R. 795 . . . . 89n
Osmanovic v DPP, unreported, High Court, July 30, 2004;
    [2006] 3 I.R. 504 (SC) 90n, 92, 107n

People (Attorney General) v Levison [1932] I.R. 158 213
People (Attorney General) v Broderick, *ex tempore,* Court of Criminal Appeal,
    July 4, 1930 . . . . 113n
People (Attorney General) v O'Brien, *ex tempore,* Court of Criminal Appeal,
    Irish Times, December 3, 1926 . . . . 113n
People (Attorney General) v Murtagh [1966] I.R. 361 . . . . 34, 35
People (DPP) v Alexiou [2003] 3 I.R. 513 . . . . 103n
People (DPP) v Connolly [2011] IESC 6 . . . . 104n
People (DPP) v Conroy (No.2) [1989] I.R. 160, [1989] I.L.R.M. 139 . . . . . . 98n, 243
People (DPP) v Cunningham [2002] 2 I.R. 712, [2003] 1 I.L.R.M. 124 . . . . 119n
People (DPP) v Duffy [2009] 3 I.R. 613, [2009] 2 I.L.R.M. 301 . . . . 241n
People (DPP) v G.K. [2008] IECCA 110 118
People (DPP) v Geasley [2009] IECCA 22, [2010] 1 I.L.R.M. 317 . . . . 157n
People (DPP) v Horgan [2007] 3 I.R. 568 . . . . 98n
People (DPP) v Kelly [2005] 2 I.R. 321, [2005] 1 I.L.R.M. 19 . . . . 81n
People (DPP) v M [1994] 3 I.R. 306, [1994] 2 I.L.R.M. 541 . . . . 81n, 91n
People (DPP) v McAuley [2001] 4 I.R. 160 . . . . 98n
People (DPP) v McCormack [2000] 4 I.R. 356 . . . . 113n
People (DPP) v Nelson, *ex tempore,* Court of Criminal Appeal, July 31, 2008 123
People (DPP) v Nolan, unreported, Court of Criminal Appeal,
    March 11, 2011 . . . . 117n
People (DPP) v P.S. [2009] IECCA 1 . . . . 119n
People (DPP) v Renald, unreported, Court of Criminal Appeal,
    November 23, 2001 . . . . 103n
People (DPP) v Sakpoba [2010] IECCA 83 . . . . 121n
People (DPP) v Shekale, *ex tempore,* Court of Criminal Appeal,
    February 25, 2008 123
People (DPP) v Stafford [2008] IECCA 15 . . . . 4n

People (DPP) v Tiernan [1988] I.R. 250, [1989] I.L.R.M. 149 . . . . 4n, 119,
120, 123, 159, 198n, 220n, 244n
People (DPP) v Whelan [2003] 4 I.R. 355 99
People (DPP) v Whitehead, *ex tempore,* Court of Criminal Appeal,
October 20, 2008 123

R v Dee (1884) 15 Cox C.C. 579 111
R v Faulkner (1877) 13 Cox C.C. 550 111
R v O'Brien (1849) 3 Cox C.C. 360 49
Rimsa v Governor of Cloverhill Prison [2010] IESC 47 . . . . 17n
Rock v Ireland [1997] 3 I.R. 484 . . . . 92n
Ryan v Governor of Limerick Prison [1988] I.R. 198 . . . . 220n

S.M. v Ireland (No. 2) [2007] 4 I.R 369 . . . . 107n, 108
State (Aherne) v Cotter [1982] I.R. 188, [1983] I.L.R.M. 17 . . . . 7n
State (Carney) v Governor of Portlaoise Prison [1957] I.R. 25 . . . . 214n
State (Cussen) v Brennan [1981] I.R. 181 . . . . 50n
State (McCormack) v Curran [1987] I.L.R.M. 225 . . . . 82n
State (O) v O'Brien [1973] I.R. 50 . . . . 220n
State (Quinn) v Ryan [1965] I.R. 70 . . . . 158n
Sweeney v Ireland, unreported, High Court, May 27, 2005 90

Whelan v Fitzpatrick [2008] 2 I.R. 678 . . . . 50n

EUROPEAN COURT OF HUMAN RIGHTS

Dickson v United Kingdom (2007) 44 E.H.R.R. 21 . . . . 231n

Easterbrook v United Kingdom (2003) 37 E.H.R.R. 40 233

Howarth v United Kingdom (2001) 31 E.H.R.R. 861 . . . . 124n

Kafkaris v Cyprus (2009) 49 E.H.R.R. 35 (p.877) 95–97
Keenan v United Kingdom (2001) 33 E.H.R.R. 38 (p.913) 10n
Kudla v Poland (2002) 35 E.H.R.R. 11 (p.198) 10n, 96n

Norris v Ireland (1991) 13 E.H.R.R. 186 . . . . 52n

Soering v United Kingdom (1989) 11 E.H.R.R. 439 . . . . 18n, 97
Stafford v United Kingdom (2002) 35 E.H.R.R. 32 . . . . 232, 233n

T and V v United Kingdom (2000) 30 E.H.R.R. 121 95
Thynne, Wilson and Gunnell v United Kingdom (1990)
13 E.H.R.R. 666 . . . . 226n, 233n
Tsirlis and Kouloumpas v Greece (1997) 25 E.H.R.R. 198 . . . . 95n

Weeks v United Kingdom (1988) 10 E.H.R.R. 293 . . . . 95n, 226n
Wynne v United Kingdom (1994) 19 E.H.R.R. 333 . . . . 232n

Yetkinsekerci v United Kingdom [2005] All E.R. (D) 232 . . . . 124n

EUROPEAN COURT OF JUSTICE

Advocaten voor de Werweld VZW v Leden von de Ministeraad,
    Case C–303/5 [2007] E.C.R. I–03633 . . . . 18n

UNITED KINGDOM

Adams v Lindsell (1818) 1 B & Ald 681 . . . . 163n

Birch Brothers v Brown [1931] A.C. 605 . . . . 158n
Bowe v The Queen [2006] 1 W.L.R. 1623 . . . . 87n
British Oxygen Co. Ltd v Minister of Technology [1971] A.C. 610,
    [1970] 3 W.L.R. 488, [1970] 3 All E.R. 165 50
Browne v The Queen [2000] A.C. 45, [1999] 3 W.L.R. 1158 . . . . 87n

DPP of Jamaica v Mollison [2003] 2 A.C. 411, [2003] 3 W.L.R. 1160 . . . . 87n
Donoghue v Stevenson [1932] A.C. 562 163

Fry v Porter (1670) 86 E.R. 898 . . . . 43n

Gee v Pritchard 36 E.R. 670 (Chan. 1818) 43n
George Wimpey & Co Ltd v British Overseas Airways Corporation
    [1955] A.C. 169 . . . . 157n

Hinds v The Queen [1977] A.C. 195, [1976] 2 W.L.R. 366 . . . . 87n
Hines v Hines and Burdett [1918] P. 364 . . . . 48n

McLoughlin v O'Brian [1983] 1 A.C. 410, [1982] 2 W.L.R. 982,
    [1982] 2 All E.R. 298 248
Matthew v The State of Trinidad and Tobago [2005] 1 A.C. 433,
    [2004] 3 W.L.R. 812 . . . . 87n
Montagu v Earl of Sandwich (1886) 32 Ch D 525 . . . . 158n

Office of the King's Prosecutor, Brussels v Cando Armas [2006] 2 A.C. 1,
    [2005] 3 W.L.R. 1079 . . . . 18n

R v Aramah (1983) 76 Cr. App. R. 190, (1982) 4 Cr. App. R. (S.) 407 . . . . . . 104, 124
R v Aranguren (1994) 99 Cr. App. R. 347, (1995) 16 Cr. App. R. (S.) 211 . . 104, 124n
R v Bailey (1988) 10 Cr. App. R. (S.) 231 . . . . 118n
R v Bieber [2008] EWCA 1601, [2009] 1 W.L.R. 223 96

R v Billam [1986] 1 W.L.R. 349, (1986) 82 Cr. App. R. 347,
(1986) 8 Cr. App. R. (S.) 48 .... 123, 124
R v Bradbourn (1985) 7 Cr. App. R.(S.) 180 .... 192, 193
R v Broady (1988) 10 Cr. App. R. (S.) 495 25
R v Cooksley [2003] 2 Cr. App. R. 18, [2004] 1 Cr. App. R. (S.) 1,
[2003] 3 All E.R. 40 127
R v Cox [1993] 1 W.L.R. 188, (1993) 96 Cr. App. R. 452, (1993)
14 Cr. App. R. (S.) 479, [1993] 2 All E.R. 19 .... 193n, 197
R v Cunningham [1993] 1 W.L.R. 183, (1993) 96 Cr. App. R. 422,
(1993) 14 Cr. App. R. (S.) 444 .... 238n
R v Home Secretary, ex parte Venables and Thompson [1998] 1 A.C. 407,
[1997] 3 W.L.R. 23, [1997] 3 All E.R. 97 25
R v Howells [1999] 1 W.L.R. 307, [1999] 1 Cr. App. R. 98, [1999]
1 Cr. App. R. (S.) 335, [1999] 1 All E.R. 50 .... 193n, 195n
R v Kelly [2000] Q.B. 198, [1999] 2 W.L.R. 1100, [1999] 2 All E.R. 13,
[1999] 2 Cr. App. R. 36, [1999] 2 Cr. App. R.(S.) 176 .... 74n
R v Johnson (1994) 15 Cr. App. R. (S.) 827 .... 160n
R v McCann [2007] 1 Cr. App. R. (S.) 4 (p.20) 195n
R v McInerney [2003] 1 Cr. App. R. 36, [2003] 2 Cr. App. R. (S.) 39 .... 197n
R v Mashaollahi [2001] 1 Cr. App. R. 6, [2001] 1 Cr. App. R. (S.) 96 .... 104n, 124n
R v Millberry [2003] 1 W.L.R. 546, [2003] 1 Cr. App. R. 25 (p. 396),
[2003] 2 Cr. App. R. (S.) 31 (p. 142), [2003] 2 All E.R. 939 127
R v Mills (1978) 68 Cr. App. R. 327 .... 46n
R v Morris [2001] 1 Cr. App. R. (S.) 87 .... 104n, 124n
R v Offen [2001] 1 W.L.R. 253, [2001] 2 All E.R. 154, [2001]
1 Cr. App. R. 24,
[2002] 2 Cr. App. R. (S) 10 .... 74n
R v Oliver [2003] 1 Cr. App. R. 28 (p. 463), [2003] 2 Cr. App. R.
(S.) 15 (p. 64) 127
R v Patel (1987) 9 Cr. App. R. (S.) 319 .... 104n, 124n
R v Port of London Authority, ex p. Kynoch [1919] 1 K.B. 176 .... 50n
R v Queen (1981) 3 Cr. App. R. (S.) 245 .... 118n
R v Rehman and Wood [2006] 1 Cr. App. R. (S.) 77 .... 74n
R v Sargeant (1974) 60 Cr. App. R. 74 .... 24n
R v Sidlow (1908) 1 Cr. App. R. 28 .... 113n
R v Sussex Justices, ex p. McCarthy [1924] 1 K.B. 256 .... 15n
R v Townsend (1995) 16 Cr. App. R. (S.) 553 .... 160n
R v Viola [1982] 1 W.L.R. 1138, 75 Cr. App. R. 125 46
R (Anderson) v Secretary of State for the Home Department [2003]
1 A.C. 837, [2002] 3 W.L.R. 1800, [2003] 1 Cr. App. R. 32,
[2002] 4 All E.R. 1089 .... 87n, 233n
R (Black) v Secretary of State for Justice [2009] 1 A.C. 949,
[2009] 2 W.L.R. 282, [2004] 4 All E.R. 1 .... 231n
R (Brooke) v Parole Board [2008] 1 W.L.R. 1950, [2008] 3 All E.R. 289 232
R (Smith and West) v Parole Board [2005] UKHL 1 .... 223n, 231n
R (Wellington) v Secretary of State for the Home Department
[2009] 1 A.C. 335, [2009] 2 W.L.R. 48, [2009] 2 All E.R. 436 .... 97n
R v Wilkes (1770) 4 Burr 2527 .... 48n

Roberts v Hopwood [1925] A.C. 578 . . . . 49n
Roodal v The State of Trinidad and Tobago [2005] 1 A.C. 328,
    [2004] 2 W.L.R. 652 . . . . 87n
Rooke's Case (1598) 5 Co. Rep. 100a 48n

Sharp v Wakefield [1891] A.C. 173 . . . . 49n
Stoker v Stoker (1889) 14 P.D 60 . . . . 48n

Taylor, *Re* (1876) 4 Ch D 157 . . . . 48n

NORTHERN IRELAND

Walsh v Curry [1955] N.I. 112 . . . . 157n

AUSTRALIA

Duncan v R (1983) 47 A.L.R. 746 . . . . 191n

Kable v DPP for New South Wales [1996] HCA 24, (1996) 189 C.L.R. 51 109

Palling v Corfield (1970) 123 C.L.R. 52 87

R v Douar [2005] NSWCCA 455 . . . . 205n
R v Zamagias [2002] NSWCCA 17 . . . . 205n

CANADA

R v Beauregard [1986] 2 S.C.R. 56 256
R v Chaulk [1990] 3 S.C.R. 1303 . . . . 91n
R v Ferguson [2008] 1 S.C.R. 96 . . . . 90n
R v Goltz [1991] 3 I.R. 485 93
R v L.M. 2008 SCC 31, [2008] 2 S.C.R. 163 . . . . 29n
R v Latimer [2001] 1 S.C.R. 3 87
R v McVeigh (1985) 22 C.C.C.(3d) 145 . . . . 241n
R v Miller and Cockriell [1977] 2 S.C.R. 680 . . . . 89, 90n
R v Morales [1992] 3 S.C.R. 711 . . . . 49n
R v Proulx [2000] 1 S.C.R. 61 . . . . 189n
R v Ramage (2008) 53 C.R.(6th) 342, 2010 ONCA 488 . . . . 241n
R v Smith [1987] 1 S.C.R. 1045 . . . . 87, 89, 90, 105
R v Valente [1985] 2 S.C.R. 673 . . . . 256n
Reference re Remuneration of Provincial Judges [1997] 3 S.C.R. 3 . . . . 256n
Royal Prerogative of Mercy upon Deportation Proceedings,
    Re [1933] S.C.R. 269, [1933] 2 D.L.R. 269 . . . . 213n

JAMAICA

R v Carnegie, unreported, November 20, 2003 87

NEW ZEALAND

R v Clode [2009] 1 N.Z.L.R. 312 .... 126n
R v Fatu [2006] 2 N.Z.L.R. 72 .... 125n
R v Mako [2000] 2 N.Z.L.R. 170 .... 125n
R v Smail [2007] 1 N.Z.L.R. 411 .... 99n
R v Taueki [2005] 3 N.Z.L.R. 372 .... 125, 126
R v Terewi [1999] 3 N.Z.L.R. 62 .... 125n, 241n
Reid v New Zealand Parole Board [2006] NZCA 232 .... 223n

SOUTH AFRICA

Centre for Child Law v Minister for Justice and Constitutional
    Development [2009] ZACC 18 .... 74n
Dodo v The State [2001] ZACC 16, 2001 (3) SA 382 (CC) 80n, 87, 88n, 94

State v Ferreira 2004 (2) SACR 454 (SCA) 73
State v Malgas 2001 (2) SA 1222, 2001 (1) SACR 469 (SCA), [2001] ZASCA 30 ... 73

UNITED STATES OF AMERICA

Apprendi v New Jersey 530 U.S. 466 (2000) 141n, 149

Barber v Thomas 560 U.S. – (2010) 135n, 146n
Blakely v Washington 542 U.S. 296 (2004) 141n, 149

Citizens United v FEC 130 S. Ct 876 (2010) 138
Cunningham v California 549 U.S. 270 (2007) 141

Dorszynski v United States 418 U.S. 424 (1974) 136n

Estelle v Gamble 429 U.S. 97 (1976) 89n
Ewing v California 538 U.S. 11 (2003) 77

Gall v United States 552 U.S. 38 (2007) 141n, 150n
Geraghty v United States Parole Commission 719 F.2d 1199 (1983) 135n
Gore v United States 357 U.S. 386 (1957) 135, 136
Graham v Florida 560 U.S. – (2010) 89, 97, 152
Gurera v United States 40 F.2d 338 (1930) 110, 136

Harmelin v Michigan 501 U.S. 957 (1991) 77, 89
Hutto v Davis 454 U.S. 370 (1982) 158n

Kimbrough v United States 552 U.S. 85 (2007) 141n, 150, 155n
Koon v United States 518 U.S. 81 (1996) 148

Lockyer v Andrade 538 U.S. 63 (2003) 77

McCleary v State 49 Wis. 2d 263, 182 N.W. 2d 512 (1971) 50n
Mistretta v United States 488 U.S. 361 (1989) 152
Murray v Buell 41 N.W. 1010 (1889) 46n

Nelson v United States 555 U.S. – (2009) 150n
New State Ice Co. v Liebmann 285 U.S. 262 (1932) 184n

People v Superior Court (Romero) 917 P2d 628 (1996) 77n
People v Williams (1998) 17 Cal.(4th) 148, 948 P2d 429 .... 77n
Pepper v United States 562 U.S. – (2011) 150n, 253n
Planned Parenthood v Casey 505 U.S. 833 (1992) 158n

Rita v United States 551 U.S. 338 (2007) 141n, 150n
Roe v Wade 410 U.S. 113 (1973) 33n
Roper v Simmons 543 U.S. 551 (2005) 89n
Ross v United States 37 F.2d 557 (1930) 110n

Simonds v Simonds 380 N.E.2d 189 (1978) 42n
Smith v United States 273 F.2d 462 (1959) 136
Spears v United States 555 U.S. 261 (2009) 150n
State of Arizona v Berger 212 Ariz. 473, 134 P.3d 378 (2006) 152, 153
State v Gallion 678 N.W. 2d 197 (Wis. 2004) 50n, 131n

Trop v Dulles 356 U.S. 86 .... 89n

United States v Angelos 433 F.3d 738 (2006) 5, 6
United States v Booker 543 U.S. 220 (2005) 141, 142, 147, 149, 153
United States v Dorvee 616 F. 3d 174 (2010) 153n
United States v Grayson 438 U.S. 41 (1977) 135n
United States v Henderson, Court of Appeals, Ninth Circuit,
      April 29, 2011 .... 147n, 150n, 153n
United States v Raby 575 F. 3d 376 (2009) 147
United States v Reedy 304 F. 3d (2002) 187n
United States v Rosenberg 195 F.2d 583, 344 U.S. 838 (1952) 136
United States v Vasquez U.S.D.C. EDNY, March 30, 2010 .... 6n, 81
United States v Watts 519 U.S. 148 (1997) 148, 149

Wade v United States 504 U.S. 181 (1992) 94n
Williams v New York 337 U.S. 241 (1949) 134n, 139n
Witte v United States 515 U.S. 389 (1995) 148n

TABLE OF LEGISLATION

CONSTITUTION OF IRELAND

Art.13.6 212
Art.15.2.1 . . . . 246n
Art.15.5.2 . . . . 241n
Art.35. 2 256
Art.40.4. 1 . . . . 9n

IRELAND—STATUTES

Civil Law (Miscellaneous Provisions) Act 2008
  s.32 . . . . 251n
Control of Dogs Act 1986 . . . . 53n
Control of Dogs (Amendment) Act 1992 . . . . 53n
Courts and Court Officers Act 1995 . . . . 33n
Courts (Establishment and Constitution) Act 1961
  s.4 . . . . 251n
  s.5 . . . . 251n
Courts (Supplemental Provisions) 1961
  s.28 . . . . 251n
Courts of Justice Act 1924 . . . . 113n
  s.34 . . . . 113n
Criminal Justice Act 1951 . . . . 102, 212, 216, 219
  s.4 . . . . 10n
  s.23 . . . . 212n
Criminal Justice Act 1960 . . . . 102, 215, 219
  s.2(1) 215n
  s.5 . . . . 215n
Criminal Justice Act 1964 . . . . 34, 241n
  s.2 34
  s.4 . . . . 91n
Criminal Justice Act 1984 40
  s.11 . . . . 4n, 35n, 109n, 111n, 257n
  s.12 . . . . 7n, 116n
Criminal Justice Act 1990 . . . . 45n, 241n
  s.2 . . . . 34, 64n
  s.5 218
Criminal Justice Act 1993 . . . . 106n
  s.6 . . . . 35n
Criminal Justice Act 2006 . . . . 17n, 72, 111
  s.84 . . . . 102, 111n
  s.99 35

s.100 .... 35n
s.184 .... 53n
Criminal Justice Act 2007 .... 17, 257n
s.22 .... 4n, 35n, 109n, 111n
s.33 .... 67n, 84n, 85n, 94n, 102n
Criminal Justice (Amendment) Act 2009 40
Criminal Justice (Community Service) Act 1983 .... 117n, 242
s.2 .... 187n
s.3 .... 35n
Criminal Justice (Community Service) (Amendment) Act 2011 .... 111n, 203n, 252n
Criminal Justice (Miscellaneous Provisions) Act 1997
s.17 .... 212n
Criminal Justice (Miscellaneous Provisions) Act 2009 40
Criminal Justice (Temporary Release of Prisoners) Act 2003 .... 215n, 218
Criminal Justice (Theft and Fraud Offences) Act 2001
s.4 .... 10n
s.14 .... 196n
Criminal Justice (United Nations Convention against Torture) Act 2000 .... 89n
s.1 .... 243n
Criminal Law Act 1976
s.13 .... 111n
Criminal Law (Insanity) Act 2006 .... 183n
Criminal Law (Sexual Offences) Act 1993
s.3 .... 52n
s.4 .... 52n
Criminal Law (Sexual Offences) Act 2006 .... 52n
Criminal Procedure Act 1993 213
s.3 .... 44n
s.3(2) 113n

Defamation Act 1961
s.8 .... 52n
Defamation Act 2009 .... 52n
s.36 .... 185n

European Arrest Warrant Act 2003
s.37 .... 18n

Genocide Act 1973 .... 98n

Infanticide Act 1949 .... 98n

Misuse of Drugs Act 1977
s.15A 16, 66, 67, 72, 94, 101-105, 123, 219
s.15B 102, 104n, 105, 219
s.27 .... 16n, 85n, 111n
s.27(3A)–(3k) 67n, 84n, 94n
s.27(3I) 67n

Non-Fatal Offences Against the Person Act 1997
    s.3 . . . . 34n
    s.15 . . . . 196n

Offences Against the State Act 1939
    s.34 88

Prisons Act 2007
    s.39 102

Roads Act 1993 . . . . 53n
Road Traffic Act 2006
    s.5 . . . . 53n

Sex Offenders Act 2001 . . . . 230n
Succession Act 1965 . . . . 14n

IRELAND—STATUTORY INSTRUMENTS

Prison Rules 2007 (S.I. No. 252 of 2007) 214n
Prisoners (Temporary Release) Rules 2004 (S.I. No. 680 of 2004) 215n

Rules for the Government of Prisons (Stat. R. & Ord. 320/1947) 214n

COUNCIL OF EUROPE

European Convention on Human Rights
    art.3 . . . . 89n, 95–97
    art.5 . . . . 226n, 232
    art.6 . . . . 24, 233
    art.7 95
    art.7(1) 95

EUROPEAN UNION

Charter of Rights and Fundamental Freedoms
    art.49 (3) 95n
    art.51(1) 95n
Council Framework Decision 2002/584/JHA 17, 18n, 236

UNITED KINGDOM— STATUTES

Children Act 1908
  s.12 109
Children Act 1989 46
  s.47(1) 46n
Constitutional Reform Act 2005 33
  s.3 256
Criminal Appeal Act 1907 . . . . 112n
Criminal Appeal (Scotland) Act 1926 . . . . 112n
Criminal Justice Act 1948
  s.57 . . . . 217n
Criminal Justice Act 1967 216
  ss.59–64 . . . . 216n
Criminal Justice Act 1982 192
  s.1(4) 192
Criminal Justice Act 1988 . . . . 106n
Criminal Justice Act 1991 . . . . 110, 192, 193, 197, 205, 217, 238
  s.1(2) 110n, 192n
  s.2(2)(a) 110n
  s.2(2)(b) 110n
  s.6(1) 110n
  s.6(2) 110n
  s.11 . . . . 118n
  ss.32–51 . . . . 217n
  s.34 . . . . 226n
Criminal Justice Act 1993
  s.66 . . . . 192n
Criminal Justice Act 2003 . . . . 74, 96, 100n, 128, 160, 188, 218, 233, 238, 239
  s.142 . . . . 238n
  s.148(1) 188n
  s.183 205
  s.244 . . . . 218n
  s.269 . . . . 233n
  s.287 74
Criminal Justice and Immigration Act 2008 . . . . 74n
Coroners and Justice Act 2009 . . . . 128, 160
  s.120(2) 129n
Criminal Justice and Licensing (Scotland) Act 2010
  s.17 . . . . 202n
Criminal Law Amendment Act 1885 . . . . 52n

Offences Against the Person Act 1861
  s.62 108

Powers of Criminal Courts (Sentencing) Act 2000
  s.79 . . . . 192n
Probation of Offenders Act 1907 . . . . 35n, 117n, 205, 208

Sexual Offences Act 2003
    s.67(4) 195n
Supreme Court of Judicature (Scotland) Act 1877 .... 43n

NORTHERN IRELAND—STATUTORY INSTRUMENTS

Dangerous Wild Animals (N.I.) Order 2004 .... 53n

AUSTRALIA—STATUTES

Commonwealth Crimes Act 1914
    s.17A 191n

Crimes (Sentencing Procedure) Act 1999 191
    s.5(1) 191n
Criminal Code Amendment Act (WA) 2009 .... 83n

CANADA—STATUTES

Criminal Code 238
    s.718 .... 239n
    s.718.1 .... 239n
    s.718.2(d) 191n
    s.718.2(e) 191n
    s.745 .... 100n

NEW ZEALAND—STATUTES

Parole Act 2002 223
    s.7(1) 223n
    s.7(2) 223n
    s.84 .... 229n

Sentencing Act 2002 239
    s.8 .... 110n
    s.8(e) 125
    s.16(1) 191n
    s.16(2) 191n
    s.102 .... 99n
Sentencing Council Act 2007 .... 126n

UNITED STATES OF AMERICA—STATUTES

Anti-Drug Use Act 1986 245

Fair Sentencing Act 2010 76

Sentencing Reform Act 1984 . . . . 76, 145

UNITED NATIONS

International Covenant on Civil and Political Rights
    art.7 . . . . 89n
    art.10(3) 231n

CHAPTER 1

PRINCIPLED SENTENCING: WHY IT MATTERS

Sir Thomas More's *Utopia*, published in 1516, begins with a highly critical account of prevailing sentencing practices. Raphael, the fictional voyager, tells of a conversation which he had while visiting the Archbishop of Canterbury, Cardinal Morton:

> "I once happened to be dining with the Cardinal when a certain English lawyer was there. I forget how the subject came up, but he was speaking with great enthusiasm about the stern measures that were then being taken against thieves.
>
> 'We're hanging them all over the place,' he said, 'I've seen as many as twenty on a single gallows. And that's what I find so odd. Considering how few of them get away with it, why are we still plagued with so many robbers?'
>
> 'What's odd about it?' I asked – for I never hesitated to speak freely in front of the Cardinal. 'This method of dealing with thieves is both unjust and socially undesirable. As a punishment, it's too severe, and as a deterrent it's quite ineffective. Petty larceny isn't bad enough to deserve the death penalty, and no penalty on earth will stop people from stealing, if it's their only way of getting food. In this respect you English, like most other nations, remind me of incompetent schoolmasters, who prefer caning their pupils to teaching them. Instead of inflicting these horrible punishments, it would be far more to the point to provide everyone with some means of livelihood, so that nobody's under the frightful necessity of becoming first a thief and then a corpse.'"[1]

The conversation then turned to the social impact of the Enclosure Acts which had the effect of fencing off common lands for pasture thereby making them unavailable for crop cultivation. However, even in the short passage just quoted we find many themes that still resonate today. The lawyer seems generally in favour of subjecting thieves to capital punishment but remains puzzled by its ineffectiveness. Doubtless he would have recommended a more severe punishment if such were possible. Raphael believes that the death penalty for theft is both disproportionate and ineffective. People are forced to steal, he argues, out of economic necessity. A just social order would be far more efficient

---

[1] More, *Utopia*, translated by Turner (London: Penguin Books, 1965), pp.43–44.

in addressing certain problems which the criminal justice system, with all its harsh and inhumane penalties, has manifestly failed to resolve. Those whose property was stolen are certainly victims, but so too are most of the thieves themselves.

Five centuries on, we continue to debate the relationship between crime and poverty, the extent to which problems of social justice are treated as problems of criminal justice, and the deterrent effect of harsh penalties. Indeed, we are no closer to universal consensus on the moral justification for state punishment than when Plato first discussed the matter two and a half thousand years ago.[2] Philosophers continue to debate this issue while newer disciplines such as psychology, criminology and economics have greatly enriched our under-standing of the nature and consequences of criminal punishment. Sentencing is treated in this book as an exercise in decision-making but it is, of course, much more than that. It is also a social practice that reflects the values, beliefs, biases and methodologies of the various actors who contribute to the overall sentencing process. That process is much more extensive than its customary portrayal as a discretionary judicial power might suggest. The imposition of sentence is indeed a critically important step, but its meaning and impact are shaped by other decisions made at earlier and later points along the continuum that constitutes the criminal process. Legislators will have decided to criminalise some kinds of conduct, but not others. Investigating and prosecuting authorities will have decided to initiate proceedings in respect of some alleged offences, but not in respect of others. The manner in which and the extent to which a sentence, once imposed, is executed will be determined by the executive branch of government.

Judicial sentencing discretion attracts a great deal of public and academic attention but, in one important respect, it is the least discretionary aspect of the entire process. Legislators have a choice in deciding which kinds of potentially injurious conduct should be criminalised; victims may decide not to report the commission of an offence; prosecutors may decide not to initiate or continue criminal proceedings; and a jury, having heard all the evidence during trial, may decide to disagree. A trial judge, by contrast, can never decline to sentence a person who has been convicted following a trial or a guilty plea. Sentence may be adjourned to allow for the preparation of professional reports or for some similar reason, but sooner or later the judge must select an appropriate penalty. Even where a non-punitive measure such as a discharge is ordered, a considered judicial choice has nonetheless been made. Decision-making is also, of course, mandatory in relation to bail, mode of trial and other interim decisions, but sentencing stands out as one area where the making of a terminating decision which may be of great consequence for the accused and society at large cannot be avoided. The manner in which that decision is reached is therefore of the highest importance, and this in turn means that the allocation of decision-making

---

[2]   Mackenzie, *Plato on Punishment* (Berkeley, CA: University of California Press, 1981).

functions within the overall sentencing process is a matter worthy of sustained reflection.

Most of us, as committed democrats, would agree that the creation and definition of criminal offences as well as the stipulation of maximum sentences should remain solely within the province of the legislature. As liberal democrats, committed to basic human rights and individualised justice, most of us prefer to leave the selection of specific penalties to the judiciary. However, we disagree, sometimes quite sharply, over who should decide upon the policies and principles that are to determine or guide judicial sentencing decisions. This, of course, is another way of asking how much discretion sentencing judges should retain. Some are inclined to argue that, for certain serious or prevalent offences at least, sentencing policy should be made exclusively by the legislature in the sense that more serious offences should attract mandatory sentences. Proponents of this view are effectively arguing that sentencing discretion should be exercised by elected representatives rather than by unelected judges. Legislators might be surprised to see themselves described as exercising sentencing discretion. Yet, that is precisely what they do when they decide, for example, that a given offence should always attract 10 years' imprisonment as opposed to five years, seven years or some other quantity. Mandatory sentences, in the true sense, seldom abolish discretion; they usually relocate it from one branch of government to another.[3] Once a person is convicted of an offence governed by a mandatory sentence, the judge has no option but to impose the penalty previously selected by legislators who, in turn, may have devoted far less attention to the level at which it should be set than a judge would typically devote to the selection of sentence in an individual case.

Murder is the only commonly-prosecuted offence that carries a truly mandatory sentence in Ireland, though a very small number of other offences now attract presumptive or mandatory minimum sentences.[4] For the vast majority of offences, the only formal limitations on judicial discretion are the maximum sentence prescribed by law and, where relevant, the general statutory limitation on the sentencing jurisdiction of the District Court. Many believe that judges should be subject to more external constraints than currently apply when sentencing individual cases. The manifestos of all the main opposition parties during the 2007 Irish general election included promises on sentencing reform, most of them referring to legislative guidelines as a means of generating consistency.[5] None of these parties, nor any other advocate of sentencing reform for that matter, has gone so far as to spell out precisely what form the guidance

---

[3] Chapter 4 below.

[4] Chapter 4 below.

[5] This was true of the Fine Gael, Labour and Sinn Fein manifestos. The Green Party, which ended up as a government coalition partner after the election, promised to implement guidelines requiring judges to give reasons for their decisions. This was something of political mantra at the time despite the fact that judges sentencing serious cases always give reasons for their decisions.

should take, and it is highly improbable that any of them have devoted much thought to the matter. They might, for all we know, have been referring to an increased use of mandatory minimum or presumptive sentences, as were already introduced for certain drug and firearms offences. They might have been referring obliquely to the possibility of establishing some sort of sentencing commission to establish more detailed guidelines which would be binding on the courts. Or, more palatably, they might have meant to direct the courts themselves to develop more specific principles and standards for the sentencing of prevalent offences. Those who advocate any of these strategies are essentially arguing for a further division of sentencing decision-making functions. They would commit the formulation of policy to one body, let it be the legislature itself, a statutory commission or an appeal court and, while leaving the selection of sentence in specific cases to trial judges, they would require those judges to apply the rules, principles or standards established by the relevant policy-making authority.

One might, of course, argue that such an arrangement already exists. Trial judges do not have an entirely free hand in selecting sentence. They are constrained by statutory maximum sentences, by a few specific statutory rules such as that requiring consecutive prison sentences for offences committed while on bail,[6] and by general principles established by the Supreme Court and the Court of Criminal Appeal. This counter argument has some merit, but what many advocates of change are seeking differs in one vital respect from the present system. What they want is a set of guiding standards which are much more specific and binding than those currently existing. Right now, a judge sentencing a rape offence is required, in the absence of exceptional circumstances, to impose an immediate and substantial custodial sentence because that is what the Supreme Court decided in 1988.[7] Yet there is little, if any, meaningful guidance on what might amount to a "substantial" sentence in any particular case, and the court expressly refrained from establishing "any standardisation or tariff of penalty for cases."[8] Twenty years later, the Court of Criminal Appeal observed with some satisfaction that, while other jurisdictions had adopted different approaches, Ireland had been well served by the present discretionary system.[9] The question therefore is whether the court was justified in its implicit conclusion that the present unstructured system is adequate to ensure that trial court sentencing practice meets the demands of legality, fairness and consistency.[10]

---

[6]   Criminal Justice Act 1984 s.11 as amended by Criminal Justice Act 2007 s.22.
[7]   *People (DPP) v Tiernan* [1988] I.R. 250, [1989] I.L.R.M. 149.
[8]   *People (DPP) v Tiernan* [1988] I.R. 250 at 254, [1989] I.L.R.M. 149 at 152.
[9]   *People (DPP) v Stafford* [2008] IECCA 15.
[10]   We are referring, of course, to consistency of approach rather than uniformity of outcome.

PRINCIPLED DISCRETION

The argument advanced in this book is that sentencing, in order to comply with the demands of justice, must remain discretionary. The selection of sentence in specific cases must therefore remain exclusively a judicial task. However, to comply with other important values including procedural fairness, equality and the rule of law, judicial sentencing must reform itself in order to produce consistency of approach, to reduce (if not eliminate) unwarranted disparity and to develop rational criteria for deciding on the nature and severity of appropriate sanctions. Custody thresholds, which are largely neglected in modern sentencing jurisprudence, call for particular attention and are discussed in Chapter 8. To link individualised sentencing with the demands of justice is not, of course, to deny that justice also calls for distributional equity. A truly holistic concept of justice requires that similar sentences be imposed on similarly situated offenders, with the important qualification that a range of offence- and offender-related factors must be considered when attempting to locate any one case on the relevant scale of gravity. The challenge is to achieve consensus on acceptable methodologies for assessing offence gravity and other ethically relevant factors, on the weight to be attributed to those factors, and on the kind and quantum of punishment appropriate for various categories of offender. This is the essence of *principled* discretion. Uniformity of outcome is not the desired goal. In fact, experience teaches us to be suspicious of any structure which promises such uniformity. Principled discretion calls for judgment—informed judgment admittedly—and that comes at the price of tolerating some element of disparity in sentencing outcomes.[11] Some might argue that this approach is insufficiently ambitious and that more radical steps are needed to generate consistency. More radical steps have indeed been taken elsewhere, most notably in the United States, but experience there shows that uniformity, no less than inconsistency, can cause its share of injustice. Critics of the present Irish system might look with some envy to the grid-style guidelines operating in some American jurisdictions which, from afar, appear simple and straightforward (assuming one ignores the 1,000-page manual governing the federal guidelines). However, consider the judge who, in 2004, was faced with sentencing Weldon Angelos, a Utah music producer, for three offences of selling small amounts of marijuana. Because Angelos was also found in possession of a firearm on each occasion, though without any indication that he either used or threatened to use it, he had to be sentenced to at least 55 years' imprisonment. While the trial judge, who later resigned from the federal bench, declined to hold the relevant guideline unconstitutional, he described the 55-year sentence which he was required to

---

[11] This was argued by James Fitzjames Stephen in the late nineteenth century when there was a vibrant debate in England, rather similar to that now taking place in Ireland, about the most appropriate means of channelling judicial sentencing discretion. See Stephen, "Variations in the Punishment of Crime" (1885) 17 *The Nineteenth Century* 755.

impose as "unjust, cruel and even irrational". He urged the defendant to seek executive clemency, as parole was no longer available in the federal system.[12] The sentence was upheld on appeal and the United States Supreme Court declined to grant further review.[13] A similar offender appearing before an Irish court—and assuming that the drugs were worth no more than a few thousand Euro—could legally be sentenced to anything from a probation order to life imprisonment. Granted, an appeal court might later vary the sentence if it were found to be contrary to principle, manifestly excessive or unduly lenient. However, there is still no comparison between the breadth of discretion accorded to Irish sentencing judges and the strictures imposed on their federal counterparts in the United States. Few, if any, of us would welcome the kind of regime which required the imposition of such an unjust and crushing sentence on Weldon Angelos. Many of us might, however, be willing to support measures designed to make the exercise of discretion more structured and predictable.

The challenge then is to develop a set of principles that will give effect to the animating purposes of the sentencing system, and do so in a fair and coherent fashion. By present-day standards, those purposes should include not only the traditional moral justifications for punishment, such as desert or deterrence, but also a commitment to treating similar cases in a similar fashion. Excessive preoccupation with reducing disparity and promoting consistency can, to be sure, lead to reforms which will prevent judges from taking account of genuinely differentiating factors, and from crafting sentences designed to reduce the risk of recidivism. However, this concern cannot justify the retention of a completely unstructured system because of the important issues of justice at stake. It is scarcely defensible in a constitutional democracy for two offenders convicted of practically identical offences to receive radically different sentences simply because they are dealt with by different judges.

THE DISPARITY QUESTION

Recommendations for systemic change in any area of public administration require rational justification, so advocates of a more closely regulated sentencing system bear the burden of demonstrating the need for such reform. In structural terms, the present system is currently defined by two primary characteristics:

---

[12] The trial judge noted the much lower sentences which several more serious offences would attract, e.g. a maximum of 24 years and 5 months for aircraft hijacking. The US federal sentencing system is described in Ch.6 below.

[13] *United States v Angelos* 433 F. 3d 738 (10th Cir. 2006). See Nilson, "Indecent Standards: The Case of *U.S. versus Weldon Angelos*" (2006) 11 Roger Williams Univ. L.R. 537 and, more recently, the remarks of Gleeson J. of the United States District Court (EDNY) when he was compelled to sentence Roberto Vasquez to five years' imprisonment for cocaine distribution despite the presence of many mitigating factors which had to be ignored but which would have warranted a much lower prison sentence: *United States v Vasquez,* U.S. District Court, EDNY, March 30, 2010 (2010 WL 1257359).

the extensive, though not unlimited, statutory discretion conferred on trial judges, and the availability of defence and prosecution appeals based on error of law and error of principle. Even at this point, an important qualification must be entered. The appeals system just outlined applies only to those convicted following indictment for serious offences. Most offences, over 90 per cent of them in fact, are disposed of in the District Court from which an appeal lies to the Circuit Court. Appeals to that court are heard *de novo* and, in an appeal against sentence only, the court hears as much evidence as is necessary for that purpose.[14] Although a court of summary jurisdiction, the District Court has extensive criminal jurisdiction and may, in certain circumstances, impose a cumulative sentence of up to two years' imprisonment for a combination of offences.[15] In 2009, the District Court disposed of more than 520,000 offences, including almost 70,000 indictable offences. The overall figure was slightly lower than that for 2008 but the figures for both of those years represented a very significant increase over 2007. The differential was particularly noticeable in public order and assault offences (69,000 in 2008 and 65,000 in 2009 compared with 36,000 in 2007), road traffic offences (358,000 in 2008 and 333,000 in 2009 compared with 282,000 in 2007) and sexual offences (2,000 in 2008 and 1,352 in 2009 compared with 500 in 2007).[16] In 2009, the District Court sentenced almost 12,500 defendants to imprisonment or detention although the figures do not differentiate between immediate and suspended sentences, nor do they indicate the terms actually imposed. It must be recalled that everyone convicted or sentenced in the District Court has an automatic right of appeal to the Circuit Court where some convictions are quashed and many sentences varied. On the other hand, there were 11,000 committals under sentence to Irish prisons in 2009, an increase of 35 per cent on the previous year, which means that a very considerable number of offenders sentenced in the District Court actually went to prison. The number of persons sentenced in the higher criminal courts would come nowhere near the overall committal figure.

The most fundamental justification that can be offered for structural reforms within our present system is that it currently lacks any formal and effective mechanism for generating consistency of approach. Allegations of sentencing disparity are admittedly easy to make, but difficult to prove. Disparity arises when similarly-situated offenders convicted of similar offences receive significantly different sentences.[17] Differential treatment may sometimes be

---

[14] *State (Aherne) v Cotter* [1982] I.R. 188, [1983] I.L.R.M. 17.

[15] Criminal Justice Act 1984 s.12.

[16] These figures have been rounded up or down, as appropriate. The exact statistics are set out in the Courts Service *Annual Report 2009*, p.56.

[17] Blumstein, Cohen, Martin and Tonry (eds), *Research on Sentencing: The Search for Reform* Vol. 1 (Washington D.C.: National Academy Press, 1983), p.72 ("Disparity exists when 'like cases' with respect to case attributes – regardless of their legitimacy – are sentenced differently"). This work has an illuminating discussion (pp.72–77) on the distinction between discrimination and disparity and on different types of disparity.

explained by adherence to different penal policies. The judge who orders a first-time, drug-addicted offender convicted of robbery to probationary supervision probably does so in the belief that the case calls for a rehabilitative measure. The judge who sentences a similar offender to a term of imprisonment may do so in the belief that robbery calls for a deterrent measure. Some might argue that there is no disparity when judges are entitled to select any one of several permissible penal purposes ranging from just deserts to rehabilitation, and when there is no statutory guidance as to when one purpose should take precedence over the others. This argument has some formal validity but it fails to convince when viewed from the perspective of offenders who are surely entitled to expect some measure of distributional equity from the sentencing system. Various research strategies might be used to investigate the existence or extent of sentencing disparity. By surveying the sentencing practices at selected court venues which deal with significant numbers of commonly-prosecuted cases, it is possible to identify variations in the kind and severity of sanctions imposed on different categories of offender, e.g. the percentage of robbers who received prison sentences and the average length of those sentences in each court venue. The number of cases included in such a pilot study must be sufficiently large to produce reliable results; otherwise, a few genuinely exceptional cases could present a distorted picture of normal sentencing practice. Another research strategy would be to get a group of judges from the same court jurisdiction to participate in a simulated sentencing exercise by presenting them with a detailed set of facts about a selection of cases and then comparing the results. Many such exercises have been conducted internationally, one of the best-known being a study carried out among Second Circuit judges in the United States in 1972. The results were said to show glaring disparities, although some critics who point to its methodological shortcomings suggest that the true levels of disparity may not have been as great as the official report concluded.[18]

Available data are insufficient to support any reliable conclusion on the existence or extent of sentencing disparity in Ireland, and the same is true of many other countries. However, the existence of some degree of disparity may be inferred from certain organisational aspects of the system, and it is occasionally exemplified by individual cases suggesting a lack of any unified or coherent approach towards the sentencing of certain offences. Those cases, however, unless particularly numerous, are seldom adequate in themselves to ground any conclusion about the existence of disparity. Media reports of trial court sentencing decisions usually lack sufficient detail to assess the

---

[18] Partridge and Eldridge, *The Second Circuit Sentencing Study: A Report to the Judges and Justices of the Second Circuit* (Washington D.C.: Federal Judicial Centre, 1974). For a critical analysis, see Stith and Cabranes, *Fear of Judging: Sentencing Guidelines in the Federal Courts* (Chicago: University of Chicago Press, 1998), Ch.4. Other traditional methods for measuring disparity are described in Diamond and Zeisel, "Sentencing Councils: A Study of Sentence Disparity and its Reduction" (1975) 43 Univ. Chicago L.R. 109.

appropriateness of specific sentences in light of all the material facts. The same holds true of most ex tempore appeal court decisions. Apart from the relatively few cases disposed of in the Central Criminal Court and Special Criminal Court, all Irish criminal trials and sentencing hearings are held in either the District Court or the Circuit Court. Formally, there is only one District Court and one Circuit Court, but their regional distribution and the practice of assigning judges permanently to districts and circuits mean that individual judges can, up to a point, develop their own practice largely in isolation from and independently of their colleagues. There are 64 District Court judges divided among 24 districts, and 38 Circuit Court judges divided among 8 circuits. They must of course remain within the law in terms of observing maximum penalties and abiding by the relevant procedural rules. They must also apply the general principles of sentencing established by the superior courts, and their decisions are subject to appeal. But even allowing for these restrictions, trial judges still retain significant discretion when it comes to choosing the kind and amount of sanction in any one case. Judicial sentencing discretion must be retained if justice is to be done in individual cases, but further measures are needed to generate more consistency of approach and to cultivate a more principled consensus on appropriate penalty levels. We may well lack empirical evidence on the existence of sentencing disparity, however defined, but the absence of this principled consensus coupled with the failure of appeal courts to indicate any benchmark or tariff penalties provide such a fertile environment for the growth of disparity that we may safely assume its existence.

JUSTIFICATIONS FOR REFORM

Constitutional justice and the rule of law

A criminal conviction usually entails the loss of one or more rights to which the offender is otherwise entitled. He no longer enjoys a presumption of innocence in respect of the offence of conviction and, if lawfully imprisoned, he must also lose his right to personal liberty and its associated privileges. However, offenders retain those rights that are compatible with their status as convicted persons or prisoners as the case may be. Their rights to natural justice, fair procedures and the observance of the rule of law remain intact. The Constitution states quite peremptorily: "No citizen shall be deprived of his personal liberty save in accordance with law".[19] This is one provision in which the word "citizen" may safely be read as "person", especially in light of the remainder of Art.40.4. Literally construed, the Constitution tolerates any deprivation of liberty permitted by law. Any sentence of imprisonment should therefore be compatible with the Constitution, provided it is within the maximum permitted by statute

---

[19]   Article 40.4.1°.

and within the jurisdiction of the sentencing court. The District Court, for example, may not impose a prison sentence in excess of 12 months for an indictable offence disposed of summarily, irrespective of the statutory maximum.[20] Few would nowadays subscribe to the forfeiture theory of sentencing which holds that the commission of a crime leaves the offender liable to any punishment up to the prescribed maximum. According to this view, a court may exercise mercy by imposing something less than the maximum but the offender cannot expect any leniency as a matter of right.[21] Modern concepts of justice demand that punishment should be calibrated to the gravity of the offence and the culpability of the offender. A criminal conviction certainly entails forfeiture of the right to be free of all punishment but it does not deprive the offender of his right to commensurate punishment. Because criminal offences are nowadays defined in broad terms, maximum sentences tend to be quite high. Theft, for example, is very broadly defined in most jurisdictions and in Ireland carries a maximum sentence of 10 years' imprisonment.[22] It can scarcely have been the legislative intent that everyone convicted on indictment of any theft whatsoever, no matter how small the value of the stolen property, should be liable to any sentence up to the maximum at the whim of the sentencing judge. By stipulating such a broad punishment range, parliament must be presumed to have intended that sentences imposed in specific cases would reflect the particular offender's guilt. The idea that convicted persons retain many constitutional rights is now so well accepted as to require little elaboration. It is reflected, for example, in both domestic and international law on prisoners' rights[23] and in those jurisdictions where proportionality is formally recognised, constitutionally or otherwise, as the main distributive principle of punishment. Constitutional justice must also require that similarly-situated offenders are treated in a similar fashion without necessarily insisting on exact uniformity of outcome in all similar cases. Such a requirement would seem to flow from the exigencies of the rule of law to which convicted as well as accused persons are constitutionally entitled.[24] By any standard, the concept of legality as encapsulated in the phrase "in accordance with law", calls for more than formal compatibility with the governing statutes.

---

[20] Criminal Justice Act 1951 s.4.

[21] Kadish, "Legal Norms and Discretion in the Police and Sentencing Processes" (1962) 75 Harvard L.R. 904 at 919 et seq. referring to the "grace conception" of criminal punishment; Byrne, Hessick and Hessick, "Recognizing Constitutional Rights at Sentencing" (2011) 99 California L.R. 47.

[22] Criminal Justice (Theft and Fraud Offences) Act 2001 s.4.

[23] *Keenan v United Kingdom* (2001) 33 E.H.R.R. 38 (p.913); *Kudla v Poland* (2002) 35 E.H.R.R. 11 (p.198); *Murray v Ireland* [1985] I.R. 532 (HC), [1991] I.L.R.M. 465 (SC); *Holland v Governor of Portlaoise Prison* [2004] 2 I.R. 573. The Eighth Amendment to the United States Constitution prohibiting cruel and unusual punishment applies to the sentencing stage of a criminal trial and to prison conditions.

[24] *G v DPP* [1994] 1 I.R. 374 at 381, per Denham J. ("No matter how heinous the crime, or how disturbing the facts, every man, woman and child suspected, charged or convicted of an offence is entitled to the rule of law and has constitutional rights").

The rule of law is an essentially contested concept, a term developed by Gallie to denote a concept which undoubtedly exists but which provokes deep divisions over its precise meaning and content in particular circumstances.[25] Concepts such as justice, liberty, power, even medicine have also from time to time been described as essentially contestable.[26] The rule of law has proved to be especially contentious, despite the frequency and passion with which it is now almost universally invoked.[27] To describe the rule of law as a protean concept would be something of an understatement but, viewed in broad terms, it may be interpreted either in a purely formal or in a more substantive way. Advocates of the more formal or "thin" version, including Dicey, Raz and Fuller, view the rule of law largely in procedural terms. By their account, law should be created by a legitimate authority, and should be clear, accessible, and capable of being observed by rational beings, prospective in its application and applicable to governors and governed alike.[28] Even this basic menu might not command universal agreement among supporters of the more formal version. All of these qualities are essentially concerned with the rule of law as opposed to the rule of *good* law, to invoke a distinction once drawn by Raz.[29] A more substantive version of the rule of law would include additional value-based elements ranging from a democratic (or even liberal democratic) system of government to the protection of human rights including in some cases social and economic rights.[30] In a well-known lecture delivered in 2006, Lord Bingham included respect for fundamental human rights

---

[25] Gallie, "Essentially Contested Concepts" (1955) 56 *Proceedings of the Aristotelian Society* 167; Gallie, *Philosophy and the Historical Understanding* (London: Chatto and Windus, 1964); Waldron, "Is the Rule of Law an Essentially Contested Concept (in Florida)?" (2002) 21 *Law and Philosophy* 137.

[26] See, for example, McDonald, "Is 'Power' Essentially Contestable?" (1976) 6:3 *British Journal of Political Science* 380; McKnight, "Medicine as an essentially contested concept" (2003) 29 *Journal of Medical Ethics* 261.

[27] Tamanaha, *On the Rule of Law* (Cambridge: Cambridge University Press, 2004), where the rule of law is described (p.3) as "an exceedingly elusive notion", has a good historical account of its evolution. The same author's "The Rule of Law for Everyone" (2002) 25 *Current Legal Problems* 97 considers, amongst other things, the variety of political contexts in which the rule of law has been invoked.

[28] For further analysis of the various versions of the rule of law and the problems associated with them, see Waldron (fn.25 above); Tamanaha (fn.27 above); Goldsworthy, "Legislative Sovereignty and the Rule of Law" in Campbell, Ewing and Tomkins (eds), *Sceptical Essays on Human Rights* (Oxford: Oxford University Press, 2002), Ch.4; Raz, "The Rule of Law and its Virtue" (1977) 93 L.Q.R. 195; Rose, "The Rule of Law in the Western World: An Overview" (2004) 35 *Journal of Social Philosophy* 457; Shklar, "Political Theory and the Rule of Law" in Hutcheson and Monahan (eds), *The Rule of Law: Ideal or Ideology* (Toronto: Carswell, 1987); Fuller, *The Morality of Law* (New Haven: Yale University Press, 1964); Ewing, *Bonfire of the Liberties: New Labour, Human Rights and the Rule of Law* (Oxford: Oxford University Press, 2010), p.3 et seq.; Craig, "Formal and Substantive Conceptions of the Rule of Law: An Analytical Framework" (1997) *Public Law* 467.

[29] Raz (fn.28 above).

[30] Exponents of this view would certainly include Ronald Dworkin. See, in particular, *A Matter of Principle* (Cambridge, MA: Harvard University Press, 1985).

and compliance by the State with its international obligations among the essential ingredients of the rule of law.[31] Although not particularly expansive, Bingham's version is certainly concerned with good law, and as such falls into the substantive category.

Either version of the rule of law might plausibly be invoked to defend a rational and coherent sentencing system, though the more substantive approach obviously provides a richer set of arguments. Even the most elementary version would require that criminal offences and the punishments attaching to them must be clearly defined and adequately published. This does not necessarily entail the advance stipulation of exact penalties—another way of saying that all penalties should be mandatory. What it does require is that the outer limits of available penalties should be clear and prospectively applicable. All of this, of course, is encapsulated in the two classic principles of legality: *nullum crimen sine lege; nulla poena sine lege* (no crime without law, no penalty without law). While the rule of law, in whatever guise, readily tolerates the allocation of sentencing discretion to judges (and some of the more substantive versions might even require such allocation), it must also require them to exercise that discretion according to principles that are settled, consistently applied and reasonably predictable. Few would nowadays dispute the compatibility of confined discretion with the rule of law. There can scarcely be any developed legal system, past or present, which has not found it necessary to temper the application of its formal rules with some measure of administrative or judicial discretion.[32] Unless discretion is exercised impartially, however, and in accordance with settled principles, it risks creating a "government of men" without the law's restraining influence.

Rawls has very plausibly argued that the rule of law "also implies the precept that similar cases be treated similarly."[33] This, as he says, significantly limits the discretion of judges and other authorities. Such a precept assumes even greater importance within a constitutional framework which places a high premium on rights to liberty, property and due process. The Irish Constitution strongly guarantees all of these rights although it clearly tolerates restrictions on personal liberty and property in order to advance such legitimate social purposes as the effective punishment of convicted offenders. But a genuine commitment to protecting such rights imposes two related constraints on public decision-makers, including judges. The first is that any incursion on an individual's

---

[31] Bingham, "The Rule of Law" (2007) 66 Cambridge L.J. 67. His views are further elaborated in Bingham, *The Rule of Law* (London: Allen Lane, 2010).

[32] Davis, *Discretionary Justice: A Preliminary Inquiry* (Baton Rouge: Louisiana State University Press, 1969), p.17 ("Every governmental and legal system in world history has involved both rules and discretion. No government has ever been a government of laws and not men in the sense of eliminating all discretionary power. Every government has always been *a government of laws and of men*" (emphasis in original)).

[33] Rawls, *A Theory of Justice* (Oxford: Oxford University Press, 1972), p.237.

personal liberty or property should be free of arbitrariness, and the second is that those rights must be restricted to the least extent necessary in the particular circumstances. Neither principle restricts the general power to punish but if, as the Supreme Court has held, convicted offenders as well as defendants are entitled to the rule of law,[34] both principles combine to demand that sentencing discretion be exercised in a particular way. It must be both principled and parsimonious. Arbitrariness is inconsistent with any version of the rule of law which, in turn, means that discretion must be exercised in a non-arbitrary fashion. The conditions necessary to achieve this goal have already been noted: discretion must be exercised according to settled, evenly-applied principles. Rights to personal liberty and property will be inadequately vindicated if the extent to which they are restricted in a given case bears no relation to the overall gravity of the criminal conduct or to the punishment typically imposed on similarly situated offenders. An offender can scarcely complain merely because one or two others in similar circumstances have been punished somewhat more leniently in the past. Perfect consistency is seldom achievable within any discretionary system. What the rule of law requires is consistency of approach, though this is a more demanding requirement than we sometimes acknowledge. There is a certain tendency to treat consistency of approach as little more than a rule of recognition, the idea being that it requires no more than broad judicial consensus on general sentencing principles. That is certainly an important element of it, and one that is generally observed. Most judges agree, for example, that a guilty plea is a mitigating factor, that the deployment of a dangerous weapon in the commission of an offence is ordinarily an aggravating factor and so forth. True consistency of approach, however, also includes a strong interpretative or evaluative element, meaning that substantial agreement should also exist over the weight to be accorded to those factors which determine the ultimate decision. This does not necessarily entail the creation of numerical guidelines similar to those in the United States federal system which are very specific in terms of the enhancements or, much more rarely, the deductions warranted by certain offence- and offender-related factors. Narrative guidance, preferably incorporating some indications of appropriate benchmarks for commonly-prosecuted offences, is much more appropriate in a jurisdiction committed to maintaining a healthy level of judicial discretion, but it must amount to something more than a collection of broadly-stated principles.

Instrumental value of procedural fairness

Observance of fair procedures, whether in a legal or administrative context, has an instrumental as well as an inherent value. Because public officials are acting on behalf of the broader community when they make decisions or resolve

---

[34] Footnote 24 above.

disputes within their jurisdictional competence, they are bound by certain ethical standards which do not apply, either at all or to the same extent, in purely private transactions. A person making a will is not obliged to leave his property to those who might reasonably seem to deserve it most. Legislation may intervene to override the testator's express instructions as to provide for some of his immediate family members but, aside from that, the law protects testamentary freedom. Subject to any formal legal constraints, people may do what they want with their own property, a right which succession law generally protects even after the owner's death.[35] Public authorities, when exercising their official duties, are never dealing with their own property nor are they there to give effect to their own personal preferences. They are either engaged in the distribution of public property in the broad sense of that term (which would include employ-ment, pensions, benefits and licences) or else making decisions which materially affect the rights and liabilities of citizens and others.[36] They must consequently comply with certain standards of procedural fairness as traditionally encap-sulated in the twin maxims of natural justice: nobody should be a judge in their own case, and both sides to a dispute must adequately be heard. While these still apply, they have been greatly amplified in light of evolving standards of justice and also in recognition of the expanding remit of the state.

Overt procedural fairness is defensible on the purely moral ground just mentioned, but it also has the further, and no less important, benefit of enhancing public confidence in the decision-making processes of courts and other state agencies. Some theorists would go further and argue that people are more likely to comply with the law when they accept the legitimacy of law enforcement agencies. Legitimacy, in turn, is created and fostered by punctilious adherence to legal rules and fair procedures. This, however, is a relatively new area of research and its conclusions must be treated with some caution. More normative and philosophical questions about whether, and why, people should obey the law have long been debated.[37] Only in more recent times have social psychologists begun to investigate why people do obey the law. Tyler, a leading exponent of the relationship between legitimacy and compliance, claims that the behaviour of actual and potential offenders is strongly influenced by their perceptions of how fairly the police and other official agencies discharge their duties.[38] In so far as this amounts to a claim that consistent observance of legality and fairness may have a deterrent impact superior to that of ordinary criminal sanctions, it is probably over-optimistic. Many convicted offenders accept that they have received due process and a fair sentence without

---

[35]   The current Irish law is contained in the Succession Act 1965 Pt IX, as amended.
[36]   Reich, "The New Property" (1964) 73 Yale L.J. 733.
[37]   Raz, *The Authority of Law: Essays on Law and Morality* (Oxford: Clarendon Press, 1979).
[38]   Tyler, "Procedural Justice, Legitimacy, and the Effective Rule of Law" in Tonry (ed.), *Crime and Justice: A Review of Research* (Chicago: University of Chicago Press, 2003), Vol.30, p.283; Tyler, *Why People Obey the Law* (Princeton, NJ: Princeton University Press, 2006).

simultaneously expressing any resolve to mend their ways. The claims made by Tyler and others may well be valid in certain circumstances, and more evidence may gradually emerge to support their credibility. There can be little doubt, however, about another, closely-related instrumental value of procedural fairness, and this has to do with the manner in which law enforcement is perceived and evaluated by the public at large. The principle that justice must not only be done but be seen to be done lies at the root of many public law doctrines.[39] A sentencing system, like any other facet of public administration, may well be inherently just but that will count for little unless it is also perceived to be so. To retain public confidence, it must be open to fair evaluation, and that in turn calls for the fulfilment of three conditions. First, sentencing practice must be governed by clearly-established principles which trial courts, subject to the supervision of appeal courts, must routinely apply. Secondly, those principles should be sufficiently detailed to permit the hypothetical informed observer, apprised of all the relevant details, to predict, subject to a reasonable margin of error, the sentence likely to be imposed for a given offence. Thirdly, the system must be accountable in the sense of allowing for public analysis of the sentences imposed and an assessment of their compatibility with governing norms and principles. Research studies have repeatedly shown that members of the public routinely underestimate the severity of sentences imposed by the courts for serious offences.[40] It is precisely this kind of public misunderstanding which leads to pressure for statutory restrictions on judicial sentencing discretion, although if the truth were known it would probably show that such restrictions were unnecessary and might well turn out, as they often do, to be counter-productive.

Public accountability

Writing in support of the draft United States Constitution in 1788, Alexander Hamilton described the judiciary as the "least dangerous" branch which had "no influence over either the sword or the purse".[41] True enough, the judiciary can neither declare war nor raise taxes which was probably what Hamilton had in mind when referring to the sword and the purse. Judicial decisions can, of course, have far-reaching economic and financial consequences. Decisions on matters such as the entitlement of indigent offenders to free legal aid or on the constitutional validity of revenue legislation are obvious examples. Sentencing decisions also have major implications for the exchequer and ultimately for the tax payer. They are no less valid or legitimate on that account; in fact, popular opinion, at least when superficially measured, generally supports the widespread

---

[39] *R v Sussex Justices, Ex p. McCarthy* [1924] 1 K.B. 256.
[40] Page 25 below.
[41] Federalist No. 78, reprinted in Rossiter (ed.), *The Federalist Papers* (New York: Mentor Books, 1961).

use of imprisonment, the most expensive sanction of all. Before considering the public accountability dimensions of sentencing, it is worth recalling a few of the more salient financial statistics in this area. In 2009, the current expenditure of the Courts Service was just over €97 million. This covers the entire service, and not just the criminal courts, and it must also be recalled that the service itself generates considerable revenue. In the same year, for example, it collected almost €27 million in fines. This money is transferred to the exchequer or to designated state agencies. Net expenditure on the Irish Prison Service in 2009 was almost €358 million, while approximately €52 million was allocated to the Probation Service. The average cost of an available prison place in 2009 was €77,000, down from almost €93,000 in 2008, while cost of a community service order was estimated at €4,295 per offender. A recent value for money study found that, even in a worst case scenario, the cost of community service was unlikely to exceed one-third of the cost of imprisoning the relevant offenders.[42] In short, therefore, sentencing has enormous financial implications. Responsibility for the growing prison population cannot, of course, be attributed solely to the courts. Account must also be taken of the statutory regime governing the sentencing of certain categories of offender, a matter over which the courts may have little or no control. For instance, we know that on December 4, 2009 there were 760 prisoners serving sentences for drug offences (compared with 567 in 2008 and 472 in 2007), accounting for about 22 per cent of the sentenced prisoner population. Not only that, but 420 of those prisoners were serving sentences of five years or more, and 119 were serving sentences of 10 years or more. It is reasonable to suppose that the vast majority of those prisoners—and probably all of those serving the longer sentences—had been convicted of a so-called section 15A offence (possessing for sale or supply controlled drugs with a street value of €13,000 or more).[43] In the vast majority of cases, however, courts are subject to few formal restraints in selecting sentence, and the choices they make have obvious financial consequences. Awareness of those consequences should not deflect judges from imposing sentences which they believe to be necessary and proper, but it is certainly a matter to which those responsible for framing sentencing policies and principles should rightly have regard.

The European dimension

Before the creation of the European Union under the Maastricht Treaty in 1993, the pre-existing European Community institutions had little competence in the

---

[42] Department of Justice, Equality and Law Reform, *Value for Money and Policy Review of the Community Service Scheme* (Dublin, 2009). The other statistics mentioned have been drawn from the most recent annual reports of the Courts Service, the Irish Prison Service and the Probation Service. According to figures just released, the average cost of a prison place in 2010 declined to €70,513.

[43] Misuse of Drugs Act 1977 s.15A and s.27, as inserted and amended by the Criminal Justice Act

area of criminal justice.[44] The Council of Europe had been much more active in that field, having produced a wide range of recommendations, declarations and treaties negotiated on an intergovernmental basis. Conferring competence on the European Community to legislate on criminal justice matters had been a much more sensitive issue because those matters were seen as closely connected with state sovereignty. With the Maastricht Treaty, a compromise was reached whereby the European Union would have three pillars, the third of which was Justice and Home Affairs (JHA). All that this permitted was intergovernmental co-operation in the areas of justice and home affairs, and the European Commission was not granted any right of initiative on criminal law matters. The Treaty of Amsterdam, while retaining this basic policy, aimed to enhance co-operation in this area, particularly through the creation of new legal instruments such as the framework decision which was similar to a directive in the sense of being binding as the result to be achieved, though it did not have direct effect.[45] The Commission, as well as member states, was granted a right of initiative in third pillar matters. Most importantly, perhaps, for present purposes, was the fundamental principle that enhanced co-operation among member states in criminal matters was best achieved by way of mutual recognition. Rather than aim for a system of harmonisation of laws, the leaders of the Union decided to opt for a system which allowed judicial decisions of one member state to be enforced by another with the minimum of formality. Mutual recognition, as Mitsilegas remarks, "does not involve a commonly negotiated standard".[46] The best known manifestation of the mutual recognition principle is the European Arrest Warrant (EAW), introduced by way of a framework decision in the aftermath of 9/11.[47] This has effectively replaced extradition within the European Union and requires that when one member state requests another to hand over a person who is wanted for prosecution or to undergo sentence, it may achieve this purpose by issuing a certificate to the requested State. The latter state must then comply with the request, and do so expeditiously, unless satisfied as to the existence of one or more of the few grounds on which it is permitted to refuse

---

1999, Criminal Justice Act 2006 and Criminal Justice Act 2007. See Ch.4 below. According to the Courts Service *Annual Report*, 51 sentences of 10 years or more were imposed in the Circuit Court in 2009, mostly for drug offences.

[44] More detailed accounts of this topic are provided by Mitsilegas, *EU Criminal Law* (Oxford: Hart Publishing, 2009); Peers, *EU Justice and Home Affairs* (Oxford: Oxford University Press, 2006); Lavenex, "Justice and Home Affairs: Communitarization with Hesitation" in Wallace (ed.), *Policy Making in the European Union*, 6th edn (Oxford: Oxford University Press, 2010), Ch.19; Eckes and Konstadinides (eds), *Crime within the Area of Freedom, Security and Justice: A European Public Order* (Cambridge: Cambridge University Press, 2011).

[45] *Rimsa v Governor of Cloverhill Prison* [2010] IESC 47.

[46] Footnote 44 above, p.124 where he also claims: "Agreeing on the *procedure* to recogise *national* decisions, rather than *substantive rules* in the field of criminal law reflects a legitimacy and democracy deficit."

[47] Council Framework Decision 2002/584/JHA, OJ L190/1 18.7.2002.

to execute the warrant.[48] More recent framework decisions have dealt with the mutual recognition of financial penalties, freezing orders and confiscation orders, as well as the European Evidence Warrant. The Lisbon Treaty has now abolished the pillar-based system; criminal justice matters will henceforth be dealt with by ordinary EU legislation.

Mutual recognition arrangements, we are constantly reminded, are founded on mutual trust. The Directorate-General for Justice of the European Commission describes the EAW system of surrender as being made possible by "a high level of mutual trust and co-operation between countries who share the same highly demanding concept of the rule of law."[49] National and European courts have echoed this sentiment in leading judgments on the operation of the EAW system.[50] Trust cannot be cultivated or sustained to any meaningful extent without some awareness of the laws, practices and custodial regimes operating in other member states. A person may not be surrendered to another State if any of his rights under the Constitution or the European Convention on Human Rights would thereby be violated.[51] A person may therefore resist surrender if he can establish that the prison conditions in the requesting state at the time of his likely surrender are such as to establish reasonable or substantial grounds for believing that he would suffer inhuman or degrading treatment or punishment (or a fortiori, torture) if surrendered.[52] Although there appears to be little authority so far on the matter in the context of the EAW, a court must surely be entitled also to have regard to sentencing practices in requesting states.[53] Given the widespread acceptance of proportionality as the primary distributive principle of punishment, it would scarcely be compatible with prevailing

---

[48] Spencer, "The European Arrest Warrant" in Bell and Kirkpatrick (eds), *The Cambridge Yearbook of European Legal Studies* Vol. 6 (2003–2004), p.201; Blekxtoon (ed.), *Handbook of the European Arrest Warrant* (The Hague: TMS Asser Press, 2005); Mitsilegas (fn.44 above), p.120 et seq. On the more recently-introduced European Evidence Warrant, see Murphy, "The European Evidence Warrant: Mutual Recognition and Mutual (Dis)trust" in Eckes and Konstadinides (fn.44 above), p.224. A report issued by the European Commission in April 2011 (Com (2011) 175 final) showed that between 2005 and 2009, almost 54,700 arrest warrants were issued by member states and 11,630 were executed. More than half of the requested persons consented to their surrender.

[49] *http://ec.europa.eu*. A similar principle is expressed in recital (10) of the Preamble to the Framework decision itself.

[50] *Advocaten voor de Werweld VZW v Leden van de Ministeraad* (Case C–303/5) [2007] E.C.R. I–03633 at [57]; *Office of the King's Prosecutor, Brussels v Cando Armas* [2005] 3 W.L.R. 1079; *Minister for Justice, Equality and Law Reform v Stapleton* [2007] IESC 30, [2008] 1 I.R. 669 at 684.

[51] European Arrest Warrant Act 2003 s.37.

[52] *Minister for Justice, Equality and Law Reform v Rettinger* [2010] IESC 45.

[53] The matter has occasionally arisen in connection with extradition to the United States, e.g. *Re Blake*, ex tempore, High Court, November 16, 2006 (*Irish Times*, November 17, 2006) (extradition refused); *Attorney General v Doyle aka West* [2010] IEHC 212 (extradition granted). *Soering v United Kingdom* (1989) 11 E.H.R.R. 439 is the leading European Court of Human Rights authority on the matter.

constitutional and human rights norms to surrender a person to a country where he would be subject to a manifestly excessive or crushing sentence which was out of all proportion to the gravity of the offence. This is not to suggest that all sentencing systems should be the same or that the likely punishment for a given offence may not legitimately vary from one country to another. As the Supreme Court has said, those provisions in EAW legislation prohibiting surrender where it would violate a person's constitutional rights must be treated as recognising national differences in the content to be ascribed to certain key concepts such as a fair trial and proportionate punishment.[54] However, as it also indicated in the same judgment, exceptional cases might arise where a rights violation appeared so egregious that surrender should be refused. This, in turn, demands that the sentencing practices as well as the sentencing laws of member states should be transparent and capable of evaluation. The appropriate authorities of each state should consequently take the steps necessary to ensure that its sentencing laws, principles and standards are both identifiable and accessible. It is also noteworthy that the Stockholm Programme adopted by the Council of the European Union in December 2009, setting out the Union's priorities in the areas of justice, freedom and security for the period 2010 to 2014, expresses the need for "adequate, reliable and comparable statistics" as a necessary prerequisite for evidence-based decisions in these areas.

The prison population

Significant increases in the prison population, unless accompanied by similar increases in recorded crime levels or in the general population or both, are often regarded as symptoms of a defective or malfunctioning criminal justice system. As against this, it must be recalled that there is no general consensus on optimal levels of imprisonment. As Tonry has written:

> "There is no value-free or scientific way to determine optimal levels of imprisonment in any country. Imprisonment patterns change over time in individual countries and vary widely between countries. No single or several factors, including changes in crime or conviction rates, in the age composition of the population, or in economic trends or employment rates, explain differences over time or across national boundaries."[55]

For comparative purposes, imprisonment rates are conventionally presented as the annual average number of prisoners per 100,000 of the population. Even when presented in this format, they must be treated with some caution.[56]

---

[54] *Minister for Justice, Equality and Law Reform v Brennan* [2007] IESC 21, [2007] 3 I.R. 732.

[55] Tonry, "Controlling Prison Population Size" (1996) 4:3 *European Journal on Criminal Policy and Research* 26.

[56] Indyk and Donnelly, *Full-time Imprisonment in New South Wales* (Judicial Commission of New South Wales, 2001), p.7.

Cross-national evaluations of sentencing practices must always be sensitive to definitional and computational differences. Some countries may treat various forms of juvenile detention as imprisonment for statistical purposes; others may not. Some may base their statistics on a pinpoint or snapshot census which counts the number of prisoners in custody on a particular date whereas others may apply the average daily population approach. Where the total prison population is covered, as in Ireland, it obviously includes a significant number of remand as well sentenced prisoners which means that it also reflects the impact of prevailing bail laws.

In 2008, the rate of imprisonment varied from 756 in the United States (the undisputed world leader in this regard) to 33 in India, and even lower in a few other countries. Ireland at that time had an imprisonment rate of 85, which was lower than that of most other European countries outside of Scandinavia. It is now believed to be in the region of 100 which is above the Western European average.[57] Bare statistics of this nature reveal little about state sentencing policy. Granted, many people both within and outside the United States would find it difficult to justify present levels of incarceration in that country, especially when so many non-violent offenders are locked up for very long periods of time.[58] Optimal levels must be identified by reference to the purpose for which imprisonment is used, and the length of custodial sentences typically imposed for various offence categories. A country which, for some reason, is constantly targeted or frequented by high-level drug dealers or persons engaged in human trafficking or child prostitution, or which is experiencing high levels of violence may well be justified in having higher than average levels of imprisonment. This leads to a second observation about the link between crime levels and prison population. What drives the prison population most is not the overall amount of recorded crime but rather the number of offenders processed through the criminal courts and the crimes of which those offenders are convicted. Prison populations are determined by the number of prisoners committed by the courts, the length of time for which they are committed and the length of time for which they are actually detained. The first and second of these factors will be determined by some combination of legislative and judicial policy. A jurisdiction with a large number of mandatory, mandatory minimum or presumptive prison sentencing provisions or which has some form of judicially-developed guide-lines heavily biased towards the use of imprisonment will almost inevitably experience significant growth in its prison population. The third factor, the length of time for which prisoners are actually detained, may also be influential. A liberal parole or early release policy will help to ease the prison population even where committal numbers are increasing and sentences are getting longer. More restrictive parole policies will have the opposite effect.[59]

---

[57]   This figure is based on the number of prisoners in custody and does not include those on temporary release.

[58]   The United States prison population has attracted a good deal of adverse comment both at home and abroad. See, for example, "Rough Justice in America", *The Economist,* July 22, 2010.

[59]   Chapter 9 below.

Ireland's prison population has risen more than ten-fold over the past half-century, and the growth has been particularly dramatic during the past few years. The average daily population reached an estimated 4,256 in June 2010 compared with 3,321 for 2007.[60] Famously, our prison population was at an all-time low in the late 1950s and indeed it remained very low right down to the mid-1970s. The average daily population at five-year intervals since 1955 is set out in Table 1.

TABLE 1

Year	Average Daily Population	Year	Average Daily Population
1955	356	1985	1,863
1960	366	1990	2,108
1965	561	1995	2,124
1970	749	2000	2,948
1975	1,019	2005	3,151
1980	1,215	2010	4,290

As can be seen from these figures, the prison population has risen steadily since 1975 when it exceeded the 1,000 mark. Viewed in purely numerical terms, the increase over the 55-year period is quite striking, but it must of course be considered in light of certain other factors. First, there has been a significant increase in the general population which stood at 2.8 million in 1960 compared to 4.2 million in 2006, the last year for which official census figures are available and an estimated 4.5 million today.

Secondly, there has been a significant increase in the volume of recorded crime. The numbers of recorded indictable offences (and, for recent years, headline offences) coming to police attention at five-year intervals since 1955 are set out in Table 2.

TABLE 2

Year	No. of recorded offences	Year	No. of recorded offences
1955	11,531	1985	91,285
1960	15,375	1990	87,658
1965	16,736	1995	102,484
1970	30,756	2000	73,276
1975	48,387	2005	101,659
1980	72,782	2010	272,191

[60] Again, these figures relate to the actual number in custody. There were only 153 prisoners on ordinary temporary release in 2007 compared with about 750 in 2010.

The remarkably high figure for 2010, the latest year for which official statistics are available, must be attributed in part to changes in recording practice. Crime statistics are now produced by the Central Statistics Office, rather than directly by the Gardaí, and are based on a recently-introduced classification scheme. The tables of recorded offences now include road traffic offences (or, at least the more serious ones) as well as public order offences, breaches of court orders and other matters which would not previously have been included in the category of serious crime. Nonetheless the 2010 figures reveal certain levels of recorded crime which would have been unthinkable 30 years earlier, such as 86 homicide offences, 358 murder threats, almost 2,400 sex offences, more than 20,000 drug offences and 30 human trafficking offences (49 in 2009).[61] Until the early 1970s, the number of recorded murders was usually in single figures and, with the exception of 1974 (the year of the Dublin and Monaghan bombings), did not exceed 30 until 1995. In recent years, the number of recorded homicides (including manslaughter and dangerous driving causing death as well as murder) has been as high as 126 in 2005, although it fell to 88 in 2009.[62] The pattern is even more pronounced in relation to sex offences and drug offences.

Thirdly, it would be a mistake to treat the late 1950s as a time "during which the condition of the human race was most happy and prosperous", as Gibbon characterised the second century AD.[63] The social environment which produced the historically low prison population of 1958 cannot be understood without attending to other forms of confinement which were flourishing at that time. It is only when due account is taken of those detained in psychiatric hospitals, industrial schools, reformatory schools and other institutions that the true extent of incarceration in mid-twentieth century Ireland can properly be assessed. Narratives of the growth of the asylum system have been a fertile site of conflict between Whig historians who have cast the growth of the asylum and the development of psychiatric expertise in a positive or benevolent light, and more radical revisionists such as Foucault and Szasz who view psychiatry and the setting in which it was practised as reflecting professional domination and increasing state control. Recent scholarship adopts a more balanced and probably a more accurate approach by acknowledging the variety of roles, custodial and therapeutic, which the asylum was called upon to discharge.[64]

---

[61] Figures drawn from most recent quarterly bulletin of the Central Statistics Office, *Recorded Crime Quarter 1 2011* (April 2011) which includes overall figures for two previous years.

[62] Central Statistics Office, *Garda Recorded Crime Statistics 2005–2009* (Dublin, 2011).

[63] Gibbon, *The Decline and Fall of the Roman Empire,* abridged edn (London: Penguin Books, 1985), p.107.

[64] For a review of these competing historical assessments, see Porter "Introduction" in Porter and Wright (eds), *The Confinement of the Insane: International Perspectives 1800–1965* (Cambridge: Cambridge University Press, 2003). The Whig approach is reflected in Roberts, *Victorian Origins of the British Welfare State* (New Haven: Yale University Press, 1960). Leading critical and revisionist works include Foucault, *Madness and Civilisation; A History of Insanity in the Age of Reason* translated by Howard (New York: Random House, 1965);

Families and communities were often more influential than public authorities in securing committal. In the absence of more appropriate services and facilities, the asylum could be a refuge from poverty, neglect or domestic violence as well as a place for detaining and treating the mentally ill.[65] Yet the characterisation of the psychiatric hospital as "a convenient place to get rid of inconvenient people"[66] remained accurate, in some measure at least, in Ireland right down to the 1970s. The Richmond Asylum, now St. Brendan's Hospital, was established in 1814 as our first purpose-built asylum—in fact it was one of the earliest in Europe—and by 1871 a further 21 county institutions were in place.[67] During the second half of the nineteenth century, the asylum population increased by 337 per cent. At one point, there was in-patient rate of 63 per 100,000 of the population and numbers did not begin to decline significantly until the late twentieth century.[68] The number of long-stay patients may be inferred from the fact that between 1965 and 2002 more than 28,000 patients died in psychiatric hospitals.

A survey of Irish prison and psychiatric hospital populations from 1960 to the early years of this century reveals a steady rise in one and an even steeper decline in the other. In 1961, when the prison population was still less than 500, there were more than 21,000 patients in psychiatric hospitals.[69] From that point onwards, the hospital population declined very gradually, dipping below 10,000 for the first time in 1988. By 2002, it was slightly less than 4,000 and today the number of beds available nationally for long-stay patients is just over 1,000.[70] Statistics on reformatory and industrial schools tell a similar story. In 1955, for example, Ireland had three reformatory schools and 49 industrial schools with a combined inmate population of about 5,500. By 1970, this had declined to about 2,000.[71] The number of children now in residential care and various kinds

---

Szasz, *The Manufacture of Madness* (London: Routledge & Kegan Paul, 1971); Szasz, *The Myth of Mental Illness* rev. edn (London: Perennial Library, 1974); Scull, *The Most Solitary of Afflictions: Madness and Society in Britain 1700–1900* (New Haven: Yale University Press, 1993).

[65] Finnane, "Asylums, Families and the State" (Autumn 1985) *History Workshop* No. 20, 134.

[66] Scull, "A convenient place to get rid of inconvenient people: the Victorian lunatic asylum" in King (ed.), *Buildings and Society* (London: Routledge & Kegan Paul, 1980), p.19.

[67] Bartlett and Wright, "Community Care and its Antecedents" in Bartlett and Wright, *Outside the Walls of the Asylum: the History of Care in the Community 1750–2000* (London: Athlone Press, 1999), p.5.

[68] Malcolm, "'Ireland's Crowded Madhouses': the institutional confinement of the insane in nineteenth- and twentieth-century Ireland" in Porter and Wright (fn.64 above), p.315.

[69] *Report of Commission of Inquiry on Mental Illness* (Dublin: Department of Health, 1966).

[70] Walsh and Daly, *Mental Illness in Ireland 1750–2002: Reflections on the Rise and Fall of Institutional Care* (Dublin: Health Research Board, 2004), pp.68–69; Mental Health Commission, *Annual Report 2008*. The present-day figure does not include those being treated in other psychiatric facilities.

[71] According to a *Tuairim* report, *Some of Our Children* (London, 1966), there were 3,419 children in industrial and reformatory schools in 1965. For further statistics, see *Report on Reformatory and Industrial Schools Systems,* Prl 1342 (Dublin, 1970).

of young offender institutions is probably in the region of 500.[72] Meanwhile, as we have seen, the prison population has risen quite steeply but the overall number of persons in state custody is now a fraction of what it was 50 years ago. This pattern is by no means unique to Ireland, although there is no inevitable or causal relationship between a decline in the numbers in institutional care and a rise in the numbers in penal detention.[73]

Public opinion

The relationship between public opinion and sentencing is a now a major area of study in itself, but a few salient points emerging from international research are worth noting, though few of them, in fact, are likely to cause much surprise. At the outset, two dimensions of the relationship must be distinguished: the impact of public opinion on judicial sentencing practice, and public perceptions of the sentencing process. As to the first of these, it is well accepted that a court should not allow anticipated public reaction to influence the choice of sentence in any one case. The right to be tried and, if convicted, to be sentenced by an independent and impartial tribunal, a right protected under the Constitution of Ireland and art.6 of the European Convention on Human Rights, entails the entitlement to have one's sentence selected in accordance with objective criteria by an authority which is legally and actually insulated from the pressure and vagaries of public opinion. At the same time, the courts' obligation to maintain and promote public confidence in the administration of justice means that they cannot entirely ignore public opinion on sentencing practices in general. As Lawton L.J. (for the English Court of Appeal) said in a leading authority on the matter: "The courts do not have to reflect public opinion. On the other hand courts must not disregard it. Perhaps the main duty of the court is to lead public opinion."[74] In a later case, the same court expressly approved the following statement by the trial judge:

> "Judges are not here to gain approval or avoid disapproval from the public, and thus decide their sentences perhaps, on the basis of the lowest common denominator of public opinion. But, at the same time, public abhorrence of behaviour like the defendant's [inflicting grievous bodily harm on his baby son] should not be, and must not be, disregarded by the courts, who also have a duty to the public to pass judgment in a way which is generally acceptable

---

[72] Health Information And Quality Authority, *National Children in Care Inspection Report 2008*, p.30 (5,449 children in care of health authorities, but almost 90 per cent of these in foster care with the remaining 400 in residential care).

[73] Harcourt, "From the Asylum to the Prison: Rethinking the Incarceration Revolution" (2006) 84 Texas L.R. 1751.

[74] *R v Sargeant* (1974) 60 Cr. App. R. 74 at 77. See also Shute, "The Place of Public Opinion in Sentencing" [1998] Crim. L.R. 465; Ashworth and Hough, "Sentencing and the Climate of Opinion" [1996] Crim. L.R. 776.

amongst right-thinking, well-informed persons. There are matters of public interest and public policy here which I have to consider ... [and a custodial sentence must be imposed]".[75]

The same matter arose, even more famously or infamously, in *R v Home Secretary, Ex p. Venables and Thompson*[76] which involved the tariff period to be served by two youths who had been convicted in 1993 of the murder of an infant, James Bulger. While the Lord Chief Justice had recommended a 10-year tariff, the Home Secretary increased it to 15 years, largely as a result of a media campaign waged by certain tabloid newspapers. The House of Lords held, first, that a sentence of detention during the pleasure of the Crown was not to be equated with the mandatory life sentence for murder committed by an adult. Secondly, it held that the Home Secretary was required to act in a judicial manner when exercising his functions in relation to offenders such as the applicants. He should not, therefore, have allowed public petitions or protests to influence his decisions in this regard. Lord Goff summed up the position in these terms:

> "I wish to draw a distinction in the present context between public concern of a general nature with regard to, for example, the prevalence of certain types of offence, and the need that those who commit such offences should be duly punished; and public clamour that a particular offender whose case is under consideration should be singled out for severe punishment. It is legitimate for a sentencing authority to take the former concern into account, but not the latter. In my opinion, by crossing the boundary from one type of public concern to the other, the Secretary of State erred in the present case."[77]

The second dimension of the issue under discussion—public perceptions of prevailing sentencing practices—has been the subject of much empirical research.[78] The findings emerging from opinion polls and other surveys in which respondents are asked straightforward questions, without being furnished with any additional information, have been reasonably consistent, throughout most of the English-speaking world at least. The public generally overestimate the

---

[75] *R v Broady* (1988) 10 Cr. App. R.(S.) 495 at 498.

[76] [1998] 1 A.C. 407, [1997] 3 W.L.R. 23, [1997] 3 All E.R. 97.

[77] [1998] 1 A.C. 407 at 491. See Shute (fn.74 above).

[78] See, in particular, Roberts and Hough, *Changing Attitudes to Punishment: Public Opinion, Crime and Justice* (Cullompton: Willan, 2002); Roberts and Hough, *Understanding Public Attitudes to Criminal Justice* (Maidenhead: Open University Press, 2005); Maruna and King, "Public Opinion and Community Penalties" in Bottoms, Rex and Robinson (eds), *Alternatives to Prison: Options for an Insecure Society* (Cullompton: Willan Publishing, 2004); de Keijser and Elffers, "Cross-Jurisdictional Differences in Punitive Public Attitudes?" (2009) 15 *European Journal on Criminal Policy and Research* 47.

incidence of crime, and of serious crime in particular.[79] A clear majority believe that judges are out of touch with social reality and that sentences imposed are unduly lenient.[80] Mandatory sentences often emerge as the preferred option for creating a safer society, the underlying belief being that such sentences are likely to have a strong deterrent impact. Misunderstandings also abound in relation to the length of time served by serious offenders before being granted temporary release from prison and about levels of recidivism among certain categories of offender. However, these views prevail when members of the public are asked for their instinctive responses to the relevant questions, and it has rightly been remarked that "too much credence tends to be given to the results of polls that manage to chart only people's unreflecting views".[81] Indeed, it has also been pointed out that some literature on the topic is all too ready to ascribe public attitudes to public ignorance. Many experts in the field also disagree strongly on certain fundamental issues, and furthermore there is little reason to believe that most of us are any more knowledgeable about other important public issues (such as social welfare entitlements) than the public in general are about crime and punishment.[82] However, what research also shows fairly consistently is that the more information respondents are given about sentencing practices, about the true nature of particular sanctions and about the background and circumstances of offenders, the more their responses tend to approximate to the actual sentencing practices of the courts. Sometimes, in fact, the sentences which informed respondents suggested in actual or hypothetical cases were more lenient that those that had been, or might have been, imposed by the courts. Another significant finding from one research exercise was that respondents who were required to suggest sentences in response to given sets of facts were primarily concerned to identify a just sentence. They did not seek information about existing sentencing patterns which, in turn, suggests that public concern about inconsistency may not be as strong as it is sometimes portrayed.[83]

---

[79] Hutton, "What do the Scottish Public Think about Sentencing and Punishment?" (2003) 9 *Scottish Journal of Criminal Justice Studies* 41 at 42. ("Seventy five per cent of the sample thought that crime had risen over the last five years when in fact it had fallen steadily over the last ten years").

[80] A MORI poll conducted in Britain in 2003 showed that 60 per cent of the public thought that sentences were too lenient. A Populus poll in March 2011 showed that 85 per cent of respondents felt that judges were out of touch and that politicians should take steps to ensure that criminals did not get off so lightly (*The Times*, April 12, 2011). A Canadian study conducted in 2005 found that 74 per cent responded that sentencing was too lenient: Roberts, Crutcher and Verbrugge, "Public Attitudes to Sentencing in Canada: Exploring Recent Findings" (January 2007) 49 *Canadian Journal of Criminology and Criminal Justice* 75. The authors show that the percentage of the public who regard sentencing as too lenient has remained remarkably stable over several decades.

[81] Hough and Park, "How malleable are attitudes to crime and punishment? Findings from a British Deliberative Poll" in Roberts and Hough (eds), *Changing Attitudes to Punishment* (fn.78 above).

[82] Maruna and King (fn.78 above).

[83] Hutton (fn.79 above).

The importance of these findings and considerations in the present context derives from the reality that political decisions to introduce mandatory penalties and other measures designed to increase sentence severity (including restrictions on parole or early release) are often strongly influenced by public attitudes reflected in opinion polls.[84] The problem is greatly aggravated when, as is often the case in Ireland, there is no ready source of information on the levels of punishment actually imposed for particular offences or on the length of time served by those sentenced to imprisonment. Worse still, one cannot point to any formal yardsticks or benchmarks for the sentencing of offences. A system like this is uniquely vulnerable to abrupt and ultimately unwise political initiatives to assuage public concern about the perceived leniency of a particular sentence or a pattern of sentencing for some offence or other. This is not to suggest that more information or the existence of guidelines or benchmarks will provide a panacea to all of these problems. However, public and political debate is likely to be much more rational and even-handed when it is possible to draw upon reliable data on existing practices and to point to the principles or benchmarks which are meant to guide trial courts and which will be employed by appeal courts to correct unduly lenient or severe sentences.

---

[84] See also p.190 below.

CHAPTER 2

THE VALUE OF JUDICIAL SENTENCING

Sentencing may be approached from many different disciplinary perspectives. Philosophers have long argued over the most defensible moral justification for state punishment, some favouring retribution or desert, others championing more utilitarian goals such as deterrence or rehabilitation. Lawyers tend to focus on the statutory framework of sentencing and the general principles developed by appeal courts. Criminologists try to draw broader conclusions from quantitative or qualitative analyses of sentencing patterns and outcomes. Less attention has been paid to the essential nature of the judicial sentencing task. General theories of adjudication are of some, though limited, explanatory assistance. Posner in a recent work identifies no less than nine theories of judicial behaviour ranging from the attitudinal which claims that "judges' decisions are best explained by the political preferences that they bring to their cases", to the legalistic which holds that legal decisions are determined by pre-existing law as applied objectively to the facts.[1] The last-mentioned theory probably reflects the orthodox conception of adjudication. Other scholars have been content to adopt a less elaborate binary classification of formalism and realism.[2] Formalism effectively corresponds to legalism as used by Posner, and is often presented as a mechanical exercise in which relevant rules are applied to particular facts in order to resolve disputes. Realism, on the other hand, is usually associated with the notion of the hunch as articulated by Hutcheson in the 1920s.[3] According to this theory, "judges follow an intuitive process to reach conclusions which they only later rationalise with deliberative reasoning."[4] Few

---

[1] Posner, *How Judges Think* (Cambridge, MA: Harvard University Press, 2008), pp.19–21 and 41. The listed theories include the attitudinal, the strategic, the sociological, the economic, the psychological, the phenomenological, pragmatism and legalism. See also Friedman, "The Politics of Judicial Review" (2005) 84 Texas L.R. 257.

[2] Guthrie, Rachlinski and Wistrich, "Blinking on the Bench: How Judges Decide Cases" (2007) 93 Cornell L.R. 1 (proposing a third, "intuitive-override" model); Neuborne, "Of Sausage Factories and Syllogism Machines: Formalism, Realism, and Exclusionary Selection Techniques" (1992) 67 N.Y.U. L. Rev. 419; Leiter, "Positivism, Formalism, Realism" (1999) 99 Columbia L.R. 1138.

[3] Hutcheson, "The Judgement Intuitive: The Function of the 'Hunch' in Judicial Decision" (1929) 14 Cornell L.J. 274. See also Radin, "The Theory of Judicial Decision: or How Judges Think" (1925) 11 Am. B.A.J. 357 (referring to how judges proceed "from a desirable conclusion back to one or another of a stock of logical premises").

[4] Guthrie, Rachlinski and Wistrich (fn.2 above), p.2.

deny that intuition has some role, at times perhaps a significant one, in the adjudication process. The challenge is to cabin it within appropriate confines.[5] Intuition essentially entails the production of a conclusion or solution without engaging in a logical thought process.[6] Both formalism and realism (in so far as realism may be equated with intuitive decision-making) could obviously provide explanatory frameworks for judicial sentencing. Sociologically oriented theories have also provided valuable insights. The concept of sentencing as a social practice, for example, would hold that decisions are not determined by legal rules but "through the routine, largely unreflective, day-to-day practices of judges working in a distinctive legal culture and in a local court environment."[7] By this account, sentencing is at best an intuitive exercise, with the most dominant influence being the judge's immersion in a particular professional culture sometimes associated with the notion of *habitus*.[8]

The "sentencing as a social practice" school of thought is correct in assuming that judges have necessarily imbibed certain values, thought patterns and problem-solving approaches through their education, training and experience, not to mention the occupational culture in which they will have been immersed since they began to practice law. The same may be said, mutatis mutandis, of most other occupational groups. The assertion that that sentencing decisions are never the product of legal rules is more contestable. The real problem is that the legal rules that do apply, whether of statutory or common-law origin, are sufficiently open-textured to permit a wide variety of outcomes in most cases. Judges themselves, when asked to describe the nature of their sentencing function, routinely emphasise its practical and pragmatic nature which must remain resistant to close constraint because of the diversity of factual circumstances and legal principles to which due consideration must be given.[9]

---

[5] Guthrie, Rachlinski and Wistrich (fn.2 above), p.5 ("Eliminating all intuition from judicial decision making is both impossible and undesirable because it is an essential part of how the human brain functions. Intuition is dangerous not because people rely on it but because they rely on it when it is inappropriate to do so" (internal footnote omitted)).

[6] Hammond, *Human Judgment and Social Policy* (Oxford: Oxford University Press, 1996), p.60.

[7] Hutton, "Sentencing as a Social Practice" in Armstrong and McAra (eds), *Perspectives on Punishment: The Contours of Control* (Oxford: Oxford University Press, 2006), p.155 at p.173.

[8] "Habitus", a concept derived from the work of Pierre Bourdieu, and used by Hutton (fn.7 above), refers to the phenomenon whereby our dispositions and decision-making processes are formed by internalising the values of class, family, education and other social structures to which we are exposed. It was described by Webb et al. (quoted in Hutton at p.162) as a "feel for the game".

[9] This, in turn, explains why some appeal courts remain strongly deferential towards the sentencing decision of trial judges. The Supreme Court of Canada has held that because of the "profoundly contextual nature of the sentencing process", the standard of review should be based on a policy of deference. It said:"(t)he sentencing judge has 'served on the front lines of our criminal justice system' and possesses unique qualifications in terms of experience and the ability to assess the submissions of the Crown and the offender ..." and that "(f)ar from being an exact science or an inflexible predetermined procedure, sentencing is primarily a matter for the trial judge's competence and expertise." (*R v L.M.* [2008] 2 S.C.R. 163, 2008 SCC 31 at [15], [17]).

They draw attention to the diversity of circumstances that may exist in apparently similar cases and the range of factors to be considered when selecting sentence. However, this leaves unanswered the critical question of how to go about choosing an appropriate response or sanction in an individual case. Again, most judges would probably reply that this is one area where they are called upon to exercise judgment in order to achieve justice which is, after all, their primary constitutional function. Many critics of the system find this response thoroughly unsatisfactory. Yet, as Kronman remarked, in the context of legal ethics, the highest compliment we can usually pay to any lawyer, whether judge or advocate, is to say that he or she is a person of sound judgement.[10]

This brings us back to the nature of judgement itself and, in particular, to the tension between formalism and intuition as positive or descriptive theories of adjudication. Traditionally, legal analyses of adjudication have been predomi-nantly normative while other disciplines have adopted more descriptive or behavioural approaches.[11] The normative approach does, of course, have an important critical value by pointing to ways in which the judgment process may be improved, provided it pays due attention to the practical contexts in which that process unfolds. Judicial pragmatism, in the sense of making decisions by reference to their likely or anticipated consequences, usually attracts strong support from the judiciary and most notably, of course, from Posner.[12] He defines practical reason as "the methods by which people who are not credulous form beliefs about matters that cannot be verified by logic or exact observation."[13] As might be expected, this has attracted its share of critics, mainly from the academic world. Levit, for example, dismissed Posner's version of practical reason as relying on "untutored and nonreflective" reasoning techniques which wrongly assume that the judiciary and the general population share the same values.[14] Yet, the notion of practical reason has a distinguished intellectual pedigree extending back to Aristotle's *Ethics*. In Book Six, entitled "Intellectual Virtues", Aristotle distinguishes between different kinds of knowledge and cognitive skills which include insight or intuition (*nous*), scientific knowledge (*epistemē*), theoretical wisdom (*sophia*), technical skill (*technē*) and what he calls *phronesis*, usually translated as practical wisdom or prudence.[15] The essence of *phronesis* is that it combines sound deliberation with prudent action.[16] Aristotle himself was at pains to stress that prudential reasoning pays at least as much attention to particulars as to universals:

---

[10] Kronman, "Living in the Law" (1987) 54 Univ. Chicago L.R. 835.
[11] Friedman (fn.1 above); Fallon, *Implementing the Constitution* (Cambridge, MA: Harvard University Press, 2001), p.2.
[12] Posner, *The Problems of Jurisprudence* (Cambridge, MA: Harvard University Press, 1990) and *How Judges Think* (Cambridge, MA: Harvard University Press, 2008).
[13] Posner, *The Problems of Jurisprudence* (fn.12 above), p.21.
[14] Levit, "Practically Unreasonable – A Critique of Practical Reason: A Review of the *Problems of Jurisprudence* by Richard Posner" (1991) 85 Northwestern Univ. L.R. 494.
[15] Aristotle, *Ethics*, trans. by Thomson (London: Penguin Books, 1976), esp. pp.206–225.
[16] Wiggins, "Deliberation and Practical Reason" (1975–1976) 75 *Proceedings of the Aristotelian*

"Again, prudence is not concerned with universals only; it must also take cognizance of particulars, because it is concerned with conduct, and conduct has its sphere in particular circumstances. That is why some people who do not possess [theoretical] knowledge are more effective in action (especially if they are experienced) than others who do possess it."[17]

Elsewhere in the same work, Aristotle says that virtue makes us aim at the right target, while practical wisdom makes us use the right means. Drawing on this concept, Kronman defines judgment as "the process of deliberating about and deciding personal, moral and political problems."[18] The notion of prudence, grounded on deliberation but with proper regard to both particulars and universals, seems to reflect the essence of the judicial sentencing task.

Some theorists will undoubtedly reject this identification of adjudication with practical reason or prudence as being insufficiently rigorous and leaving far too much scope for unexplained discretionary decision-making. They should recall, however, that practical reason consists, first and foremost, of deliberation and that, in turn, requires reflection on principles as well as facts. The ultimate goal, at least within the realm of sentencing, must be to produce decisions which are governed by principles transcending the facts of the particular case.[19] Legal decisions in general derive their legitimacy from being grounded on "impersonal and durable principles" of law.[20] Coherent decision-making requires the application of the same relevant principles to all similar cases in order to produce consistency of approach. Consistency of outcome, which is what many critics of the present sentencing system seem to want, is a more tendentious concept. Crudely defined in the sense that everyone convicted of offence X committed in certain circumstances should receive punishment Y, it could be profoundly unjust for failing to take account of genuinely differentiating circumstances. True consistency is achieved when the same principles or standards are routinely applied in assessing the gravity of offences, the personal circumstances of offenders and other ethically-relevant variables such as the nature of the plea or the level of co-operation, if any, tendered to law enforcement authorities. The main challenge currently facing the Irish sentencing system is to decide on the level of specificity with which those principles should be formulated. Many

---

Society 29; Polansky, "'Phronesis' on Tour: Cultural Adaptability of Aristotelian Ethical Notions" (2000) 10:4 *Kennedy Institute of Ethics Journal* 323.

[17] Aristotle, *Ethics* (fn.15 above), p.213.

[18] Kronman (fn.10 above), p.846.

[19] Wechsler, "Toward Neutral Principles of Constitutional Law" (1959) 73 Harv. L.R. 1 at 15 ("[T]he main constituent of the judicial process is precisely that it must be genuinely principled, resting with respect to every step that is involved in reaching judgment on analysis and reasons quite transcending the immediate result that is achieved.") See also Siegel, "The Virtue of Judicial Statesmanship" (2008) 86 Texas L.R. 959.

[20] Henry Hart, "The Supreme Court 1958 Term – Foreword: The Time Chart of the Justices" (1959) 73 Harv. L.R. 84 at 99.

general principles, such as the grant of a discount for a guilty plea, are already well established though subject to occasional exceptions. But should we go further by indicating appropriate levels of discount, say one-quarter or one-third or perhaps varying fractions depending on predefined circumstances? Would this in turn make any practical difference in the absence of agreed sentencing benchmarks to which those discounts could be applied? This looks like remaining a source of considerable disagreement for the foreseeable future, as the articulation of benchmarks could be interpreted as a move towards the creation of guidelines which many are determined to avoid but which others, mainly outside the legal system, would gladly support. As will later be argued, the debate over benchmarks must be placed on hold until more reliable information becomes available on the consistency or otherwise of existing sentencing practices, and that is unlikely to emerge until a reasonably extensive data bank on those practices has been established and analysed.[21]

To defend the value of practical wisdom or practical reasoning is not to suggest that all judges naturally possess it or to deny that many other decision-makers in the public and private spheres must exercise it in their day-to-day work. Indeed, it is a quality more often associated with statesmanship than with adjudication. Among modern theorists, it is most closely associated with the work of Isaiah Berlin who, in the context of defending his general political philosophy of value pluralism, envisaged practical wisdom as an exercise in synthesis rather than analysis, a capacity to respond to particular circumstances and problems, and with a strong focus on the consequences of any decision made.[22] What we value therefore is the virtue itself as opposed to any naïve assumption that everybody appointed, by whatever means, to a particular office somehow becomes endowed with it. Solum, who has analysed the concept more fully than most others, identifies six judicial virtues: "(1) judicial intelligence, (2) judicial wisdom, (3) judicial integrity, (4) judicial temperament, (5) judicial impartiality, and (6) justice."[23] He also remarks that "[t]he virtue of judicial wisdom includes the ability to assess the consequences of one's decisions and take them into proper account. A virtue-centred theory of judging permits a judge to attend to the considerations advanced by rival theories".[24] One practical corollary of placing such a high premium on practical reasoning is that great care must be taken in the selection of judges. Judicial selection processes vary

---

[21] Chapter 10 below.

[22] See, in particular, Berlin's essay, "Political Judgment" in *The Sense of Reality: Studies in Ideas and their History* (London: Pimlico, 1997), and also *Russian Thinkers* (London: Hogarth Press, 1978). For an analysis of this aspect of his work, see Aarsbergen-Ligtvoet, *Isaiah Berlin* (Amsterdam: Editions Rodopi B.V., 2006).

[23] Solum, "Equity and the Rule of Law" in Shapiro (ed.), *The Rule of Law*, NOMOS XXXVI (New York: New York University Press, 1994), p.120 at p.130. See also Macedo, "The Rule of Law, Justice, and the Politics of Moderation" in the same volume, p.148.

[24] Solum (fn.23 above).

greatly throughout the world, though in most common-law countries judges are drawn mainly or entirely from the ranks of the practising legal profession. They may be elected (as in some American states, though not in the federal system), appointed directly by the executive or chosen by an independent, expert body. The present Irish system is less than ideal because, although there has been a Judicial Appointments Advisory Board in place since 1995, the decision to nominate a person for a judicial appointment rests exclusively with the Government.[25] Selection processes should be rigorously directed towards choosing the best appointees in terms of legal knowledge, the capacity to reach careful, impartial and reasoned decisions, and the possession of the right judicial temperament. Political loyalty or affiliation should have no influence whatever, formally or informally. A system like that introduced in England and Wales under the Constitutional Reform Act 2005 which effectively commits the selection of judges to a statutory commission, with very limited residual powers left to the Lord Chancellor, could usefully be adopted in Ireland as well.

Any defence of adjudication must confront the issue of democratic legitimacy. This is a familiar theme within the realm of constitutional theory, particularly when applied to legal systems such as those of Ireland and the United States where courts are entitled to invalidate democratically-enacted legislation which is found to conflict with the terms of a written constitution. Such judicial decisions provoke little controversy when a clear conflict has emerged between a statutory provision and an express constitutional norm. An Irish law requiring that a general election be held at least every eight years would undoubtedly conflict with Art.16.5 of the Constitution which states that the Dáil (the house of representatives) shall not continue for longer than seven years or such shorter period as may be prescribed by law. By contrast, a decision striking down a ban on contraception or abortion in circumstances where neither matter is expressly mentioned in the constitutional document itself is likely to produce allegations of judicial legislation.[26] Decisions of the latter kind have produced deep fault lines among constitutional theorists, including many senior American judges, over the most defensible approach to constitutional interpretation.[27] Conservative theorists tend to favour some kind of "original meaning" approach which would focus attention on what the relevant constitutional provision meant, or probably meant, at the time of its adoption. When confronted with the argument that their interpretation may produce a socially undesirable result, originalists typically respond that the remedy rests with the political branches of government and, ultimately, with the citizenry at large who can exercise the power of amendment. (Members of the United States

---

[25] Courts and Court Officers Act 1995.

[26] This is exemplified by responses to *McGee v Attorney General* [1974] I.R. 284 in Ireland and *Roe v Wade* 410 U.S. 113 (1973) in the United States.

[27] There is a voluminous American literature on this topic, but much of the best of it is digested and analysed in Garvey, Aleinikoff and Farber (eds), *Modern Constitutional Theory: A Reader*, 5th edn (St. Paul, Minn.: Thomson West, 2004).

judiciary who adopt this argument do so in the clear knowledge that the federal constitution is almost impossible to amend.) Liberal theorists generally favour a more dynamic or progressive approach towards the interpretation of a constitutional text, though they may differ over the degree of latitude which the courts should be permitted to exercise for that purpose. Debates about the appropriate parameters of constitutional interpretation on the one hand and judicial sentencing discretion on the other have certain points in common. In both instances, unelected judges are making decisions which some citizens, though not all, would prefer to see allocated to more democratically accountable branches of government. In the case of sentencing this would presumably entail much greater reliance on mandatory or mandatory minimum sentences.

However, there are more differences than similarities between the two situations. Those charged with constitutional interpretation are typically faced with a set text which may have been adopted decades or centuries earlier and which may, in traditional terminology, be "rigid" in the sense that it cannot easily be amended.[28] Constitutional challenges to modern legislation or administrative decisions frequently require judges to provide answers to questions and controversies upon which the constitutional text itself is entirely silent. Interpretation is therefore inevitable, and those claiming to be guided by the original meaning or something similar are engaging in just as much interpretation as their more liberal colleagues, save that they are applying their minds to a different set of historical materials. The exercise of sentencing discretion, by its nature, never calls for textual interpretation. Cases may well arise where courts must interpret a sentencing statute to discover its true meaning. The Criminal Justice Act 1964 (s.2), for instance, provided that a person "who but for this Act would be liable to suffer death shall be liable to penal servitude for life". In *People (Attorney General) v Murtagh*,[29] the Supreme Court had to decide if this meant that penal servitude for life was the mandatory or merely the maximum sentence for murder. The court decided that it was mandatory, and the matter has since been put beyond doubt by the Criminal Justice Act 1990 (s.2). The question in *Murtagh*, however, was about the existence rather than the exercise of discretion. When it comes to exercising the discretion that is available for all but a handful of offences, sentencing judges are bound by few formal limits, principally the maximum sentence prescribed by statute and, where applicable, more general limits on the sentencing powers of summary jurisdiction courts. Such limits are usually clear and unambiguous. An Irish court sentencing a person convicted on indictment of a single offence of assault causing harm may not, in any circumstances, impose a prison sentence in excess of five years.[30] The same statutory provision allows for the imposition

---

[28] On the concepts of rigid and flexible constitutions, see Jenkins, "From Unwritten to Written: Transformation in the British Common-Law Constitution" (2003) 36 Vanderbilt J. Transnational L. 863 at 922 et seq.

[29] [1966] I.R. 361.

[30] Non-Fatal Offences Against the Person Act 1997 s.3.

of an unlimited fine whether in addition to or instead of a period of imprisonment, and the general law permits the court to select some other measure such as a suspended prison sentence or a community service order. The latter, if chosen, may not involve more than 240 hours of unpaid work.[31] This is not to suggest that sentencing statutes are inherently less problematic than others. One can point to the problem which arose in *Murtagh* in relation to the life sentence and the ongoing interpretative problems associated with s.99 of the Criminal Justice Act 2006 which provided a statutory foundation for the suspended sentence.

The meaning of discretion is discussed at more length in the next chapter but it essentially entails the authority to choose between several options, and when it comes to sentencing that choice is usually quite extensive. In Ireland at present, a court sentencing an adult convicted on indictment of a single offence of assault causing harm may impose: (1) any period of immediate imprisonment not exceeding five years; (2) a fully suspended term of imprisonment not exceeding five years; (3) a partly suspended term of imprisonment provided the aggregate does not exceed five years; (4) a fine which is de jure without limit but which, in accordance with settled principles, must reflect the means of the offender and the gravity of the offence; (5) a fine coupled with a term of imprisonment; (6) a community service order not exceeding 240 hours in length; (7) a compensation order on its own or coupled with another punishment[32]; (8) a fine coupled with a deferred prison sentence[33]; (9) a probation order.[34] Further options might be available in particular cases but those listed are sufficient to reveal the breadth of choice typically available to a sentencing judge. The most appropriate measure in any specific case will be determined by the particular facts and by the application of general principles to those facts. A guilty plea, the absence of previous convictions and the presence of provocation at the time of the assault would all ordinarily count as mitigating factors. The judge is therefore engaged in an interpretative exercise but one which differs quite radically from the task of interpreting a constitutional document. He or she is essentially required to interpret the evidence in light of any specific statutory rules (such as the requirement to impose consecutive prison sentences for offences committed while on bail[35]) or general principles (such as the treatment of a guilty plea as a mitigating factor).

Those who would remove or diminish the power vested in judges to engage in this interpretative exercise bear the burden of explaining how justice can otherwise be done in specific cases. Let us leave aside for the present other adjudication mechanisms such as a panel system whereby sentence might be selected by a group of people including, but not necessarily confined to, judges.

---

[31] Criminal Justice (Community Service) Act 1983 s.3.
[32] Criminal Justice Act 1993 s.6.
[33] Criminal Justice Act 2006 s.100.
[34] Probation of Offenders Act 1907.
[35] Criminal Justice Act 1984 s.11 as amended by the Criminal Justice Act 2007 s.22.

The Scottish Children's Hearing system,[36] which appears to have worked remarkably well, would be one such model though one cannot be sure how well it might translate to adult courts. The important point, however, is that discretion would still have to be exercised, though collectively, rather than individually. Opponents of judicial discretion seldom have this kind of model in mind. They would prefer to make sentencing more amenable to political control by means of mandatory penalties, statutory guidelines or other constraining measures. This in turn reflects a belief in the capacity of the democratic process to yield a more effective, whatever about a more just, sentencing system. Before proceeding to analyse this assumption, we must pause to note that the concept of effectiveness in sentencing is much more problematic than most advocates of the legislative model are willing to acknowledge. They may want the system to be effective by reducing crime through deterrent sentences, by incapacitating those likely to commit future crimes or by ensuring that convicted persons are punished to a degree which reflects communal assessments of offence gravity. All of these approaches would probably result in heavy sentences but it is by no means certain that they would all result in the same sentence. Nor, for that matter, can it be assumed that fixed or presumptive sentences would adequately fulfil any one or all of these social expectations. (By presumptive sentences in this context I mean sentences or sentence ranges prescribed in advance by legislation or by an administrative agency which the courts are bound to apply in the absence of defined exceptional circumstances.) When the requirement of individualised justice is added to the equation, as most people who have reflected on the matter agree that it must be the inadequacy of fixed and presumptive sentences becomes all the more apparent. The logical conclusion therefore is that reasoned and principled adjudication, as opposed to prior legislative prescription, is the best means of delivering just and effective sentences. But we must still confront the incompatibility which is sometimes alleged to exist between discretionary judicial decision-making and democratic principles.

Democracy may literally mean rule by the people, but the term itself tells us little about how that rule is to be exercised or, for that matter, about the people who are meant to exercise it. At one end of the spectrum, in both historical and participatory terms, is the concept of direct democracy which is most strongly associated with classical Athens in the fifth and fourth centuries BC. The people (*demos*) exercising this direct rule consisted solely of male citizens who in turn accounted for approximately 10 per cent of the overall population. They met regularly in assemblies where all matters relating to the governance of the city state (*polis*) were vigorously debated and decided.[37] Participation in assembly debates was regarded as a badge of good citizenship.[38] Apart from town

---

[36] Originally introduced by the Social Work (Scotland) Act 1968 in response to the Kilbrandon Report (1964).

[37] Dunn, *Setting the People Free: The Story of Democracy* (London: Atlantic Books, 2006), p.37.

[38] The duty to participate was most famously expressed in Pericles' speech as recorded by

meetings which evolved early on as the main instrument of government in colonial New England, the modern age has known few examples of direct democracy. In fact, following its demise at Athens in the late fourth century BC, democracy did not re-emerge in any meaningful form until the French Revolution and the American War of Independence more than two thousand years later. Changed social circumstances and vastly increased populations meant that Athenian-style direct democracy was no longer possible; democracy had henceforth to be representative in nature. Civic participation was still theoretically at the core of the political system but in practice it was confined to choosing rulers, a far remove from active self-government. Popular participation in a representative democracy is therefore episodic rather than continuous, and those elected to political office are representatives rather than proxies of those who have elected them.[39]

Some would argue that the electronic age has brought us back closer than we imagine to the direct democracy of classical Athens, but without the deliberation. Never in the modern era have members of the public had so many opportunities to express and register their opinions on virtually any topic. Opinion polls are no longer conducted solely in the traditional manner of soliciting the views of a representative sample of the population; they are also run continuously on websites, satellite television and elsewhere. Add to this the opportunities available to communicate instant opinions and grievances, publicly and privately, to politicians and other decision-makers by way of radio talk shows, email, text messages, internet blogs and the growing range of social media. In the mid-1990s, when the fax machine and telephone answering machine were still the principal means of speedy communication, the term "hyperdemocracy" was used, if not then invented, to describe this phenomenon of direct connection between government and the governed.[40] As one commentator summed up the situation:

> "The political system has become sensitive—indeed, hypersensitive—to the public's opinions and anxieties. The traditional parties and interest groups, as well as the Constitution, have been pushed into the background, as polls, the media and ideological activists and advocacy groups have moved to the forefront."[41]

Thucydides, *History of the Peloponnesian War*, trans. by Warner (London: Penguin Books, 1972), p.147. See also, Hansen, *The Athenian Democracy in the Age of Demosthenes*, trans. by Crook (Oxford: Blackwell Publishers, 1991), and Finley, *Democracy Ancient and Modern*, 2nd edn (London: Hogarth Press, 1985).

[39] Urbinati, *Representative Democracy: Principles and Genealogy* (Chicago: University of Chicago Press, 2006).

[40] Wines, "Washington Really is in Touch: We're the Problem", *New York Times*, October 16, 1994; Wright, "Hyperdemocracy", *Time*, January 23, 1995. Just around the time of writing, Bob Geldof has weighed in on the topic telling an American audience that hyperdemocracy "is a bust", adding: "Everyone has got the means to say anything they want but nobody has anything to say." (*New York Times*, March 17, 2011).

[41] Heclo, "Hyperdemocracy" (1999) 23 *Wilson Quarterly* 62.

Criminal justice issues, and sentencing in particular, have been particularly vulnerable to popular pressure exerted in this fashion. Public opinion, when measured or transmitted at random, is likely to reflect the view that sentencing is unduly lenient, that judicial sentencing practices are riddled with inconsistency and that harsher punishment would be effective in reducing crime.[42] To cite but one recent example, a Populus opinion poll conducted in England and Wales for *The Times* in March 2011 showed that 85 per cent of respondents agreed with the statement: "Judges are out of touch and politicians should make sure that they do not let criminals off too lightly." When it came to choosing the measure likely to be most effective in reducing crime, 40 per cent favoured "making punishment harsher to deter reoffending".[43] This, it should be recalled, was in a country which already has a prison population in excess of 85,000 (up from 45,000 in 1990) and one of the highest imprisonment rates in Western Europe. At least the Populus poll appears to have been conducted along reasonably conventional lines involving a random sample of 1,509 adults. It was therefore a more reliable indicator of public opinion than most electronic polls which make no attempt at random selection and usually pose single questions which are often phrased so as to encourage the desired response.

Disenchantment with existing forms of democracy has led many political scientists and philosophers to argue for a system of deliberative democracy in which decisions would be taken following rational debate and deliberation which endeavoured to accommodate different points of view. Representative democracy, particularly when combined with a tightly controlled political party system, operates and survives through the aggregation of preferences. Nowadays, as well, it often produces a political system in which the executive is far more powerful and influential than the legislature. Several different models and ideas of deliberative democracy have emerged since the term was introduced by Bessette in 1980.[44] However, it is essentially about active and informed discussion among engaged citizens over contentious matters of public concern. At the heart of the concept is the value of persuasion. Rather than simply aggregate preferences as to whether solution A, B or C should be adopted, a deliberative model allows proponents of different viewpoints an opportunity to explain their position, to listen to the views of others, to seek common ground and, as a best case scenario, to develop a satisfactory consensus

---

[42]   Page 24 et seq. above.

[43]   *The Times*, April 12, 2011. The poll was carried out in light of an ongoing controversy over Government Green Paper, *Breaking the Cycle: Effective Punishment, Rehabilitation and Sentencing of Offenders* Cm 7972 (London: Stationery Office, 2010).

[44]   Bessette, "Deliberative Democracy: The Majority Principle in Republican Government" in Goldwin and Schambra (eds), *How Democratic is the Constitution?* (Washington D.C.: American Enterprise Institute, 1980), pp.102–116. Other leading works include Gutmann and Thompson, *Why Deliberative Democracy?* (Princeton, NJ: Princeton University Press, 2004); Bohman, *Public Deliberation* (Cambridge, MA: MIT Press, 2000); Macedo (ed.), *Deliberative Politics: Essays on Democracy and Disagreement* (Oxford: Oxford University Press, 1999).

on the best way forward. Participants who approach the exercise in good faith may be persuaded to change their initial stance in light of the arguments they have heard. The system is premised on the idea that legitimacy of outcome depends on the nature and quality of the decision-making procedure.

Most advocates of deliberative democracy nowadays are realistic enough to accept that it is likely to function solely as a supplement to, rather than a replacement for, existing representative models of democracy. Its most practical application to date has been in the form of deliberative polling where participants (chosen as a representative sample of the relevant population) are brought together, often over one or two weekends in large scale, well-funded projects, and given the opportunity to hear a variety of advice and perspectives from specialists and others on the topic under discussion. They are also allowed ample time to debate the issues themselves in small group and plenary sessions. The topic might be political (e.g. which party to support in a forthcoming election), ethical (perhaps involving some aspect of medical practice), scientific (e.g. the pros and cons of nuclear power) or indeed a purely local issue such as the location for a waste disposal facility. Research has shown that engaged participants can be willing to change their minds, even where they held fixed or entrenched positions at the outset.[45]

It becomes apparent, therefore, that bald invocations of democracy mean little in themselves unless they specify more precisely the decision-making process in which we are being asked to place our trust. Representative democracy, which operates mainly through an aggregation of preferences, is suitable for some kinds of decision-making, but not for others. It is an efficient means of establishing general rules to guide human conduct and regulate social interaction. But it cannot operate either fairly or efficiently in circumstances where decisions and responses must be carefully calibrated to a specific set of facts. Nor is it always effective in devising rules and principles which must be sufficiently comprehensive and pliable to accommodate a wide variety of future contingencies. One of the lessons learned from experiments in deliberative democracy is that policy preferences may change and adapt, sometimes quite dramatically, when participants are alerted to the range of situations and circumstances to which the rule or decision under consideration is likely to apply. The realities of modern political practice and discourse seldom accommodate this kind of deliberative, evolutionary approach towards policy making. Adjudication, on the other hand, is a reasoned response to reasoned argument. Within an adversarial system, judicial decisions amount, in effect, to an evaluation of opposing arguments, and it may be assumed that those responsible for advancing those arguments will have mustered every legal and factual point that might assist their case. The adjudication process also operates vertically in the sense that trial

---

[45] Fishkin, *When the People Speak: Deliberative Democracy and Public Consultation* (Oxford: Oxford University Press, 2009); Ghosh, "Deliberative Democracy and the Countermajoritarian Difficulty: Considering Constitutional Juries" (2010) 30 Oxford J. Leg. Stud. 327 at 336 et seq.

court decisions are subject to review by appeal courts which, in turn, have the opportunity to develop principles, of greater or lesser degrees of specificity, in the context of real, fact-bound cases and controversies. Principles so developed can be much more finely tuned than broad legislative rules and, equally importantly, they are created in an environment which is largely immune from popular pressure to respond instantly to transient fears and concerns.

The deliberative nature of adjudication and the manner in which it permits the gradual elaboration of rules and principles contrasts sharply with the manner in which some key pieces of criminal justice legislation have been enacted in this country in recent years. Very little of this legislation was preceded by genuine deliberation, in parliament or elsewhere. In fact, over a 30-year period we have witnessed a marked decline in both the extent and quality of public and political debate in this area. The Criminal Justice Act 1984 was intensely debated in both parliament and the media, though its most controversial provision at the time, permitting suspects to be detained for questioning for up to 12 hours, was in retrospect quite tame. Contrast this with the half dozen significant criminal justice statutes enacted between 2006 and 2009. Despite introducing far more radical reforms than anything contained in the Criminal Justice Act 1984, they received no more than cursory consideration in parliament and very little critical attention from the media. The most striking example of this phenomenon occurred in July 2009 when the Criminal Justice (Amendment) Bill, which made very significant changes in relation to the detention of suspects and removing the right to jury trial for certain organised crime offences, was rushed through the Dáil with very little debate and passed on the day that the Dáil rose for its summer recess on July 10. It then proceeded to the Seanad where it passed all stages on July 14, 2009. No amendment proposed in the Seanad had any practical hope of success because that would have entailed deferring the enactment of the Bill until the Dáil reconvened in the autumn to consider the Seanad amendments. The Government had made clear its intention to have the Bill enacted into law immediately and that is what happened. To be fair, this chain of events (as well as the content of the Bill itself) attracted a good deal of public criticism from the legal professions, civil liberties groups and others. The President also convened a meeting of the Council of State to discuss whether the Bill should be referred to the Supreme Court to test its constitutionality. She decided not to refer it and duly signed it into law. The Criminal Justice (Miscellaneous Provisions) Act 2009, which made important changes to the European Arrest Warrant, firearms legislation and other matters, also proceeded through Parliament at alarming speed. It received a second reading on May 20, 2009 and was briefly debated on a few occasions thereafter before being signed into law on July 21, 2009.

Important lessons can be drawn from this chain of events. Legislation made and enacted in such a perfunctory manner may claim democratic legitimacy in purely formal terms, but little more than that. The Criminal Justice (Amendment) Act 2009, for example, was introduced mainly in response to the tragic murder of a Limerick businessman in April 2009,[46] an event that illustrated the ruthless nature of organised crime in that locality at the time. (As it happens, the person responsible for the killing was quickly apprehended and put on trial in the Central Criminal Court where he pleaded guilty to murder in May 2010. There is nothing to suggest that the new legislation assisted the process in any way.) Legislation of this kind, which fundamentally alters the balance of the criminal process, should be preceded by a detailed policy analysis carried out by a specialised unit of the kind recommended in Chapter 10 below. When statutory sentencing reform is effected in this manner, it suffers from the same absence of deliberation and reflection, even though it will invariably have far-reaching consequences for individual offenders and, on an institutional level, for the prison system well into the future. The range of factors and consider-ations which must be considered when framing sentencing policy means that legislation is seldom suited for establishing anything more than general directive rules. Sentencing principles, including those indicating tariffs or presumptive sentences, are best developed and elaborated by the judiciary through a process of deliberation and evidence-based decision-making, qualities that are seldom apparent in the legislative process nowadays.

---

[46] See remarks by Minister for Justice during the Second Reading of the Bill: 686 *Dáil Debates,* Col.177 (July 3, 2009).

CHAPTER 3

DISCRETION AND RULES IN THE CRIMINAL PROCESS

Opponents of discretion often claim to put their trust in rules, meaning a set of fairly specific norms established in advance by a recognised authority. Those rules should be capable of yielding a clear and predictable answer in every case to which they apply once the facts have been authoritatively established. While such a regime might just about be theoretically possible, it could scarcely exist in the real world without causing considerable injustice to many civil litigants and to virtually everyone accused or convicted of criminal wrongdoing. Writing in the fourth century BC, Aristotle defended equity as "a rectification of legal justice".[1] He said that since all law is universal, problems and disputes will inevitably arise for which just legal solutions cannot be prescribed in advance. The early development of the common law, amongst other historical episodes, illustrates the truth of this insight. Although that law had developed organically as a set of rules and principles derived from judicial decisions in specific cases, it eventually became so rigid, particularly in relation to property rights, that a parallel system of justice was introduced. This new system, designed to mitigate the rigour of legal rules, became known as equity and was inspired by classical notions of that concept as found in Aristotle and other ancient writers. In fact, the history of equity and its relationship to the common law make instructive reading for anyone interested in the proper role of sentencing discretion today. It illustrates the enduring need for some form of individualised justice to counteract the restrictive limitations of formal rules. In early English law, equitable remedies were granted by the chancellor—in the early days a senior ecclesiastic but later almost always a lawyer—who acted, in theory at least, as the conscience of the monarch. A person aggrieved by a decision of a common-law court could seek redress from the chancellor who was empowered to set aside the court's decision. Rather than adhere to pre-existing rules, the chancellor acted in accordance with conscience and his own notion of right.

That this new equitable jurisdiction could be both benign and beneficial was beyond doubt. But over time it, too, attracted critics including the English jurist John Selden who remarked that equity was "a roguish thing" and that because

---

[1] Aristotle, *Ethics*, Book 5, Ch.1, trans. by Thomson, rev edn (London: Penguin Books, 1976). In *Simonds v Simonds* 380 N.E.2d 189 at 192 (1978), a New York appeals court, having cited Aristotle, wrote: "Since adherence to principles of 'law' does not invariably produce justice, equity is necessary."

it depended so much on the conscience of individual chancellors, it was just as if the standard measure for a foot became the chancellor's foot.[2] There were indeed times when Selden's criticism was well justified and perhaps unduly charitable, particularly during the chancellorships of Cardinal Wolsey (1515–1529) who never failed to show his disdain for lawyers and legal principles, and Lord Ellesmere (1596–1617) who, although a lawyer by background, seemed to delight in antagonising the common-law judges.[3] Others, such as Bacon, were more conciliatory and helped to develop some measure of harmony between the two parallel systems of adjudication. At one time, chancellors and chancery judges were adamant that equity, unlike the common law, did not operate through a system of precedent. As late as 1670, we find Vaughan C.J. declaring that equity was "a universal truth and there can be no precedent in it."[4] Later judges, mindful perhaps of Selden's critique, took a different view. In 1818 Lord Eldon maintained that equitable doctrines should be as settled as those of the common law which were laid down as fixed principles, so that they did not change with each succeeding judge.[5] This view ultimately prevailed, and in the late nineteenth century it became possible to merge both legal and equitable jurisdiction in the same set of superior courts.[6] Even today, however, equity plays a useful role if only because equitable remedies are discretionary in nature and, through the various maxims of equity, courts are entitled to have regard to the conduct of the parties as well as to the substantive issues in dispute.[7]

Equity may have arisen from a need to ameliorate the rigidity of common-law rules through the exercise of discretion and the individualisation of justice. But over time, it too became rule-bound in its own way. The publication of law reports had sometimes been cited as one of the contributing causes to the formalisation of the common law. In due course, the chancery courts had their own reports, and equitable precedents became binding, even if not to the same extent as their common-law counterparts. What we see then is an interplay between discretion and rules. The failure of common-law rules to adapt to new conditions and to right obvious wrongs necessitated the introduction of a parallel system of justice less inhibited by precedent and formality. But over time, the

---

[2] Pollock (ed.), *Table Talk of John Selden* (London: Quaritch, 1927), p.43. See also Holdsworth, *Some Makers of English Law* (Cambridge: Cambridge University Press, 1938); Powell, "'Cardozo's Foot': The Chancellor's Conscience and Constructive Trusts" (1993) 56:3 *Law and Contemporary Problems* 7; Rundell, "The Chancellor's Foot: The Nature of Equity" (1958) 27 Univ. of Kansas City L.R. 71. On the history of equity, see Baker, *An Introduction to English Legal History*, 2nd edn (London: Butterworths, 1979), Ch.6.

[3] Baker (fn.2 above), p.92.

[4] *Fry v Porter* (1670) 86 Eng. Rep. 898 at 902.

[5] *Gee v Pritchard* (1818) 36 Eng. Rep. 670, 674.

[6] Supreme Court of Judicature (Ireland) Act 1877 (40 & 41 Vict. c.57).

[7] On the continuing vitality of equity in shaping doctrines such as unjust enrichment, see Sherwin, "Restitution and Equity: An Analysis of the Principles of Unjust Enrichment" (2001) 79 Texas L.R. 2083. As she writes, at p.2092: "[E]ven the best possible rules will be imperfect in some of their applications."

practices followed by that parallel system gradually developed into rules or something closely resembling them. In fact, a broader survey of legal history and, indeed, more modern developments reveal a strong tendency to classify. Ancient civilisations developed codes, most of which probably emerged from existing practices, customs and beliefs, the Code of Hammurabi drawn up in Babylonia about 1,700 BC being a leading surviving example.[8] In the middle of the fifth century BC, for example, a specially appointed commission produced the 12 tables of ancient Rome, with the apparent purpose of providing a clear and public statement of law so as to prevent the misuse of patrician powers. Over the next millennium or so, the bare precepts set out in the 12 tables were subject to constant interpretation and analysis by jurists. The writings of some of these jurists were treated as authorities in themselves. Eventually, in the period 525 to 535 AD, the Emperor Justinian appointed yet another commission to draw up a new and comprehensive legal code which systematised and replaced all existing laws. This formed the basis for many continental European codes.[9]

This cyclical pattern of rule-bound and more discretionary systems of regulation was noted by Roscoe Pound in a landmark address dating from 1906.[10] Pound's main concern was to attack what he saw as the stultifying and counterproductive emphasis on procedure at the expense of substantive justice within the American legal system at the time. Under the so-called Exchequer rule, the slightest procedural irregularity could be held to justify a re-trial. (This rule was expressly abandoned in these islands through the adoption of the proviso in criminal appeals, whereby a procedural flaw which has not resulted in a miscarriage of justice may be ignored.)[11] An important component of his argument was that a just legal system requires a sensible balance between fixed rules and discretionary decision-making by authorised officials:

> "The most important and most constant cause of dissatisfaction with all law at all times is to be found in the necessarily mechanical operation of legal rules. This is one of the penalties of uniformity. Legal history shows an

---

[8]   Davies, *The Codes of Hammurabi and Moses* (Cincinnati: Jennings and Graham, 1905).

[9]   Watson, *Rome of the XII Tables: Persons and Property* (Princeton, NJ: Princeton University Press, 1975); Jolowicz and Nicholas, *Historical Introduction to the Study of Roman Law*, 3rd edn (Cambridge: Cambridge University Press, 1952).

[10] "The Causes of Popular Dissatisfaction with the Administration of Justice", delivered to the American Bar Association on August 29, 1906. It has recently been reprinted in (2007) 48 South Texas L.R. 853 in connection with a symposium to mark the centenary of the address. On the significance of this address and its impact, see Tidmarsh, "Pound's Century, and Ours" (2006) 81 Notre Dame L.R. 513; Alfini, "Centennial Reflections on Roscoe Pound's 1906 Address to the American Bar Association: Fanning the Spark that Kindled the White Flame of Progress" (2007) 48 South Texas L.R. 849; Clark, "A Tribute to Roscoe Pound" (1964) 78 Harvard L.R. 1. Pound (1870–1964) would later become Dean of Harvard Law School and is recognised as one of the foremost legal scholars of the twentieth century.

[11] The present Irish law on the matter is governed by the Criminal Procedure Act 1993 s.3.

oscillation between wide judicial discretion on the one hand and strict confinement of the magistrate by minute and detailed rules on the other. From time to time more or less reversion to justice without law becomes necessary in order to bring the public administration of justice into touch with changed moral, social, or political conditions. But such periods of reversion result only in new rules or changed rules. In time the modes of exercising discretion become fixed, the course of judicial action becomes stable and uniform, and the new element, whether custom or equity or natural law, becomes as rigid and mechanical as the old. This mechanical action of the law may be minimised, but it cannot be obviated. Laws are general rules; and the process of making them general involves elimination of the immaterial elements of particular controversies ... Hence the law has always ended in a compromise, in a middle course between wide discretion and over-minute legislation. In reaching this middle ground, some sacrifice of flexibility of application to particular cases is inevitable."[12]

Present as well as past experience illustrates the wisdom of his remarks. Few would seriously contest the need for some measure of discretion in order to deliver justice in most branches of law. The challenge, as we shall see when we come to consider the more recent work of Kenneth Culp Davis, is how best to regulate discretion in order to make it as compatible as possible with rule-of-law values.

THE NATURE OF DISCRETION

If there were a game of legal word association in which participants had to state one word or phrase immediately prompted by another, "sentencing" might well be the most common response to "discretion" and vice versa. However understandable this intuitive association may be, it fails to reflect the pervasiveness of discretion within the legal system and, indeed, throughout the entire system of public administration. One need only point to the discretion vested in judges, and sometimes in juries, to determine monetary compensation awards for defamation, and to make matters worse, the Supreme Court in this country has held that juries should not be given guidelines on the appropriate quantum of damages in such cases.[13] Judges dealing with family and matrimonial disputes are routinely required to exercise discretion in child custody decisions, the distribution of family property and other matters of that nature. Other officials

---

[12] Pound (fn.10 above), pp.855–856.

[13] *De Rossa v Independent Newspapers plc* [1999] 4 I.R. 432; *O'Brien v Mirror Group Newspapers Ltd* [2001] 1 I.R. 1. This situation has now become quite critical because of some extraordinary high awards made by juries in recent times, such as the €10 million award in *Kinsella v Kenmare Resources Plc, Irish Times* (November 18, 2010).

must often make important decisions of far-reaching consequences, but which also call for the exercise of discretion. Initial decisions taken by social workers and other professionals engaged in child protection usually determine the future course of any judicial or administrative proceedings in which the needs of a child are identified and addressed. The English Children Act 1989, for example, provides that a local authority must make enquiries regarding a child's welfare in any case where it has reasonable cause to suspect that a child is suffering, or likely to suffer, "significant harm".[14] This formulation was intended to strike an appropriate balance between excessive intervention and effective supervision. Yet an assessment of what amounts to *significant* harm must necessarily be subjective, to some extent at least.

Judges and other professionals might argue that when making decisions in relation to child custody, matrimonial property disputes and similar matters, they are essentially exercising judgement rather than discretion. They are not free to reach conclusions or decide cases according to their own preferences but must, instead, take decisions in accordance with statutory criteria. This distinction between discretion and judgement was emphasised by the English Court of Appeal in *R v Viola*[15] which dealt with the proper interpretation of a statute which prohibited evidence being adduced in a rape trial about the complainant's previous sexual experience with anybody other than the accused. Such evidence might be adduced if and only if the judge was satisfied that it would be unfair to the defendant to exclude it. An earlier authority had referred to the matter being at the discretion of the trial judge,[16] but the court in *Viola* was adamant (and apparently all parties agreed) that this was the wrong approach. It said that the judge has to make a judgement and, once he has done that, he has no discretion in the matter. If he was satisfied on the facts that it would be unfair to exclude the evidence, then he should allow it, but not otherwise. Irrespective of whether it is classed as an exercise in discretion or as judgement, a decision of this kind clearly calls for an objective evaluation of the facts and an application of the governing statute law accordingly. There is no guarantee that all judges would evaluate the facts in the same way or make the same findings; some might conclude that excluding the evidence would cause an injustice while others might conclude the opposite.

This supposed tension between judgement and discretion clearly raises definitional problems, and these certainly abound in the general literature on the topic. At one end of the spectrum, discretion may be said to exist when, in the words of one American court, there is "an exclusive right to decide as [the] court pleases".[17] Most of the better-known definitions, on the other hand, presuppose

---

14   Children Act 1989 s.47(1). The equivalent Irish law is contained in the Child Care Act 1991 as amended.
15   [1982] 1 W.L.R. 1138, 75 Cr. App. R. 125.
16   *R v Mills* (1978) 68 Cr. App. R. 327.
17   *Murray v Buell* 41 N.W. 1010 (1889) at 1011–1012.

some formal restrictions on the choices available to the decision-maker. Hart and Sachs defined discretion as "the power to choose between two or more courses of action each of which is thought of as permissible."[18] This suggests that all the available choices must, in themselves, be legitimate, in the sense of having some legal or official source. A similar assumption appears to underlie Dworkin's claim that discretion properly exists only "when someone is in general charged with making decisions subject to standards set by a particular authority."[19] He vividly illustrated that point by comparing discretion to the hole in a doughnut, saying that discretion does not exist "except as an area left open by a surrounding belt of restriction".[20] This is vastly different from the idea of discretion as an untrammeled power vested in a court or other authority to decide a matter howsoever it wishes. Both forms of discretion can, of course, coexist. Dworkin, for example, distinguishes between strong discretion which is exercised by a decision-maker who is not bound by any pre-existing standards, and various forms of weak discretion such as where a decision-maker must exercise judgement in deciding how authoritative standards should be applied in specific cases.[21] Rosenberg likewise draws a distinction between primary and secondary discretion which is similar in substance to Dworkin's classification.[22] The multitude of contexts in which decision-makers within the criminal justice system (let alone the broader legal system) must exercise discretion cannot readily be categorised under such neat headings. It is certainly true that the kinds of discretion exercisable at various points of the criminal process vary enormously in scope and amenability to review or correction, though the difference is often one of degree.

Prosecutors are usually endowed with extensive and virtually unreviewable discretion in deciding if charges should be brought and, if so, the nature of those charges. If certain problems arise in the course of a trial, the judge has discretion to decide if the jury should be discharged and a mistrial declared. The latter might seem to be an example of strong discretion in the sense that even if an appeal court were later to hold that the judge erred in discharging the jury, it can never, as Rosenberg says, "put Humpty Dumpty together again" once the jury has disbanded.[23] On the other hand, trial judges do not have untrammelled discretion, in the sense of being able to do as they please, when it comes to discharging a jury. There are some guiding rules and principles on the matter,

---

[18] Hart and Sachs, *The Legal Process: Basic Problems in the Making and Application of Law* (unpublished edn, 1958), p.162.
[19] Dworkin, "The Model of Rules" (1967) 35 Univ. of Chicago L.R. 14 at 32; and *Taking Rights Seriously* (Cambridge, MA: Harvard University Press, 1977), p.31.
[20] Dworkin, "The Model of Rules" (fn.19 above).
[21] Dworkin, "The Model of Rules" (fn.19 above).
[22] Rosenberg, "Judicial Discretion of the Trial Court, Viewed from Above" (1971) 22 Syracuse L.R. 635.
[23] Rosenberg (fn.22 above), p.650.
[24] *Dawson v Irish Brokers' Association*, unreported, Supreme Court, November 6, 1998.

though they are seldom phrased in very specific terms.[24] After all, while appeal courts cannot take any meaningful steps to correct an erroneous decision to discharge a jury, they can quash a conviction if they conclude that a jury should have been discharged but was not. The same may be said of prosecutors who enjoy significant but not untrammeled discretion; they are usually subject to pre-determined guidelines and, *in extremis*, to judicial review.[25] The exercise of peremptory jury challenges, where they are still permitted, is also highly discretionary. In Ireland, where each party to a case may challenge up to seven jurors without cause, the challenging party has complete discretion in deciding who to eliminate from the jury which is about to be sworn. Subject only to the upper number of permissible challenges, the party (usually acting through their solicitor) need not abide by any standards relating to gender balance, racial representation or anything of that nature. But that is the exception rather than the rule. Most discretionary decisions are subject to some form of appeal or review, if only to ensure that they were made in accordance with basic public-law principles described below.

PROPER EXERCISE OF DISCRETION

Once discretion, however defined, is legally conferred on a public authority, it must be exercised in a principled and rational manner. As far back as 1598, we find Coke declaring that even where public officials had statutory authority to act according to their discretion, "their proceedings ought to be limited and bound with the rule of reason and Law." He went on to say:

> "For discretion is a science or understanding to discern between falsity and truth, between right and wrong, and between shadows and substance, between equity and colourable glosses and pretences, and not to do according to their wills and private affections; for one saith, *talis discretio discretionem confundit.*"[26]

Many more recent authorities have stressed the same point. Foremost among them is Lord Mansfield's statement that discretion, when applied to a court of justice, "means sound discretion guided by law. It must be governed by the rule of law, and

---

[25] O'Malley, *The Criminal Process* (Dublin: Round Hall, 2009), Ch.12.

[26] *Rooke's Case* (1598) 5 Co. Rep. 100a. *Talis discretio discretionem confundit* may be translated to mean: "discretion exercised in this (capricious) way runs counter to the true meaning of discretion".

[27] *R v Wilkes* (1770) 4 Burr. 2527 at 2539. See also *Re Taylor* (1876) 4 Ch D 157 at 160, per Jessel M.R. ("The discretion of the judge is to be exercised on judicial grounds – not capriciously, but for substantial reasons"); *Stoker v Stoker* (1889) 14 P.D. 60 at 61, per Butt J. ("I must not forget that the discretion given to me must be exercised judicially, not fancifully, or arbitrarily"); *Hines v Hines and Burdett* [1918] P. 364; *Dennehy v Independent Star Ltd* [2009] IEHC 458.

not by humour; it must not be arbitrary, vague or fanciful, but legal and regular."[27] In the case of William Smith O'Brien, decided by the Irish Court of Queen's Bench in 1849, we find Crampton J. saying that he is "certainly not alarmed at this doctrine of discretion, temperately and properly used, as it ought to be according to adjudged cases and according to law."[28] The consistent message has been that discretion, however broadly conferred, must be exercised in accordance with reason as opposed to the private whims or preferences of the decision-maker.[29] As the Canadian Supreme Court once said, "cloaking whims in judicial robes is not sufficient to satisfy the principles of fundamental justice."[30] In other words, legal discretion in the true sense has little to do with the Weberian concept of Khadi justice under which cases are decided on an ad hoc basis, and not in accordance with general rules. At issue in the Canadian case was the grant of bail, but the observation is equally applicable, if not more so, to sentencing. In fact, sentencing is one area where there has been a perceptible resistance to the notion that discretionary decision-making must be informed by objectively-identified principles and standards. Granted, sentencing judges often have to consider a much wider range of factors than other decision-makers in the public sphere. But this makes it all the more imperative to have a principled consensus on the factors that are truly relevant to sentence and on the weight to be attributed to those that are deemed relevant. In the absence of such a consensus, judges are apt to vary widely—some would say wildly—in their assessments of relevance and weight and this, in turn, produces the kind of disparity which diminishes public confidence in the fairness and rationality of the system itself. It also furnishes both an excuse and impetus for those in the political sphere and elsewhere who are anxious to remove or curtail judicial discretion to accomplish their aim through the introduction of mandatory or mandatory minimum penalties. Sentences that are not chosen in accordance with settled principles become literally indefensible in the sense that anyone who is minded to defend discretionary sentencing as an institution is left helpless in the face of evidence, anecdotal or otherwise, which reveals very different sentences being imposed on similarly-situated offenders. The principled use of sentencing discretion should not, of course, be equated with the elimination or a significant curtailment of discretion by way of mandatory penalties or binding guidelines. What it entails instead is the selection of sentence according to established

---

[28] *R v O'Brien* (1849) 3 Cox C.C. 360 at 417.

[29] *Roberts v Hopwood* [1925] A.C. 578 at 613 where Lord Wrenbury said discretion does not authorise a decision-maker to do what he likes. Instead, he must "by use of his reason, ascertain and follow the course which reason directs". See also *Sharp v Wakefield* [1891] A.C. 173 at 179–180 (Lord Halsbury). Lord Bingham likewise says that a judge has no discretion in finding facts or making legal rulings but if, having done these things, he has to choose between different courses of action, whether in relation to sentencing or anything else, he must then exercise discretion (Bingham, *The Business of Judging: Selected Essays and Speeches* (Oxford: Oxford University Press, 2000), p.36).

[30] *R v Morales* [1992] 3 S.C.R. 711.

principles and benchmarks and, where relevant, an explanation as to why one or more circumstances peculiar to the case have justified a departure from the type or amount of punishment which those principles or benchmarks would ordinarily indicate. The proper exercise of discretion also entails the articulation of reasons for the choice of sentence; otherwise, it will be impossible to identify the factors taken into account, the weight attributed to them and any exceptional circumstances justifying a departure from any agreed norms.[31]

Nor is there any reason to suppose that judicial sentencing practices are immune from certain well-established public-law rules governing the exercise of discretion. In brief terms, those rules require, first and foremost, that a public official on whom discretion is legally conferred must actually exercise it. Adherence to rigid self-imposed rules or guidelines, blind adherence to rules or guidelines established by others, or an unauthorised delegation to decision-making would ordinarily amount to a failure to exercise discretion, and any resulting decision is liable to be quashed by way of appeal or review. This principle does not preclude the adoption of internal guidelines, which may indeed be necessary in order to bring a measure of fairness and equity to administrative decision-making, provided the relevant official or authority is willing to consider each case on its merits to see if there is any exceptional factor which might justify a departure from the guidelines. As one leading authority put it, the decision-maker must always be astute to discover if an individual applicant (or party) has something new to say.[32] Secondly, the decision-maker must take all relevant considerations into account and exclude all irrelevant considerations.[33] In an administrative context, this generally requires close attention to the wording of the relevant statutory provisions. For sentencing purposes, the relevant considerations are more likely to be found in appeal court jurisprudence or, where they exist, official guidelines. Obviously, any statutory rules or constraints must be punctiliously observed as well.

DISCRETION IN THE CRIMINAL PROCESS

Robert M. Hutchins, a former president of the University of Chicago, is said to have described the typical university of his day as an aggregation of separate sovereignties connected only by a common heating plant. Much the same may be said of the criminal justice system which consists essentially of a collection of separate institutions, notably the police, prosecuting agencies, courts, prisons,

---

[31] *McCleary v State* 49 Wis. 2d 263, 182 N.W. 2d 512 (1971), (sentencing discretion "must be exercised on a rational and explainable basis", and a valid sentence depends on there being "a statement by the trial judge detailing his reasons for selecting the particular sentence imposed"). See also *State v Gallion* 678 N.W. 2d 197 (2004).

[32] *British Oxygen Co. Ltd v Minister of Technology* [1971] A.C. 610, [1970] 3 W.L.R. 488, [1970] 3 All E.R. 165. See also *R. v Port of London Authority, ex p. Kynoch* [1919] 1 K.B. 176.

[33] *State (Cussen) v Brennan* [1981] I.R. 181; *Whelan v Fitzpatrick* [2008] 2 I.R. 678.

probation services and parole authorities. These institutions are not entirely autonomous and independent; they interconnect and overlap in various complex ways. The manner in which any one of them, such as the police, discharges its functions will probably determine, or strongly influence, the operation and workload of the others. They are also subject to various checks and balances, with the courts as the main controlling agency. Thus, an authoritative judicial decision that evidence obtained in breach of a person's constitutional rights must be excluded should, in principle at least, influence the manner in which police conduct their investigations. It may also influence prosecution decisions which are primarily determined by the availability of sufficient admissible evidence to support a realistic prospect of conviction. Parole authorities, in turn, may be envisaged as exercising a check on judicial sentencing practice. Prisoners are often released after serving no more than a fraction of the sentences imposed upon them following conviction or appeal. Criminal justice systems differ profoundly in this respect from the typical business corporation which may also have several different units operating largely independently of one another, but which is ultimately characterised by its hierarchical structure and common objectives. All units and individuals within the corporation have a common purpose which is to contribute to its commercial success and maximise its profits. At the apex of the corporation is an individual or body empowered to direct and control the organisation in its entirety as well as its constituent members and units. Granted, the criminal justice system may be said to have public safety as its overriding common goal, though efforts to realise it must be tempered by the observance and promotion of other important social values such as respecting the rule of law and according due process of law to those suspected, accused or convicted of crime. However, the criminal justice system is characterised by the absence of an overall hierarchical structure. There are, of course, hierarchies within the individual units but there is no general directing authority. The courts might sometimes be seen as fulfilling this role but their supervisory functions are limited to ensuring that the other agencies do not exceed their legal powers and that they comply with the demands of legality and fairness in their decision-making processes. It would therefore be a mistake to view the courts as a kind of supreme governing authority. They have no power to frame criminal justice policy, and there are many areas of discretionary decision-making, notably in relation to the investigation and prosecution of offences, which are effectively immune from judicial review. The executive branch of government, acting through the ministry of justice, has significant policy-making functions, but in modern democratic systems it is usually prohibited from attempting to determine or influence operational decision-making by police, prosecutors and courts. This diffusion of power among separate agencies has certain advantages but it also illustrates the ubiquity of discretion which is by no means confined to the exercise of judicial power.

While the criminal justice system may thus be viewed in structural or institutional terms, the criminal process, once invoked, is best seen as a continuum beginning at the point at which a crime is reported or detected and ending with a final verdict. That final verdict may be reached by a trial court, an appeal court or at a retrial following a successful appeal. Needless to say, many allegations of crime never result in a verdict of any kind. In fact, in so far as discretion is concerned, the process may be said to begin with the legislative decision to classify certain forms of behaviour as criminal offences meriting prescribed punishments. We seldom refer to such legislative decisions as discretionary, and some would insist on treating them solely as rules, but they do, after all, represent a choice. Legislators select certain acts and omissions to be labelled as crimes, and they have no all-encompassing moral or social criterion to guide them in that exercise.[34] Morality, even if we could achieve consensus on its precise contours, is scarcely the guiding lodestar because of the clear lack of fit between criminal behaviour and moral wrongdoing. To tell harmful lies, to take away a person's character, or to engage in marital infidelity are generally regarded as morally wrong. Yet mendacity, defamation and adultery do not feature in our calendar of crimes. There is nothing inevitable about this. In some American states with legal traditions largely similar to our own, adultery and fornication remain criminal offences and, until fairly recently at least, were occasionally prosecuted.[35] In these islands, such matters remain beyond the scope of the criminal law. Likewise, we rely on the private law of torts to provide a remedy for ordinary defamation, although until recently an exception was made for criminal libel which, subject to certain procedural constraints, might result in a prosecution.[36] In 1885, the Westminister Parliament chose to criminalise certain sexual acts between consenting adult males; in 1993, its Irish counterpart chose to decriminalise the same acts unless they amounted to exploitation of young or other vulnerable persons.[37] At one time, it was an

---

[34] Reitz makes a useful distinction between "systemic discretion" and "case-specific discretion". He writes that legislative discretion (which is of the systemic variety) "is in play when a legislature defines an offence, fixes a maximum statutory penalty for an offence, or sets a mandatory penalty for an offence – and all such actions are discretionary choices at the multiple case level." Case-specific discretion arises when another actor within the system, such as a prosecutor or judge, must make a decision in relation to a particular individual. See Reitz, "Modeling Discretion in American Sentencing Systems" (1998) 20 *Law & Policy* 389 at 392.

[35] In Michigan, one of several American states to retain the crime, adultery is defined as "the sexual intercourse of two persons, either of whom is married to a third person" (Michigan Penal Code, §750.29). The last conviction took place in 1971, but rather controversially, in *People v Waltonen*, decided on November 7, 2006 and available at *http://courtofappeals.mijud.net*, the Michigan Court of Appeals warned that adultery remained an offence punishable with a heavy prison sentence.

[36] Defamation Act 1961 s.8, now abolished by the Defamation Act 2009. On the former law, see *Hilliard v Penfield Enterprises Ltd* [1990] 1 I.R. 138; *Dennehy v Independent Star Ltd* [2009] IEHC 458.

[37] Criminal Law Amendment Act 1885 which was repealed and replaced by the Criminal Law (Sexual Offences) Act 1993 ss.3 and 4 which have now, in turn, been repealed and replaced by the Criminal Law (Sexual Offences) Act 2006. The 1993 amendments were, admittedly, made in response to the European Court of Human Rights decision in *Norris v Ireland* (1991) 13 E.H.R.R. 186.

offence to have an ordinary radio receiver without a licence; this has long since been repealed but it remains an offence to have a television without a licence. One cannot legally own a dog without a licence, but owners of poisonous reptiles are subject to no such requirement.[38] Not only do legislators exercise choice when deciding which forms of behaviour to criminalise, they also make crucial choices in relation to the consequential sanctioning arrangements and, for this purpose, they have significant leeway in deciding how much discretion to vest in the courts.

Before proceeding to mention other discretionary decisions by various actors at different stages of the criminal process, it is well to remind ourselves of the extent to which judicial discretion is being removed or, at least, eroded in the treatment of many summary and regulatory offences. This is reflected in the recent practice of introducing fixed penalty notices, mainly for road traffic and public order offences. Typically, a person issued with such a notice has the option of paying the specified amount within a stated period or else face prosecution. While going to court remains a possibility, it is usually accompanied by the disincentive that conviction will leave the defendant subject to a considerably higher penalty than the standard amount specified in the notice and may, of course, include the possibility of imprisonment. Similar systems, usually known as prosecutor fines, have existed for quite some time in other European jurisdictions, including Scotland where it is issued by the prosecutor, the procurator fiscal, and therefore known as a fiscal fine.[39] In Ireland, many road traffic offences are subject to fixed charges and even, in some drink-driving cases, fixed disqualification notices issued administratively.[40] Fixed charges have also been introduced for some public order offences.[41] This practice of punishment without prosecution is the very antithesis of individualised punishment. It operates mechanically and, from the State's perspective, efficiently as it relieves the court system of a vast number of minor cases. It has been variously described as a liberal-bureaucratic[42] and an administrative-bureaucratic[43] approach to criminal justice. No attempt is made to tailor the punishment to the offender's personal circumstances and there is nothing resembling the totality

---

[38] Control of Dogs Act 1986, as amended by the Control of Dogs (Amendment) Act 1992. In Northern Ireland, on the other hand, the Dangerous Wild Animals (Northern Ireland) Order 2004 makes it an offence to keep an unlicensed "dangerous wild animal", which includes many species of reptile.

[39] Duff, "The Prosecutor Fine" (1994) 14 Oxford J. Leg. Stud. 565.

[40] Road Traffic Act 2006 s.5. Under s.14 of the same Act, the relevant Ministers have extensive powers to declare any summary offence under the Road Traffic Acts or the Roads Act 1993 to be fixed charge offences.

[41] Criminal Justice Act 2006 s.184.

[42] Bottoms, "Neglected Features of Contemporary Penal Systems" in Garland and Young (eds), *The Power to Punish* (London: Heinemann, 1983), p.166.

[43] Duff, "The Prosecutor Fine and Social Control: The Introduction of the Fiscal Fine in Scotland" (1993) 33 Brit. J. Crim. 481.

[44] Australian Institute of Criminology, *Criminal Justice on the Spot: Infringement Notices in Victoria* (Canberra, 1995), Ch.1.

principle in the case of multiple offending.[44] The offender can, of course, allow the matter to go to court but that, as already noted, may carry the risk of much heavier punishment. Even more pertinent in the present context is the growth of privatised law enforcement, most strongly reflected in the practice of local authorities to "outsource" parking control to private clamping companies. Once this transfer has taken place, enforcement policies and practices become motivated by the imperative of maximising profit as opposed to the maintenance of public order, let alone any concern for individualised justice.

DISTRIBUTION OF DISCRETION

Discretionary power is distributed unevenly throughout the criminal process. During the trial process which, for present purposes, may be treated as beginning when an accused person is first brought before a court and ending with a verdict, decision-making is constrained by various rules and norms dictated by the requirements of due process. Even during this phase, however, significant pockets of discretion remain, some of which have already been mentioned. They include the untrammelled power vested in the parties to challenge a certain number of potential jurors without cause and the power vested in the jury itself to reach a decision which may be seriously at odds with the evidence. Perverse or apparently inexplicable acquittals are commonly treated as jury nullification.[45] Judicial decisions on the grant or withholding of bail, on applications for an acquittal by direction, on whether a corroboration warning should be given in a sex offence case and many other matters arising in the course of a trial are, of course, governed by rules and often quite detailed rules at that, but all of them call for some measure of discretionary judgment. Discretion exists in its strongest forms before charge and after conviction.[46] At the earlier stages of the process, police and prosecutors make crucial decisions on whether to embark upon or persevere with an investigation, and on the charges, if any, to be brought, decisions which will determine the course and outcome of any subsequent proceedings. The police are the principal gate-keepers of the criminal process, a function that has assumed even greater importance with the adoption and expansion of cautioning practices which keep many offenders out of the mainstream criminal justice system.[47] Many crimes

---

[45] O'Malley (fn.25 above), Ch.21.

[46] Kadish, "Legal Norm and Discretion in the Police and Sentencing Process" (1962) Harvard L.R. 904.

[47] Juvenile cautioning existed in Ireland on an administrative level since the early 1960s before being placed on a statutory footing by the Children Act 2001. Adult cautioning was introduced, again on an administrative basis, in 2006. The relevant document, *Adult Cautioning Scheme*, is available at *www.garda.ie*. The widespread use of cautions and informal warnings may result in official crime statistics understating the true incidence of the offences to which the cautions and warnings apply. See, for example, Farrington and Burrows, "Did Shoplifting Really Decrease?" (1993) 33 Brit. J. Crim. 57.

will never come to police attention unless victims or others decide to report them. In such a case, the all-important discretionary decision is made by a private party. And, to add a further layer of complexity, decisions to report are often determined by public perceptions of how victims are treated within the criminal process. At the other end of that process, discretion reasserts itself quite strongly as soon as a conviction is entered. Unless the offence of conviction carries a mandatory sentence, as rarely happens, the judge will have extensive discretion in selecting the kind and amount of penalty. No less extensive, though much less visible, is the discretion vested in the executive branch of government to grant early release to prisoners and to allow remission of fines.[48]

The hydraulic metaphor is commonly invoked to describe the distribution of discretion throughout the criminal justice system.[49] More specifically, it is invoked by those who claim that discretion can never be eradicated from the system as a whole, but merely redistributed. Sentencers could, in theory, be deprived of all discretion through the prescription of mandatory penalties but the system would very quickly adapt, probably through increased prosecutorial discretion at one end of the spectrum, increased executive discretion at the other end or both. History lends strong support to this claim, as we shall see in later chapters dealing with mandatory penalties and sentencing guideline systems. But one need not have recourse to history to illustrate this phenomenon and, indeed, to appreciate the problems which it can sometimes cause. Formal restrictions on judicial sentencing discretion, particularly through the intro-duction of mandatory and mandatory minimum sentences, can certainly increase prosecutorial power and discretion. Nowadays, an offender's liability to a mandatory minimum sentence depends upon the existence of some specified factor (often described as a cliff) over and above the commission of the basic offence. It may, for example, depend on the amount or estimated value of the drugs seized, the possession or use of a firearm, or the age of the victim.[50] In many such instances, the prosecution will have considerable leeway in deciding whether to bring a charge which includes the relevant aggravating factor or a lesser charge which attracts a lower or entirely discretionary penalty. Add to this a strong culture of plea bargaining, as exists in most American jurisdictions, and one can quickly see how the prosecutorial choice of charge may effectively determine the ultimate sentence or, at any rate, the likely range of sentence.

Most jurisdictions allow for the executive reduction of prison sentences

---

[48]　The executive power to remit fines has, admittedly, been somewhat curtailed as a result of *Brennan v Minister for Justice* [1995] 1 I.R. 612, [1995] 2 I.L.R.M. 206.

[49]　Miethe, "Charging and Plea Bargaining Practices under Determinate Sentencing: An Investigation of the Hydraulic Displacement of Discretion" (1987) 78 *Journal of Criminal Law and Criminology* 155; Alschuler, "Sentencing Reform and Prosecutorial Power: A Critique of Recent Proposals for 'Fixed' and 'Presumptive' Sentencing" (1978) 126 Univ. Pennsylvania L.R. 550.

[50]　Chapter 4 below.

[51]　Chapter 9 below.

through some form of remission, parole or temporary release.[51] While decisions to revoke parole or early release, once it has been granted, must conform with the requirements of natural justice, the initial grant of release is often entirely discretionary. In Ireland, temporary release has been described as "a quintessentially executive function"[52] and, more significantly, as a privilege rather than a right.[53] Executive discretion need not, of course, be entirely untrammelled; its precise scope will depend on the presence or absence of a formal parole system and the extent to which parole authority recommendations are binding. But in a country with no formal parole system or a weak one (as Ireland's may justly be described), the executive usually determines the length of sentence which a prisoner will actually serve. Taken to an extreme, this might result in the typical prisoner serving no more than a small fraction of the judicially-imposed sentence or, depending on prevailing government policy, serving every day of it, less any standard remission. Such extensive executive power, unless exercised in accordance with clearly-articulated principles and standards, has obvious disadvantages, particularly in a jurisdiction which claims to treat proportionality as its overarching sentencing norm. Judicial efforts to craft sentences that reflect offender culpability or that will promote some defensible social goal such as deterrence are largely wasted if there is no meaningful relationship between the sentence imposed and the sentence served. It was this concern that spawned the "truth in sentencing" initiatives undertaken in many countries throughout the 1990s.[54] Another drawback of very generous early release practices is that they reduce the deterrent and incapacitative impact of prison sentences. On the other hand, the abolition or severe curtailment of executive release powers causes its own problems. Early release is an important safety valve, often indeed a vital one, at times of prison overcrowding. Even when the prison system is operating within capacity, the possibility of early release can be an effective incentive to prisoners to obey prison rules or use their time productively by participating in work programmes, training or treatment. In Ireland right now, those sentenced for presumptive or mandatory minimum terms of imprisonment are entitled to standard remission but are otherwise ineligible for early release.

A holistic assessment of the discretionary powers dispersed throughout the criminal process, as opposed to a narrow concentration on judicial sentencing discretion, reveals the extent to which the process is designed to counteract any measures adopted to eliminate or reduce the exercise of discretion at any particular point. Even if the system is not deliberately designed to achieve such a result, that at any rate is how it tends to operate in practice. And, to reprise a recurring theme in this book, one of the key advantages of leaving discretion to sentencers is that their decisions and decision-making processes have much

---

[52] *O'Neill v Governor of Castlerea Prison* [2004] 1 I.R. 298 at 313.

[53] *Lynch and Whelan v Minister for Justice, Equality and Law Reform* [2010] IESC 34.

[54] Beck and Greenfeld, *Violent Offenders in State Prison: Sentences and Time Served* (Washington DC: Dept. of Justice, 1995); Wood and Dunaway, "Consequences of truth-in-sentencing" (2003) 5:3 *Punishment and Society* 139.

higher levels of visibility (and the accountability that goes with it) than apply at any of the other points in the criminal process towards which discretion would probably migrate if eliminated from sentencing.

THE REDISCOVERY OF DISCRETION

The criminal process thus understood—beginning with the reporting or detection of an offence—consists of a continuum that is punctuated at several key points by discretionary decisions. The multiplicity of decision-points along the continuum and the exercise of discretion at each of them are matters seldom recognised by those who insist on locating all the perceived ills of the process at the sentencing stage. It is therefore worth digressing briefly to recall the circumstances in which the discretionary nature of the criminal process was rediscovered or, at any rate, more fully realised in the mid-twentieth century. Discretion had long been recognised as an important aspect of our legal system. In the late nineteenth century, as debate over judicial sentencing practices intensified in England, judicial discretion was robustly defended by James Fitzjames Stephen among others.[55] Roscoe Pound's 1906 address has already been noted as a significant reminder of the historical interplay between discretion and rules.[56] This was a recurring theme in his later writings which proved remarkably influential in generating more flexible and substance-oriented codes of procedure.[57] At that time, however, he was largely preoccupied with civil procedure, though his insights on the relationship between rules and discretion illuminate developments in all branches of law. Another half-century was to elapse before the centrality of discretion within the criminal process was subjected to thorough empirical investigation.

In 1953, Justice Robert Jackson of the United States Supreme Court, and then a much respected figure because of his role as chief prosecutor at the Nuremberg War Crimes Tribunal, addressed the American Bar Association on the many serious defects, as he saw them, in the criminal justice system. These included the failure of many victims to report crimes, the high level of discretion vested in police and prosecutors, the discretion of trial judges to grant a new trial following conviction (a common American phenomenon at the time), systemic delays and, of course, inconsistent sentencing. In fact, more than 50 years later, many of his observations still ring true. He candidly acknowledged, for example, that he would be reluctant to encourage a family member to report a rape given the trauma which the complainant would suffer within the criminal process. His speech also contained the following passage of enduring relevance:

---

[55] Stephen, "Variations in the Punishment of Crime" (1885) 17 *The Nineteenth Century* 755.
[56] Page 44 above.
[57] See, in particular, Pound's essay "Mechanical Jurisprudence" (1908) 8 Columbia L.R. 605, and also Tidmarsh (fn.10 above).

"I have often said that the real problem in criminal law is not the criminal; it is the good people. The difficulty is that our good citizens tend to sway between sentimentalism and savagery. When they get excited about a crime wave, the only thing that occurs to them is tough sentences and shortcuts to conviction. They utterly forget that the more severe the penalties, the stronger the urge to acquit, and the greater the difficulty of conviction. After a little period of toughness, the public suddenly gets sentimental about some case where the punishment seems severe. Then comes a period of laxity. If we could have a sound and consistent understanding among the law-abiding citizens of the difficulties and needs of this problem, I think society could take care of the evil persons much better."[58]

By then, Jackson was heading up a special committee of the American Bar Association which had received foundation funding for an exploratory study of the criminal justice system. In another address delivered about the same time, he mapped out the scope of that study, a hallmark of which would be its concentration on the actual operation of the system.[59] It was not intended to be a criminological exercise examining the possible causes of crime; in fact, there was a good deal of such research being done at that time in any event. Instead, the existence of crime and the legal definitions of specific crimes would be taken as given. The ABA study could therefore concentrate on the manner in which the system responded to suspected or detected crime. As Walker, the leading historian of the ABA initiative, has explained, earlier investigations of the criminal justice system had adhered to a "progressive model" which was characterised by reliance on official sources of information, as opposed to direct observation of the system in action, and by a reformist ideology which was probably naïve in its belief that a public spirited citizenry could inject higher standards of integrity into criminal justice practices.[60]

Major studies dating from this era include those by LaFave on arrest, Joseph Goldstein and Herman Goldstein on police discretion, and Newman on plea bargaining.[61] The full title of Joseph Goldstein's article, "Police Discretion Not to

---

[58] Robert Jackson, "Serving the Administration of Criminal Justice", speech to the Criminal Law Section of the American Bar Association, Boston, August 26, 1953, reprinted in (1953) 17 *Federal Probation* 3. See also "Criminal Justice: The Vital Problem of the Future" (August 1953) 39 *ABA Journal* 743, which is the text of a further address by Justice Jackson setting out the scope of the exploratory study. There is an excellent website devoted to Jackson, including the texts of many of his speeches, at *www.roberthjackson.org*.

[59] Walker, "Origins of the Contemporary Criminal Justice Paradigm: The American Bar Foundation Survey, 1953–1969" (1992) 9:1 *Justice Quarterly* 47; Walker, *Taming the System: The Control of Discretion in Criminal Justice 1950–1990* (Oxford: Oxford University Press, 1993).

[60] Walker, "Origins of the Contemporary Criminal Justice Paradigm", fn.59 above, pp.52–54.

[61] LaFave, *Arrest: The Decision to take the Suspect into Custody* (Boston: Little, Brown, 1953); J. Goldstein, "Police Discretion not to Invoke the Criminal Process: Low-Visibility Decisions in the Administration of Justice" (1959–1960) 69 *Yale Law Journal* 543; H. Goldstein, "Police Discretion: the Ideal versus the Real" (1963) *Public Administration Review* 148; Newman, *Conviction: The Determination of Guilt or Innocence without Trial* (Boston: Little Brown, 1966).

Invoke the Criminal Process: Low Visibility Decisions in the Administration of Justice" was instructive in itself. First, it drew attention to an important discretionary police power, the power *not* to proceed with a prosecution. Until then, critical attention had focused mainly on positive decisions to arrest or prosecute. Secondly, it captured one of the essential qualities of this discretionary power, namely, its low visibility. Decisions to arrest or prosecute may occasionally attract some publicity even if they never result in a trial or a verdict; decisions not to invoke the criminal process almost invariably remain hidden from public scrutiny. The opening lines of the article boldly set out the importance of the topic:

> "Police decisions not to invoke the criminal process largely determine the outer limits of law enforcement. By such decisions, the police define the ambit of discretion throughout the process of other decision makers—prosecutor, grand and petit jury, probation officer, correction authority, and parole and pardon boards."[62]

This remains equally true today, reflecting the situation in most Western countries, including Ireland. Police discretion should not always, of course, be viewed negatively; it has many advantages provided it is not used to cover up improper or discriminatory practices.

In 1969, Kenneth Culp Davis, one of the leading American administrative lawyers of the twentieth century, published his classic work, *Discretionary Justice*.[63] By then, Davis had spent some decades studying administrative agencies and their workings. He recognised the inevitability of discretion in public decision-making processes and somewhat grudgingly valued it, but he had an optimistic belief that it could be curtailed and structured through administrative rule-making. His working definition of discretion was clear and uncomplicated:

> "A public officer has discretion whenever the effective limits of his power leave him free to make a choice among possible courses of action."[64]

Like Goldstein before him, he recognised the enormous amount of discretion vested in the police; in fact, he later wrote a book on that specific topic.[65] But unlike Dicey, he did not consider the existence of discretion to be incompatible with the rule of law.[66] Discretion in the right measure and subject to appropriate

---

[62] J. Goldstein (fn.61 above), p.543 (internal reference omitted).

[63] Davis, *Discretionary Justice: A Preliminary Inquiry* (Baton Rouge: Louisiana University Press, 1969, republished by Illinois University Press, Urbana, Ill, 1976). Davis also wrote the leading administrative law treatise in the United States. For a critical appreciation of his work, see Levin, "The Administrative Law Legacy of Kenneth Culp Davis" (2005) 42 San Diego L.R. 315, also available at *http://ssrn.com/abstract=560783* [Last accessed September 27, 2011].

[64] Davis (fn.63 above), p.4.

[65] Davis, *Police Discretion* (St. Paul, Minn.: West Publishing Company, 1975).

[66] Dicey, *Introduction to the Study of the Law of the Constitution*, 10th edn (London: Macmillan, 1959). See also, Bingham, *The Rule of Law* (London: Allen Lane, 2010), Ch.4.

controls was essential and, indeed, desirable in the modern state. Davis proposed a tripartite strategy of confining, structuring and checking discretion in an effort to achieve an appropriate balance between rule-bound and discretionary decision-making. Discretion must be confined so as to prevent arbitrariness and inequality but permitted to a degree necessary to permit sufficient individualisation.[67] Even where it must exist, discretion should be structured through the development of open, transparent standards and criteria to shape the manner in which it is exercised. Finally, discretionary decisions should be checked in the sense of being subject to review. Obviously, in a legal context, this is best accomplished by appeal courts.

The insights offered by Davis's work are particularly valuable in a criminal justice context although that was not one of his main areas of concern in *Discretionary Justice*. Nobody who is familiar with the operation of the justice system would seriously suggest that all discretion should be eliminated from it, though most experienced participants could point to instances where unstructured discretion has produced arbitrary and incompatible results. An acceptable balance between discretion and rules requires, first and foremost, that as many norms as possible should be prescribed in advance, leaving the appropriate decision-makers with sufficient discretion to deliver justice in those cases where individual circumstances must be taken into account. Those decision-makers, in turn, should endeavour to create standards which, while embodying adequate levels of flexibility, will bring some order and coherence to the manner in which they exercise their discretionary powers. Specific decisions should, in turn, be subject to a system of review the principal purpose of which should be to ensure that decisions were made within legal limits and in accordance with the prescribed or agreed general standards. Such a strategy is eminently suitable for application to common-law sentencing systems and provides the basis for the structural reforms suggested in the final chapter of this book. The other major works which resulted from the ABA initiative, including the studies on police discretion and arrest policies, are also of enduring significance because they serve as a reminder of the extent to which decisions made at one point in the process shape or influence decisions made at later stages.

INFLUENCING DISCRETIONARY DECISIONS

Public commentary on discretionary decision-making, and on sentencing in particular, generally focuses on the ultimate decision-maker, the judge in the case of sentencing. Yet, few decisions by key actors in the overall criminal process can properly be understood or evaluated without taking account of the material on which those decisions are based and the manner in which that material, whether it be in the form of evidence, reports, recommendations or

---

[67] Davis, *Discretionary Justice* (fn.63 above), p.52.

submissions, is selected and presented.[68] In addition, therefore, to adopting a telescopic view of the criminal process as a series of decisions extending from the legislative creation of an offence to the ultimate disposal of a specific charge, we must also be prepared to subject particular decisions to a microscopic analysis. Before selecting sentence for a serious offence, a judge will have heard evidence about the facts of the offence (either in the course of the trial, by way of police evidence at the sentencing hearing or both) and about the circumstances of the offender. There may well be a probation report or, in other jurisdictions, a pre-sentence or social inquiry report, and often a victim impact statement or report as well. Social inquiry reports may well include a risk assessment of future offending.[69] Defence counsel will have made submissions, generally in the form of a plea in mitigation, and prosecution counsel may have made general observations on the nature and gravity of the offence. Each of these actors has the opportunity to influence the ultimate decision to a significant degree. They may exercise this influence individually or, sometimes, collectively such where, in return for a guilty plea, police evidence or prosecution submissions are so tailored as to omit certain aggravating aspects of the offence or the offender's character. It is not uncommon for police witnesses to be asked on the basis of their local knowledge about the offender's general character, his work record, his relationship with his family and related matters. The tone and language used to convey this information to the court, apart altogether from the opportunity to be factually selective, may well influence the judge's overall assessment of the offender. The same holds true, to an even greater extent, of written reports. Court culture and relationships between the various actors may have more influence on sentencing outcomes than formal principles.[70] Little detailed research appears to have been carried out in this country on probation reports and victim impact statements. Research findings elsewhere have revealed evidence of racial and ethnic stereotyping in pre-sentence and risk-assessment reports.[71] This may not hold true here, but the findings remain instructive as an indication of the extent to which subjective evaluations by non-judicial actors may influence the ultimate judicial decision. There is, however, a tendency, even among judges to treat non-legal personnel as the only "honest brokers" in the entire process. In a remarkably candid and enlightening account of his experience as a sentencer, an American trial judge recently described

---

[68] Hawkins, "The Use of Legal Discretion: Perspectives from Law and Social Science" in Hawkins (ed.), *The Uses of Discretion* (Oxford: Clarendon Press, 1994), p.29 ("Since discretion is diffused among those supplying information, evaluations, and recommendations to the proximate or ultimate decision-makers, it is important to distinguish the real exercise of discretion from mere ratification").

[69] On pre-sentence reports, see special issue of *Punishment and Society*, Vol. 12(3), 2010, edited by Tata and Field, and in particular, Tata, "A Sense of Justice: The Role of Pre-Sentence Reports in the Production (and Disruption) of Guilt and Guilty Pleas" at p.239 et seq.

[70] Rumgay, "Custodial Decision Making in a Magistrates' Court: Court Culture and Immediate Situational Factors" (1995) 35 Brit. J. Crim. 201.

probation officers as "the one unbiased sounding board available to judges for hugely important sentencing decisions that must be made otherwise alone."[72] But surely it cannot be denied that all professionals, however high their levels of personal integrity, bring certain cognitive, cultural and occupational biases to their work. This is not to suggest that the system is necessarily any the worse for that. What matters is that they, and all other participants, should be conscious of the assumptions and criteria which may inform their assessments, conclusions and recommendations. Any research agenda on the operation of sentencing discretion must therefore include a close examination of the roles played by all actors within the process, of the opportunities available to each group of actors to influence the eventual outcome and of any prejudices, conscious or otherwise, which may be reflected in advice tendered to sentencing courts.

USING DISCRETION CONSTRUCTIVELY

The relationship between discretion and rules is a highly intricate one. Both have their advantages. Rules are often seen as the best means of achieving enlightenment or rule-of-law ideals such as predictability, consistency, openness and rationality, though they are not always very effective in delivering individualised justice. Discretion, on the other hand, has the merit of flexibility, and it permits decision-makers to respond to individual needs in a way which an entirely rule-bound system will seldom facilitate. One aspect of the relationship between the two, which is often overlooked, is that each can strengthen and legitimate the other. Within a constitutional democracy, discretion should be conferred by duly enacted laws, thereby legitimating its exercise. Furthermore, as Davis argued persuasively, those laws should confer no more discretion than is needed to achieve the desired goals.[73] What is less obvious or, at least, less explored, is the opportunity furnished by the availability of discretion to promote the adoption of better rules and principles. This is what Schneider has described as "rule-building discretion".[74] A dynamic and constructive process can evolve whereby rule-makers decide initially to adopt laws which grant considerable discretion to decision-makers, but with a view to later taking advantage of the experience of those decision-makers in order to create more detailed rules. Having used their discretion in applying a broadly-constructed rule to many specific cases, decision-makers are in a good position to advise on how more efficient, effective or fairer rules could be developed. This rule-building dimension of discretion

---

[71] See, in particular, Hudson and Bramhall, "Assessing the 'Other': Constructions of 'Asianness' in Risk Assessments by Probation Officers" (2005) 45 Brit. J. Crim. 721.

[72] Hornby, "Speaking in Sentences" (Winter 2011) 14 *Green Bag* 147 at 157.

[73] Davis (fn.63 above).

[74] Schneider, "Discretion and Rules: A Lawyer's View" in Hawkins (ed.), *The Uses of Discretion* (Oxford: Clarendon Press, 1994), pp.47, 64.

has particular relevance to sentencing, though the result need not be in the form of revised statutory provisions. To be sure, the experience of decision-makers (judges in the case of sentencing) and others deeply involved in the process (such as lawyers and probation officers) may well point to the need for legal reform. But it can also be used productively to generate guiding principles to shape the future exercise of discretion. In effect, this is very similar to Davis's argument for structuring discretion through norms and standards adopted by those charged with its exercise.[75]

Criminal appeal courts are particularly well placed to engage in this constructive exercise. Because they hear appeals from decisions taken by many judges in one or more lower courts, they come to learn about the variety of circumstances in which particular offences are committed, the diversity of offender characteristics, and variations among trial judges in identifying relevant factors, in assigning weight to those factors and in selecting the penalties ultimately imposed. At the same time, appeal courts are at a remove from the coal face of sentencing, a factor which some regard as weakening their credibility, but which also has the advantage of enabling them to adopt a more generalised, principle-based perspective on recurring problems and issues. They are in a position to draw from the collective experience of many different trial judges in order to shape and refine general principles which, in turn, will create more consistency of approach on the part of trial judges in the future. The legitimacy and public acceptability of adjudication, as opposed to legislative direction, depend heavily on the willingness of appeal and review courts to engage actively in this function of elaborating and refining principles. When they reach a point at which it becomes possible to set down presumptive tariffs or benchmarks, they should not shrink from doing so, provided they have the necessary empirical data and research findings.[76] However, with or without benchmarks, they can do much to transform a largely discretionary system into a more principled one.

---

[75] Davis (fn.63 above).
[76] Chapter 5 below.

CHAPTER 4

MANDATORY PENALTIES

Mandatory penalties take a variety of forms. Strictly speaking, a penalty is mandatory when it is the only sanction which a court may lawfully impose for a given offence. The life sentence for murder under Irish law is truly mandatory because, irrespective of the circumstances of the offence or the offender, a court has no option but to impose it once a conviction for murder is entered.[1] The judicial imposition of a life sentence does not, of course, mean that the offender will spend the rest of his natural life in prison. In all probability, he will be released under some kind of parole or temporary release arrangement after serving a certain number of years. This is one characteristic of mandatory penalties to be noted at the outset. They certainly tie the hands of the judiciary by prohibiting the exercise of discretion in the selection of penalty but they do not necessarily preclude the later exercise of executive clemency or, where it exists, a statutory parole power. Mandatory minimum sentences, which are becoming more prevalent, require the imposition of a specified minimum punishment, usually expressed in terms of years' imprisonment, when certain conditions are fulfilled. A qualifying condition may consist merely of a conviction for a specified offence or, more commonly nowadays, the presence of an aggravating factor such as a previous conviction for a similar offence. Thus, while a maximum sentence places a ceiling on the amount of punishment that may lawfully be imposed, a mandatory minimum sentence raises the floor of permissible punishment while allowing for the imposition of a heavier sentence up to and including the prescribed maximum. Presumptive sentences are sometimes, though erroneously, classified as mandatory. Typically, a presumptive sentencing arrangement requires the courts, when selecting punishment for a given offence, to consider imposing a specified mandatory or mandatory minimum sentence unless they are satisfied that the interests of justice call for a more lenient measure. There is, to be sure, a mandatory dimension to such sentences in so far as they require courts to consider the imposition of a specified sanction or, perhaps, to adopt that level of sanction as their benchmark. But presumptive minimums cannot strictly be classified as mandatory when they permit downward departures in exceptional circumstances.

Mandatory sentences attract most controversy when they require the imposition of fixed or minimum terms of imprisonment, but other mandatory penalties and orders, such as disqualification from driving following conviction

---

[1] Criminal Justice Act 1990 s.2.

for a serious road traffic offence, may also have a severe punitive impact. It has been remarked that mandatory penalties tend to operate without controversy at the upper and lower reaches of the scale of gravity, and there is probably some truth in that. The mandatory life sentence for murder at the upper end of the scale and the mandatory disqualification for drunken-driving towards the lower end (not that this offence should be treated as trivial) attract relatively little criticism. The attachment of mandatory minimum sentences to middle-ranking offences is usually considered more objectionable. Yet, for analytical purposes, it is difficult to draw distinctions of this kind. Removing or curtailing judicial discretion produces the same problems irrespective of the nature or gravity of the offence. This is not to deny the possibility that mandatory sentences and other ancillary orders might be objectively justified in some circumstances provided they are supported by reliable evidence as to their deservedness or effectiveness.

The first and most compelling argument against mandatory sentences is that by removing or substantially curtailing judicial discretion, they strip courts of the power and opportunity to select sentences that reflect all the relevant circumstances of specific cases. When the legislature stipulates a fully mandatory sentence for an offence, it effectively assumes the role of sentencer, thereby displacing the judge for that purpose. It is, after all, predetermining the sentence which everyone convicted of that offence must receive. A mandatory minimum sentence has much the same effect save that it permits the courts to impose heavier sentences when so minded. Here we can immediately identify one fundamental problem with mandatory sentencing, and it is the problem of distance. The greater the experiential distance between the framers of a rule and those charged with its implementation, the less efficient the rule is likely to be in accommodating the diversity of circumstances to which it applies. The varied personal circumstances of the unidentified individuals being targeted by a mandatory provision are seldom given much thought before the relevant law is enacted. Needless to say, in a sentencing context, personal circumstances include the degree of moral guilt attending the commission of the offence. In the comfort of the parliamentary chamber and emboldened by the high-minded rhetoric of their colleagues, legislators can easily reach the conclusion that everyone who commits a given offence should receive sure and severe and uniform punishment. Yet, even a modicum of exposure to day-to-day proceedings in the criminal courts would quickly displace this presumption. Legislators tend to concentrate on offences rather than offenders and, also, to determine mandatory or maximum penalties by reference to the most serious manifestations of the criminal activity in question.

Mandatory penalties have a long history but they have operated differently over time. At one time, conviction of a designated offence was the only condition necessary to qualify for a mandatory sentence. This remains true of murder which automatically attracts a life sentence irrespective of the circumstances, and it once held true of most other felonies when they were capital crimes. Nowadays, eligibility for a mandatory or mandatory minimum sentence is much more likely to depend on the existence of certain facts or circumstances over and above the commission of the crime itself. Previous convictions for a similar offence and the presence of some other aggravating element, such as having drugs of certain kind or amount, are the most common triggering factors in modern mandatory sentencing schemes. Indeed, both of these factors may occasionally be required. In Ireland, for example, a repeat section 15A drug offender must be sentenced to a prison term of 10 years or more.[2] To qualify for such a sentence, an adult offender must have had a previous conviction for one of two specified offences, and the offence of conviction (like the previous ones) is so defined as to require that the drugs had a street value of €13,000 or more. Mere possession of controlled drugs for sale or supply will not, in the absence of both of these factors, leave the offender liable to a mandatory sentence. This arrangement reflects another well-recognised drawback of modern mandatory sentencing provisions. They typically isolate one or two aggravating factors to the exclusion of all other relevant circumstances, and it is the presence or absence of those factors which will determine an offender's liability to the mandatory punishment.[3] Far from promoting sentencing consistency, such provisions can in fact create considerable disparity. In most common-law jurisdictions no more than a handful of offences, usually drug-related and firearms offences, attract mandatory or mandatory minimum sentences. In the absence of a successful constitutional challenge, the courts must impose those sentences in the manner specified by the legislature. The sentencing of virtually all other offences, including more serious ones, remains discretionary. Let us consider, for example, the consequences of the 10-year mandatory minimum for repeat section 15A drug offenders. A person caught in possession of, say, €15,000 worth of cocaine who had previously been convicted of a similar offence must now receive a prison sentence of 10 years or longer. Yet, another person appearing in an adjoining court on the same day on a manslaughter, rape or robbery charge might well receive a much shorter sentence, even though he had previous convictions for similar offences. Violent offences of this nature usually attract heavy prison sentences, but courts are always entitled to exercise leniency when there are clear and exceptional mitigating factors. The repeat section 15A offender may also be able to point to exceptional mitigating factors but, unlike the person convicted of a serious violent offence, he can receive no leniency on that account. The most a repeat section 15A offender can expect is that the trial judge will order review at the mid-point of the sentence. However, to qualify for such review, the offender must have been addicted to drugs when he committed the offence, and there can be no guarantee in any event that release will be ordered on the review date. To make matters worse, the only remaining avenue of redress also remains closed to him. One common response

---

[2] The relevant law is summarised at p.101 et seq. below.
[3] Lowenthal, "Mandatory Sentencing: Undermining the Effectiveness of Determinate Sentencing Reform" (1993) 81 California L.R. 61 at 67 et seq.

to complaints about inflexible sentencing provisions is that the executive branch of government may extend clemency in appropriate cases. However, the statutory provisions governing section 15A offences clearly provide that temporary release may not be granted "unless for a grave reason of a humanitarian nature" and only for such limited duration as is justified by that reason.[4]

THE LESSONS OF HISTORY

By early nineteenth century, more than 200 capital felonies were formally known to English law, although the true number was substantially lower as many of the relevant statutory provisions were targeting the same kind of behaviour.[5] They were mostly crimes against property which had either been created or declared capital throughout the eighteenth and early nineteenth centuries. The Waltham Black Act of 1723[6] was by far the most notorious eighteenth-century criminal statute, not only because of its speedy enactment and the range of offences which it rendered capital, but also because of the manner in which it was judicially interpreted. The common name of the Act indicates the mischief it was intended to address. It was aimed primarily at gangs known as Blacks because they blackened their faces when going about their activities which consisted mainly of illegal deer-hunting, other forms of poaching, causing damage to forests and fences, and various kinds of public disorder. They appear to have been short-lived and to have been confined to a few parts of England, one of which was Epping Forest near Waltham in Essex.[7] At a conservative estimate, the Act created more than 50 capital offences although Thompson in his classic study claims that the true number should be somewhere between 200 and 250 given the range of circumstances in which some of them could be committed.[8] Many of them already existed but were non-capital, so the Black Act truly

---

4   Misuse of Drugs Act 1977 s.27(3I) as substituted by the Criminal Justice Act 2007 s.33.
5   Tonry, "Mandatory Penalties" in Tonry (ed.), *Crime and Justice: A Review of Research*, Vol.16 (Chicago: University of Chicago Press, 1992), p.243 at p.247 (in 1819 English law recognised 220 capital offences, most of them property crimes). Stephen, in his *History of the Criminal Law of England*, Vol.1, p.470, had made the point that the capital offences in existence in the mid-eighteenth century might "be reduced by careful classification to a comparatively small number". See Langbein, "*Albion's* Fatal Flaws" (1983) 98:1 *Past and Present* 96 at 118.
6   9 Geo. I, c. 22 ("An Act for the more effectual punishing wicked and evil disposed Persons going armed in Disguise, and doing Injuries and Violences to the Persons and Properties of His Majesty's Subjects, and for the more speedy bringing the Offenders to Justice"). See Radzinowicz, "The Waltham Black Act: A Study of the Legislative Attitude towards Crime in the Eighteenth Century" (1945) 9 Cambridge L.J. 56. Lecky describes the Act as "a special and most sanguinary law" (*A History of England in the Eighteenth Century* (London, 1892), Vol.1, p.488).
7   Blackstone, *Commentaries on the Laws of England* (1765) Bk 4, Ch. 17.
8   Thompson, *Whigs and Hunters: The Origin of the Black Act* (New York: Pantheon Books, 1975), p.23.

consisted of a "bloody code" by prescribing the death penalty for virtually all property and protest-related criminal activities. It had been rushed through Parliament in a matter of weeks with very little debate, and was not fully repealed until 1827.[9] While historians have differed over the most likely political motivation for the legislation, they have all recognised its draconian nature.[10] This was an era when the right to private property was being glorified by leading intellectual and political figures. John Locke had gone so far as to claim that government had "no other end but the preservation of property."[11] Criminal legislation enacted by the propertied classes to safeguard their own interests certainly reflected this ideology.

Despite the vast increase in the number of capital crimes during this era, the number of executions was relatively small, and lower, in fact, than it had been a century earlier. Several neutralising and adaptive techniques had emerged over time to mitigate the rigours of the formal code.[12] In much more recent times, Reisman has drawn a distinction between what he describes as the myth system and the operational code. The myth system reflects the law as it might appear from a study of purely formal sources such as statutes, while the operational code refers to what actually happens in practice and that, in turn, may differ sharply from what the formal sources appear to demand.[13] This provides a useful analytical framework for understanding eighteenth-century penal laws and practices. One important component of the operational code was a practice dating back to the fourteenth century, if not earlier, and this was the benefit of clergy.[14] It originated as a means of transferring from the royal courts to the

---

[9] Thompson, *Whigs and Hunters: The Origin of the Black Act* (New York: Pantheon Books, 1975), p.21 ("At no stage in its passage does there appear to have been debate or serious division; a House prepared to debate for hours a disputed election could find unanimity in creating at a blow some fifty new capital offences").

[10] In addition to Radzinowicz, "The Waltham Black Act: A Study of the Legislative Attitude towards Crime in the Eighteenth Century" (1945) 9 Cambridge L.J. 56 and Thompson, *Whigs and Hunters: The Origin of the Black Act* (New York: Pantheon Books, 1975); see Broad, "Whigs and Deer-Stealers in Other Guises: A Return to the Origins of the Black Act" (May 1988) 119 *Past and Present* 56; Cruickshanks and Erskine-Hill, "The Waltham Black Act and Jacobitism" (1985) 24 *Journal of British History* 358; Rogers, "The Waltham Blacks and the Black Act" (1974) 17:3 *The Historical Journal* 465.

[11] Locke, *Two Treatises of Government,* rev. edn by Laslett (Cambridge: Cambridge University Press, 1963), Second Treatise, §94. See also §124.

[12] Lecky, *History of England in the Eighteenth Century* (London, 1892), Vol.II, p.134; Cross, "The English Criminal Law and Benefit of Clergy During the Eighteenth and Early Nineteenth Centuries" (1917) 22 *American Historical Review* 544.

[13] Reisman, *Folded Lies: Bribery, Crusades, and Reforms* (New York: The Liberty Press, 1979); Reisman and Schreiber, *Jurisprudence: Understanding and Shaping Law: Cases, Readings and Commentary* (New Haven: New Haven Press, 1987).

[14] Langbein, "Shaping the Eighteenth-Century Criminal Trial: A View from the Ryder Sources" (1983) 50 Univ. of Chicago L.R. 1 at 37–41; Beattie, *Crime and the Courts in England 1660–1800* (Oxford: Clarendon Press, 1986), esp. pp.141–146; Bellamy, *Criminal Law and Society in Late Medieval and Tudor England* (New York: St. Martin's Inc., 1984); Gabel, *Benefit of Clergy in England in the Later Middle Ages* (New York: Octagan Books, 1969, first published

ecclesiastical courts defendants who were attested to be clergy in holy orders. At first the benefit of clergy could be granted prior to trial, but it later applied solely after conviction. It was also gradually extended to apply to anyone, lay or clerical, who could read and, in due course, the literacy test itself became a mere formality as it always consisted of reciting the same short passage from scripture. Later developments confirmed the status of the benefit as a means of extending leniency to those convicted of certain felonies and property offences in particular. It survived the removal of ecclesiastical jurisdiction over criminal charges and it was extended to women as well as men, although women would not have been eligible to take holy orders. It became, as Langbein writes, "a rubric by which nonecclesiastical courts mitigated the law of felony for non-ecclesiastical persons."[15] In theory, a person could himself avail of the benefit only once and, in the absence of more sophisticated record-keeping systems, the defendant's thumb was branded to indicate that the benefit had been conferred. However, the one-chance rule does not appear to have been very rigorously observed. The true nature of the benefit as a leniency measure was reflected in various sixteenth-century statutes which made certain felonies including murder, highway robbery and rape, non-clergyable. In 1699, the benefit was withdrawn from those convicted of stealing from shops where the stolen goods were worth five shillings or more, and in 1713 from those convicted of stealing from dwelling houses where the goods were valued at 40 shillings or more. An Act passed in 1717 permitted the courts to impose a sentence of seven years' transportation on a person given the benefit of clergy. Some years earlier the reading test had been abandoned, and so by the early eighteenth-century, the availability of the benefit depended on the offence of conviction as opposed to the status of the offender. The crucial question from now on was whether or not an offence was clergyable. If it was not (and most offences under the Waltham Black Act were not), then the convicted offender was liable to be hanged.

Because of the large number of commonly-prosecuted felonies that were non-clergyable during the eighteenth century, one might have expected a commensurate increase in executions. But other practices and strategies combined to ensure that this did not happen. We must recall, first and foremost, that until well into the nineteenth century, most prosecutions were undertaken by private individuals in the absence of organised police forces and prosecution services. Victims might often be persuaded to refrain from prosecuting, especially where the offender was willing to offer some form of compensation or redress. The courts, for their part, became increasingly strict in the interpretation of capital statutes and even more punctilious in their insistence on formal propriety in the drafting of indictments. As Hay remarks, many prosecutions "though founded

---

1929); Sawyer, "'Benefit of Clergy' in Maryland and Virginia" (1990) 34 American J. Legal History 49.
[15] Langbein, "Shaping the Eighteenth-Century Criminal Trial: A View from the Ryder Sources" (1983) 50 Univ. of Chicago L.R. 1 at 38.

on excellent evidence and conducted at considerable expense failed on minor errors of form in the indictment, the written charge."[16] Juries also played their part in mitigating the rigours of the formal legal code by returning partial verdicts which had the effect of saving the offender from liability to the death penalty or some other severe punishment.[17] Finally, of course, there was a well-established pardoning and clemency system which saved most of those actually condemned to death from being hanged. Recommendations for clemency were often made by the judge who had pronounced the death penalty (having had no other option under the prevailing law). In other cases petitions were submitted to the Crown by or on behalf of the convicted person. Recent historical analyses of archive material dating mainly from the eighteenth century suggest that judicial reprieves (essentially recommendations for a full or conditional pardon which were generally accepted) did not operate randomly or arbitrarily as some had previously suggested. The gravity of the offence appears to have been the predominant consideration, followed by other factors such as the age and antecedents of the offender. Judges seldom granted reprieves in homicide cases except where they felt that the accused had been wrongly convicted or where they could identify exceptional mitigating circumstances.[18] While many capital offences were created in Ireland between the late seventeenth and early nineteenth centuries, they were not so numerous as to amount to anything like the bloody code operating in England during much of this period.[19] The number of capital offences was steadily reduced in the first-half of the nineteenth century and, from 1861 onwards, murder was the only commonly-prosecuted capital offence remaining on the statute books. However, studies of murder trials in late nineteenth-century Irish show a familiar pattern of discrepancy between the number of death sentences imposed and the number executed.[20]

The main lesson to be drawn from the historical evidence is that mandatory sentences seldom accomplish anything of value. They may eliminate or curtail judicial sentencing discretion but other compensatory mechanisms quickly evolve to restore some measure of justice to the overall system. Judges may be deprived of discretion, but other actors within the system including victims, prosecutors, juries and the executive branch of government can tailor their decisions in such a way as to spare of the suspect or accused from the excesses

---

[16] Hay, "Property, Authority and the Criminal Law" in Hay et al. (eds), *Albion's Fatal Tree: Crime and Society in Eighteenth Century England* (London: Penguin Books, 1977), Ch.1.

[17] Cross (fn.12 above); Langbein (fn.5 above) at 106; King, "Decision-Makers and Decision-Making in the English Criminal Law, 1750–1800" (1984) 27 *The Historical Journal* 25 at 41 (where he records the example of a woman accused of stealing five shillings and sixpence. Her defence was that she had "a bad husband and three children ready to starve with hunger". The jury returned a verdict in which the value of the stolen money was reduced to tenpence).

[18] Beattie (fn.14 above), p.430 et seq.; King (fn.17 above); King, *Crime, Justice and Discretion in England 1740–1820* (Oxford: Oxford University Press, 2000).

[19] Garnham, *The courts, crime and the criminal law in Ireland 1692–1760* (Dublin: Irish Academic Press, 1996); Vaughan, *Murder trials in Ireland 1836–1914* (Dublin: Four Courts Press, 2009).

[20] See, in particular, Vaughan (fn.19 above), pp.375–379.

of the formal law. Of course, the reason why these neutralising techniques developed in the first place was that the mandatory penalties in question were often unduly harsh and arbitrary, and usually failed to reflect the true circumstances of the offences and offenders to which they applied. Studies of mandatory penalties introduced in American jurisdictions at various times between the 1950s and 1990s reveal a similar pattern. As Tonry writes:

> "Evaluated in terms of their stated substantive objectives, mandatory penalties do not work. The record is clear from research in the 1950s, the 1970s, the 1980s and the 1990s that mandatory penalty laws shift power from judges to prosecutors, meet with widespread circumvention, produce dislocations in case processing, and too often result in imposition of penalties that everyone involved believes to be unduly harsh. From research in the 1970s and 1980s, the evidence is also clear that mandatory penalties have either no demonstrable marginal deterrent effects or short term effects that rapidly waste away."[21]

The transfer of discretion from judges to prosecutors mentioned by Tonry remains one of the more salient characteristics of mandatory penalty systems and is discussed further below. Wherever there is a heavy dependence on plea bargaining, as is true of the United States, prosecutors can use the availability of a mandatory penalty as a powerful bargaining chip to secure a plea to a lesser offence. Perhaps the most damning indictment of mandatory penalties and other severe sentencing arrangements is that they have seldom, if ever, been shown to have any appreciable impact on the incidence of the offences to which they apply.

MANDATORY PENALTIES TODAY

Many Western countries have introduced mandatory minimum sentences during the past 20 years and most have done so in defiance of strong and compelling evidence as to the injustice and ineffectiveness of such measures. A Canadian survey published in 2006 described various kinds of mandatory penalties then in force in Canada itself, England and Wales, Scotland, Ireland, South Africa and some Australian jurisdictions.[22] The United States, which was not covered in that particular survey, also has many mandatory minimum sentencing provisions at both state and federal level, some of which are described below. The short section devoted to Ireland in the Canadian survey was manifestly inadequate as it dealt solely with murder offences and made no reference to the

---

[21] Tonry, *Sentencing Matters* (Oxford: Oxford University Press, 1996), p.135. For a more recent analysis, see Tonry, "The Mostly Unintended Consequences of Mandatory Penalties: Two Centuries of Consistent Findings" in Tonry (ed.), *Crime and Justice: A Review of Research* Vol. 38 (Chicago: University of Chicago Press, 2009), p.65.

[22] *Mandatory Sentences of Imprisonment in Common Law Jurisdictions: Some Representative Models* (Research and Statistics Division, Department of Justice, Ottawa, 2005).

presumptive sentences for section 15A drug offences introduced in 1999. It also stated, rather optimistically, that there appeared to be no likelihood of further mandatory sentences being introduced here in the near future. Less than a year later, the Criminal Justice Act 2006 would introduce absolute mandatory minimum sentences for repeat section 15A drug offenders and several new presumptive minimum sentences for firearms offences. When evaluating the presence and impact of mandatory sentencing regimes internationally, a distinction must first be drawn between those minimum sentences that are invariably mandatory and those that are tailored to allow courts some residual discretion to impose more lenient measures in exceptional circumstances. Canada itself, as it happens, provides a good example of the former situation. Since 1995, in particular, it has introduced several mandatory minimum sentences, principally for firearms offences, sexual offences against children and repeat offences of impaired driving.[23] Most of them, however, are reasonably short, at least when compared to our five- and 10-year sentences for drug and firearms offences. In a parliamentary fact sheet produced in 2006, the longest mandatory minimum sentence listed was one of four years' imprisonment for the using of a firearm in the commission of certain serious offences. Most others were of one year's duration or less and included, for example, one year (on indictment) or 90 days (on summary conviction) for producing, distributing, importing or exporting child pornography. Possession of child pornography also attracts a minimum sentence (45 days following conviction on indictment and 14 days following summary conviction). Over the past few years, the Canadian government has been making determined efforts to introduce mandatory minimum sentences for certain drug offences. Bill S-10, passed by the Senate in December 2010, is the most recent version of the draft legislation in question. It proposes a one-year mandatory minimum prison sentence for trafficking in drugs such as cocaine and heroin when certain aggravating factors are present. The minimum increases to two and three years in certain circumstances, such as when there is a risk to health or safety. Marijuana production will also attract mandatory minimums—six months' imprisonment, for example, for the cultivation of six to 200 plants. A few aspects of this proposed legislation are particularly interesting from an Irish perspective. First, the prescribed minimums are relatively low, compared to those applicable to section 15A offences in Ireland. Secondly, a court will have discretion to depart from a specified minimum where the offender enters and successfully completes a drug treatment programmes. Thirdly, it is proposed that within five years of the legislation entering into force, it should be subject to a

---

23 On the history of mandatory minimum prison sentences in Canada up until 2000, see Crutcher, "Mandatory Minimum Penalties of Imprisonment: An Historical Analysis" (2001) 44 Crim. L.Q. 279. See also Doob and Cesaroni, "The Political Attractiveness of Mandatory Minimum Sentences" (2001) 39 Osgoode Hall L.J. 287; Roberts, Crutcher and Verbrugge, "Public Attitudes to Sentencing in Canada: Exploring Recent Findings" (2007) 49 *Canadian Journal of Criminology and Criminal Justice* 75.

comprehensive review, including a cost-benefit analysis of mandatory minimum sentences.[24]

South African law, by contrast, provides for much harsher mandatory sentences for a reasonably wide range of offences, but compensates for this by allowing for a downward departure where "substantial and compelling circumstances" are found to exist. The Criminal Law Amendment Act 1997, which became operative in 1998, was originally to remain in force for two years only but it has regularly been renewed ever since.[25] Essentially, s.51 of the Act provides that a person convicted of murder or rape, with certain aggravating circumstances in both instances, must be sentenced to life imprisonment. Another set of offences including robbery with aggravating circumstances, drug trafficking, firearms, fraud and related offences attract minimum sentences of 15, 20 and 25 years for first-time, second-time and third or subsequent offenders respectively. Other offences attract somewhat lower mandatory minimums. Rape, unless it falls within the category requiring a life sentence, attracts a sentence of 10, 15 or 20 years depending on whether the person is a first-time or repeat offender. The criterion by which courts may department from the prescribed minima, "substantial and compelling circumstances" appears to be borrowed from the Minnesota Sentencing Guidelines, but is otherwise left undefined. This has inevitably led to different judicial interpretations but following the decision of the Supreme Court of Appeal in *State v Malgas*[26] it appears accepted that such circumstances exist where the prescribed sentence would result in an injustice. However, the court cautioned that this was not lightly to be inferred and that weighty and convincing circumstances were needed to warrant a downward departure. A later decision of the same court illustrates how sentencers may differ over the presence or absence of substantial and compelling circumstances. In *State v Ferreira*[27] the appellant had been found guilty of the murder of her partner and sentenced

---

[24] *Debates of the Senate (Hansard)*, 3rd session, 40th Parliament, Vol.147, Issue 27 (May 11, 2010).

[25] The text of the Act is available in South Africa's *Government Gazette* (No. 18519) available at: *www.info.gov.za*. Some amendments have been made by the Criminal Law (Sentencing) Amendment Act 2007 (No. 38 of 2007) (South Africa). More detailed analysis of this legislation and its application is provided by Terblanche and Mackenzie, "Mandatory Sentences in South Africa: Lessons for Australia" (2008) 41 *Australian and New Zealand Journal of Criminology* 402; Roth, "South African Mandatory Minimum Sentencing: Reform Required" (2008) 17 Minnesota J. of International L. 155; Terblanche and Roberts, "Sentencing in South Africa: Lacking in principle but delivering justice?" (2005) 18 *South African Journal of Criminal Justice* 187; Terblanche, *Research on the Sentencing Framework Bill* (Newlands, SA: Open Society Foundation for South Africa, 2008); O'Donovan and Redpath, *The Impact of Minimum Sentencing in South Africa* (Newlands, SA: Open Society Foundation for South Africa, 2006); Giffard and Muntingh, *The Effect of Sentencing on the Size of the South African Prison Population* (Newlands SA: Open Society Foundation for South Africa, 2006).

[26] 2001 (1) SACR 469 (SCA); [2001] ZASCA 30.

[27] 2004 (2) SACR 454 (SCA). For a detailed comment, see Terblanche and Roberts (fn.25 above).

to life imprisonment despite clear evidence that she had been subjected to severe and prolonged violence at his hands. The Supreme Court of Appeal varied this to six years' imprisonment with half of that term suspended. More recently the Constitutional Court of South Africa has invalidated an amending law that applied the minimum sentencing regime to 16- and 17-year-olds.[28]

Mandatory or, more precisely, presumptive minimum sentences were introduced for certain repeat offenders in England and Wales under the Crime (Sentences) Act 1997.[29] As originally enacted, the most draconian aspect of this legislation was a requirement that anyone sentenced for a second "serious offence" had to receive life imprisonment unless there were exceptional circumstances to justify a more lenient measure.[30] The two provisions which remain in force are essentially "three strikes" laws in so far as they require certain minimum sentences for third-time Class A drug offenders and third-time domestic burglars (at least seven years' imprisonment for the first group and at least three years' imprisonment for the second). However, these provisions are not truly mandatory as a court is not required to impose the sentences in question if it would be "unjust to do so in all the circumstances". The Criminal Justice Act 2003 introduced a rather complicated sentencing regime for "dangerous offenders" and obliged the courts, depending on the circumstances, to impose life sentences, indeterminate sentences for public protection (IPP) and extended sentences on dangerous offenders convicted of specified offences. Many offenders found themselves subject to these provisions and the IPP provision in particular. Significantly, however, the system was reformed in 2008 so as to give the courts discretion in imposing these measures on dangerous offenders.[31] One significant measure introduced by the Criminal Justice Act 2003 (s.287), however, was a requirement to impose minimum sentences (five years for an adult offender) for certain firearms offences, including possession. However, this is also subject to the qualification that a court need not do so if satisfied that there are exceptional circumstances relating to the offence or the offender which would not justify such a sentence.[32]

Some continental European countries also have introduced various minimum sentencing arrangements. France, for example, has recently introduced presumptive minimum sentences for specified assault offences, all of them having certain

---

[28] *Centre for Child Law v Minister for Justice and Constitutional Development* [2009] ZACC 18.

[29] On this and more recent developments in England and Wales, see Ashworth, *Sentencing and Criminal Justice*, 5th edn (Cambridge: Cambridge University Press, 2010), pp.224–238.

[30] On the interpretation of this section, see *R v Kelly* [2000] Q.B. 198, [1999] 2 W.L.R. 1100, [1999] 2 All E.R. 13, [1999] 2 Cr. App. R. 36, [1999] 2 Cr. App. R. (S.) 176, and, with reference to the European Convention on Human Rights, *R v Offen* [2001] 1 W.L.R. 253, [2001] 2 All E.R. 154, [2001] 1 Cr. App. R. 24, [2002] 2 Cr. App. R. (S.) 10.

[31] Criminal Justice and Immigration Act 2008 Pt 2.

[32] *R v Rehman and Wood* [2005] EWCA Crim 2056, [2006] 1 Cr. App. R. (S.) 77. Both this case and *Offen* (fn.30 above) are useful for their definitions of "exceptional circumstances".

aggravating features.[33] The statute introducing these measures was referred to the *Conseil Constitutionnel* which upheld the constitutionality of the presumptive sentences as they applied to adult offenders, but deemed several other provisions, including minimum sentences for juveniles, to be contrary to the Constitution. The section introducing presumptive sentences provides that an aggravated assault offence carrying a maximum sentence of 10 years' imprisonment shall henceforth be punished with at least two years' imprisonment while such an offence carrying a maximum of seven years' imprisonment shall be punished with at least 18 months' imprisonment. However, there is a saving clause permitting a court to impose a lower sentence, or a non-custodial sentence, in light of the circumstances of the offence or the offender provided it articulates its reasons for doing so. It was argued that this provision ran counter to art.8 of the Declaration of the Rights of Man 1789 which prohibits excessive sentences.[34] The *Conseil* noted, first, that the new arrangements applied solely to assaults with certain aggravating factors, that the presumptive minimum sentences were reasonably low, and that, in any event, trial courts retained some measure of discretion to impose lower sentences in appropriate circumstances. It therefore found the relevant provisions to be compatible with the Constitution.

American experience of mandatory penalties, at federal level at least, dates from the late eighteenth century. The first federal mandatory minimum sentence was adopted in 1790 for piracy, but it was only in the 1950s that Congress first turned to mandatory minimums in the fight against drugs. The Boggs Act 1951 and, more particularly, the Narcotic Control Act 1956 introduced severe mandatory minimum sentences for drug importation and distribution. Significantly, however, Congress repealed almost all of these in 1970, having realised that they were unjust and ineffective. It discovered, for example, that such sentences led to fewer convictions because prosecutors were often unwilling to charge suspects with offences attracting such heavy penalties.[35] Unfortunately, Congress regained its appetite for mandatory sentencing in the mid-1980s, and the timing

---

[33] Loi d'orientation et de programmation pour la performance de la securité interieure (*Loppsi2*), available at *www.senat.fr/petite-loi-ameli/2010-2011/262.html* [Last accessed August 19, 2011]. The sentencing provisions under discussion are in art.37. The decision of the *Conseil Constitutionnel* (Décision No. 2011-625 DC du 10 mars 2011) is available at *www.conseil-constitutionnel.fr* (under "Les Décisions"). For a comment on the decision, see *Le Monde*, March 12, 2011, p.10. The new sentencing arrangements apply mainly to certain assault offences defined in art.222 of the Penal Code.

[34] Article 8 provides: "La loi ne doit établir que des peines strictement et évidemment nécessaires ..." (The law should not prescribe penalties other than those that are strictly and manifestly necessary).

[35] Oliss, "Mandatory Minimum Sentencing: Discretion, the Safety Valve, and the Sentencing Guidelines" (1995) 63 Univ. Cincinnati L.R. 1851. See also Wallace, "Mandatory Minimums and the Betrayal of Sentencing Reform: A Legislative Dr Jekyll and Mr Hyde" (1993) 57 *Federal Probation* 9; Miller and Freed, "Editors' Observations: The Chasm between the Judiciary and Congress over Mandatory Minimum Sentences" (1993) 6 *Federal Sentencing Reporter* 59.

could scarcely have been more ironic. After a decade of debate and deliberation, the Sentencing Reform Act 1984 introduced federal sentencing guidelines which certainly constrained judicial discretion but which still required sentencers to consider in detail the facts of the particular offence, the offender's criminal history and related matters. Yet, at the very same time, it introduced some mandatory minimum sentences and that trend continued for many years afterwards.[36] Most of these mandatory minimums, in practice at least, were directed at drug and firearms offences. Most notorious were the Anti-Drug Abuse Acts 1986 and 1988, the first of which introduced severe mandatory minimum penalties for drug possession. More controversially still, it introduced a 100:1 ratio for crack and powder cocaine, meaning in effect that the same mandatory sentence (five years) applied to the offence of dealing five grams of crack or 500 grams of powder cocaine. Persons found in possession of 50 grams of crack or 5,000 grams of powder cocaine faced a mandatory 10-year sentence. Critics of this law had consistently pointed to its racial impact. Many members of the Congressional Black Caucus had supported its enactment because of the devastating effect which crack was having on African American communities. However, the discriminatory impact of the law soon became apparent. In 2006, 82 per cent of crack cocaine defendants were African American,[37] and they consequently served much longer prison sentences than those served by white offenders convicted of similar or more serious offences. The Fair Sentencing Act 2010 has now eliminated the mandatory minimum sentence for simple possession of crack cocaine and increased the weight required to trigger a mandatory sentence. It reduces the disparity between powder and crack cocaine in sentencing terms from 100 to one to 18 to one, a move that has generally been welcomed.

Mandatory minimums have also proliferated in most American states in recent decades.[38] Most notable, and indeed notorious, of these were the so-called Rockefeller drug laws, introduced in 1973, which imposed harsh mandatory sentences for selling even small quantities of drugs. Michigan introduced a similar regime some years later. Another highly significant development, dating

---

[36] The serious drawbacks associated with mandatory minimums within the federal system were clearly outlined by the United States Sentencing Commission in a report to Congress, *Mandatory Minimum Sentences in the Criminal Justice System* (Washington, 1991). See also statement of Jay Rorty of the American Civil Liberties Union at a public hearing of the Sentencing Commission on May 27, 2010, available at *www.aclu.org.*

[37] Sentencing Project, *Federal Crack Cocaine Sentencing,* available at *www.sentencingproject.org* [Last consulted April 2, 2010]. The same paper states (p.4): "Between 1994 and 2003, the average time served by African Americans for drug offences increased by 62 per cent, compared with an increase of 17 per cent for white offenders. Moreover, African Americans now serve virtually as much time in prison for a drug offence (58.7 months) as whites do for a violent offence (61.7 months)" (internal citations omitted).

[38] Bjerk, "Making the Crime Fit the Penalty: The Role of Prosecutorial Discretion Under Mandatory Minimum Sentencing" (2005) 48 *Journal of Law and Economics* 591.

from the 1990s, was the widespread introduction of "three strikes" laws. Between 1993 and 1995, 24 states and the federal system introduced such laws although their precise terms vary from one jurisdiction to another. Under the Californian law, adopted in 1994, any felony can qualify as a third strike which means that a person convicted of a felony who has two or more prior convictions for a serious or violent felony must receive a sentence of 15 years to life imprisonment. Second time offenders, those with two strikes, receive twice the standard sentence. One notable feature of California's three strikes law is the power vested in both prosecutors and trial courts to disregard a previous felony conviction in furtherance of the interests of justice in a deserving case.[39] Any hope that these laws might fall foul of the Eighth Amendment of the federal Constitution (the cruel and unusual punishment clause) was comprehensively shattered by the Supreme Court decisions in *Ewing v California*[40] and *Lockyer v Andrade.*[41] Ewing was sentenced to 25 years to life imprisonment for stealing goods worth approximately $1,200 in total while Andrade was sentenced to 50 years for stealing $150 worth of goods from two different stores. Both were caught by the three-strikes law. Delivering the court's judgment in *Andrade*, O'Connor J. said that when sentences of terms of years' imprisonment are being evaluated against the Eighth Amendment, a "gross disproportionality principle" applies and this in turn "reserves a constitutional violation for only the extraordinary case."[42] Four members of the court dissented, but the majority holding continues to apply. In recent years, many states have begun to repeal mandatory minimum sentencing laws, especially for low-level drug offences.[43] New York, for example, significantly amended the Rockefeller drug laws in 2009 so that prison is no longer mandatory in less serious cases. Legislators in some states have probably been swayed by arguments about the injustice and futility of mandatory minimums for low- and medium-level offending, and organisations such as FAMM (Families Against Mandatory Minimums) have been very effective advocates of reform. But financial considerations have been at least as influential; the cost of the prison system in many states had become unsustainable.[44]

Ireland has relatively few mandatory penalties, at least when compared to the United States, Canada and South Africa. Aside from mandatory disqualification orders for certain road traffic offences, the only commonly-prosecuted offence carrying a truly mandatory sentence is murder which attracts life imprisonment.

---

[39] *People v Superior Court (Romero)* 917 P 2d 628 (1996); *People v Williams* (1998) 17 Cal. 4th 148.

[40] 538 U.S. 11 (2003).

[41] 538 U.S. 63 (2003).

[42] 538 U.S. 63 at 72 and 77 (2003). See also *Harmelin v Michigan* 501 U.S. 957 (1991).

[43] Austin, *Criminal Justice Trends: Key Legislative Changes in Sentencing Policy 2000–2010* (New York: Vera Institute, 2010).

[44] Porter, *The State of Sentencing 2010: Developments in Policy and Practice* (Washington: The Sentencing Project, 2011).

Those murders which were capital offences between the partial abolition of the death penalty in 1964 and its complete abolition in 1990 are punishable with life imprisonment coupled with a mandatory requirement that the offender serve at least 40 years' imprisonment to which standard remission may be applied.[45] As described in more detail below, certain drug-trafficking offences attract a presumptive minimum sentence of 10 years' imprisonment on a first conviction and a mandatory minimum of 10 years' imprisonment on a second or subsequent conviction. Some firearms offences also attract presumptive minimum sentences of five or 10 years' imprisonment. There are also several provisions in Irish law, and in the laws of many other countries, requiring the imposition of mandatory ancillary orders following conviction for certain offences such as drink-driving. Despite being ancillary in nature, these orders are often in effect the most severe, and the most feared, consequence of a conviction for such an offence. To that extent they certainly have some deterrent value.

Impact of Mandatory Penalties

Deterrence and incapacitation are the penal purposes most commonly invoked by supporters of mandatory penalties. All of the traditional justifications for criminal punishment rest on certain moral and empirical premises, and these two are no exception. Deterrence—and we are referring here to general rather than individual deterrence—assumes that the end justifies the means. If the consistent imposition of harsh punishment reduces the incidence of the conduct to which it applies, then the practice is morally justifiable. That is fundamentally the argument used to support deterrence as the sole or dominant justification for punishment. The individual offender is treated instrumentally in order to convey a message to the wider society as to the consequences that will follow conviction. Such an approach is morally problematic and it certainly offends against the Kantian principle that individuals should be treated as ends in themselves rather than as means. Granted, there is room for philosophical debate about the respective merits of teleological and deontological approaches towards punishment. But there is a more immediate objection which may defeat the teleological argument on its own territory and that is the absence of any convincing evidence that harsh punishment does in fact deter. There can be no doubt but that deterrence works in general terms. In fact, the entire purpose of the criminal law is to deter people from engaging in injurious and antisocial conduct. But this is far from saying that more severe sentences, mandatory or otherwise, have a direct impact on crime levels. Most of the empirical research shows that increases in punishment have no more than a marginal impact on offending, and that the likelihood of detection has a more significant behavioural

---

[45]   Criminal Justice Act 1990.

impact than the probable or anticipated level of punishment.[46] Admittedly, the deterrent effect of particular penalties is always difficult to measure with any degree of precision, not least because of varying levels of awareness among the general public about the existence and nature of such penalties. The criminal conduct to which they apply might well be more prevalent in their absence. What can be said with more certainty, however, is that harsh penalties, mandatory or otherwise, do not significantly affect recorded levels of offending. In Ireland, murder attracts a mandatory sentence of life imprisonment. Yet, the number of recorded murders has increased very substantially over the past decade or so, and so has the number of prosecutions. In 2009, 53 new murder cases came before the Central Criminal Court, the highest since 2002.[47] The same holds true, and even more so, of drug dealing offences. In 2009, 732 defendants were dealt with in the Circuit Court for drug offences which, by virtue of having been dealt with in that court, must have been serious in nature. Ninety-seven per cent of them were convicted; in fact, 94 per cent pleaded guilty. Of those convicted, more than 500 received prison sentences, 171 of these sentences being for five years or longer.[48] The same pattern has now prevailed for a number of years, and it scarcely induces much confidence in the deterrent effect of lengthy prison sentences.

Incapacitation brings its own share of well-documented problems. Every custodial sentence incapacitates in the sense that it prevents the prisoner from offending against the general community for the duration of the sentence. In this sense, incapacitation is an incident of custodial punishment rather than a justification for it. But those who advocate mandatory sentences as a means of incapacitating certain categories of offender usually have something different in mind. They believe that the public can best be protected by obliging the courts to impose prison sentences of a certain length, or a certain minimum length, for specified offences. One problem with this approach is that mandatory sentences tend to be prescribed quite selectively and not always for the most serious offences. Why have mandatory minimum sentences for repeat drug dealers, even those with a low level of involvement in the drugs trade, but not for repeat armed robbers or repeat rapists? Secondly, there are well-known problems associated with predictions of recidivism. Such predictions are difficult enough in individual cases, whether made on the basis of clinical or actuarial assessments. They obviously become much more problematic when applied indiscriminately to a wide category of offenders who, apart from having been convicted of the same type of offence, may have little else in common. In a recent review of the relevant literature, von Hirsch writes:

---

[46] Von Hirsch, Bottoms, Burney and Wikstrom, *Criminal Deterrence and Sentence Severity* (Oxford: Hart Publishing, 1999).
[47] Courts Service, *Annual Report 2009* (Dublin: Courts Service, 2010), p.40.
[48] Courts Service (fn.47 above), p.55.

"Although statistical forecasting methods can identify groups of offenders having higher than average probabilities of recidivism, these methods show a disturbing incidence of 'false positives'. Many of those classified as potential recidivists will, in fact, not be found to offend again. The rate of false positives is particularly high when forecasting serious criminality—for example, violence."[49]

The problem of false positives is, indeed, a serious one given the fallibility of most prediction techniques. The Floud Report, a seminal work in this area, accepted that false positive rates in predicting serious violent crime was at least 50 per cent and could be as high as 66 per cent.[50] The more recent Halliday Report suggests that prediction still remains an inexact science.[51] Incapacitation may also conflict with proportionality as the most defensible distributive principle of punishment. A prison sentence can, of course, serve both purposes quite harmoniously. Even if chosen on proportionality grounds, it will incapacitate the offender for whatever term he is required to serve. But an offender sentenced to a period longer than a strict application of the proportionality principle may demand is being punished for conduct which he has not committed and which, contrary to predictions, he might never have committed even if he were at liberty. These are just some of the more fundamental problems of principle associated with mandatory sentences, but it would be a mistake to treat them as largely theoretical in nature. On the contrary, they point very clearly to the ineffectiveness of mandatory sentences in general, at least when effectiveness is measured in terms of reducing the incidence of criminal behaviour.

Conflict with fundamental principles of justice

When the legislature prescribes a mandatory penalty, it is effectively pre-sentencing every person thereafter convicted of the relevant offence. The injustice of this arrangement scarcely needs elaboration but it was well summarised by a judge of the United States District Court when faced with the prospect of imposing harsh mandatory and guideline sentences on low-level drug dealers:

"The factual record before the Court clearly demonstrates the injustice that results from a system that has the sentence of a defendant predetermined by people who have never seen the defendant, know nothing of the defendant's background and are unaware of the particular factual circumstances of his crime."[52]

---

49 Von Hirsch, "Incapacitation" in Ashworth, von Hirsch and Roberts (eds), *Principled Sentencing: Readings on Theory and Policy*, 3rd edn (Oxford: Hart Publishing, 2009), pp.75, 76.

50 Floud and Young, *Dangerousness and Criminal Justice* (London: Heinemann, 1981).

51 Halliday, *Making Punishments Work: Report of a Review of the Sentencing Framework for England and Wales* (London: Home Office, 2001).

52 *United States v Genao* 6 Fed. Sent. R. 85 (1993), S.D.N.Y. (Martin J.). See Miller and Freed (fn.35 above). In *Dodo v The State* (2001) 3 SA 382, Smuts J. of the South African High Court

More recently, in *United States v Vasquez*, Judge Gleeson of the same court, this time in the Eastern District of New York, who found himself compelled to ignore clear mitigating factors and impose a sentence which he regarded as excessively harsh, began his statement of reasons with the following remark:

> "When people think about miscarriages of justice, they generally think big, especially in this era of DNA exonerations, in which wholly innocent people have been released from jail in significant numbers after long periods in prison. As disturbing as those cases are, the truth is that most of the time miscarriages of justice occur in small doses, in cases involving guilty defendants. This makes them easier to overlook. But when they are multiplied by the thousands of cases in which they occur, they have a greater impact on our criminal justice system than the cases you read about in the newspapers or hear about on *60 Minutes*. This case is a good example."[53]

Such a system clearly runs counter to the principle of proportionality which is supposed to be the most fundamental distributive principle of sentencing in many Western jurisdictions. Ireland, in fact, adheres to a remarkably strong version of proportionality which requires every sentence to reflect not only the gravity of the particular offence but also the personal circumstances of the particular offender.[54] Even in the absence of a legally- or constitutionally-entrenched proportionality principle, basic notions of fairness should alert us to the injustice of precluding sentencing courts from taking account of the specific circumstances of individual cases and tailoring punishments accordingly. Presumptive sentences leave some element of discretion to the courts, but purely mandatory sentences leave them with none.

Displacement of discretion

Mandatory sentences are commonly promoted as a means of removing discretion from the sentencing of the offences to which they apply, the implication being that as long as judges have discretion they will be inclined to impose unduly lenient sentences. This calls for two comments. First, politicians and others who rely on this argument seldom, if ever, produce any empirical evidence to support it. They may, at best, be able produce anecdotal evidence of a few recent cases where lenient sentences appear to have been imposed. Even then, a closer examination of the facts might well reveal circumstances which justified the sentences in question but which were not adequately covered in media reports.

---

is recorded as saying of mandatory sentences, "… the robes are the robes of the judge, but the voice is the voice of the Legislature."

[53] *United States v Vasquez*, U.S. District Court, EDNY, March 30, 2010 (2010 WL 1257359).
[54] *People (DPP) v M* [1994] 3 I.R. 306, [1994] 2 I.L.R.M. 541; *People (DPP) v Kelly* [2005] 2 I.R. 321, [2005] 1 I.L.R.M. 19.

This problem is particularly acute in Ireland because of the sheer absence of reliable data on existing practices apart from some very raw statistics from which no meaningful conclusions can safely be drawn. The second comment relates to the fallacy of removing discretion. True enough, one set of actors within the system, namely judges, are being fully or substantially deprived of discretion in relation to the sentencing of the relevant offences. Absolute mandatory sentences deprive judges of all discretion. Mandatory minimums, even when accompanied by some kind of safety valve to cater for exceptional cases, significantly reduce the scope of judicial discretion. More often than not, however, discretion is merely transferred to other actors within the criminal justice system. A legislative scheme which makes liability to a mandatory penalty contingent on the presence of a specified factor, such as possessing a firearm while committing the basic offence, confers enormous discretion on prosecutors in deciding if they should charge the basic offence or the enhanced version, i.e. including the firearm element.

Prosecutors in most common-law jurisdictions enjoy extensive discretion in deciding on the charges to be preferred in specific cases and, in the absence of a serious vitiating factor such as bad faith or invidious discrimination, the exercise of this discretion is generally immune from judicial review.[55] Prosecution decisions are also seriously lacking in visibility, at least when compared to sentencing decisions which must be announced in open court and are thereby subject to public scrutiny.[56] The extent to which discretion is transferred to prosecutors depends on the precise terms of the sentencing provision. Western Australia, for example, has recently introduced mandatory minimum sentences for assaults on police, prison and public transport officers. An assault on such a person, provided it caused bodily harm, carries a mandatory minimum sentence of six or nine months' imprisonment (depending on the circumstances), whereas an assault causing grievous bodily harm carries a mandatory minimum sentence of 12 months, provided the defendant has reached the age of 18 years. Lower minima apply to persons aged between 16 and 18 years. A person's liability to these punishments will depend on whether he is convicted of a minor assault not resulting in bodily harm (in which case the mandatory sentencing regime does not apply), an assault causing bodily harm or an assault causing grievous bodily harm. Obviously, the offence with which the person is initially charged will strongly influence, if not determine, the eventual offence of conviction and,

---

[55] O'Malley, *The Criminal Process* (Dublin: Round Hall, 2009), Ch.12. Leading Irish authorities on prosecutorial discretion include *State (McCormack) v Curran* [1987] I.L.R.M. 225; *H v DPP* [1994] 2 I.R. 589, [1994] 2 I.L.R.M. 285.

[56] Schulhofer, "Rethinking Mandatory Minimums" (1993) 28 Wake Forest L.R. 199; Beale, "What's the Law Got to Do with It? The Political, Social, Psychological and other Non-Legal Factors Influencing the Development of (Federal) Criminal Law" (1997) 1 Buffalo Crim L.R. 23; Bjerk (fn.38 above).

consequently, the sentence.[57] The same applies in circumstances where liability to a mandatory minimum sentence depends on the possession of a specified amount of drugs or the possession of a firearm in the course of committing another offence. Discretion may also be transferred to those charged with the execution of sentence. Again, much depends on the terms of the relevant statutory provision. Irish statutes introducing such sentencing regimes have consistently included provisions to the effect that a sentenced person is not entitled to discretionary early release except for grave reasons of a humanitarian nature and then only for such limited period as is strictly necessary. In the absence of such a provision, and particularly at times of prison overcrowding, many of those who had to receive minimum sentences following conviction could end up being released long before the minimum term had expired.

Disparity

It may seem strange at first sight to accuse mandatory penalties of producing disparity since that is precisely what they are commonly intended to remove or diminish. Legislators introduce mandatory penalties with the avowed purpose of ensuring that everyone convicted of the relevant offence will receive the same sentence or, at least, a sentence which does not fall below a specified level. To that extent, their efforts will have been successful. Unless found to be constitutionally invalid, mandatory sentences must be faithfully imposed and upheld by the courts. All the legislation will have achieved, however, is a crude level of uniformity of outcome. Suppose the law were to provide that everyone convicted of dealing in drugs had to receive a fixed sentence of three years' imprisonment provided the amount of drugs involved either reached or exceeded the prescribed threshold. Once that threshold was reached, all judges would have to impose the same sentence and to that extent the possibility for inter-judge disparity would be eliminated. But a more invidious form of disparity would thereby be created. The three-year sentence would have to be imposed on everybody irrespective of the amount of drugs involved, provided the statutory threshold was reached. A big-time dealer found in possession of millions of Euro

---

[57] Criminal Code Amendment Act (WA) 2009. There have been mixed reactions to this legislation since it came into effect. It has been claimed that the number of assaults against police officers dropped by almost 30 per cent in the first year (*www.southernthunderer.com.au/2010/09/mandatory-sentencing-laws-taking-effect/* [Last accessed August 19, 2011]). However, there have also been allegations that some of those charged have been persons suffering from mental illness and other problems. One of the more notorious examples of mandatory sentencing occurred in the Northern Territory of Australia where, between 1997 and 2001, juvenile repeat property offenders were subject to mandatory terms of detention varying from 28 days to 12 months. On this and other mandatory sentencing laws in Australia, see Warner, "Mandatory Sentencing and the Role of the Academic", paper delivered to International Society for the Reform of the Criminal Law, July 2006, and available at *www.isrcl.org/*.

worth of drugs would receive the same sentence as the addict found transporting €20,000 worth (assuming this reached or exceeded the prescribed threshold) in return for a paltry monetary reward. The repeat offender would receive the same penalty as the hardened recidivist; the kingpin of the entire enterprise would receive the same sentence as the penniless runner; the defendant who pleaded guilty and gave valuable assistance to the police would receive the same sentence as one found guilty after a long and expensive trial. This may seem a rather fanciful scenario, but it is not entirely unrealistic considering some of the statutory provisions now applicable in Canada and elsewhere. The mandatory minimum 10-year sentence currently applicable to repeat drug traffickers in Ireland applies irrespective of the nature of the plea, the level of participation, the amount of drug involved (provided the combined street value is €13,000 or more), or criminal record save to the extent that the offender must have at least one previous conviction for a similar offence.[58] There are, admittedly, two saving factors. One is that a court may impose a sentence well in excess of 10 years' imprisonment in particularly serious cases, but this may not prove very significant if, in practice, the minimum comes to be regarded as the norm rather than the starting point. The other is that in the case where addiction was a substantial factor, the court may list the case for review once at least half of the sentence has been served. Advocates of mandatory penalties tend to view disparity solely in terms of like cases being treated differently, though they seldom take much trouble to investigate if this has actually been happening. Disparity also arises when courts choose or are compelled to treat different cases alike. In fact, this can be the most noxious form of disparity because it virtually guarantees that many defendants will be sentenced as severely as those with much higher levels of guilt.

Impact on the criminal justice system

Adversarial systems of criminal justice are valued for the protection they afford to accused persons and, in particular, for the opportunities they furnish to the defence to mount a comprehensive challenge to the prosecution case during a criminal trial. The adversarial process is probably at its most developed in common-law jurisdictions but, rather paradoxically, many of those jurisdictions would find it impossible to manage their criminal justice systems with any degree of efficiency were it not for a high rate of guilty pleas. Everyone charged with a criminal offence is entitled to plead not guilty and to put the prosecution on proof, an entitlement which explains the near universal practice of rewarding those who plead guilty with a reduced sentence. Few common-law criminal justice systems would continue to function without a high rate of guilty pleas. Of the 3,489 defendants who appeared before the Irish Circuit Criminal Court

---

[58]   Misuse of Drugs Act 1977 s.27(3A)–(3K), as substituted by the Criminal Justice Act 2007 s.33.

in 2009, 3,026 (87 per cent) pleaded guilty. The rate varied from 94 per cent for drug offences to 62 per cent for sex offences.[59] Of the 463 trials, 120 resulted in conviction, 170 in an acquittal and 173 in a *nolle prosequi*. Mandatory sentences may, depending on their severity and the circumstances in which they apply, create a serious disincentive to plead guilty. A person who knows that he will get the same sentence irrespective of the nature of his plea may as well contest his guilt. He might, after all, manage to secure an acquittal, perhaps because of a so-called technical hitch in the conduct of the trial or because the jury, if they are aware of the penal consequences of a conviction, may use their untrammelled power to acquit even in the face of compelling prosecution evidence. The higher rate of guilty pleas to serious drug charges in Ireland may seem to contradict this proposition given that a conviction for the sale or supply of drugs which have a street value of €13,000 or more attracts a presumptive minimum sentence of 10 years' imprisonment. However, the relevant legislation expressly provides that a court, in considering whether there are exceptional and specific circumstances to justify a lower sentence, may have regard to a number of factors including a guilty plea and the stage at which it was entered.[60] There has also been a slight growth in the number of guilty pleas to murder in recent years despite the presence of an entirely mandatory life sentence. This is probably due to an expectation that the plea may later have some bearing on the granting of parole. However, when a sentence is entirely mandatory, the incentive to plead guilty diminishes substantially.

Depending upon their nature and prevalence, mandatory penalties may have a significant impact on prison populations. As noted in Chapter 1, prison populations are determined by the number of persons sentenced to imprisonment by the courts, the length of sentences imposed and the length of time for which prisoners are held. A severe mandatory sentencing regime, especially when coupled with statutory restrictions on early release, can only have a highly inflationary impact on prison numbers. Irish prison statistics bear out this trend. They show that what has contributed most to the present record-high prison population is not the large number of short sentences imposed by the District Court, although these bring their own share of problems, but the growing number of long-term prisoners serving sentences for homicide, sex offences and drug offences. A snapshot of the sentenced prisoner population on December 4, 2009 showed that there were 1,343 serving sentences of five years or longer, and of these 941 (70 per cent) were imprisoned for murder, manslaughter, sexual offences or drug offences. In fact, drug offenders (420) were by far the largest group of long-term prisoners. By contrast, there were only about 140 prisoners in custody on that date serving sentences of six months or less, though this was probably due to a large number of others being on temporary release.

---

[59] Court Service, *Annual Report 2009*, p.55.
[60] Misuse of Drugs Act 1977 s.27 as substituted in part by the Criminal Justice Act 2007 s.33.

Finally, it is reasonable to suppose that the statutory prescription of high mandatory or presumptive sentences for selected offences may have the effect of ratcheting up sentencing levels generally. This is a difficult proposition to prove empirically, but it seems intuitively plausible that judges who find themselves constrained to impose heavy sentences for certain offences would conclude, logically in some respects, that more serious offences should attract at least the same, if not higher, levels of punishment. Aside from murder, the offences attracting various kinds of mandatory sentences are not always, or indeed typically, the most serious. Drug and firearms offences are far more likely be singled out for special treatment than serious offences against the person or against property. Courts which find themselves obliged to consider a 10-year sentence for possessing drugs with an estimated street value of €13,000 for sale or supply might reasonably conclude that a serious assault or robbery should not be treated any more leniently. Indeed, a robust doctrine of proportionality might even suggest as much. Proportionality requires first and foremost that the offence of conviction should be located on its own scale of gravity, but it must surely require also that attention be paid to other offences with similar or identical maximum sentences. Yet this is a factor which legislatures routinely ignore when deciding to introduce mandatory minimum and presumptive sentences for selected offences. It also underscores yet again the value of having an advisory body charged with making recommendations on sentencing policy which are based on empirical research and which take account of the wider ramifications of any proposed reforms.[61]

CONSTITUTIONAL DIMENSIONS

Constitutional challenges to mandatory penalties may rest on a separation of powers argument or, more likely, on a claim that the relevant statutory provision conflicts with a substantive constitutional norm such as a prohibition on inhuman or degrading treatment, or a requirement that punishment should be proportionate to the offence of conviction. Separation of powers arguments rarely succeed as courts are not easily convinced that legislatures lack the constitutional competence to prescribe fixed punishments for criminal offences. Throughout the common-law world at least, it is widely accepted that all three branches of government have essential roles in the sentencing process. Legislatures must decide on the penalties—mandatory, maximum or minimum—to attach to particular offences; the judiciary is responsible for the selection of sentence, when there is a selection to be made; and the executive is responsible for the implementation of sentence. No modern constitutional scheme provides for an absolute separation of powers; some system of checks and balances is generally

---

[61] Chapter 10 below.

thought desirable. The idea that the judicial branch should be exclusively entitled to decide on sentence finds little support in modern constitutional jurisprudence and has, in fact, been decisively rejected in some leading decisions beginning, as it happens, in Ireland with *Deaton v Attorney General and Revenue Commissioners*.[62] There, the Supreme Court held:

> "There is a clear distinction between the prescription of a fixed penalty and the selection of a penalty for a particular case. The prescription of a fixed penalty is the statement of a general rule, which is one of the characteristics of legislation; this is wholly different from the selection of a penalty to be imposed in a particular case."[63]

The court reiterated the same point in *Lynch and Whelan v Minister for Justice*,[64] considered further below. Importantly, however, it was also held in *Deaton* that where the legislature provides for a choice of punishment, that choice may not be exercised by any authority other than the trial court. Similar conclusions as to the per se constitutionality of mandatory penalties have been reached by the High Court of Australia in *Palling v Corfield*,[65] the Supreme Court of Canada in *R v Smith*,[66] and *R v Latimer*,[67] the Constitutional Court of South Africa in *Dodo v The State*,[68] and (implicitly at least) the Court of Appeal of Jamaica in *R v Carnegie*.[69] The matter was considered in some depth by the Constitutional Court of South Africa in *Dodo* where it had been argued that the legislative

---

[62] [1963] I.R. 170. This decision, especially in so far as it insists that the choice of punishment is a judicial act, has been widely cited elsewhere. See, for example, *Hinds v The Queen* [1977] A.C. 195, [1976] 2 W.L.R. 366; *Roodal v The State of Trinidad and Tobago* [2005] 1 A.C. 328, [2004] 2 W.L.R. 652; *Matthew v The State of Trinidad and Tobago* [2005] 1 A.C. 433, [2004] 3 W.L.R. 812; *R (Anderson) v Secretary of State for Home Department* [2002] 3 W.L.R. 1800; *Bowe v The Queen* [2006] 1 W.L.R. 1623; *DPP of Jamaica v Mollison* [2003] 2 A.C. 411, [2003] 3 W.L.R. 1160; *Browne v The Queen* [2000] A.C. 45, [1999] 3 W.L.R. 1158.

[63] [1963] I.R. 170 at 182. See O'Malley, "The Power to Punish: Reflections on *Deaton v AG (1963)*" in O'Dell (ed.), *Leading Cases of the Twentieth Century* (Dublin: Round Hall Sweet and Maxwell, 2000), p.196.

[64] [2010] IESC 34.

[65] (1970) 123 C.L.R. 52 at [10], Barwick C.J. said: "It is beyond question that the Parliament can prescribe such penalty as it thinks fit for the offences which it creates. It may make the penalty absolute in the sense that there is but one penalty which the court is empowered to impose and, in my opinion, it may lay an unqualified duty on the court to impose that penalty. The exercise of the judicial function is the act of imposing the penalty consequent upon conviction of the offence which is essentially a judicial act. If the statute nominates the penalty and imposes on the court a duty to impose it, no judicial power or function is invaded: nor, in my opinion, is there any judicial power or discretion not to carry out the terms of the statute."

[66] [1987] 1 S.C.R. 1045 at [65], Lamer J. ("The legislature may, in my view, provide for a compulsory term of imprisonment upon conviction for certain offences without infringing the rights protected by s. 12 of the Charter".)

[67] [2001] 1 S.C.R. 3.

[68] (2001) 3 SA 382 (CC).

[69] Unreported, Constitutional Court of South Africa, November 20, 2003.

prescription of a life sentence for murder (though with the qualification that a lesser sentence could be imposed where there were "substantial and compelling circumstances") violated the separation of powers because "[s]entencing is pre-eminently the prerogative of the courts".[70] The Constitutional Court rejected this argument, holding that all three branches of government have legitimate roles in the sentencing process. However, it also said that "the legislature ought not to oblige the judiciary to impose a punishment which is wholly lacking in proportionality to the crime".[71]

A consistent theme running through all of the leading authorities is that acceptance of the general legislative competence to prescribe mandatory penalties must not be interpreted as conferring an unrestricted legislative power to impose fixed penalties without due regard to their rationality, fairness and humanity. Penalties should not be disproportionately severe having regard to the nature of the offence or, at a minimum, there must be a rational connection between penal severity and offence gravity. A penalty must not be so severe in nature or so degrading in the manner of its implementation as to violate a convicted person's fundamental rights, and it must not discriminate invidiously or unfairly against one particular category of offender. In *Cox v Ireland*,[72] for example, the Supreme Court found s.34 of the Offences Against the State Act 1939 to be invalid having regard to the Constitution. It did so, however, because the secondary penalty which that section imposed operated in an unfair and capricious manner. The court did not hold that the legislature was constitu-tionally prohibited from enacting such a measure, provided it had due regard to those rights expressly and implicitly protected by the Constitution.

Mandatory penalties are more often challenged on the basis that they violate a particular substantive norm protected by a state constitution or an international human rights instrument. The criteria applied by the courts and, consequently, the likelihood of the applicant succeeding, depend on the wording of the particular constitutional or treaty provision relied upon. Both the federal Constitution of the United States and the Canadian Charter of Rights and Freedoms have directly adopted the wording of s.10 of the English Bill of Rights 1688 ("Excessive Bail ought not to be required, nor excessive Fines imposed, nor cruel and unusual Punishments inflicted"). This was incorporated verbatim in 1791 into the Eighth Amendment to the US Constitution, and it was clearly the source of s.12 of the Canadian Charter ("Everyone has the right not to be subjected to any cruel and unusual treatment or punishment").[73] Most international human rights instruments, on the other hand, outlaw torture and "inhuman or degrading

---

[70] This was the view of the High Court in *Dodo* where the provision in question was found unconstitutional.

[71] (2001) 3 SA 382 at [26].

[72] [1992] 2 I.R. 503.

[73] The Constitution of South Africa s.12(1)(e) likewise provides that everyone has the right not to be punished "in a cruel, inhuman or degrading way".

treatment or punishment".[74] The Irish Constitution, strangely enough, has no provision equivalent to any of these, but there is authority to the effect that it implicitly prohibits torture as well as other cruel, inhuman or degrading treatment or punishment.[75] In any event, torture is now a criminal offence under Irish law[76] and the State has ratified the United Nations Convention Against Torture and Other Cruel, Inhuman or Degrading Treatment or Punishment (1984). Eighth Amendment jurisprudence in the United States is complicated by two factors. First, somewhat different criteria apply depending on whether the challenge involves the death penalty or a term of years' imprisonment. Secondly, it is affected by a broader underlying disagreement as to how the Constitution should be interpreted. Some Supreme Court justices favour an original meaning approach, while others prefer to apply more contemporary standards. In *Harmelin v Michigan*[77] a majority of the court held that the Eighth Amendment did not require "strict proportionality between crime and sentence" because the Amendment "forbids only extreme sentences that are grossly disproportionate to the crime".[78] However, there is also majority agreement, as reflected in *Graham v Florida*,[79] that the Eighth Amendment must be interpreted in accordance with "the evolving standards of decency that mark the progress of a maturing society".[80] Applying this criterion, the majority in *Graham* held that the Eighth Amendment prohibits the imposition of life imprisonment without the possibility of parole on a juvenile offender convicted of a non-capital offence, the offences in that case being armed burglary and attempted armed robbery. The court has likewise held that it is not constitutionally permissible to impose the death penalty on a person convicted of a capital offence committed while he was a juvenile.[81]

The test applied by the Canadian Supreme Court when deciding if a statutory sentencing provisions offends against s.12 of the Charter is, on the face of it, similar to that applied by its American counterpart, in that the question is whether the required sentence is "grossly disproportionate". As the court said in *R v Smith*:

> "The criterion which must be applied in order to determine whether a punishment is cruel and unusual within the meaning of s. 12 of the *Charter* is, to use the words of Laskin C.J. in *Miller and Cockriell, supra*, at p. 688, 'whether the punishment prescribed is so excessive as to outrage standards of

---

[74] International Covenant on Civil and Political Rights art.7; European Convention on Human Rights art.3.

[75] *Oguekwe v Minister for Justice, Equality and Law Reform* [2008] 3 I.R. 795.

[76] Criminal Justice (United Nations Convention Against Torture) Act 2000.

[77] 501 U.S. 957 (1991).

[78] 501 U.S. 957 (1991) at 1000–1001.

[79] 560 U.S. — (May 17, 2010).

[80] *Trop v Dulles* 356 U.S. 86 at 101 (1958); *Estelle v Gamble* 429 U.S. 97 at 102 (1976).

[81] *Roper v Simmons* 543 U.S. 551 (2005).

decency'. In other words, though the state may impose punishment, the effect of that punishment must not be grossly disproportionate to what would have been appropriate … In assessing whether a sentence is grossly disproportionate, the court must first consider the gravity of the offence, the personal characteristics of the offender and the particular circumstances of the case in order to determine what range of sentences would have been appropriate to punish, rehabilitate or deter this particular offender or to protect the public from this particular offender."[82]

Significantly, however, in *Smith* itself, the Supreme Court struck down a seven-year mandatory minimum sentence for the importation of narcotics, a decision which its southern neighbour, even at its most liberal, would scarcely contemplate.[83] This, admittedly, was something of an exception and later challenges to mandatory minimum sentences have been mainly unsuccessful.[84] The great difference between Canada and the United States in this regard lies in the realm of sensibility and culture rather than in form. Viewed in purely linguistic terms, the tests applied in both jurisdictions are much the same but the values which inform the application of those tests differ profoundly between the two jurisdictions.

Until recently, there was little Irish authority on the circumstances in which a mandatory penalty might be found unconstitutional. *Deaton* was largely a separation of powers case and it did not consider proportionality issues, while *Cox* was largely about the discriminatory application of particular ancillary measure.[85] In *Sweeney v Ireland*,[86] the High Court rejected a challenge to mandatory fine specified by law for a customs offence. However, the court's decision appears to have been reached primarily on the ground that the application was premature although it also briefly rejected any argument that the legislative prescription of a mandatory penalty was per se unconstitutional. The matter later came before the Supreme Court in a combined set of appeals where it was held that the applications were not premature, but that they should be dismissed primarily because the relevant statutory provision, when properly interpreted, did not impose a fixed penalty.[87] The court did, however, accept obiter that "the courts might be entitled to strike down a mandatory sentence if they were convinced that its purpose or effect was to leave offenders liable to disproportionately heavy punishment. In the view of the court, that issue does not arise and should not be considered in this case."[88] While clearly obiter, this statement

---

[82] [1987] 1 S.C.R. 1045 at 1072. *Miller* is reported at [1977] 2 S.C.R. 680 at 688.

[83] For a detailed analysis of *R v Smith* and its implications, see Roach, "Searching for *Smith:* the Constitutionality of Mandatory Sentences" (2001) 39 Osgoode Hall L.J. 367.

[84] See, for example, *R v Ferguson* [2008] 1 S.C.R. 96.

[85] *Deaton v Attorney General and Revenue Commissioners* [1963] I.R. 170; *Cox v Ireland* [1963] I.R. 170.

[86] Unreported, High Court, Ó Caoimh J., May 27, 2004. See also *Osmanovic v DPP*, unreported, High Court, Ó Caoimh J., July 30, 2004.

[87] *Osmanovic v DPP* [2006] 3 I.R. 504.

[88] [2006] 3 I.R. 504 at 518.

afforded some ground for optimism that any future challenge to a mandatory penalty would be decided on proportionality grounds. However, the most recent Supreme Court decision on the matter must seriously dent any such optimism. *Lynch and Whelan v Minister for Justice*[89] involved a long-awaited challenge to the constitutionality of the life sentence for murder, and seldom has a challenge been so comprehensively rejected. At the outset the court rightly drew a distinction between two separate streams of proportionality jurisprudence which have developed here and elsewhere. First, there is what might be described in Ireland as *Heaney*-type proportionality, a juridical criterion which apparently originated in nineteenth-century Prussia, for assessing the compatibility of sub-constitutional rules with a constitution or other higher form of law.[90] To survive constitutional challenge, the restrictions imposed by the challenged rule must serve a legitimate social objective and must not entrench upon protected rights any more than is strictly necessary in the circumstances. Independently of this, there is a principle extending back to classical times that a punitive or disci-plinary measure should not be disproportionate to the gravity of the wrong which prompted its imposition. Drawing on this longstanding tradition, Irish law requires that sentences be proportionate to the circumstances of the offence and of the offender.[91]

The Supreme Court held that the legislative prescription of a mandatory life sentence for murder was consistent with the Constitution on account of the uniquely serious nature of that offence. It expressly agreed with a statement of the High Court judge in the same case that "… there can be nothing offensive in the Oireachtas promoting the respect for life by concluding that any murder even at the lowest end of the scale, is so abhorrent and offensive to society that it merits a mandatory life sentence …". Both courts accepted that murder could vary in its gravity, and they could scarcely have decided otherwise, if only because a person may be convicted of murder without necessarily intending to kill. An intention to cause serious injury will suffice.[92] Aside from that, context and motive may render some murders more or less egregious than others, irrespective of the specific intention of the killer. Such considerations might legitimately point to the need for a more nuanced punishment regime. However, the court got around this argument, though not very convincingly, by holding that the principle of proportionality applies only where a sentencing judge is entitled to exercise discretion, something that does not arise when a sentence is fixed by law. Yet, if proportionality, in the second sense in which it was described earlier and as it applies to punishment, is a constitutional as well as a legal

---

[89] [2010] IESC 34.

[90] *Heaney and McGuinness v Ireland* [1994] 3 I.R. 593, [1994] 2 I.L.R.M. 420 (High Court); [1996] 1 I.R. 580, [1997] 1 I.L.R.M. 117 (Supreme Court). The High Court drew upon the leading Canadian decision in *R v Chaulk* [1990] 3 S.C.R. 1303 in relation to the meaning of proportionality for the purpose of evaluating the constitutionality of legislation.

[91] *People (DPP) v M* [1994] 3 I.R. 306, [1994] 2 I.L.R.M. 541.

[92] Criminal Justice Act 1964 s.4.

principle, as has sometimes been judicially held,[93] it would surely demand that all statutory penalty regimes, mandatory or otherwise, should be so structured as to avoid the necessity of imposing excessive or unwarranted punishment in any given case. Murder could still be treated as a special case but in view of the variety of circumstances in which it may be committed—a reality acknowledged by the Supreme Court—it could be made punishable with a presumptive life sentence with the possibility of downward departure in defined and exceptional circumstances. This is on the assumption that the legislature does not wish to make life imprisonment the maximum rather than the mandatory sentence for murder, a most unlikely development for the foreseeable future.

More significantly for present purposes, the Supreme Court had this to say in relation to the constitutionality of mandatory sentences generally:

> "The Court is satisfied, as Ó Dálaigh C.J. explained in [*Deaton*], that the Oireachtas in the exercise of its legislative powers may choose in particular cases to impose a fixed or mandatory penalty for a particular offence. That is not to say that legislation which imposed a fixed penalty could not have its compatibility with the Constitution called in question if there was no rational relationship between the penalty and the requirements of justice with regard to the punishment of the offence specified."[94]

The language of proportionality is strikingly absent from this passage, which is scarcely surprising in light of the court's decision to confine the application of proportionality to those cases where a sentencing court may lawfully exercise discretion. Instead the test has now been reframed in terms of a "rational relationship" between the punishment and the requirements of justice. In effect, this may not differ a great deal from the proportionality test mentioned obiter in *Osmanovic*.[95] However, as we know from administrative law contexts, irrationality can be much more difficult to prove than a lack of proportionality.[96] Much will depend also on how future courts interpret the "requirements of justice" in respect of an offence carrying a mandatory penalty. Again, it is difficult to imagine how the concept of proportionality could realistically be avoided when determining what a just penalty might be. The precise test to be applied when assessing the constitutionality of mandatory sentences, by whatever criterion, has yet to be properly clarified in this jurisdiction. Generally speaking, a statutory provision may be attacked if it has the purpose or effect of violating a constitutional right. A statutory provision which required that members of a particular racial or religious group should be punished more heavily than others

---

[93]   *Rock v Ireland* [1997] 3 I.R. 484 at 500 ("The principle of proportionality is by now a well-established tenet of Irish constitutional law").

[94]   *Lynch and Whelan v Minister for Justice* [2010] IESC 34.

[95]   See text accompanying fn.88 above.

[96]   *O'Keeffe v An Bord Pleanála* [1993] 1 I.R. 39; *Meadows v Minister for Justice, Equality and Law Reform* [2010] IESC 3, [2010] 2 I.R. 701.

convicted of the same offence would clearly have a discriminatory purpose and, in all likelihood, an unconstitutional one as well. A much more probable scenario is that a mandatory penalty will have an unconstitutional effect by, for example, requiring courts to sentence certain offenders so heavily as to be incompatible with the requirements of justice (if that is to be the new criterion).

This still leaves unresolved the question of whether the courts should test the constitutionality of a statutory provision solely by reference to its impact on the particular plaintiff or whether it should be prepared to consider other, hypothetical cases as well. As constitutional lawyers well know, the success of any challenge can depend crucially on finding the right plaintiff. Yet, the success of such a constitutional challenge should not be entirely contingent on the particular facts. There is much to be said for the adoption of a "reasonable hypothetical" approach as favoured by the Canadian Supreme Court and described in the following terms in *R v Goltz*:

> "If the particular facts of the case do not warrant a finding of gross disproportionality, there may remain another aspect to be examined, namely a *Charter* challenge or constitutional question as to the validity of a statutory provision on grounds of gross disproportionality as evidenced in *reasonable hypothetical circumstances*, as opposed to far-fetched or marginally imaginable cases.
>
> A reasonable hypothetical example is one which is not far-fetched or only marginally imaginable as a live possibility. While the Court is unavoidably required to consider factual patterns other than that presented by the respondent's case, this is not a licence to invalidate statutes on the basis of remote or extreme examples. Laws typically aim to govern a particular field generally, so that they apply to a range of persons and circumstances. It is true that this Court has been vigilant, wherever possible, to ensure that a proper factual foundation exists before measuring legislation against the *Charter* ... Yet it has been noted above that s. 12 jurisprudence does not contemplate a standard of review in which that kind of factual foundation is available in every instance. The applicable standard must focus on imaginable circumstances which could commonly arise in day-to-day life."[97]

This approach has the advantage of preventing the failure of a constitutional challenge solely on account of the specific facts of a case, as opposed to the broader context in which the challenged measure applies.

The safety valve

As noted at the beginning of this chapter, several different kinds of sentencing regime are colloquially grouped under the general heading of mandatory sentences or penalties. Many jurisdictions take the precaution of including a so-called

---

[97] [1991] 3 S.C.R. 485. Emphasis in original and internal references omitted.

safety valve in any statutory provision mandating severe penalties. The South African scheme of mandatory penalties, as noted earlier, illustrates this practice. Many of its penalties are very severe indeed but their rigour is somewhat mitigated by the concession that the court may impose a lesser sentence where there are "substantial and compelling circumstances". In Ireland likewise, the 10-year minimum sentence for section 15A drug offences need not apply where there are "exceptional and specific circumstances" relating to the offence or the offender.[98] It might be going too far to say that the presence of a safety valve will invariably render the relevant sentencing provision immune from constitutional challenge, but it will certainly make any such challenge exceedingly difficult. Mandatory sentences are usually attacked on the ground that they oblige courts to impose disproportionately severe punishment. Such an argument is very difficult, if not impossible, to sustain once courts have some degree of latitude to depart from the specified sentence in defined circumstances. In *Dodo v The State*[99] the Constitutional Court of South Africa refused to invalidate a law requiring life imprisonment for certain offences because trial courts may impose a lesser sentence when satisfied as to the presence of substantial and compelling circumstances. Statutory provisions permitting departure from otherwise fixed sentences should be clearly phrased and should operate in a rational, equitable manner. Federal law in the United States permits the imposition of a sentence below the statutory minimum where the defendant has given substantial assistance in the investigation or prosecution of another offender. This can only be done, however, "upon motion of the government" which means that prosecutors have wide discretion in deciding whether to ask a court to give credit for assistance. The United States Supreme Court has held that the prosecutor's discretion is reviewable, but only where it is alleged to have been based on an unconstitutional motive, such as an intention to discriminate on the grounds of race or religion.[100] Such a provision would scarcely be constitutionally acceptable in Ireland or in many other countries as it leaves the offender almost entirely at the mercy of the prosecution when it comes to securing some reduction on the fixed sentence. As noted earlier, the decision of the French *Conseil Constitutionnel* in March 2011 to uphold the constitutionality of minimum sentences for aggravated assault offences was motivated in part by the presence of a saving clause empowering courts to impose lower sentences in certain circumstances.[101]

EUROPEAN CONVENTION ON HUMAN RIGHTS

The European Convention on Human Rights makes few overt references to the punishment of offenders. Article 6 which guarantees the right to a fair trial by

---

[98] Misuse of Drugs Act 1977 s.27(3A)–(3K) as substituted by the Criminal Justice Act 2007 s.33.
[99] (2001) 3 SA 382.
[100] *Wade v United States* 504 U.S. 181 (1992).
[101] Page 74 above.

an independent and impartial tribunal lists a number of specific ingredients such as the right to be presumed innocent, the right to legal representation and legal aid, and the free assistance of an interpreter but makes no reference to just punishment. This may be contrasted with the EU Charter of Fundamental Rights which provides that "[t]he severity of penalties must not be disproportionate to the criminal offence."[102] The European Convention does however proscribe the imposition of a heavier penalty than applied when the offence was committed,[103] and it also outlaws torture and inhuman or degrading treatment or punishment.[104] Article 5 of the Convention protects the right to personal liberty and security and has been interpreted by the European Court of Human Rights to include protection from arbitrary detention.[105] The Court has also occasionally indicated that it would be prepared to intervene where a sentence was so disproportionately severe in the circumstances as to amount to inhuman or degrading treatment, but there is little substantial authority on this point.[106] The absence of an express proportionality requirement in the text of the Convention renders it very difficult to challenge a sentence on the merits, at least in the absence of some truly exceptional factor, and it has proved remarkably difficult to convince the court that the severity of punishment violates art.3. This became apparent in *T and V v United Kingdom*[107] (better known as the Jamie Bulger case) where the court declined to hold that a sentence of detention at Her Majesty's Pleasure imposed on two 11-year-old boys, admittedly for the rather gruesome murder of an infant, was inhuman or degrading within the meaning of the Convention. More relevant, for present purposes, is the Court's decision in *Kafkaris v Cyprus*[108] where the applicant was serving three life sentences for murder and, under the prevailing Cypriot law, the decision as to when, if ever, he would be released was entirely at the discretion of the country's president. While the applicant succeeded on a point under art.7 of the Convention, he failed in his principal arguments which were grounded on art.3. As to the proper interpretation of art.3 in general, the Court said:

> "The Court has consistently stressed that the suffering and humiliation involved must in any event go beyond that inevitable element of suffering or humiliation connected with a given form of legitimate treatment or punishment. Measures depriving a person of his liberty may often involve such an element.

---

[102] Article 49(3). However, the provisions of the Charter apply solely to the institutions of the European Union and to member states only when they are implementing European Union law (art.51(1)).

[103] Article 7(1).

[104] Article 3.

[105] *Tsirlis and Kouloumpas v Greece* (1997) 25 E.H.R.R. 198 at para.56.

[106] For a detailed discussion, see Emmerson, Ashworth and Macdonald, *Human Rights and Criminal Justice*, 2nd edn (London: Sweet & Maxwell, 2007), p.664 et seq., discussing *Weeks v United Kingdom* (1988) 10 E.H.R.R. 293 in particular.

[107] (2000) 31 E.H.R.R. 121.

[108] (2009) 49 E.H.R.R. 35 (p.877).

In accordance with Article 3 of the Convention the State must ensure that a person is detained under conditions which are compatible with respect for his human dignity and that the manner and method of the execution of the measure do not subject him to distress or hardship exceeding the unavoidable level of suffering inherent in detention."[109]

It then held that a life sentence was not in itself incompatible with art.3 or any other provision of the Convention, but that the imposition of an irreducible life sentence on an adult "may raise an issue under Art. 3", as indicated in previous cases.[110] Significantly, for this purpose, it added:

"It follows that a life sentence does not become 'irreducible' by the mere fact that in practice it may be served in full. It is enough for the purposes of Art. 3 that a life sentence is *de jure* and *de facto* reducible."[111]

Arrangements for sentence review, according to the Court, are a matter for member states provided they do not contravene Convention principles, though going by the general tenor of this judgment, those principles would allow for considerable flexibility in framing early release rules. The Court also noted that there was then no clear standard among member states in relation to the review of life sentences. Here the court was falling back on the consensus principle which it often applies when uncertain as to whether a particular law or practice complies with Convention standards. This, however, is one area where the Court might have been expected to lead rather than to follow, but unfortunately it did not see fit to do so on this occasion. Ultimately, however, the Court found that the sentence in this case was not irreducible as it could be remitted at the President's discretion, and the applicant's claim under art.3 failed. This aspect of the decision was reached by 10 votes to seven. Five of those who dissented refused to accept that the existence of the discretionary presidential power which had swayed the majority provided the applicant with a "real and tangible prospect of release".

In *R v Bieber*,[112] the applicant had been sentenced to a whole life term for murder even though the governing legislation, the Criminal Justice Act 2003, permitted the judge to specify a minimum term to be served before an adult convicted of murder became eligible for parole. He challenged the sentence on the ground that it violated art.3 of the European Convention and, needless to say, *Kafkaris* figured prominently in both argument and judgment. The Court of Appeal held that an irreducible life sentence might raise an issue under art.3 where it results in the offender being held beyond a term which is justified by the legitimate objects of the sentence, but otherwise it will not. In any event,

---

[109]   (2009) 49 E.H.R.R. 35 at [97], p.923, referring to *Kudla v Poland* (2002) 35 E.H.R.R. 11.
[110]   (2009) 49 E.H.R.R. 35 at [98].
[111]   (2009) 49 E.H.R.R. 35 at [99].
[112]   [2008] EWCA 1601, [2009] 1 W.L.R. 223.

under English law, the secretary of state is empowered to release any life prisoner on exceptional grounds and also has a practice of reviewing the tariff of whole-life prisoners when they have served 25 years. The court therefore concluded that the appropriate time to challenge such a sentence was not at the point of its imposition but much later when the prisoner may be able to argue that, having regard to all the circumstances, his continued detention amounts to a violation of art.3 of the European Convention. In so far as it was of any comfort to the applicant in this case, the Court of Appeal then decided on the facts to vary his sentence to the extent of specifying 37 years as the term to be served before being eligible for release on licence.

A similar issue has arisen in the context of extradition requests, particularly when they come from the United States where life without parole (LWOP) is widely available and commonly imposed. In 2008, more than 41,000 prisoners were serving LWOP sentences, though in 2010, the Supreme Court held that this sentence was unconstitutional for most juvenile offenders.[113] According to *Soering v United Kingdom*[114] a state party acts in violation of the European Convention if it extradites a person to another country where he is at risk of being tortured or subjected to inhuman or degrading treatment or punishment. Again, however, the *Kafkaris* principle has come to the rescue in relation to the extradition of persons to jurisdictions where they risk being sentenced to LWOP. The House of Lords dismissed a challenge to extradition in the case of a person wanted in Missouri on a number of charges including first-degree murder which would have left him liable to the death penalty. An undertaking was given that the death penalty would not be sought, but the applicant would be liable to LWOP. The Law Lords held that since this sentence was de jure reducible in Missouri through the Governor's powers of pardon and commutation (which, it was accepted, were very rarely exercised), extradition would not violate art.3 of the Convention.[115] Indeed, they went further and held that in a case of extradition as opposed to one dealing with sentencing arrangements in the requested state itself, an irreducible life sentence would not be treated as a bar to extradition unless the sentence was likely, on the facts to be clearly disproportionate. *Kafkaris* and its progeny are, of course, primarily concerned with the indeterminate life sentence and do not necessarily indicate the future impact of the European Convention on Human Rights on mandatory sentences generally. In future years, the European Court may well develop its currently embryonic jurisprudence on the need for sentences to be proportionate (or, at least, not to be manifestly disproportionate) in order to comply with the terms of arts 3, 5 and 6 of the Convention.

---

[113] O'Hear, "The Beginning of the End for Life without Parole?" (2010) 23:1 Fed. Sent. Rep. 1; *Graham v Florida* 560 U.S. – (2010).
[114] (1989) 11 E.H.R.R. 439. See Lillich, "The *Soering* Case" (1991) 85 Am. J. Int. Law 128.
[115] *R (Wellington) v Secretary of State for the Home Department* [2008] UKHL 72, [2009] 1 A.C. 335. See Milanovic, "Extradition and Life Imprisonment" (2009) 69 Cambridge L.J. 248.

THE SENTENCE FOR MURDER

The unanimous Supreme Court decision in *Lynch and Whelan* leaves the mandatory life sentence for murder constitutionally secure, but that should not foreclose further discussion on its policy implications.[116] After all, there is nothing in the court's judgment to suggest that the replacement of the mandatory sentence with a maximum sentence of life imprisonment would pose any constitutional difficulty. Murder is, indeed, the most serious offence known to our law, apart from genocide which, thankfully, has never become an issue in this country since it was criminalised in 1973.[117] Like all serious offences, murder may be committed in a wide variety of circumstances and with varying levels of moral culpability. As noted earlier, an intention to cause serious injury suffices as the mens rea of murder as, needless to say, does an intention to kill. There is often a very fine line between assault, manslaughter and murder because of the difficulty in identifying the precise intention of the accused at the time of the killing. This is reflected in leading sentencing decisions which recognise that, in terms of gravity, manslaughter may sometimes be virtually indistinguishable from murder and at other times amount to little more than an accident.[118] Moral culpability may also vary according to motive. The orthodox approach to criminal liability demands a strict separation of motive and intention. A person may have a good, even if misguided, motive for performing a particular act but will be held to have had the necessary intention if he acted purposively. An act of so-called mercy killing may have been influenced by a benign motive—to save a terminally-ill person from further suffering—but the person who carries out the killing will ordinarily be treated as having acted intentionally and therefore guilty of murder. Yet, it is scarcely deniable that there is a considerable difference between the moral culpability of a mercy killer and that of somebody who, for example, ruthlessly executes the carefully-planned murder of a rival in the drugs trade. The point is not that mercy killers should be treated with impunity; public policy may demand some measure of punishment, if only for deterrent purposes. The point is that the mercy killer does not deserve the same punishment as other, patently more culpable, murderers. Defences such as infancy, provocation and, more recently, diminished responsibility as well as the special verdict of infanticide,[119] were introduced to save certain categories of offender from the mandatory death penalty which historically attached to murder and many other offences, just as today they save certain offenders from the mandatory life sentence.

---

[116]   For a more detailed discussion, see O'Malley "Sentencing Murderers: The Case for Relocating Discretion" (1995) 5 I.C.L.J. 31. On the development of English law on sentencing for murder, see Hart, "Murder and the Principles of Punishment: England and the United States" in *Punishment and Responsibility*, 2nd edn (Oxford: Oxford University Press, 2008), p.54.

[117]   Genocide Act 1973.

[118]   *People (DPP) v Conroy (No.2)* [1989] I.R. 160, [1989] I.L.R.M. 139; *People (DPP) v McAuley* [2001] 4 I.R. 160; *People (DPP) v Horgan* [2007] 3 I.R. 568.

[119]   Infanticide Act 1949.

The introduction of discretionary sentencing for murder would not necessarily lead to more lenient punishment. The law might, for example, specify life imprisonment as the presumptive sentence for murder while leaving the courts with some measure of discretion to impose a lesser sentence in a genuinely exceptional case. Alternatively, it might simply replace the mandatory life sentence with a maximum life sentence and leave the appeal courts to develop appropriate principles and tariffs. Right now, the multiple murderer can receive no more than concurrent life sentences; the idea of consecutive life sentences would be a contradiction in terms. The background to *People (DPP) v Whelan*[120] is instructive in this regard. The applicant had pleaded guilty to murder and attempted murder involving two different victims. He was originally sentenced to 15 years' imprisonment for the attempted murder and this was ordered to take effect as soon as the life sentence for murder came to an effective end (meaning, presumably, the date on which he would be eligible for temporary release). The Court of Criminal Appeal reversed the order of these sentences, an arrangement which provided more certainty as to the commencement dates of each sentence. Suppose, however, that the applicant had been convicted of two or more murders. In that case, he would have received concurrent life sentences and while the number of offences might well influence the executive when it eventually came to consider his eligibility for release, there can be no formal certainty that he would serve any longer than somebody convicted of a single murder. If, on the other hand, murder were punishable with a discretionary life sentence, a court could impose consecutive determinate sentences. The multiple murderer might then receive a cumulative sentence of 30 to 40 years rather than the indeterminate life sentence which must now be imposed.

Several Australian jurisdictions have abolished the mandatory life sentence for murder. New South Wales abolished it in 1982, followed by Victoria in 1986.[121] In Victoria, for example, murder may attract either a life sentence or a determinate sentence with the possibility of a non-parole period being fixed in either case. In Western Australia, on the other hand, a person convicted of murder must be sentenced to life imprisonment unless the court is satisfied that such a sentence would be unjust in light of the circumstances and that the person is unlikely to be a threat to the community when released. In that event, the person is liable to imprisonment for 20 years.[122] New Zealand has a rather similar provision.[123] These are examples of a presumptive life sentence which

---

[120] [2003] 4 I.R. 355. The applicant was also the appellant in *Lynch and Whelan v Minister for Justice, Equality and Law Reform* [2010] IESC 34.

[121] For a detailed analysis of sentencing for murder in Victoria, see Fox and Freiberg, *Sentencing: State and Federal Law in Victoria*, 2nd edn (Oxford: Oxford University Press, 1999), p.876 et seq.

[122] Criminal Code of Western Australia s.239. See Mackenzie and Stobbs, *Principles of Sentencing* (Annandale, NSW: Federation Press, 2010), p.217 et seq.

[123] New Zealand Sentencing Act 2002 s.102 (life sentence mandatory unless it would be "manifestly unjust" in light of the circumstances of the offence and the offender); *R v Smail* [2007] 1 N.Z.L.R. 411.

was suggested earlier as a possibility in Ireland. Rather tellingly, most Australian jurisdictions have now abolished the partial defence of provocation, leaving evidence of provocation, where it exists, as a relevant sentencing factor.[124] Other strategies are also possible. In Canada, for example, a person convicted of first-degree murder or second-degree murder with certain aggravating features such a previous conviction for homicide, must be sentenced to life imprisonment without eligibility for parole until 25 years' imprisonment has been served. In other circumstances, second-degree murderers may qualify for parole after serving shorter periods.[125] This approach is rather similar in effect to allowing for the imposition of determinate sentences for murder, the significant difference being that, on completion of the non-parole period, the offender remains subject to the life sentence and presumably to the possibility of recall to prison for breach of a parole condition. A modified version of the Canadian model might be worth considering in Ireland where it is difficult to foresee much political support for abolishing the mandatory life sentence. The possibility of allowing trial courts to set non-parole periods could be considered as part of an overall review of the parole system as recommended in Chapter 9. There is, admittedly, the danger that legislators might take that opportunity to set very high non-parole periods which would leave many murderers serving longer sentences than they do now.[126] It would be preferable therefore if the courts were left to develop guidelines on appropriate non-parole periods for different categories of offender.

Sentencing discretion tempers of the rigour of binary verdicts. Unless a jury are unable to agree, or in a position to return a special verdict such as not guilty on the ground of insanity, they are generally confined to bringing in a verdict of guilty or not guilty. Traditionally, juries have been informally entitled to add riders to their verdicts recommending clemency or mitigation of punishment, but judges are not obliged to adopt such recommendations and, in any event, are entirely precluded from doing so following a murder verdict which inevitably entails a life sentence. A guilty verdict means that the jury were convinced beyond a reasonable doubt that the accused performed the actus reus of the offence charged and did so with the necessary mens rea. It is a finding of legal guilt but does not include or imply any evaluation of moral guilt which can only be assessed by reference to the precise nature of the accused person's behaviour, the motivation for that behaviour, personal characteristics, previous record and related matters. Judges are vested with sentencing discretion so that they can place all of those factors in the balance when deciding where the specific

---

[124] Mackenzie and Stobbs (fn.122 above), pp.218–219; Stewart and Freiberg, "Provocation in Sentencing: A Culpability-Based Framework" (2008) 19 *Current Issues in Criminal Justice* 283.

[125] Criminal Code of Canada s.745. See Roach, *Criminal Law*, 4th edn (Toronto: Irwin Law, 2009), p.353.

[126] This is arguably what happened in England and Wales as a result of the statutory minimum periods (varying from 15 years to a whole life term) specified by the Criminal Justice Act 2003 Sch.21.

offence should be located on the overall scale of gravity and, in consequence, how much punishment the offender deserves. This arrangement applies to the sentencing of virtually all criminal offences right across the spectrum of gravity. It is very difficult to justify a different sentencing regime for murder unless one believes that all murders are of equal gravity but, as already indicated, that is patently not the case. In making positive recommendations at this juncture, one must accept the reality that replacing the mandatory life sentence with discretionary sentencing shaped by judicially-developed guidelines would not, in all probability, be politically acceptable. A somewhat more realistic possibility would be to treat the life sentence as the presumptive penalty for murder, but with the qualification that a determinate sentence might be imposed in exceptional circumstances. If necessary, the range of factors capable of being treated as exceptional for this purpose might be specified in advance by statute. Another possibility would be to leave the mandatory life sentence intact and concentrate instead on parole release arrangements. However, in order to calibrate the seriousness of the particular offence to the term which the offender should be required to serve, courts could be charged with task of specifying at the outset the minimum term to be served. Again, in the interests of coherence and rationality, they should be required to develop guidelines for this purpose.

DRUG AND FIREARMS OFFENCES

Many references have been made throughout this chapter to the special sentencing arrangements for section 15A drug offences and it is therefore appropriate to conclude with some thoughts on their constitutional and policy implications. Until the entry into force of the Criminal Justice Act 1999, the sentencing of drug trafficking offences in Ireland was quite straightforward, in formal terms at least. Unlawful possession of controlled drugs for sale or supply carried a maximum sentence of life imprisonment, irrespective of the nature of the drugs involved. The 1999 Act introduced a new offence of having for sale or supply controlled drugs with an estimated street value of €13,000 or more.[127] Every adult offender convicted of this offence remains liable to a maximum of life imprisonment but must now be ordered to serve at least 10 years' imprisonment unless the court is satisfied that there are exceptional and specific circumstances which would make the presumptive 10-year minimum sentence unjust in the circumstances. The legislation, as amended, provides a non-exhaustive list of factors which a court may consider for this purpose including the nature of the plea, assistance given to the police, any previous conviction for a drug trafficking offence and the public interest in preventing drug trafficking. A court must also have regard in particular to whether the offender has previously been convicted

---

[127]   The amount was originally set at £10,000 but this was translated to €13,000 with the currency changeover to the Euro in 2002.

of a drug trafficking offence and "whether the public interest in preventing drug trafficking would be served by the imposition of a lesser sentence."[128]

Since the entry into force of s.84 of the Criminal Justice Act 2006, an adult who is convicted of a second or subsequent section 15A or section 15B offence, or who is convicted of either offence for the first time, having previously been convicted of the other, must be sentenced to a minimum of 10 years' imprisonment. This is a truly mandatory minimum, as opposed to a presumptive, sentence. There is no safety valve for repeat offenders. The one concession made (and this also applies to first-time offenders sentenced to 10 years or more) is that if the court is satisfied that drug addiction was a substantial factor leading to the commission of the offence, it may list the sentence for review after the expiry of at least half of the sentence specified by the court. To this extent, the legislation acknowledges differences in culpability between those who become involved in drug dealing in order to feed their own habit (and they are the ones most likely to be arrested) and those further up the hierarchy who, in many cases, have no addiction problem themselves.

A similar sentencing structure was introduced in 2006 for certain firearms and offensive weapons offences except that for some of these offences the presumptive minimum for a first offence and the mandatory minimum for repeat offences is five rather than ten years. One particularly stringent aspect of these sentencing arrangements, for both drug and firearms offences, is that offenders sentenced to the minimum terms are ineligible for special remission or commutation under the Criminal Justice Act 1951, or for early release under the Criminal Justice Act 1960 for the duration of the sentence imposed by the court. Standard remission is however applied to the minimum period.[129] Thus, a person sentenced to 10 years' imprisonment can ordinarily expect release after seven-and-a-half years but will not be eligible for earlier release through the operation of executive clemency or parole. Very short periods of temporary release may be granted but only for "a grave reason of a humanitarian nature" and only for such limited period as is justified by that reason. They are also presumably eligible for periodic release under the Prisons Act 2007 (s.39).

The presumptive sentences for section 15A offences have caused serious difficulties for the courts, and not least because politicians, including some who were party to the introduction of the relevant legislation, have insisted on characterising those sentences as mandatory. Yet, the legislation itself clearly allows for the imposition of sentences less than 10 years for first-time offenders where there are exceptional and specific circumstances, which are not that well defined, which would render the presumptive minimum unjust. The Court of Criminal Appeal has held that even in such cases, a trial court should have regard to the 10-year minimum indicated in the legislation, a principle which

---

[128]   Section 27(3D)(c)(ii). The relevant law is now restated in the Criminal Justice Act 2007 s.33.
[129]   The various forms of remission and early release available to prisoners are described in Ch.9 below.

results in reasonably heavy sentences being imposed even where there are strong mitigating circumstances.[130] Suspended prison sentences and short custodial sentences have been imposed and upheld in a small number of cases,[131] but most section 15A offenders have received lengthy prison terms. The history of this legislation and its subsequent application illustrate vividly a point made at the outset about mandatory sentencing in general. Those responsible for introducing mandatory penalties generally concentrate on the most serious manifestations of the offences to which they will apply, with little regard to the less serious offenders who are likely to be the main recipients of those penalties. In fact, it is probably fair to say that most of those sentenced for section 15A offences over the past decade or so have had quite a low level of involvement in the drug distribution enterprises in which they found themselves ensnared. This reflects international experience as well. As Roberts et al. put it, "[t]he penal net has caught the wrong fish" as it is the small fry that usually become enmeshed.[132]

The presumptive and mandatory minimum sentences introduced for drug dealing since 1999 may have swollen the long-term prison population, but they have done little to diminish drug crime. In 1999, proceedings were instituted in respect of about 7,000 drug offences.[133] Cannabis accounted for more than 60 per cent of the drugs seized that year, and 96 per cent of heroin offences were recorded in the Dublin area. Five years later, the number of recorded drug offences was about the same, but by then only 83 per cent of heroin offences were confined to Dublin which means that this drug was now spreading to other parts of the country.[134] Recorded drug offences have trebled in the meantime, with 18,554 recorded in 2007, 23,405 in 2008, 21,983 in 2009 and 20,057 in 2010. Possession of drugs for personal use typically accounts about 75 per cent of recorded drug offences but the number of drug dealing offences also remains high, typically in the region of 4,000 in recent years.[135] Offending levels might well be higher in the absence of special sentencing arrangements; this is always an imponderable argument in respect of any set of laws designed to deter specific crimes. What remains clear, however, is that recorded levels of drug crime have increased greatly during the decade or so that the present sentencing arrangements have been in force. It is also, of course, widely recognised that the quantity of drugs seized by law enforcement agencies represents no more than a fraction of the overall amount being distributed and consumed in any one year.

---

[130] *People (DPP) v Renald,* unreported, Court of Criminal Appeal, November 23, 2001.
[131] See, for example, *People (DPP) v Alexiou* [2003] 3 I.R. 513. On the sentencing of drug offences generally, see O'Malley, *Sentencing Law and Practice,* 2nd edn (Dublin: Thomson Round Hall, 2006), Ch.15.
[132] Footnote 23 above, p.80.
[133] An Garda Síochána *Annual Report 1999,* p.101. This figure includes indictable and non-indictable offences.
[134] An Garda Síochána *Annual Report 2004,* p.73.
[135] Central Statistics Office, *Recorded Crime: Quarter 3 2010* (Dublin, 2010).

Perhaps the most objectionable feature of the section 15A regime is that the principal triggering factor is the estimated street value, as opposed to the weight, of the drugs. Ireland seems to be unique in this regard. Other common-law jurisdictions typically adopt the active weight of the drug as the key consideration.[136] This is reflected, for example, in the various American guidelines systems and in guideline judgments of the English Court of Appeal (Criminal Division). Admittedly, in *R v Aramah*,[137] sentencing guidance for class A drugs was expressed by reference to estimated street value, but when it came to class B drugs and cannabis in particular, it was expressed by reference to active weight. This was later explained on the basis that cannabis is not usually diluted or adulterated before use, whereas heroin and other substances may be mixed with other substances between importation and sale.[138] More recent decisions have emphasised the key importance of active weight for sentencing purposes, with estimated street value being described as no more than a rough guide.[139] Of particular significance in this respect is *R v Aranguren*,[140] where the Court of Appeal, having heard expert evidence on the matter, concluded quite emphatically that weight was a better and more reliable measure for assessing the significance of any seizure of class A drugs. Irish courts have yet to face this problem directly in the context of section 15A offences, largely because the estimated value of the drugs in prosecutions to date have usually been well above the €13,000 threshold. However, the underlying policy remains fundamentally flawed. When the draft legislation was being debated in 1998, the Minister for Justice said that the street value of drugs could be determined by a court following evidence from a police or customs officer who had knowledge of the illegal drugs trade.[141] This was, and remains, an unacceptably casual and unscientific manner of establishing the nature and quantity of drugs involved in any given case. By virtue of their illegality and the clandestine manner in which they circulate, prohibited substances cannot be valued, except in the crudest terms, like other commodities. Street value may vary over time and, also, from one part of the country to another. There can be no guarantee that the amount of drugs (or any particular kind of drug) that could be bought for £10,000 in 1999 would approximate to what can now be bought for €13,000. Perhaps it is roughly the same, but it could also be substantially more or less. The limited discretion currently available to courts when dealing with first-time section 15A offenders has probably saved that section from a serious constitutional challenge to date.

---

[136] The need for reliable evidence in regard to the active weight of drugs was confirmed by the Supreme Court in *People (DPP) v Connolly* [2011] IESC 6, although it was not necessary in that case to deal with the constitutionality of street value as the triggering factor for conviction of a section 15A or section 15B offence.

[137] (1983) 76 Cr. App. R. 190, (1982) 4 Cr. App. R. (S.) 407.

[138] *R v Aranguren* (1994) 99 Cr. App. R. 347, (1995) 16 Cr. App. R. (S.) 211.

[139] *R v Morris* [2001] 1 Cr. App. R. (S.) 87; *R v Patel* (1989) 9 Cr. App. R. (S.) 319.

[140] (1994) 99 Cr. App. R. 347. See also *R v Mashaollahi* [2001] 1 Cr. App. R. (S.) 96.

[141] 499 *Dáil Debates*, Cols 536–537 (June 11, 1998).

However, if more cases emerge involving repeat offenders who are liable to an absolute mandatory minimum sentence of 10 years' imprisonment, the rationality and, consequently, the constitutionality of using estimated street value as the qualifying condition may well come under attack. A person who was alleged to have had drugs worth little more than €13,000 and who had a previous conviction for such an offence would have good grounds for mounting a constitutional challenge on this ground alone. Indeed, if the courts were to adopt an approach similar to that of the Canadian Supreme Court in *R v Smith*,[142] the mandatory minimum for repeat section 15A and section 15B offences might prove to be constitutionally vulnerable irrespective of the amount of drugs involved in any given case.

---

[142]   [1987] 1 S.C.R. 1045. See p.89 above.

CHAPTER 5

STATUTORY AND JUDICIALLY-DEVELOPED PRINCIPLES

Sentencing guidelines, in the various forms in which they now exist in some American jurisdictions and in England and Wales, are a relatively recent phenomenon. The practice of controlling judicial sentencing discretion through general principles established by appeal courts and, to a lesser extent, by statute has a much longer history in most common-law countries. Strangely enough, appellate review of sentence was largely unknown in the United States federal system and in many individual states throughout much of the twentieth century, but it assumed considerable importance in England after 1907 and in this country after 1924 with the establishment of appeal courts empowered to entertain defence appeals against sentence.[1] Prosecution appeals came much later in both jurisdictions.[2] Judicially-developed principles are almost always expressed in narrative form, a quality which renders them more flexible and malleable than grid-based, numerical guidelines. This narrative quality has the advantage of being compatible with common-law methods of adjudication and with the progressive development of precedent, a topic considered further in Chapter 7. It fits easily into existing legal culture and is readily understood by judges, lawyers and most other actors in the sentencing process. General principles, whether originating in statute or case law, suffer from the drawback that they seldom provide much guidance to trial courts as to the nature or quantum of punishment appropriate for particular offences or categories of offender. As such they have a limited capacity to generate a coherent sentencing system and to eliminate genuine disparity. To achieve desired levels of systemic coherence and consistency of approach, judicially-developed principles, in particular, must be expressed in more specific terms, and this is best achieved in the first instance by strengthening the advisory and information services available to senior appeal courts.

STATUTORY GUIDANCE

Subject to very few constitutional constraints, the legislature has tremendous scope for shaping judicial sentencing practice. It fulfils this function primarily

---

[1] Chapter 6 below.
[2] Criminal Justice Act 1988 (England and Wales); Criminal Justice Act 1993 (Ireland).

by stipulating maximum or, much more rarely, mandatory penalties for particular offences. It is difficult to imagine a statutory maximum sentence, no matter how high, being deemed unconstitutional on grounds of quantum.[3] Any such challenge would undoubtedly be met with the argument that judges are never obliged to impose the maximum in any one case and that they are always empowered, indeed obliged, to tailor their sentences to reflect the specific circumstances of the offence and the offender. Mandatory and mandatory minimum sentences, and obligatory secondary penalties such as disqualification or forfeiture orders, are more vulnerable to constitutional attack. There can be little doubt about the formal legitimacy of such measures or about their compatibility with the separation of powers doctrine.[4] Their vulnerability is more likely to reside in their disproportionately severe impact in specific cases. Thus, a mandatory seven-year prison sentence might not in all circumstances be a disproportionate punishment for offence A, but it might well be disproportionate if imposed on offender B following conviction for offence A. This is one important consequence of the proportionality principle as it has been enunciated in Ireland that a sentence must be proportionate not only to the gravity of the offence but also to the personal circumstances of the offender. Few opportunities have so far arisen to test the constitutional implications of this principle. The Supreme Court decision in *Cox v Ireland*,[5] however, and certain *dicta* in later judgments of the same court strongly suggest that mandatory penalties, regardless of whether they are classified as primary or secondary punishments, will be unconstitutional if they have a disproportionately severe impact or if they operate in an arbitrary or irrational manner.[6] The marked political preference for presumptive rather than mandatory sentences, as reflected in recent statutory provisions governing drug and firearm offences, has no doubt been influenced by an awareness of the constitutional vulnerability of absolute mandatory penalties. Presumptive minimum sentencing provisions, as long as they allow the courts reasonable latitude to take account of particular extenuating circumstances, probably comply with any constitutional requirement of proportionality.

Two aspects of statutory maximum penalties merit attention in the present context. The first is the frequent lack of co-ordination between the maxima for

---

[3] *Re Art. 26 and the Regulation of Information (Services outside the State for the Termination of Pregnancies) Bill 1995* [1995] 1 I.R. 1 at 53, [1995] 2 I.L.R.M. 81 at 116 ("The question of the determination of the appropriate penalty for the commission of an offence created by statute is a matter purely for the Oireachtas and the adequacy or otherwise of any such penalty cannot be regarded by this Court as a ground for holding that the provision in regard to the creation of the offence and providing the penalty therefor is repugnant to the provisions of the Constitution."). A challenge might succeed if, for instance, there was a clear gender-based disparity in the maximum sentences attaching to two variants of the same offence as happened in *S.M. v Ireland (No.2)* [2007] 4 I.R. 369. See p.108 below.

[4] Chapter 4 below.

[5] [1992] 2 I.R. 503.

[6] *Osmanovic v DPP* [2006] 3 I.R. 504; *Lynch and Whelan v Minister for Justice, Equality and Law Reform* [2010] IESC 34. See p.91 above.

different offences. As far back as 1861, when our present system was taking shape, we find Greaves, a leading figure in the criminal law consolidation movement, remarking:

> "The truth is, that whenever the punishment of any offence is considered, it is never looked at, as it always ought to be, with reference to other offences, and with a view to [establishing] any congruity in the punishment of them, and the consequence is that nothing can well be more unsatisfactory than the punishments assigned to different offences …".[7]

Rarely is much consideration devoted to maximum penalties during parliamentary debate on draft criminal legislation, apart from occasional and predictable opposition claims that the proposed penalties are too low. Officials and legal advisors who prepare criminal legislation may well have regard to maximum penalties for cognate offences, but there is little evidence of political concern about such matters. Identifying appropriate maximum sentences will never be an exact science, but those who make the selection should try, as best they can, to ensure that maximum sentences reflect the relative gravity of the offences to which they are attached. After all, the statutory maximum is one of the factors, and arguably an important one, which courts must consider when selecting sentence in specific cases. Unwarranted discordance between maximum sentences might therefore lead to less serious offences attracting heavier punishment than more serious ones. Unjustified differences between maximum sentences which conflict with a constitutionally protected right may lead to the relevant statutory provision being invalidated. The Offences Against the Person Act 1861 (s.62) provided a 10-year maximum sentence for indecent assault upon a male, but only a two-year maximum for indecent assault upon a female. The latter maximum had been increased to 10 years in Ireland in 1981, but a first-time offender convicted of having committed an indecent assault against a male before that date would have faced a maximum sentence five times higher than someone convicted of having indecently assaulted a female during the same era. It is generally accepted that the relevant maximum sentence is that which applied when the offence was committed. In *S.M. v Ireland (No.2)*[8] the applicant faced charges of indecent assault against a male allegedly committed during the period 1966 to 1976. The High Court declared s.62 of the 1861 Act to be inconsistent with the Constitution in so far as it prescribed a higher maximum sentence for indecent assault upon a male, and made an ancillary declaration to the effect that the applicant, if convicted, should not face a maximum in excess of what would have been available for the offence of indecent assault upon a female at the relevant time. The second noteworthy aspect of maximum

---

[7]   Greaves, *The Criminal Law Consolidation and Amendment Acts* (London: Stevens & Sons, 1861), p.xlvi.
[8]   [2007] 4 I.R. 369.

penalties in the present context is that they are strictly binding upon the courts. No matter how low the maximum may appear, a court must not exceed it for any one offence and must, indeed, impose a sentence which is proportionate having regard to the maximum. This is no longer much of a problem because of the recent wave of criminal law reform but, before that, courts occasionally found themselves frustrated by statutory provisions, often dating from the nineteenth century or earlier, laying down maximum fines which were exceedingly low by modern standards or maximum prison sentences which failed to reflect modern views on the seriousness of the relevant offences. The low maximum penalties for child neglect under the Children Act 1908 (s.12) which lasted into the early years of this century would be one such example.

Our primary concern in this chapter, however, is with the utility of general principles as a means of shaping judicial discretion. Most of these principles are judicially-created but some also derive from statute. Again, the legislature has extensive constitutional competence to lay down general principles as long as it does not seek to influence the choice of sentence in any one case, and provided also that the principle or rule will not lead inexorably to disproportionately severe punishment. Neither eventuality is very likely. It would (hopefully) be unthinkable in a modern constitutional democracy that the legislature would try to dictate the sentence to be imposed on any particular person, although the background to *Kable v DPP for New South Wales*[9] shows that, even today, it is not entirely beyond the bounds of possibility. (In that case the High Court of Australia declared unconstitutional on jurisdictional grounds a statute which authorised the continued detention of a named individual following completion of his prison sentence.) Secondly, even when statutory principles are expressed as rules, such as the Irish rule requiring consecutive custodial sentences for offences committed while on bail, they rarely point to any specific quantum of punishment.[10] For instance, the rule just mentioned in relation to bail does not require that a custodial sentence be imposed in the first place or that it be of any particular length. It merely says that if the judge considers a custodial sentence, of whatever length, to be warranted for the later offence, he must order it to run consecutively to any subsisting custodial sentence.

A survey of statute law, past and present, in common-law jurisdictions reveals many examples of general statutory rules and principles aimed at influencing, rather than determining, the nature or amount of sanction to be imposed in prescribed circumstances. In 1929, towards the end of the Prohibition era, the United States Congress passed the Jones Act which significantly increased penalties for offences involving the sale or transportation of alcohol. The Act also provided that it was the intent of Congress "that the court, in imposing sentence hereunder, should distinguish between casual or slight violations and habitual sales

---

[9] [1996] HCA 24, (1996) 189 C.L.R. 51.
[10] Criminal Justice Act 1984 s.11 as amended by Criminal Justice Act 2007 s.22.
[11] (1929) 45 Stat. 1446. Prohibition was introduced by the Eighteenth Amendment to the United States Constitution in 1919 and abolished by the Twenty-First Amendment in 1933.

of intoxicating liquor, or attempts to commercialize violations of the law."[11] This provision survived at least one constitutional challenge based on the rather implausible argument that it delegated legislative power to trial courts but, apart from that, it was generally accepted as a legitimate form of statutory guidance.[12] As one appeal court said, it was designed to distinguish between the "making of a quart of wine by a housewife for private household or medicinal purposes" and large scale transactions.[13]

Statute law may endeavour to influence judicial sentencing practice in a variety of ways. It might, for instance, specify the predominant moral purpose or the primary distributive principle of punishment. The nature and content of statutory direction or guidance will obviously depend on prevailing political ideologies and on the institutional relationship between the judicial and political branches of government. At one time, for example, the Czechoslovakian Criminal Code provided that the first goal of punishment was "to make the enemy of the working people harmless."[14] On a more practical level, the English Criminal Justice Act 1991 provided that a custodial sentence should be commensurate with the seriousness of the offence or with a combination of relevant offences.[15] A similar provision was made in relation to community sentences.[16] This was viewed as an official endorsement of a just deserts theory of punishment to the extent that it required sentencing courts to focus on the gravity of the offence as opposed to more forward-looking considerations such as deterrence or rehabilitation. By way of exception to this general policy, where the offence was of a violent or sexual nature, the court could impose such longer term as it considered necessary to protect the public from serious harm from the offender.[17] As a rule, however, neither a custodial nor a community-based sentence was to be imposed unless the court was satisfied that the offence was serious enough to warrant such a measure.[18] The New Zealand Criminal Justice Act 1985 had somewhat similar though less elaborate provisions stating that violent offenders should ordinarily be imprisoned in the absence of special circumstances whereas property offenders should not ordinarily be imprisoned in the absence of special circumstances. Although since repealed,[19] these general principles illustrate the kind of guidance which legislators can legitimately offer to courts on the sentencing of various categories of offender.

Statutory provisions of this sort in Ireland vary from the mandatory to the

---

[12]   *Ross v United States* 37 F. (2d) 557 (1930).

[13]   *Gurera v United States* 40 F. (2d) 338 at 340 (1930).

[14]   Quoted in Mueller and Le Poole, "Appellate Review of Legal but Excessive Sentences: A Comparative Study" (1968) 21 Vanderbilt L.R. 411 at 429.

[15]   Section 2(2)(a). On the current English law, see Ashworth, *Sentencing and Criminal Justice*, 5th edn (Cambridge: Cambridge University Press, 2010).

[16]   Section 6(2).

[17]   Section 2(2)(b)

[18]   Section 1(2) and section 6(1).

[19]   New Zealand's Sentencing Act 2002 s.8 has a more elaborate set of general principles on the choice of sentence.

hortatory. In the former category are those rules requiring consecutive prison sentences for offences committed while on bail[20] or while the offender was serving a sentence of imprisonment or detention.[21] In the latter category are provisions such as that introduced by the Criminal Justice Act 2006 requiring a court when deciding if a minimum 10-year sentence should be imposed for a drug-trafficking offence to consider if the offender has previously been convicted of such an offence and, also, if the public interest in preventing drug trafficking would be served by the imposition of a lesser sentence.[22] Courts must obviously take these factors into account once they are required by statute to do so, but they remain free to decide on the weight to be attributed to them in any given case. The impact of general statutory directives is seldom possible to evaluate, let alone quantify, although if faithfully followed they may be expected to have some influence on overall sentencing patterns. Directive principles are often intended to encourage heavier sentences—that seems a fair interpretation of the provision regarding drug-trafficking offences—but they might also tend in the opposite direction by, for example, requiring courts to consider all available community-based options before imposing a short prison sentence.[23] General statutory principles of this kind are not without value but they are seldom of much practical use in eliminating unwarranted disparity.

JUDICIALLY-DEVELOPED PRINCIPLES

The creation of a Court of Criminal Appeal, first in England in 1907 and later in Ireland in 1924, provided a clear opportunity for the development of a sentencing jurisprudence which had hitherto been lacking. Numerous unsuccessful efforts had been made throughout the second half of the nineteenth century to establish such a court in both jurisdictions.[24] The Court of Crown Cases Reserved, which was formally set up in 1848, had few opportunities to consider legal issues of any description as the decision to refer a case rested entirely with the trial judge, and the court was mainly concerned in any event with points of substantive criminal law and criminal procedure. The Irish Court of Crown Cases Reserved issued a few judgments of lasting significance. *R v Dee*,[25] for instance, remains an important authority on rape committed through impersonation, and *R v Faulkner*[26] is occasionally cited in relation to the test for recklessness. However,

---

[20] Criminal Justice Act 1984 s.11 as amended by the Criminal Justice Act 2007 s.22.
[21] Criminal Law Act 1976 s.13.
[22] Misuse of Drugs Act 1977 s.27 as amended by the Criminal Justice Act 2006 s.84.
[23] The Criminal Justice (Community Service) (Amendment) Act 2011 falls into this category. See also Ch.8 below.
[24] Thomas, *Constraints on Judgment: The Search for Structured Discretion in Sentencing, 1860–1910* (Cambridge: Institute of Criminology, 1979), p.75 et seq.
[25] (1884) 15 Cox C.C. 579.
[26] (1877) 13 Cox C.C. 550.

the court appears to have sat very infrequently throughout the first two decades of the twentieth century.[27] With the virtual disappearance of the death penalty except for murder by the mid-nineteenth century, and the growing legislative preference for maximum as opposed to mandatory sentences, the need for some mechanism to structure judicial sentencing discretion became increasingly obvious. At one point it was felt that a textbook on sentencing might go a considerable way towards achieving this purpose, and such a work was indeed produced by the redoubtable Edward Cox, one of those remarkably energetic individuals who seem to have flourished in the late nineteenth century.[28] Explaining his motivation for writing *The Principles of Punishment* (1877), he wrote:

> "In the course of my practice, I had noted the extraordinary diversity of sentences passed upon criminals, not only by different courts but by judges of the same court, for offences apparently alike. But I was aware also how difficult it is for any person, not being in the position of the judge who tries the case, to form a fair opinion of the propriety of the sentence. So many circumstances, not admissible at the trial, are to be taken into account for the purpose of punishment—so many inquiries into the antecedents of the convict and general history of the case are to be made—that divers considerations often present themselves to affect the sentence, of which the public can know nothing."[29]

In fact, there are few statements in his lengthy introduction which could not plausibly be made of Irish sentencing practice today, though not all of the ideas expressed elsewhere in the book would now command approval. His views on domestic violence, in particular, have been criticised by social historians who are far from persuaded by his opinion that the female victim had typically "made her husband's home an earthly hell" while the husband had been "tortured and taunted to the verge of madness".[30] However, most reformers put their faith in the establishment of an appeal court which would have jurisdiction to review sentences on their merits. Such a court, as noted, was eventually established in

---

[27] Greer, "A Security Against Illegality: The Reservation of Crown Cases in Nineteenth-Century Ireland" in Dawson (ed.), *Reflections on Law and History* (Dublin: Four Courts Press/The Irish Legal History Society, 2006), p.163 at p.201.

[28] In addition to his work as a barrister and part-time judge, Cox (1809–1879) founded the *Law Times*, the law report series *Cox's Criminal Cases* and other publications. He also founded what became the British Psychological Society. See Spiller, *Cox and Crime* (Cambridge: Institute of Criminology, 1985).

[29] Cox, *The Principles of Punishment* (London: Law Times Office, London, 1877) pp.viii–ix.

[30] Cox (fn.29 above), pp.99–102. See Tomes, "A 'Torrent of Abuse'; Crimes of Violence between Working-Class Men and Women in London, 1840–1875" (1978) 11 *Journal of Social History* 328.

[31] Criminal Appeal Act 1907 (7 Edw. 7 c.23). A similar court was established in Scotland under the Criminal Appeal (Scotland) Act 1926 (16 & 17 Geo. V c.15). On the events leading to the establishment of the English Court of Criminal Appeal and its early history, see Smith

England in 1907[31] and this provided a model for the Irish Court of Criminal Appeal established under the Courts of Justice Act 1924.[32] The sentencing jurisdiction of the latter court is now expressed in the following terms:

> "On the hearing of an appeal against sentence for an offence the Court may quash the sentence and in place of it impose such sentence or make such order as it considers appropriate, being a sentence or order which could have been imposed on the convicted person for the offence at the court of trial."[33]

While the early history of the Irish Court of Criminal Appeal remains to be fully explored, it appears that following its formal establishment, it got down to work without undue ceremony, or indeed without any at all. The first sitting is reported to have occurred on July 16, 1924 to hear an application connected with an appeal against a murder conviction by one Felix McMullen.[34] Counsel for the applicant had appeared in the Supreme Court two days earlier and asked for a Court of Criminal Appeal to be constituted, which request was granted. A problem arose because of the absence of rules of court (not the last time an Irish court faced such a predicament) but the case was heard within a few days, and the appeal was dismissed on July 27. McMullen was hanged, as scheduled, on August 1, 1924. From then on, the court proceeded to deal with appeals in a businesslike manner and does not appear to have made any significant pronouncements on sentencing principles. Most of the sentences appealed against in non-capital cases were relatively short. In 1926, the court reduced a sentence for bigamy from two years to six months "on account of mitigating circumstances"[35] but in 1930 it apparently found no such circumstances when it upheld a six-month sentence imposed on a man convicted of receiving a stolen bicycle.[36] At some early point in its history, however, the court seems to have adopted a rule which had been laid down by its English counterpart in 1908 which was to the effect that a sentence, assuming it was lawful and within jurisdiction, would not be varied unless it was shown that the trial court had committed an error of principle.[37] This remains the law and has been applied to prosecution as well as defence appeals.[38]

"Criminal Law" in *The Oxford History of the Laws of England* Vol. XIII (Oxford: Oxford University Press, 2010), pp.12–137.

[32] Section 34 of the 1924 Act originally provided: "The Court of Criminal Appeal shall have jurisdiction to affirm or to reverse the conviction in whole or in part, and to remit, or to reduce, or to increase or otherwise vary the sentence, and generally to make such order, including any order as to costs as may be necessary for the purpose of doing justice in the case before the court."

[33] Criminal Procedure Act 1993 s.3(2).

[34] *Irish Times*, July 15 and 17, 1924. McMullen had been convicted, following a short trial where the jury had deliberated for 40 minutes, of the murder of a member of the civic guard during a bank raid at Baltinglass in County Wicklow.

[35] *People (Attorney General) v O'Brien, Irish Times,* December 3, 1926.

[36] *People (DPP) v Broderick, Irish Times,* July 4, 1930.

[37] *R v Sidlow* (1908) 1 Cr. App. R. 28.

[38] *People (DPP) v McCormack* [2000] 4 I.R. 356.

Within the legal system generally, appeals serve a variety of purposes. In psychological terms, they provide some immediate hope to offset the disappointment of defeat. Persons who find themselves on the losing side in civil proceedings, who are convicted following a criminal trial or who receive a heavier sentence than had been anticipated can derive some consolation from knowing that they have at least one further opportunity to be heard.[39] Aside from this, an appeals system has two important practical functions. It permits specific decisions of lower courts to be reviewed and, if necessary, corrected, and it also provides the appeal court with an opportunity to explain and develop the legal principles governing the subject matter of the appeal. In practice, the second of these functions can be discharged only by a superior court of appeal. Appeals against decisions of courts of summary jurisdiction are usually heard by middle-ranking courts, such as the Circuit Court in Ireland, the decisions of which are seldom recorded or reported. This, in turn, explains the dearth of jurisprudence on the sentencing of that large category of offences falling within the exclusive jurisdiction of the District Court. Although a court of summary jurisdiction, the Irish District Court is constitutionally empowered to deal with minor offences which include a large selection of indictable offences as well as purely summary offences, and it may in certain circumstances impose up to two years' imprisonment. Granted, the general principles of sentencing apply in the District Court as in all other trial courts, and it is also possible to have District Court decisions brought up for consideration by the High Court and Supreme Court by way of case stated or judicial review proceedings. Having said this, there are several categories of commonly-prosecuted offences, particularly public order, road traffic, minor theft and assault offences, which are dealt with exclusively by the District Court. The superior courts have therefore no meaningful opportunity to identify the circumstances in which such offences should ordinarily attract immediate imprisonment or to establish other relevant sentencing principles. Because of the significant growth in judicial review and case stated proceedings in recent years, the High Court and Supreme Court have been able to establish a significant body of jurisprudence in relation to arrest, summons procedure, drink-driving prosecutions, the grant of legal aid and other such matters. Rarely, however, are they afforded an opportunity to offer the District Court any guidance on sentencing. This is scarcely surprising given that case stated and judicial review proceedings operate primarily as mechanisms for raising disputed points of law and ensuring the observance of procedural justice.

As a means of structuring judicial sentencing discretion, appellate review has undoubted strengths but it may also suffer from certain weaknesses which will be considered presently. The term "appellate review" is used here as a convenient description for the process whereby sentences imposed for serious offences may be appealed to a superior court on the ground of undue leniency

---

[39]   Shapiro, *Courts: A Comparative and Political Analysis* (Chicago: University of Chicago Press, 1986), p.52.

or undue severity. The essence of an appeal is that it entails an assessment of the merits of the challenged decision whereas judicial review, in the formal sense of that term, is concerned solely with issues relating to jurisdiction and procedure. Defence appeals against conviction and sentence have been available in these islands for a century or so, but it is only in more recent times that statutory provision has been made for prosecution appeals against unduly lenient sentences. The main strength of appellate review as a means of developing principled sentencing is that it is firmly grounded on reality. Principles are developed and refined in the context of specific cases which, over time, acquaint the appeal court with the entire range of circumstances in which certain offences are committed and with the personal characteristics of the offenders. A general principle established in one case may later have to be refined or recast if an unpredicted variation of the relevant offence comes to light. Another major strength of appellate review is that it can provide more nuanced, narrative guidance than is usually possible under grid-based guidelines. A system of the latter kind might provide, for example, that a person found in possession of a defined quantity of heroin for sale or supply should receive a prison sentence of so many months or years. Granted, it will usually list some aggravating and mitigating factors as well and may indeed go further by indicating the numerical weights to be attributed to those factors (as in the United States federal guidelines). An appeal court, on the other hand, is able to offer guidance which, while usually less prescriptive and certain than that found in grid-type systems, may be more helpful to trial courts in terms of identifying relevant factors and indicating circumstances where departures from the prescribed norm will be justified. Yet another advantage of appellate review is its capacity to respond to novel factual situations and emerging social concerns. Formal guidelines, on the other hand, are naturally a product of their time, and are often marked by a rigidity which can produce considerable injustice in specific cases. The problem is exacerbated when legislation or some other formal measure is required to amend the guidelines, as legislators and other policy-makers may be reluctant to authorise any change which might betray a tendency towards leniency. Appellate review is distinctly more flexible, although this can also be a negative quality unless appeal courts constantly strive to develop coherent principles. There is nothing more inimical to rationality in sentencing than the co-existence of conflicting precedents.

In theory, a vibrant system of appellate review can go a considerable way towards creating a rational, coherent and reasonably consistent sentencing system, particularly in those jurisdictions which allow prosecution as well as defence appeals against sentence. Unfortunately, however, most appeal courts are subject to certain practical constraints which seriously diminish their capacity to produce a useful and coherent body of sentencing jurisprudence. These constraints may be classified under three broad headings: (1) opportunity; (2) co-ordination; and (3) transmission. Each of these must be considered in turn.

Opportunity

To begin by stating the obvious, a court can only decide those cases which are brought before it for resolution. When assessing an appeal court's capacity to offer meaningful sentencing guidance, one must begin by examining the range of cases coming within its jurisdiction. Authoritative statements of principle, whether in regard to sentencing or any other aspect of law, can only emanate from a superior appellate court such as the Court of Criminal Appeal or the Supreme Court in Ireland, or the Court of Appeal (Criminal Division) in England and Wales. The right of appeal to such a court is typically limited to persons who have been convicted of serious offences and they account for no more than a small percentage of convicted offenders in any given period. In these islands at least, the vast bulk of criminal cases are handled exclusively by courts of summary jurisdiction. Magistrates' courts deal with 95 per cent of criminal prosecutions in England and Wales. Much the same holds true of the District Court in Ireland which has considerably greater sentencing powers than its English counterpart—it may impose a cumulative sentence up to two years' imprisonment in certain circumstances.[40] It also disposes of about half a million offences annually compared with 6,000 or so (admittedly more serious offences) disposed of in the higher courts.

This is not to suggest that intermediate appeal courts carry out their functions in anything other than a conscientious and principled manner. The problem is that they operate independently of one another, their decisions are never formally reported and their caseload renders it impossible for them to deliver written judgments even in a minority of cases. Yet, the statistics just mentioned also point to another important conclusion. Because more than 90 per cent of offences are dealt with summarily, courts of summary jurisdiction and intermediate appeal courts exercise enormous influence over key aspects of the sentencing process, including the use of imprisonment and other criminal sanctions. Principled sentencing is therefore just as vital, if not more so, in the lower courts as in the higher courts. Intermediate appeal courts can serve two of the three general purposes of appeals mentioned earlier. The availability of an appeal can certainly provide some comfort and hope of further redress for those convicted and sentenced in courts of summary jurisdiction. Intermediate appeal courts can also fulfil the second function, which is to take corrective action where necessary by quashing a conviction or varying a sentence. What they cannot readily fulfil is the third function, namely, the articulation and development of general principles to govern sentencing practice in the courts below them. Some Circuit Court judges have tried to create a degree of consistency in the use of custodial sentences when dealing with appeals from different district courts within their circuits. While this is a commendable endeavour, it depends very

---

[40]   Criminal Justice Act 1984 s.12.

much on the initiative of individual judges. Furthermore, any principles or policies developed for this purpose will probably apply solely within the relevant circuit, and only during the tenure of office of the particular judge. State-wide initiatives are needed to promote coherence in the use of custody and community-based sanctions in the District Court. This is a topic to which we shall return in Chapter 10, but for now it is sufficient to note that the superior courts of appeal, on which we rely for the development of sentencing principles, have very limited opportunities to offer sentencing guidance for the wide range of summary offences which are exclusively within the District Court's juris-diction or for the many indictable offences which are routinely disposed of in that court because they are deemed to be minor in nature. The same observation may be made in regard to certain dispositions such as fines, probation orders and community service orders which are much more widely used in summary jurisdiction courts than in the higher courts. If proof of this is needed, one can point to the dearth of superior court jurisprudence on the appropriate use of probation since it was introduced in its present form more than a century ago and on community service which was introduced in 1983.[41]

Another factor which traditionally restricted the capacity of the Court of Criminal Appeal to develop a coherent body of sentencing jurisprudence was that it dealt solely with defence appeals which, almost by definition, involved heavy sentences. A person given the benefit of a suspended sentence or a fine following conviction on indictment was unlikely to challenge such a sentence on appeal (although it might be the subject of comment in an appeal against conviction). The court's power to increase as well as reduce a sentence following a defence appeal, a power which it still retains though seldom uses, acted as a further disincentive to convicted persons to appeal against anything other than custodial sentences. Indeed, they would often be well advised to refrain from appealing where a particular custodial sentence might be seen as rather light in the circumstances. The introduction of prosecution appeals against unduly lenient sentences (or, strictly speaking, applications for review of such sentences) has ameliorated this situation somewhat. At the same time, it is well accepted that the prosecutorial review function is to be exercised sparingly and that the Court of Criminal Appeal must be satisfied that the sentence is *unduly* lenient to such a degree that it should not, in all the circumstances, be allowed to stand.[42] The number of prosecution appeals remains comparatively low which means that, although they have certainly enhanced the court's capacity to address issues which might not have arisen very often in defence appeals, they are not in themselves sufficient to fill the various lacunae that almost invariably occur in any system which relies on appellate review as the sole or predominant means of structuring sentencing discretion.

---

[41] Probation of Offenders Act 1907; Criminal Justice (Community Service) Act 1983.

[42] O'Malley, *Sentencing Law and Practice*, 2nd edn (Dublin: Thomson Round Hall, 2006), Ch.35. This principle has recently been restated in *People (DPP) v Nolan*, ex tempore, Court of Criminal Appeal, March 11, 2011.

Co-ordination

Sentencing principles are currently developed in the context of specific appeals and are therefore shaped and limited by the particular facts and submissions with which the appeal court is presented. This holds true in equal measure of offence-specific principles and general principles, and it also explains why the resulting case law may reveal conflicting approaches towards the same problem. It might seem eminently reasonable to classify some particular factor as aggravating or mitigating in light of one set of facts, but the same factor may seem less worthy of significance or undeserving of the same weight when considered in the context of another case involving the same offence committed in different circumstances. Add to this a less than satisfactory system for publishing or disseminating appeal court decisions and the potential for inconsistency becomes all too apparent. Bear in mind that we are here discussing appellate jurisprudence which, in theory at least, is supposed to correct or iron out inconsistencies which have emerged at trial court level. Yet the context in which that jurisprudence develops is less than conducive towards the elaboration of coherent principles. Take, for example, something as fundamental as the principle that a guilty plea should ordinarily merit a discount. The core of the principle is easily stated and widely accepted but surrounding that core (and the core of most other settled principles) is a penumbra of less settled issues such as whether an offender caught red-handed should receive any credit for a guilty plea, or whether a person convicted of a lesser offence to which he had originally offered to plead should be treated as if he had pleaded to the offence of conviction. The problem intensifies when the core principle itself is the subject of doubt or disagreement, as exemplified by questions surrounding the relevance of previous convictions or the most appropriate manner of dealing with offenders simulta-neously convicted of multiple offences. Previous convictions pose a particularly difficult dilemma. Most people agree that an offender's record should have some bearing on sentence; yet, treating previous convictions as an aggravating factor carries the risk of subjecting the offender to double punishment. The progressive loss of mitigation approach tries to accommodate both of these considerations.[43] Two recent Court of Criminal Appeal decisions on the matter illustrate the limitations of appellate review as a means of generating effective sentencing principles. In *People (DPP) v G.K.*,[44] the Court of Criminal Appeal seemed to say that, in some circumstances at least, previous convictions should be treated as an aggravating factor when assessing the seriousness of the offence of conviction. Six months later, when faced with a rather similar set of facts, the court seemed to retreat to the more conventional position that, rather than

---

[43]   *R v Queen* (1981) 3 Cr. App. R.(S.) 245, 255; *R v Bailey* (1988) 10 Cr. App. R. (S.) 231.

[44]   [2008] IECCA 110. For further discussion, see O'Malley, "Sentencing Recidivist Sex Offenders: A Challenge for Proportionality" in Bacik and Heffernan (eds), *Criminal Law and Procedure: Current Issues and Emerging Trends* (Dublin: Firstlaw, 2009), p.106.

aggravating the offence of conviction, previous convictions should be treated as a ground for denying mitigation.[45] On both occasions, the court, like the trial judges who imposed the original sentences, was faced with a very difficult decision. Both applicants had been convicted of serious sex offences committed within a short time of completing prison sentences for similar offences. But this is precisely the kind of difficulty which makes it all the more desirable, if not imperative, to have settled principles not only for the benefit of trial courts but also for future compositions of the Court of Criminal Appeal itself.

This is not to deny that the Irish superior courts have, on occasion, established clear and coherent principles on certain aspects of sentencing. Proportionality, for example, is well established as the dominant distributive principle of punishment in all cases where the sentence is discretionary. It is also clear that matters arising between the time of sentence and the time of appeal are not ordinarily relevant for the purpose of deciding if a sentence is wrong in principle or in need of variation.[46] The leading case of *People (DPP) v Tiernan*[47] set out the fundamental principles applicable to the sentencing of rape offences and listed certain factors which are not to be treated as relevant for that purpose. Many other examples of decisions establishing reasonably firm principles could also be cited. Yet, *Tiernan*, for all its merits, happens to illustrate a problem associated with any effort to deduce appropriate sentence levels or starting points from leading cases, and it is a problem that may arise even in Ireland where the appeal courts have refrained from indicating guideline or benchmark sentences. This is the so-called anchoring effect, a form of cognitive bias which may arise when a numerical value adopted in some situation (such as the sentence substituted or upheld in a leading case) influences subsequent decisions with a similar factual matrix. It can lead to a situation in which people "come up with or evaluate numbers by focusing on a reference point (or anchor) and then [adjust] up or down from that anchor."[48] The phenomenon is best known and most widely researched in the field of negotiation. Controlled experiments have shown that when two parties are negotiating, for example, on the sale of a business premises, the price eventually agreed is often strongly influenced by whoever makes the opening offer. It is likely to be higher when the seller makes the first offer and lower when the buyer makes the first offer.[49] The same phenomenon has been identified in legal contexts. Research has shown that "a numeric value that is requested or suggested in court influences legal

---

[45] *People (DPP) v P.S.* [2009] IECCA 1.

[46] *People (DPP) v Cunningham* [2002] 2 I.R. 712, [2003] 1 I.L.R.M. 124.

[47] [1988] I.R. 250, [1989] 1 I.L.R.M. 149.

[48] Bibas, "Plea Bargaining outside the Shadow of Trial" (2004) 117 Harvard L.R. 2464 at 2515. See also Miller, "Anchors Away: Why the Anchoring Effect Suggests that Judges Should be Able to Participate in Plea Discussions" available at *http://papers.ssrn.com*.

[49] Galinsky and Mussweiler, "First Offers as Anchors: The Role of Perspective-Taking and Negotiator Focus" (2001) 81:6 *Journal of Personality and Social Psychology* 657.

decisions".[50] In those systems where personal injuries litigants can request specific amounts of compensation from a jury, the amount requested has been shown systematically to influence the amount awarded.[51] The problem, therefore, with relying on sentences approved in leading cases (even where, as in *Tiernan*, the substituted sentence was emphatically not intended as a benchmark) is that they may produce this kind of unconscious cognitive bias. In other words, later courts may treat them as benchmarks even for cases which have markedly different factual backgrounds. In evaluating the sentence substituted by the Supreme Court in *Tiernan*, for example, it must be recalled that it was imposed for a gang rape of a level of ferocity and degradation that has rarely, if ever, been surpassed in the meantime.

Transmission

However detailed, thoughtful or coherent they may be, sentencing principles developed by appeal courts will have little practical effect unless they are effectively transmitted to the relevant trial courts. A number of historical episodes reveal the inadequacy of legal principles and standards unless they are properly communicated to those who are primarily charged with their implementation. The so-called Alverstone Memorandum, drawn up by the Lord Chief Justice and judges of the Queen's Bench in 1901, represents an early judicial effort to create presumptive sentencing guidelines for a range of commonly-prosecuted serious offences. Yet, it appears to have been transmitted solely to the Home Office where it languished and eventually disappeared, but it was never circulated to the Quarter Sessions where the offences in question were tried and where, at the time, sentencing disparity was most pronounced.[52] Overall, however, English lawyers and judges have been more fortunate than their counterparts in Ireland and elsewhere in terms of access to appeal court decisions. Following the establishment of the Court of Criminal Appeal in 1907, a commercially-produced series of law reports, the *Criminal Appeal Reports*, was launched and continues to be published to this day. In the late 1970s, a companion series, the *Criminal Appeal Reports (Sentencing)*, was introduced to cover the increasing number of sentencing judgments being handed down by the Court of Appeal (Criminal Division), as it had then become.

---

[50] Englich, Mussweiler and Strack, "Playing Dice with Criminal Sentences: The Influence of Irrelevant Anchors on Experts' Judicial Decision-Making" (2006) 32 *Personality and Social Psychology Bulletin* 188 at 189.

[51] Englich, Mussweiler and Strack (fn.50 above).

[52] Smith (fn.31 above), p.127 (suggesting that the Home Office was probably unhappy with the memorandum because the suggested sentences were too lenient). The text of the memorandum is reproduced in Jackson, *Enforcing the Law* (Harmondsworth: Penguin Books, 1972), pp.391–399.

Yet, even in the mid-1980s, many English trial judges had limited awareness of the principles established by the Court of Appeal. This became clear in a pilot study conducted under the aegis of the Centre for Criminological Research at Oxford University. Following an approach from the Centre, the Home Office had agreed to fund a study of sentencing practices in the Crown Court. The Lord Chief Justice of the day, Lord Lane, agreed to a pilot study but, unfortunately and rather inexplicably, he refused to allow the research to proceed further. A report on the pilot study, later published by the Centre, will certainly repay reading by Irish criminal lawyers, judges and policy-makers today as it examined the English sentencing system at a time when it was much closer to ours than it is now.[53] One of the more interesting findings for present purposes was that many trial judges did not feel that appeal court decisions were being adequately communicated to them. As the authors write:

> "Turning to the question of communication, some of the judges and recorders who participated in the 'pilot study'—and they came from a group selected for us by the higher judiciary—strongly expressed the view that their needs were either not known or not heeded by the Court of Appeal. The 'pilot study' suggested that many judges have a poor awareness of the principles laid down by the Court of Appeal. Without assistance from counsel, who rarely cite particular decisions, judges are left to obtain for themselves a knowledge of appellate judgments which may be relevant to particular cases. The steps taken by judges to keep abreast of the case law were variable, and several criticised their book allowances as inadequate."[54]

One can only assume that this problem is at least as acute in Ireland today as it was in England back then. There has never been an effective system for communicating Irish Court of Criminal Appeal decisions, particularly in relation to sentencing. This is explained partly by the rather skeletal law reporting system that operated throughout much of the history of the State and partly also by the court's own reluctance to attribute significance to the ex tempore judgments which account for most of its output.[55] The *Irish Reports*, published in their present format by the Incorporated Council of Law Reporting for Ireland since 1894, are exclusively devoted to superior court judgments. Throughout most of their history, they appeared in one annual volume but since 1998 they have appeared in four volumes. Like all general reports series, they contain no more than a selection of reserved judgments, and traditionally included very few Court of Criminal Appeal judgments (e.g. one in 1970 and 1980, two in 1961

---

[53] Ashworth, Genders, Mansfield, Peay and Player, *Sentencing in the Crown Court: Report of an Exploratory Study* Occasional Paper No. 10 (Oxford: Centre for Criminological Research, 1984).

[54] Ashworth et al. (fn.53 above), p.49.

[55] The court has, admittedly, explained on more than one occasion why ex tempore judgments cannot be accorded the same authority as reserved judgments. See, for example, *People (DPP) v Sakpoba* [2010] IECCA 83.

and 1965). The situation has improved considerably over the past few years. The *Irish Reports* carried 20 Court of Criminal Appeal judgments in 2007 and 10 in 2008. The *Irish Law Times Reports*, which were published until 1980 and the *Irish Law Reports Monthly*, which began in 1981 with retrospective volumes dating back to 1976, also include some criminal appeal reports. Our greatest debt in this regard is owed to a former court registrar, Gerard Frewen, who brought together in two volumes hitherto unreported Court of Criminal Appeal judgments dating from 1924 to 1983. A third volume covering the years 1984 to 1989 was published after his death and this included transcripts of several ex tempore sentencing judgments.[56] No further volumes have been produced because, despite their undoubted value, they do not seem to have been commercially viable, a common problem in a small jurisdiction.

Computer-based technology held great promise for the more efficient dissemination of superior court judgments and this promise has been largely fulfilled except, unfortunately, in the case of the Court of Criminal Appeal. The Courts Service website (*www.courts.ie*) has a valuable judgments section on which most reserved judgments of the High Court and Supreme Court are published, often on the day of delivery. Because this website, as a matter of policy, includes approved judgments only, it contains relatively few Court of Criminal Appeal decisions. According to official statistics, that court disposed of 232 cases, including 158 sentence appeals, in 2007. In 2008 it disposed of 279 cases including 213 sentence appeals.[57] Only a fraction of these resulted in approved judgments. The Courts Service website carried 27 Court of Criminal Appeal judgments for 2007 (three of which resulted from the same appeal) and 24 for 2008 (two of which resulted from the same appeal). Some commercially-produced electronic services carry rather more of the court's unapproved and ex tempore judgments.[58] It would, of course, be entirely unrealistic to expect all judgments and decisions on sentence appeals to be formally published. Many of them merely confirm or marginally vary the sentence imposed by the trial court without offering any precedent-setting comment which means that there would be little point in issuing or approving formal judgments. Similar practices are followed elsewhere. Doob and Park, for example, in describing their efforts to develop a sentencing information system in Canada in the 1980s, refer to the recording practices of the various provincial appeal courts in respect of appeals against sentence.[59] Few of them managed to produce anything better than summaries of sentence appeal decisions.

---

[56] Frewen, *Judgments of the Court of Criminal Appeal 1924–1978* and Frewen, *Judgments of the Court of Criminal Appeal 1979–1983*, both published by the Incorporated Council of Law Reporting for Ireland in the early 1980s; Casey (ed.), *Judgments of the Court of Criminal Appeal 1984–1989* (Dublin: The Round Hall Press, 1991).

[57] Figures drawn from Court Service Annual Reports for 2007 and 2008.

[58] See, for example, *www.justis.com*.

[59] Doob and Park, "Computerized Sentencing Information for Judges: An Aid to the Sentencing Process" (1987) 30 *Criminal Law Quarterly* 54 at 67 et seq.

The present Irish policy on the electronic publishing of sentence appeal decisions is much too restrictive, and it would benefit from the inclusion of more ex tempore judgments. Again, it is not being suggested that all such judgments be published but a judicious selection of the more significant ones should be made available. Many useful precedents and statements of principle on the sentencing of section 15A drug offences, to take but one example, are to be found in ex tempore judgments. In *Whitehead*, the Court of Criminal Appeal, having regard to exceptional mitigating factors, halved the sentence imposed on a South African woman convicted of drugs importation. In *Shekale*, the court stressed that a person should never be penalised or appear to be penalised for having pleaded not guilty. In *Nelson*, the court was unable to identify the basis upon which the trial judge had arrived at the sentence, and it held that this in itself amounted to an error of principle.[60] There may not be anything particularly novel about these decisions but, at the very least, they are valuable for articulating and re-affirming the relevant principles. None of them is reported on the Courts Service website though all of them are available on a commercially-produced online law reporting service.

GUIDELINE JUDGMENTS

For reasons already outlined, appeal court decisions have a limited capacity to influence trial court sentencing practice. They can certainly establish, re-assert and refine those general principles applicable in most cases and occasionally, though usually indirectly, indicate the appropriate sentence range for certain offences. In fact, they seldom fulfil the latter role very effectively because their attention will necessarily be confined to some particular variant of an offence. The 17-year prison sentence substituted by the Supreme Court in *People (DPP) v Tiernan*[61] may be a useful guide for the sentencing of particularly egregious rape offences, and gang rapes in particular, but the court deliberately refrained from indicating appropriate starting points in other circumstances. Although the judgment of the English Court of Appeal in *R v Billam*[62] was brought to its attention, the Supreme Court decided that it would be inappropriate to establish any similar benchmarks in Ireland, partly because of the absence of reliable data on existing practice and partly because it was opposed in principle to curtailing the sentencing discretion of trial courts. *Billam* was typical of the guideline judgments then being handed down by the English Court of Appeal (Criminal Division). Beginning in early 1980s, the court took advantage of certain cases

---

[60] *People (DPP) v Whitehead*, ex tempore, Court of Criminal Appeal, October 20, 2008; *People (DPP) v Shekale*, ex tempore, Court of Criminal Appeal, February 25, 2008; *People (DPP) v Nelson*, ex tempore, July 31, 2008, CCA.

[61] *People (DPP) v Tiernan* [1988] I.R. 250, [1989] I.L.R.M. 149.

[62] *R v Billam* (1986) 82 Cr. App. R. 347; (1986) 8 Cr. App. R. (S.) 48.

coming before it to indicate appropriate starting points for certain variants of the offences involved, without necessarily confining its observations to the facts of the particular case, or group of cases, before it. Thus, in *R v Aramah*[63] it established certain benchmarks for the importation or supply of prohibited drugs. The guidelines for certain class A drugs were expressed by reference to estimated street value while those for class B drugs, such as cannabis, were expressed by reference to weight.[64] That, of course, was almost 30 years ago, but several more recent judgments have offered more detailed and modern guidance on sentencing serious drug offences.[65] In *Billam*, the court had indicated starting points of five years, eight years, 15 years and life imprisonment in contested rape cases, depending on the presence or absence of certain specified factors. Similar guideline judgments were issued in relation to many other commonly-prosecuted offences. While useful up to a point, these guideline judgments suffered from the limitations already mentioned in connection with appeal court judgments in general.[66] The opportunity to develop guidelines was obviously determined and limited by the cases which happened to come before the court. All of those cases would have originated in the Crown Court (which has a criminal jurisdiction more or less equivalent to that of the Irish Circuit Court and Central Criminal Court combined) and therefore involved serious offences. Secondly, most appeals were defence appeals against immediate and reasonably substantial terms of imprisonment. The introduction of prosecution appeals—in England and Wales in 1988 and in Ireland in 1993—has only marginally increased the variety of sentences being appealed. Thirdly, while the court may have endeavoured to be as comprehensive as possible, its attention was inevitably focused on the facts of the case before it, and counsel's submissions would doubtless have concentrated on the legal points relevant to that case. Fourthly, the guidance was almost invariably offered on an offence-by-offence basis, with little effort (and probably little opportunity) to relate the levels of sentence recommended for one offence to those recommended for others. Fifthly, appellants are entitled to have a reasonably speedy response to their appeal; indeed they have such a right under the European Convention on Human Rights.[67] Appeal courts can therefore seldom afford to take the time that is required to deliver comprehensive guideline judgments. Finally, few sentencing judges have any direct input to the appeals process.[68] The English system has

---

[63] (1983) 76 Cr. App. R. 190, (1982) 4 Cr. App. R. (S.) 407.

[64] The reasons for the difference in approach was explained in *R v Aranguren* (1994) 99 Cr. App. R. 347, (1995) 16 Cr. App. R. (S.) 211. Later decisions have revealed a distinct preference for guidance based on weight: *R v Morris* [2001] 1 Cr. App. R. (S.) 87; *R v Patel* (1987) 9 Cr. App. R. (S.) 319; *R v Mashaollahi* [2001] 1 Cr. App. R. (S.) 96.

[65] For an account of the main cases, see Ashworth, *Sentencing and Criminal Justice*, 5th edn (Cambridge: Cambridge University Press, 2010), pp.128–130.

[66] Young and Browning, "New Zealand's Sentencing Council" [2008] Crim L.R. 287 at 289.

[67] *Yetkinsekerci v United Kingdom,* European Court of Human Rights, October 20, 2005, [2005] All E.R.(D) 232 (Oct.); *Howarth v United Kingdom* (2001) 31 E.H.R.R. 861.

[68] In Ireland, the Court of Criminal Appeal consists of one Supreme Court judge and two High

now changed quite radically through a series of legislative innovations beginning with the establishment of the Sentencing Advisory Panel in 1998 and these will be considered presently.

The New Zealand Court of Appeal has gradually developed a body of sentencing guideline jurisprudence, rather similar to that of the English Court of Appeal prior to the establishment of the Sentencing Advisory Panel. In *R v Taueki*,[69] for example, it offered some guidance on the sentencing of serious violent offences, having first explained the purpose of the exercise in the following terms:

> "The principal objective of the guidelines set out in this judgment is consistency. Consistency has always been an objective of sentencing policy and s. 8(e) of the Sentencing Act 2002 now gives that statutory backing. We hope that this judgment will provide a single point of reference for sentencing Judges and counsel, and that this will lead to consistency in the sentencing levels imposed on offenders. What we seek to achieve is consistency in the approach adopted by sentencing Judges, which should in turn lead to consistency in sentencing levels. This does not override the discretion of sentencing Judges, but rather provides guidance in the manner of the exercise of that discretion."[70]

Following an analysis of the various factors that may legitimately be considered in assessing the seriousness of an assault offence, the court set out three sentencing bands or ranges for such offences, the first band ranging from three to six years, the second ranging from five to 10 years, and the third ranging from 9 to 14 years (the statutory maximum). It then proceeded to give examples of the kind of offences that might fall into each of these bands, and also clarified that the recommended starting points were to be treated as "the sentence appropriate for the particular offending (the combination of features) for an adult offender after a defended trial."[71] In other words, the starting point should take account of the aggravating and mitigating factors connected with the offence, but further adjustments may be made in respect of such factors as they relate to the offender. Similar guidance has been provided for other offences including drug offences.[72] The Court of Appeal has occasionally recommended the use of guidelines drawn up by the English Sentencing Guidelines Council for offences which had not yet been the subject of a guideline judgment within New Zealand

---

Court judges who may or may not have recent experience of presiding over a trial in the Central Criminal Court. Circuit Court judges who are responsible for sentencing the vast bulk of serious criminal cases in this country are not eligible to sit on the Court of Criminal Appeal.

[69] [2005] 3 N.Z.L.R. 372.

[70] [2005] 3 N.Z.L.R. 372 at 377.

[71] [2005] 3 N.Z.L.R. 372 at 377 citing *R v Mako* [2000] 2 N.Z.L.R. 170.

[72] *R v Terewi* [1999] 3 N.Z.L.R. 62 (cannabis cultivation); *R v Fatu* [2006] 2 N.Z.L.R. 72 (offences involving methamphetamine).

itself.[73] There is much to be said for the New Zealand approach which combines narrative guidance on the differentiation of offences falling into the same broad legal category (serious violent offences in *Taueki*) with concrete indications of appropriate starting points and sentence ranges. Assuming a reasonable level of compliance on the part of the trial judges and a reasonable level of vigilance on the part of appeal courts, this approach should produce a fair degree of consistency while leaving sufficient room for the exercise of discretion in exceptional circumstances. However, it also suffers from the weaknesses already identified in the English system by which it was clearly inspired. The New Zealand Court of Appeal usually alerts counsel to its intention to treat a case as an opportunity to offer a guideline judgment and often deals with a number of appeals together for this purpose. Inevitably, however, the guidance will be shaped, to some degree at least, by the facts of the cases under consideration and is generally confined to a particular offence or category of offence without reference to others. Legislation enacted in 2007 provided for the creation of a Sentencing Council charged with producing sentencing and parole guidelines.[74] The work programme envisaged for the Council was quite ambitious; it was intended to produce a comprehensive set of guidelines rather than adopt the incremental approach of the English Sentencing Guidelines Council. The guidelines were to be presumptively binding, though a court could depart from them where strict adherence would be contrary to the interests of justice. Some time after the Act came into force, a new Government, elected in 2008, decided not to proceed with creating guidelines, with the result that, so far, no sentencing council has been appointed. The Law Commission had already been working on draft guidelines and some of these have been used by the Court of Appeal in recent guideline judgments.[75]

Developments in England and Wales since 1998 illustrate how appeal courts and specialist agencies may fruitfully collaborate in providing more comprehensive sentencing guidance than appeal courts can generally manage on their own. The Crime and Disorder Act 1998 (ss.80–81) provided for the creation of a Sentencing Advisory Panel whose main function was to draft guidelines for the sentencing of particular offences and to recommend those guidelines to the Court of Appeal.[76] The Panel itself could select offences for this purpose, as it did in many cases, or the home secretary could refer an offence to it. Also,

---

[73]   *R v Clode* [2009] 1 N.Z.L.R. 312 (child pornography).
[74]   Sentencing Council Act 2007 (New Zealand).
[75]   Young and King, "Sentencing Practice and Guidance in New Zealand" (2010) 22 Fed. Sent. Rep. 254; Young and Browning (fn.66 above).
[76]   On the history of the Sentencing Advisory Panel and the Sentencing Guidelines Council up to 2008, see Ashworth, "English Sentencing Guidelines in their Public and Political Context" in Freiberg and Gelb (eds), *Penal Populism, Sentencing Councils and Sentencing Policy* (Cullompton: Willan Publishing, 2008), Ch.8. See also Robson, "The Sentencing Advisory Panel: An Under-Valued Institution" *Criminal Law and Justice Weekly,* August 15, 2009.

whenever the Court of Appeal was of the view that guidelines were needed for a particular offence, it first had to refer the matter to the Panel for its recommendations. This meant that the Court of Appeal could no longer deliver a guideline judgment based solely on the parties' submissions and its own assessment of appropriate sentence levels. It had to await the considered view of the Panel. However, the court could accept or reject, in whole or in part, the Panel's advice once it was tendered. Matters did not get off to a very good start when the court rejected the first advice offered by the Panel on sentencing environmental offences. Later, however, the court became much more receptive to the Panel's advice and many of the leading guideline judgments of the past decade, some of which such as *Millberry* on rape, *Oliver* on child pornography and *Cooksley* on dangerous driving causing death have been influential in other jurisdictions as well, resulted from the Panel's expert advice.[77] The great value of this advice was that it was based on solid research and was unconstrained by the facts of any particular case. As Ashworth and Wasik, both former Chairmen of the Panel, have written:

> "[The Panel's] distinctive approach was to examine the relevant sentencing law, to consider the statistics on sentencing for the type of offence, to consider the sentencing levels relative to comparable offences, and then to have a public consultation on a set of provisional proposals."[78]

The views of statutory consultees such as the Magistrates' Association, the Crown Prosecution Service and of other specialist organisations were also sought before any proposal was finalised. Nobody who has used or studied the Panel's reports can fail to be impressed by their quality. Most of them are of great comparative value for their penetrating analyses of the offences under consideration, of the varied circumstances in which those offences are committed, and of the relevant aggravating and mitigating factors. Leaving aside the recommended starting points and sentence ranges, which were obviously intended for application in England and Wales only, the reports provide a most useful model for other jurisdictions contemplating the introduction of a sentencing advisory system. On a few occasions, the Panel commissioned independent research on public attitudes to particular sentencing issues. Earlier research had shown that members of the public generally underestimate the severity of sentences imposed by the courts, but when they themselves are asked to suggest appropriate sentences, they generally select more lenient sentences than the courts

---

[77] *R v Millberry* [2003] 1 W.L.R. 546, [2003] 1 Cr. App. R. 25, [2003] 2 Cr. App. R. (S.) 31, [2003] 2 All E.R. 939; *R v Oliver* [2003] 1 Cr. App. R. 28, [2003] 2 Cr. App. R. (S.) 15; *R v Cooksley* [2003] 2 Cr. App. R. 18, [2004] 1 Cr. App. R. (S.) 1, [2003] 3 All E.R. 40.

[78] Ashworth and Wasik, "Ten Years of the Sentencing Advisory Panel" in *Annual Report of the Sentencing Guidelines Council and Sentencing Advisory Panel 2009/2010*, p.5. Professor Wasik was Chairman of the Panel from 1999 to 2007 while Professor Ashworth was Chairman from 2007 to 2010.

have in fact imposed. This trend was confirmed in a major study commissioned by the Panel in relation to domestic burglary (2001).[79] Similar surveys were later carried out in relation to rape (2002), offences involving death by driving (2008) and the general principles of sentencing (2009).

The Criminal Justice Act 2003 created a new body called the Sentencing Guidelines Council which was interposed between the Sentencing Advisory Panel, which remained in existence, and the Court of Appeal. Various reasons, none of them particularly convincing, were offered for this new arrangement. Certainly, it made little sense in retrospect to confine the Panel to recommending sentences for particular offences rather than granting it a wider remit to include more general issues such as reductions for guilty pleas. It might also be argued that there was a democratic deficit to the extent that Parliament did not have any formal role in the development of guidelines. All of these matters could have been addressed by way of statutory change. In any event, the Sentencing Guidelines Council, with judges forming a majority of the members, became responsible for the issue of final guidelines, having first received the Panel's advice. It then formulated draft guidelines having considered additional issues such as the consequential cost and the likely effectiveness of the recommended measures, and consulted with the Minister for Justice and the House of Commons Justice Committee. The Council would finally issue a definitive guideline to which courts were obliged to have regard. A court which passed a sentence outside of a recommended range was required to state its reasons for doing so.[80] Again, it must be said that the Council produced many useful guidelines and some of these, such as the definitive guidelines on assessing offence seriousness, credit for guilty pleas, failure to surrender to bail and the magistrates' court guidelines, are worthy of study in any common-law jurisdiction.[81]

This entire system has now been altered yet again by the Coroners and Justice Act 2009 (Part 4) which abolished the Sentencing Advisory Panel and the Sentencing Guidelines Council and replaced them with a Sentencing Council which combines the functions of both former bodies. Because the Council is charged with formulating guidelines which the courts are ordinarily bound to follow, it had originally been planned that it should consist entirely of judges in order to reflect a presumed constitutional principle that the formulation of sentencing policy is exclusively a judicial task. Eventually, however, it was

---

[79] Russell and Morgan, *Sentencing of Domestic Burglary*, Research Report 1 (London: Sentencing Advisory Panel, 2001).

[80] Ashworth (fn.76 above), p.114.

[81] Sentencing Guidelines Council, *Overarching Principles: Seriousness: Guideline* (2004); *Reduction in Sentence for a Guilty Plea: Definitive Guideline* (2007); *Failure to Surrender to Bail: Definitive Guideline* (2007); *Magistrates' Court Sentencing Guidelines* (2008 with later updates). The Council's publications, like those of the Sentencing Advisory Panel, can be accessed through the website of the present Sentencing Council at *www.sentencingcouncil. org.uk*.

decided that it should include some lay members as well, though judges form the majority.[82] The Council is charged with the creation of guidelines which "may be general in nature or limited to a particular offence, particular category of offences or particular category of offender."[83] Guidelines are supposed to specify the range of sentences appropriate for the relevant offence or for variations of that offence, and should also specify starting points. Every court "must follow" any guidelines that are relevant to the case being sentenced unless it is satisfied that it would be "contrary to the interests of justice to do so".[84] Previously, courts were merely requited to "have regard to" the guidelines created by the Sentencing Guidelines Council. The language of the 2009 Act has understandably caused concern among judges and lawyers who fear that the discretion of trial courts to fashion sentences appropriate to the circumstances of individual cases will be unduly constrained. Lord Justice Leveson has offered assurance that the Council, of which he is the Chairman, firmly recognises the need for discretion and individual judgment in sentencing, while also stressing that the guidelines are intended to promote more consistency and public confidence in sentencing.[85] Only time will tell if the new regime can manage to strike an acceptable balance between consistency and fairness.

ASSISTED APPELLATE REVIEW

The drawbacks associated with guideline development solely by way of appellate case law have already been noted,[86] and would doubtless apply to any initiative by the Irish Court of Criminal Appeal or Supreme Court to develop sentencing tariffs or benchmarks. Yet, appellate guidance remains the most promising way forward in a jurisdiction like this which suffers from a dearth of empirical information on existing sentencing practices and where there is a strong institutional resistance to any notion of externally-imposed guidelines. The challenge is to find a way of bridging the gap between the strong desire to leave the elaboration of sentencing principles to the judiciary and the undoubted need to develop more detailed and coherent principles than now exist. The answer, it is suggested, lies in some form of assisted appellate review whereby appeal courts would have access to more general information and broader policy analysis than can ordinarily be expected from submissions filed by the parties to a criminal appeal. More specifically, what is being advocated here, and elaborated upon the final chapter, is the creation of sentencing advisory or

---

[82] The Council consists of eight judicial members and six non-judicial members, all of whom have extensive experience or expertise in the area of sentencing and criminal justice.

[83] Coroners and Justice Act 2009 s.120(2).

[84] Section 125.

[85] See Lord Justice Leveson's address to Criminal Bar Association Conference, May 8, 2010, available at *www.sentencingcouncil.org.uk*.

[86] Page 115 et seq. above.

information unit charged with the ongoing task of gathering information on existing sentencing practice, collating and disseminating appeal court sentencing jurisprudence, and drawing up working documents on the problems and issues associated with the sentencing of particular offences and categories of offender. Like the Sentencing Council in England and Wales, it would also provide background documents on more general sentencing issues such as discounts for guilty pleas and the relevance of previous convictions. It would keep track of relevant sentencing jurisprudence in other common-law countries, an exercise which would be of great comparative value. This information-based function is now accepted in the United States as one of the major institutional advantages of a sentencing commission, irrespective of whether the commission is also charged with formulating official guidelines.[87]

The former Sentencing Advisory Panel of England and Wales provides a useful model for the structure being recommended here. The role, composition and remit of the two bodies need not be identical. Significant differences between the two countries in terms of overall population and the workloads of the criminal courts mean that Ireland can manage with less elaborate structures than are needed in England and Wales. However, the basic information needs are much the same. Ireland's recent experience in developing a sentencing information system clearly illustrates what can be achieved with relatively few resources. The challenge, as outlined in Chapter 7, is to find an efficient and cost-effective means of collecting trial court sentencing data on a regular, on-going basis. Achieving consistency of approach depends crucially on the quality of the guidance offered by appeal courts, and the capacity of any senior appeal court to fulfil its role as a forum of principle depends in turn on the quality of information and advice at its disposal. An advice or information unit of the kind being recommended here would not pose any constitutional difficulty, precisely because it would be doing nothing more than offering advice or information. It would not in any way attempt to influence the outcome of any specific case and its general recommendations would amount to no more than that. The Court of Criminal Appeal or, if called upon to do so, the Supreme Court would always make the final decision as to whether any particular recommendation should be adopted in whole or in part. The value of relevant empirical data and general advice was well stated by the Supreme Court of Wisconsin in 2004:

> "Information compiled by a sentencing commission will also be helpful in providing comparative data as to the length of sentence for the same crime and similarly situated defendants. The rule of law is advanced by providing advisory guidelines that channel outcomes in the majority of cases and serve as a touchstone for explaining the reasons for the particular sentence imposed.
>
> Experience has taught us to be cautious when reaching high consequence conclusions about human nature that seem to be intuitively correct at the

---

[87]   Chapter 6, fn.87 below.

moment. Better instead is a conclusion that is based on more complete and accurate information and reached by an organised framework for the exercise of discretion."[88]

That statement was made against the background of a truth-in-sentencing regime which involved, amongst other things, the abolition of parole, so not every aspect of it, such as the reference to a sentencing commission, is relevant to Ireland. But the general tenor of remarks, with their emphasis on the value of reliable data and settled principles, merits close attention.

In keeping with general public law rules and the principles of procedural justice, any advisory or information unit must operate openly and transparently. This means, in practical terms, that its reports, working papers and general advisory documents should be publicly available, preferably by means of a dedicated website. Lawyers and their clients would rightly object if, having heard submissions, an appeal court proceeded to seek advice or information on the issues raised from some other source without giving the parties an opportunity to offer further observations. In fact, the courts themselves have long since recognised the injustice of allowing any decision-making body in the public domain to rest its decision fully or partly on extraneous information.[89] Under the model being proposed here, all of the information unit's output would be publicly available, and therefore fully accessible to advocates or lay litigants wishing to incorporate relevant parts of it into their submissions. Such a system would promote a more constructive use of discretion by encouraging courts to engage in the progressive elaboration of principle. A point would eventually be reached at which fairly specific tariffs or benchmark sentences could be indicated, maybe not for all offences but at least for the more prevalent ones.

---

[88] *State v Gallion* 678 N.W. 2d 197 (Wis. 2004) at 206.

[89] O'Malley, *Sentencing Law and Practice*, 2nd edn (Dublin: Thomson Round Hall, 2006), pp.555–557. It was in recognition of this principle that the results of the pilot project on a sentencing information system were made available on a public website: *www.irishsentencing.ie*. See Ch.7 below.

CHAPTER 6

SENTENCING COMMISSIONS AND SENTENCING GUIDELINES

The most prominent characteristic of American sentencing reform over the past 30 years has been the establishment of sentencing commissions and guideline systems. While commissions, or structures very similar to them, have also been established or recommended in other countries, American-style guidelines have found few imitators elsewhere.[1] It is probably fair to say that the vast majority of Irish judges and lawyers would strongly oppose the introduction of similar guidelines here, though they might be prepared to accept less rigid structuring mechanisms. The merits and drawbacks of sentencing commissions and guideline systems cannot be understood without some appreciation of the legal and political environment in which they developed. Despite occasional references in this chapter to "American" sentencing issues, it must be recalled that the United States has 52 separate jurisdictions, and therefore as many sentencing systems. Each state has its own system, as do the federal jurisdiction and the District of Columbia. This, after all, is a country with a land mass in excess of nine million square kilometres and a population of more than 310 million. Considerable variations in legal and political culture can therefore be expected. The death penalty, for instance, is authorised in 34 states and the federal system, but is outlawed in the remaining 16 states and the District of Columbia.[2] Because of the way in which the United States was historically formed, the legal systems of the various states also have much in common. All, apart from Louisiana, are essentially common-law jurisdictions, while the federal Constitution, as interpreted by the United States Supreme Court, requires the states to protect basic civil and political rights including due process rights for criminal defendants. Most criminal law matters fall entirely within the purview of the states, each of which has its own criminal code. The federal criminal code and its associated sentencing system deal solely with offences against the federal government, offences with a cross-border dimension which do not fall directly

---

[1] An English working group established in 2007 to assess the feasibility of establishing a more structured sentencing system examined and expressly rejected the guideline systems operating in Minnesota and North Carolina, describing them as "far too restrictive of judicial discretion to be acceptable": Sentencing Commission Working Group, *Sentencing Guidelines in England and Wales: An Evolutionary Approach* (the Gage Report) (London, 2008), para.4.23.

[2] The death penalty is rarely carried out, or even imposed, in a majority of the retentionist states: Garland, "Five myths about the death penalty", *The Washington Post*, July 18, 2010.

with the jurisdiction of any one state, and certain additional matters.[3] This rather limited jurisdiction has not, however, prevented the federal prison population from undergoing a increase of 700 per cent between 1980 and 2009, rising from 24,000 to 208,000.[4]

Developments in sentencing policy within the United States over the past few decades must be considered in light of the scale and complexity of that country's criminal justice network. A few facts will suffice to illustrate its dimensions:

- The total population of the United States now exceeds 310 million.
- The overall prison population is approximately 2.3 million, including more than 760,000 held in local jails.
- The rate of incarceration, at 748 prisoners per 100,000 of the overall population in 2009, is the highest in the world, though it has declined very slightly over the past year or so.
- In 2009, one in every 135 Americans was imprisoned.
- One in ten black males aged 25 to 29 years was incarcerated in 2008, compared to one in 26 Hispanic and one in 63 white males in the same age group. A white male has a 6 per cent chance of spending time in prison at some point during his life while a black male has a 32 per cent chance.
- In 2008, 5.1 million adults were under some kind of community supervision, 84 per cent of these being probationers.
- Within the federal system alone, there are 94 district courts with 677 judges and 179 appeal court judges distributed among 13 circuits.
- There are approximately 30,000 authorised judges in all of the state courts combined, though about 18,000 of these are in limited jurisdiction courts.
- Approximately 1.4 million violent crimes, including 16,000 homicides were committed nationwide in 2008. The number of drug arrests at state and local levels in 2007 exceeded 1.8 million.[5]
- The number of persons released from state and federal prisons in 2009 was approximately 729,000, and an estimated 13 million people now have felony convictions.

---

[3] Over the years, however, the federal authorities have expanded their jurisdiction over drug offences, white-collar crime and, more recently, child pornography offences. Developments such as these have led to more federal prisoners serving longer sentences.

[4] Statistics provided by Federal Bureau of Prisons (*www.bop.gov*). See also Sentencing Project, *The Expanding Federal Prison Population* (Washington DC, 2011), available at *www.sentencingproject.org*. Only one in ten federal prisoners is incarcerated for a violent crime.

[5] Prison statistics are derived mainly from The Sentencing Project, *Facts about Prisons and Prisoners* (Washington DC, 2009) available at *www.sentencingproject.org*. Data on state courts based on *State Court Caseload Statistics, 2007* (National Centre for State Courts, 2008), available at *www.ncsonline.org*. Information on the federal court system, probation statistics and overall crime statistics are drawn from various US Department of Justice websites (*www.justice.gov*). More up-to-date information on sentencing developments at state level is provided by Porter, *The State of Sentencing 2010: Developments in Policy and Practice* (Washington DC: The Sentencing Project, 2011), available at *www.sentencingproject.org*.

The ideological chasm between certain American states and comparable European countries is illustrated by the size of their respective prison populations. Indiana, for example, has a general population of 6.3 million and a prison population of 28,000, while Ohio has a general population of 11.5 million with a prison population of 52,000. Denmark and Finland, each with a general population of roughly 5.5 million, have prison populations of approximately 3,500.[6] Ireland, with a general population of about 4.5 million currently has about 4,500 prisoners. The United States is, of course, the world leader when it comes to the use of incarceration, as is clear from the facts just outlined.[7] Russia comes next with approximately 600 prisoners per 100,000 of the population.

THE RETREAT FROM INDETERMINATE SENTENCING

The modern history of American sentencing law revolves around the adoption of indeterminate sentencing and its later replacement with more structured, determinate systems. At a slightly deeper level it is about the embrace, and then the rejection, of rehabilitation as the dominant purpose of sentencing. By most accounts, indeterminate sentencing flourished in the United States from the late nineteenth century until the late 1970s, although in some states it continues to exist in various forms.[8] The expression "indeterminate" as it is used in modern sentencing literature is apt to confuse as it often means no more than discretionary sentencing as we know it. However, indeterminate sentencing in most American jurisdictions, including the federal system, had certain characteristics which distinguished it from discretionary sentencing models elsewhere. Most notable among these was the power vested in parole authorities to decide when a prisoner should be released. A trial court could impose any sentence up to the maximum permitted by statute, but the parole board decided on the actual release date.[9] This, in theory, was perfectly compatible with a rehabilitative philosophy of punishment. Being unable to predict exactly how long it would take to reform or rehabilitate an offender, the trial judge could do no more than

---

6   Walmsley, *World Prison Population List*, 8th edn (International Centre for Prison Studies, King's College London, 2009).

7   Most striking perhaps is the contrast with Canada which has a general population of 34 million, a prison population of about 38,000, and an incarceration rate of 116 per 100,000 of the population which is about one-fifth of the equivalent rate in the United States.

8   Friedman, *Crime and Punishment in American History* (New York: BasicBooks, 1993), pp.159–161, 304–308; Anon, "The Indeterminate Sentence" (1908) 11 *Atlantic Monthly* 320; Zalman, "The Rise and Fall of the Indeterminate Sentence" (1977) 24 Wayne L.R. 45 and 857. The Supreme Court effectively approved the notion of indeterminate sentences with their reformative purpose in *Williams v New York* 337 U.S. 241, 248 (1949).

9   Tonry, "Judges and Sentencing Policy – the American Experience" in Munro and Wasik (eds), *Sentencing, Judicial Discretion and Training* (London: Sweet and Maxwell, 1992), p.137 at p.153 ("'Determinate' signifies that the duration of a prison sentence can be calculated at the time of sentencing, subject only to reduction as a result of operation of 'good time' laws").

impose a sentence of sufficient length to enable the prison system to achieve its rehabilitative mission. Release could be ordered whenever the relevant parole board considered the offender fit to rejoin the community. The sentencing function was therefore split between two authorities: the judge and the parole board. Most prisoners were released after serving a fraction of the judicially-imposed sentence, typically one-third in the federal system,[10] which meant that the parole board was often the real sentencer. Indeterminate sentencing took various forms. A judge might impose a fixed sentence, say 12 years, knowing that the parole board would grant release long before that term expired. Sometimes judicial sentences were expressed in minimum and maximum terms, such as one to seven years. In that case, the offender would serve at least one year after which the parole board was free to grant release according to its own terms.[11] In *Gore v United States*,[12] for example, it is recorded that the offender was sentenced to one to five years on each count, the sentences on the first three counts to be consecutive and the remainder to be concurrent. This amounted to a total judicial sentence of three to 15 years, but once three years had been served, the actual release date was a matter for the parole board. Similar arrangements applied in many states. In California, for example, the sentence judicially imposed for a felony was almost invariably one year to life in prison, leaving the parole authority to determine the actual duration of sentence.[13] The dominant role of parole authorities within the sentencing process was reflected in the eventual adoption of parole guidelines, especially within the federal system, which were intended to inject some measure of rationality and consistency into parole release decisions.[14]

Another important feature of the pre-guideline era, and one which accentuated the indeterminate nature of American sentencing, was the virtual absence of sentence appeals. This may seem strange from our vantage point, though we should recall that it is barely a century since appellate review of sentence was

---

[10] *United States v Grayson* 438 U.S. 41 at 47 (1977): "Thus it is that today the extent of a federal prisoner's confinement is initially determined by the sentencing judge, who selects a term from within an often broad, congressionally prescribed range; release on parole is then available on review by the United States Parole Commission which, as a general rule, may conditionally release a prisoner any time after he serves one-third of the judicially-fixed term" (Burger C.J. delivering the Opinion of the court). See also *Barber v Thomas* 560 U.S. – (June 7, 2010).

[11] *Geraghty v United States Parole Commission* 719 F.2d 1199 (1983). The court noted that the Commission operated according to guidelines under which it first determined the gravity of the offence of conviction, and secondly the likelihood that the prisoner would succeed on parole. Good institutional conduct and performance on any rehabilitative programmes were taken into account for this purpose.

[12] 357 U.S. 386 (1957).

[13] Stith and Cabranes, *Fear of Judging: Sentencing Guidelines in the Federal Courts* (Chicago: University of Chicago Press, 1998), p.21.

[14] Zalman (fn.8 above); Hoffman and DeGostin, "Parole Decision-Making: Structuring Discretion" (1974) 38:4 *Federal Probation* 7.

introduced in these islands.[15] The United States federal system in particular adhered with surprising tenacity to the common-law doctrine that sentences imposed within jurisdiction were unreviewable. For a brief period in the late nineteenth century, from 1879 to 1891 to be exact, federal appeal courts were empowered to review and reduce excessive sentences. However, there was no express mention of this power in legislation enacted in 1891 establishing the circuit appeal courts system. Appeal courts generally interpreted this as meaning that, absent an error of law or a conflict with a recognised constitutional principle, they had no power to review a sentence simply because it appeared to be excessive.[16] This often resulted in manifestly excessive sentences being left undisturbed where the applicant was unable to demonstrate legal error. In *Smith v United States*,[17] for example, a 51-year-old man with no previous record was fined and sentenced to 52 years' imprisonment for narcotics offences. While appearing to accept that the sentence was excessive, the appeals court said it was powerless to offer any redress. Some years earlier, and much more controversially, neither the Court of Appeals nor the Supreme Court was willing to interfere with the death penalty imposed by Judge Irving Kaufman on Julius and Ethel Rosenberg following their conviction for espionage, although a term of imprisonment could have been imposed instead.[18] Writing for the Court of Appeals, Judge Frank said: "Unless we are to overrule sixty years of undeviating federal precedent, we must hold that an appellate court has no power to modify a sentence."[19] The Supreme Court's view of the matter was put beyond doubt in *Gore v United States* where Frankfurter J., delivering the court's opinion, bluntly stated: "First the English and then the Scottish Courts of Criminal Appeal were given power to revise sentences, the power to increase as well as the power to reduce them ... This Court has no such power."[20] From the late nineteenth

---

[15] Chapter 5 above.

[16] Kutak and Gottschalk, "In Search of a Rational Sentence: A Return to the Concept of Appellate Review" (1974) 53 Nebraska L.R.463 (which has a detailed analysis of the 1891 legislation and the relevant case law); Labbe, "Appellate Review of Sentences: Penology on the Judicial Doorstep" (1977) 68 *Journal of Criminal Law and Criminology* 122; Weigel, "Appellate Revision of Sentences: To Make the Punishment Fit the Crime" (1968) 20 Stanford L R. 405; Mueller, "Penology on Appeal: Appellate Review of Legal but Excessive Sentences" (1962) 15 Vanderbilt L.R. 671; Mueller and Le Poole, "Appellate Review of Legal but Excessive Sentences: A Comparative Study" (1968) 21 Vanderbilt L.R. 411; Hall, "Reduction of Criminal Sentences on Appeal: I" (1937) 37 Columbia L.R. 521.

[17] 273 F 2d. 462 (10th Cir. 1959). See Note, "Appellate Modification of Excessive Sentence" (1960) 46 Iowa L.R. 159.

[18] *United States v Rosenberg* 195 F.2d 583 (2nd Cir. 1952); *Rosenberg v United States* 344 U.S. 889 (1952) where Frankfurter J. said: "A sentence imposed by the United States District Court, even though it be a death sentence, is not within the power of this court to revise."

[19] 195 F.2d 583 at 604 (1952). In *Gurera v United States* 40 F. 2d 338 at 340–341 (8th Cir. 1930), the Court of Appeals had said: "If there is one rule in the federal criminal practice which is firmly established, it is that appellate court has no control over a sentence which is within the limits allowed by statute."

[20] 357 U.S. 386 at 393 (1957). See also *Dorszynski v United States* 418 U.S. 424 (1973).

century onwards, some of the States had become more adventurous in granting rights of appeal against excessive sentences. In fact, Iowa had introduced such a law as early as 1860.[21] A survey published in 1977 showed that 23 states had some form of sentence review, though it also showed that appeals were virtually unknown in some of these states (even where sentence could be increased as well as reduced on appeal).[22] The precise circumstances in which appeal or review was permissible varied from one state to another, and certain inbuilt statutory limitations probably explain why appeals were a rarity even when formally permitted. In Colorado, to take just one example, appeals were available solely against sentences in excess of three years imposed for a felony conviction. Still, the absence of a robust system of merit-based sentence appeals within the federal system right up to the adoption of the Sentencing Guidelines in 1987 remains surprising, and it was certainly not for want of recommendations from bar associations, judges, academics and others.[23]

The availability of merit-based appeals represented a very significant difference between the British-Irish and American sentencing systems, and should give us pause for thought on the perils of unreflective policy transfer. Whether in relation to sentencing or any other aspect of social policy, innovative structures introduced elsewhere must always be examined and evaluated by reference to the particular problems or deficiencies which they were intended to address. Had there been an effective sentence appeals system within the United States federal jurisdiction, the need for guidelines might not have been so pressing.[24] Granted, it is difficult to imagine a sentence appeals system generating a great deal of consistency across such a vast territory, and significant variations would almost inevitably have materialised between, if not within, the various circuits. But the availability of merit-based appeals might have prompted policy-makers to opt for a less rigid structuring mechanism than the federal guidelines. In smaller and more manageable jurisdictions, appeals hold much more promise as a vehicle for generating consistency of approach, if nothing else. This is particularly true of a unitary jurisdiction, such as Ireland or England and Wales, where a single criminal appeal court can establish sentencing standards, of whatever degree of specificity, for the guidance of trial courts.[25]

---

[21] Mueller (fn.16 above).

[22] Labbe (fn.16 above).

[23] Sobeloff, "A Recommendation for Appellate Review of Criminal Sentences" (1954) 21 Brooklyn L.R. 2 (the author was then United States Solicitor General); Weigel (fn.16 above) (the author was then a federal District Court judge); Note, "Power of Appellate Court to Modify Sentences on Appeal" (1933) 9 Wisconsin L.R. 172.

[24] Gertner, "Supporting Advisory Guidelines" (2009) 3 *Harvard Law and Policy Review* 261 at 264 (how the absence of appeals removed the incentive for judges to create standards through written judgments, and prevented the development of effective sentencing advocacy).

[25] This, admittedly, applies to the sentencing of serious offences only, as sentencing decisions of summary jurisdiction courts are usually appealed to intermediate appellate courts which are organised on a regional basis. See Ch.5 above.

Another institutional difference between Ireland and other common-law countries on one hand, and the United States on the other, which is worth mentioning at this point is that in many American states judges are elected, and their sentencing record may play a significant role in re-election campaigns. Some 39 states elect at least some of their judges, and the recent Supreme Court decision in *Citizens United v FEC*[26] allows corporations and unions to devote unlimited funds to supporting campaigns for state and federal office, including state judicial appointments. There have been instances of senior state judges failing to secure re-election because of unpopular decisions which they made. Successful campaigns were waged against Chief Justice Rose Bird of California's Supreme Court in 1986 and Justice Penny White of Tennessee's Supreme Court in 1996 because of their perceived opposition to the death penalty. Neither was re-elected. Federal judges are appointed and, subject to good behaviour, have life tenure. However, in those states where judicial tenure lacks insulation from the whims of popular opinion and the impact of well-orchestrated opposition campaigns, it is understandable that radical steps may be necessary to control sentencing practice. In that kind of political environment, state-wide guidelines, or something similar, may be necessary to ensure that judicial sentencing is not unduly influenced by the prospect or threat of electoral defeat. That particular problem does not, however, arise where judges, once appointed, enjoy security of tenure.

THE MOVEMENT TOWARDS DETERMINATE SENTENCING

Rehabilitation and incapacitation were the animating objectives of indeterminate sentencing in the United States. Imprisonment was officially believed to have the capacity to reform, though how sincerely key decision-makers held this belief is difficult to assess. The official adoption of rehabilitation may be traced back to 1929 when the US Congress established the Federal Bureau of Prisons which was charged, amongst other things, with the provision of individualised discipline, care and treatment to inmates.[27] By this time, social work, psychology and psychiatry were coming into their own as professional and academic disciplines, and they held great promise in terms of their capacity to generate both individual and social change.[28] In 1949, the United States Supreme Court confidently proclaimed that retribution was no longer the dominant objective of

---

[26] 130 S. Ct. 876 (2010). The Brennan Center at NYU Law School has an excellent website, *www.brennancenter.org*, on judicial elections and related matters. See, in particular, Skaggs, *Buying Justice: the Impact of Citizens United on Fair Elections* (2010), available on that website. He reports (p.3) that "[f]rom 2000 to 2009, an estimated $93.6 million was spent on television advertising by candidates and interest groups hoping to sway judicial contests".

[27] Bates, *Prisons and Beyond* (New York: Macmillan Co., 1936).

[28] Frank, "The American Prison: The End of an Era" (1979) 43 *Federal Probation* 3.

the criminal law; reform and rehabilitation had become more important goals.[29] The erosion of faith in rehabilitation as a sentencing objective and in the indeterminate system that it underpinned has been well charted.[30] Suffice it to say that from the early 1970s onwards, the rehabilitative ideal came under attack from liberal critics who claimed that actions taken in the name of rehabilitation often seriously infringed prisoners' rights, and from conservative critics who saw it as producing inconsistent and, often, unduly lenient sentences. In the 1960s, sentencing councils were established in a few federal district court areas to provide a forum where judges could discuss with their judicial colleagues the sentences they might impose in forthcoming cases. A council's role was purely advisory and judges were ultimately free to impose whatever sentences they deemed appropriate.[31] In 1972, a federal District Court judge, Marvin Frankel, published a book entitled *Criminal Sentences: Law without Order*, and it is probably fair to say that few other works since Beccaria's *On Crimes and Punishments*, published in 1764, have had such a transformative impact on the sentencing system of any country. Frankel's book, the title of which was deliberately and cleverly chosen, amounted to a searing indictment of the sentencing practices prevailing at the time. Page after page, it bristles with eloquent condemnations of the pervasive and unchecked disparity which, in Frankel's view, characterised the sentencing system at that time. He called for the creation of an administrative commission that would create guidelines, though he probably did not envisage the development of guidelines as complex and binding as those which eventually became operative in the federal system in 1987. What cannot be doubted, however, is that this book ignited or at least reinvigorated political interest in sentencing and may therefore be seen as a progenitor of the federal guidelines. Some would now argue in hindsight that Frankel protested too much.[32] Although serving as a federal judge when he wrote the book, he clearly did not hold most trial judges in very high regard and, probably as a result of this, failed to balance his condemnation of disparity with an appreciation of the value of discretion.[33] He relied heavily on anecdote and offered little, if any, empirical evidence to support his claims. Federal sentencing was certainly in an unsatisfactory state at the time, particularly because of the decisive role of parole authorities, but a more nuanced critique of the system

---

[29] *Williams v New York* 337 U.S. 241, 248 (1949).

[30] Allen, *The Decline of the Rehabilitative Ideal: Penal Policy and Social Purpose* (New Haven: Yale University Press, 1981); O'Hear, "The Original Intent of Uniformity in Federal Sentencing" (2006) 74 Univ. Cincinnati L.R. 749 at 757–758

[31] Diamond and Zeisel, "Sentencing Councils: A Study of Sentence Disparity and its Reduction" (1975) 45 Univ. Chicago L.R. 109.

[32] Adelman and Deitrich, "Marvin Frankel's Mistakes and the Need to Rethink Federal Sentencing" (2008) 13 *Berkeley Journal of Criminal Law* 239.

[33] He claimed, for example, that in any given case the sentencing judge might be "punitive, patriotic, self-righteous, guilt-ridden, and more than customarily dyspeptic" (*Criminal Sentences: Law without Order*, p.23).

might have led Frankel to propose a more flexible remedy. Other influential reports and writings from this era also recommended more structured judicial sentencing, whether in the form of presumptive sentences or guidelines.[34]

Concern about sentencing disparity was by no means confined to the federal system. By the late 1970s, indeterminate sentencing had begun to fall out of favour in the United States generally and several individual states embarked on efforts to develop more structured sentencing systems.[35] Maine, for example, abolished parole in 1975 without, at the same time, establishing any kind of sentencing commission while California adopted a determinate sentencing system in 1977.[36] The immediate motivations for imposing or adopting guidelines varied from one state to another. In the mid-1970s, North Carolina had the highest imprisonment rate of any American state. A growing crisis over prison space, which at one time involved the threat of a federal takeover, and an extraordinary high level of early release for those serving sentences, led to a series of initiatives including the Fair Sentencing Act 1981 which did not have much effect and, eventually, the creation of a Sentencing and Policy Advisory Commission which remains in existence.[37] Some states experimented with commissions but decided not to retain them or later replaced them with different models.[38] The process is on-going, as individual states respond to emerging problems and policy preoccupations. Controlling and reducing the prison population has become the dominant concern of many states in recent years because of severe budgetary constraints. More and more states are taking steps to repeal at least some of their mandatory minimum sentences, to offer greater support to treatment programmes and even to expand the availability of parole. Whatever the future may hold in store for the guidelines movement, one thing seems certain and it is that the financial considerations will determine the shape of most sentencing reform initiatives for many years to come.

---

[34] Twentieth Century Fund Task Force on Criminal Sentencing, *Fair and Certain Punishment* (New York: McGraw-Hill, 1976); Fogel, *We Are the Living Proof: The Justice Model for Corrections* (Anderson, Cincinnati, 1975); von Hirsch, *Doing Justice: the Choice of Punishments: Report of the Committee for the Study of Incarceration* (New York: Hill and Wang, 1976).

[35] Frase, "Sentencing Guidelines in Minnesota, 1978–2003" in Tonry (ed.), *Crime and Justice: A Review of Research* Vol. 32 (Chicago: University of Chicago Press, 2005), p.131 at p.142: Blumstein, Cohen, Martin and Tonry (eds), *Research on Sentencing: The Search for Reform* Vol. 1 (Washington DC: National Academy Press, 1983).

[36] Page 141 below.

[37] Wright, "Counting the Cost of Sentencing in North Carolina, 1980–2000" in Tonry (ed.), *Crime and Justice: A Review of Research* Vol. 29 (Chicago: University of Chicago Press, 2002), p.39; Freeman, *The North Carolina Sentencing and Policy Advisory Commission: A History of its Creation and its Development of Structured Sentencing* (Raleigh, NC, 2009).

[38] Missouri, for example, has had three sentencing commissions since 1989. The most recent, appointed in 2003, the Missouri Sentencing Advisory Commission (MOSAC) still exists. See Wolff, "Missouri's Information-Based Discretionary Sentencing System" (2006) 4 Ohio State J. Crim. Law 95.

SENTENCING COMMISSIONS AND GUIDELINES

For a variety of reasons, the federal sentencing guidelines tend to dominate American sentencing discourse although they apply to no more than a minority of defendants convicted in American courts.[39] This is partly attributable to the lengthy and well-documented gestation period of the federal guidelines which began shortly after the publication of Frankel's book and ended with their formal adoption in April 1987, and partly also to the extensive scholarship which has developed around them over the past 20 years.[40] Other factors have contributed as well, notably the landmark Supreme Court decision in *United States v Booker*[41] which rendered the guidelines advisory rather than mandatory and some later decisions clarifying the implications of that transformation.[42] The federal guidelines and their provenance will be discussed presently, but first we should note that they represent only one species of guideline system currently operating in the United States. In fact, many states have no formal guideline system, preferring to rely on judicial discretion, appellate review, statutory prescription or some combination of these. As far back as 1977, California adopted a determinate sentencing regime whereby three possible terms of imprisonment were prescribed for most offences. The middle term must be selected in the absence of factors which justify imposing either the lower or higher term instead. In *Cunningham v California*,[43] for example, where the offence was one of continuous sexual abuse of a child, the available terms were 6 years, 12 years and 16 years. Recent suggestions that California should create a sentencing commission have failed to find sufficient political support.

In the late 1970s, Minnesota, Pennsylvania and Washington set about creating sentencing commissions and guidelines. There had been some earlier, though mainly unsuccessful, attempts in other States, but the Minnesota guidelines which entered into force in 1980 have been well regarded from the outset, and continue to provide a model of how an effective guidelines system might work.[44]

---

[39] Berman and Chanenson, "The Real (Sentencing) World: State Sentencing in the Post-*Blakely* Era" (2006) 4 *Ohio State Journal of Criminal Law* 27. They record (fn.9) that in 2002 state courts accounted for 94 per cent of all adult felony convictions in the United States.

[40] Stith and Cabranes, *Fear of Judging: Sentencing Guidelines in the Federal Courts* (Chicago: University of Chicago Press, 1998); Breyer, "The Federal Sentencing Guidelines and the Key Compromises on which They Rest" (1988) 17 Hofstra L.R. 1, 3.

[41] 543 U.S. 220 (2005). This decision, in turn, had been widely forecast following earlier decisions in *Apprendi v New Jersey* 530 U.S 466 (2000) and, more particularly, *Blakely v Washington* 542 U.S. 296 (2004).

[42] *Gall v United States* 552 U.S. 38 (2007); *Kimbrough v United States* 552 U.S. 85 (2007); *Rita v United States* 551 U.S. 338 (2007).

[43] 549 U.S. 270 (2007). In this case, the Supreme Court found that California's determinate sentencing law violated the Sixth Amendment of the federal Constitution by allowing a judge rather than a jury to engage in fact-finding which led to a higher sentence, thus applying *United States v Booker* 543 U.S. 220 (2005) to the Californian regime.

[44] On earlier efforts, see Tonry, "Structuring Sentencing" in Tonry and Morris (eds), *Crime and Justice: A Review of Research* (Chicago: University of Chicago Press, 1988), p.267.

A study undertaken by the National Centre for State Courts and published in 2008 identified 21 states with guideline systems of one kind or another.[45] Those systems vary enormously in terms of the extent to which they constrain judicial discretion and the extent to which their application is effectively monitored through appellate review. Some have been accompanied by the abolition of parole, others not. Some apply to a wide range of offences, others to a fairly narrow range of commonly-prosecuted felonies. Some manage better than others to accommodate non-custodial sanctions as well as imprisonment. The nomenclature applied to the various guideline systems is apt to confuse because it is not always clear, from a distance at least, what precisely is meant by "mandatory", "presumptive", "voluntary" and "advisory". Reitz perhaps comes closest to reality when he portrays the various state sentencing systems as operating along a continuum extending from untrammelled judicial discretion at one end to a system of fixed punishments at the other.[46] Few systems, if any, can properly be located at either extreme, but the remainder can be fixed at different points in between. Labels such as "presumptive" and "voluntary" are not particularly helpful descriptions of guideline systems without further investigation as to how they operate in practice. Prior to *Booker*, and as discussed more fully below, the federal guidelines were mandatory in the sense that trial judges had no option but to apply them. Yet, they could also be described as presumptive in the sense that some deviation from the prescribed sentence range was permissible in exceptional circumstances. Guidelines are sometimes treated as voluntary when judges are free to follow or ignore them at will, and as advisory when judges are free to depart from them provided they state their reasons for doing so.[47] Some voluntary guideline systems actually have high compliance levels.[48] In some systems departures may be subject to

---

[45] National Centre for State Courts (NCSC), *State Sentencing Guidelines: Profiles and Continuum* (Williamsburg, VA: NCSC, 2008). See also Frase, "State Sentencing Guidelines: Diversity, Consensus, and Unresolved Policy Issues" (2005) 105 Columbia L.R. 1190, who found guidelines operating in 18 states and the District of Columbia. As the NCSC remarks, it can be surprisingly difficult to identify if certain guideline systems are still operational which explains why studies may report different numbers of guideline states.

[46] Reitz, "The Enforceability of Sentencing Guidelines" (2005) 58 Stanford L.R. 155. See also Frase, "Is Guided Discretion Sufficient? Overview of State Sentencing Guidelines" (2000) 44 St. Louis Univ. L.J. 425.

[47] Hunt and Connelly, "Advisory Guidelines in the Post-Blakely Era" (2005) 17:4 Fed. Sent. Rep. 233. ("Advisory guidelines, operating in nine states and the District of Columbia, are sentencing guidelines that do not require a judge to impose a recommended sentence but that may require the judge to provide justification for imposing a sentence that is different from what is recommended.") Guidelines are sometimes classed as voluntary when adopted by judges without prompting from any other authority.

[48] Frase (fn.45 above), at 1198. In Maryland, which has voluntary guidelines, the State Commission on Criminal Sentencing Policy (MSCCSP) has a compliance goal of 65 per cent. This goal was exceeded in 2008 with most departures being below rather than above the recommended guideline: MSCCSP, *Annual Report 2008* (available at *www.msccsp.org*).

appellate review at the instance of the defence, the prosecution or both. However, there is nothing formal about this classification; regard must always be had to the precise terms of the governing legislation in each state.

Some guideline systems have been developed by sentencing commissions specifically appointed for that purpose, while others have been directly created by legislation. Commissions are worthy of close study in their own right, especially for comparative purposes, because their remit often extends well beyond the development of guidelines. One great advantage of a commission is that it is, or ideally should be, non-partisan and it can operate at a remove from the mainstream political system.[49] Because it is usually composed of judges, criminologists and other specialists, it is insulated from political pressure to respond to the shifting preferences and preoccupations of the public at large. Criminal legislation in general and sentencing legislation in particular is most likely to be enacted in a piecemeal fashion dealing with isolated offences or groups of offences. A commission, on the other hand, is usually charged with formulating policy in relation to sentencing generally or, at least, for a broad spectrum of offences. Furthermore, its conclusions and recommendations are likely to be based on a close examination of existing sentencing practices, and designed to further certain normative objectives which have been well discussed and analysed. Standing or permanent commissions have the additional advantage of being able to monitor sentencing practice on an ongoing basis, to identify trends and to assess the extent to which courts are adhering to any applicable guidelines or standards. These are among the reasons why the American Law Institute in redrafting the Model Penal Code sentencing provisions has recommended the creation of sentencing commissions whose initial task will be to formulate presumptive guidelines.[50] Few jurisdictions outside of the United States have shown much appetite for grid-based guidelines but the idea of a sentencing commission has proved to be much more palatable. Some Australian jurisdictions have bodies similar to commissions which engage in ongoing research on sentencing practices and issues, while the various bodies established in England and Wales from the former Sentencing Advisory Panel to the present Sentencing Council have been charged with carrying out research on sentencing as well as recommending or producing guidelines (though not grid-based guidelines). There are some, of course, who oppose the idea of a sentencing

---

[49] Frase, "The Minnesota Sentencing Guidelines" in Freiberg and Gelb (eds), *Penal Populism, Sentencing Councils and Sentencing Policy* (Cullompton: Willan Publishing, 2008), p.83 ("[I]ndependent sentencing commissions are valued not only for their expertise and research capacity but also because they promote a long-term, fiscally responsible perspective and help to insulate sentencing policy development from short-term political pressures driven by sudden shifts in public opinion.")

[50] American Law Institute, *Model Penal Code Sentencing* Tentative Draft 1 (Philadelphia, 2007), p.10 ("When a commission is properly constituted, it brings unique credibility to the task, due to its diverse membership drawn from all sectors of the criminal-justice system and from the broader community ... a commission brings collective, diverse, and informed judgments to the task, and is well positioned to think comparatively about offences throughout the criminal code").

commission precisely because it is non-political. They argue that within a democracy, elected politicians must be responsive to public concerns about crime and the levels of punishment meted out to convicted offenders. According to this view, politicians are reneging on one of their most fundamental responsibilities, the promotion of public safety, if they decide to delegate the formulation of sentencing policy to an independent body. Yet, the arguments in favour of an independent commission remain compelling, principally because of its capacity to adopt a holistic approach in formulating policy, and because it need not feel pressurised to respond to every public panic that happens to arise over some particular kind of crime. This is not to suggest that sentencing policy should be immune from any political control. There is, of course, considerable force in the democratic argument, but political control may be exercised by way of general directions to a commission which, in turn, should be ready to engage with the political system when it comes to creating, reformulating or revising sentencing policy.

Many state guidelines, like those operating in the federal system, are centred on a two-dimensional grid with offence seriousness measured along the vertical axis and a criminal history score along the horizontal axis. This arrangement is interesting from a common-law perspective as it reflects a clear belief that sentence severity should progressively increase according to the number of previous convictions, a principle that is by no means free of theoretical difficulties. The Minnesota Guidelines, which cover felonies only, have 11 offence levels and 7 categories of prior criminal record ranging from zero to six or more. It also has a dispositional line separating lower and higher level scores. Those offenders who fall below that line are, with some exceptions, presumptively entitled to a stayed sentence which means that they are unlikely to undergo immediate custody. State imprisonment is the presumptive sentence for those who find themselves above the dispositional line. Each cell above the line indicates a presumptive sentence in terms of months' imprisonment, together with a range from which a sentence can be selected without it being deemed a departure. Thus, third-degree murder attracts a presumptive sentence of 150 months where the offender has a criminal history score of zero, but any sentence within the range of 128 to 180 months may be imposed. Departure is permissible only where there are identifiable, substantial and compelling circumstances to justify a sentence outside the specified range, and judges must always give reasons for departure. Having only 11 categories of offence seriousness, the Minnesota guidelines are much more manageable than the federal guidelines which have 43 levels of seriousness. Minnesota now has a separate guidelines grid for sex offenders which is constructed in the same manner as the main grid and which has its own dispositional line. The guidelines are kept under constant review by a standing sentencing commission and a revised edition is issued annually.[51] The

---

[51] The Minnesota Sentencing Guidelines Commission has an excellent website where the guidelines manual and other material can be found: *www.msgc.state.mn.us*. For a detailed

North Carolina Guidelines, which came into effect in 1994 and have been revised periodically since then, are also centred on a grid rather like the Minnesota Guidelines but structured in a slightly different way. Within each cell on the principal grid which deals with felonies, there are three sentence ranges: a presumptive range, a mitigated range and an aggravated range. Imprisonment is mandatory in all those cells marked "A" (and that accounts for the vast majority of them); intermediate punishment is possible in those marked "I" and community punishment in those marked "C". There is a separate grid for misdemeanours. These guidelines appear to have had some measure of success in keeping the prison population under control. North Carolina used to have the highest rate of imprisonment in the United States. By the early years of this century, it had fallen below the national average.[52] As already noted, and as all leading American commentators emphasise, state guideline systems vary considerably in purpose and content. The Minnesota and North Caroline guideline systems have briefly been described here just to indicate what can be achieved through grid-based systems.

The federal guidelines

Following on the publication of Judge Frankel's *Criminal Sentences: Law without Order* in 1972, the idea of a federal sentencing commission started to gain congressional support most notably in a bill sponsored by Senator Edward Kennedy.[53] After many political twists and turns, Congress eventually passed the Sentencing Reform Act 1984 (SRA) which established the United States Sentencing Commission whose main task, initially at any rate, was to create sentencing guidelines. The seven-member Commission consisted of three federal judges, three professors (one each of law, sociology and economics) and a member of the United States Parole Commission which, rather ironically, was being abolished under the SRA. There was also an ex officio non-voting member representing the Department of Justice. Some of the non-judicial members were already on record as strong opponents of judicial discretion. Apparently, only one member of the Commission, the Chairman, Judge Wilkins, had any experience of sentencing at trial court level.[54] Anyone who has grown accustomed to the

---

account of the guidelines and their development, see Frase, "Sentencing Guidelines in Minnesota, 1978–2003" in Tonry (ed.), *Crime and Justice: A Review of Research* Vol. 32 (Chicago: University of Chicago Press, 2005).

[52] Wright, "Counting the Cost of Sentencing in North Carolina, 1980–2000" in Tonry (ed.), *Crime and Justice: A Review of Research* Vol. 29 (Chicago: University of Chicago Press, 2002), p.39; Wright, "*Blakely* and the Centralizers in North Carolina" (2005) 18:1 Fed. Sent. Rep. 19.

[53] The Kennedy-McClellan Bill (1977). See Tonry and Morris, "Sentencing Reform in America" in Glazebrook (ed.), *Reshaping the Criminal Law: Essays in Honour of Glanville Williams* (London: Stevens & Co., 1978), p.434.

[54] For further information on the Commissioners, see Stith and Cabranes (fn.13 above), pp.49–51.

gentle pace of Irish tribunals of inquiry can only marvel at the accomplishments of the United States Sentencing Commission between its appointment in late October 1985 and the finalisation of the proposed Guidelines in April 1987. During this time, it analysed 10,000 past cases and drew up guidelines covering virtually all federal offences. Such a short timescale also had its drawbacks. For one thing, it left the Commission with little opportunity to probe the causes of the disparity that seemed so prevalent in existing sentencing practice.

The federal Guidelines entered into force in November 1987 and their purpose, according to the SRA, was to "provide certainty and fairness in meeting the purposes of sentencing, avoiding unwarranted sentencing disparities among defendants with similar records who have been found guilty of similar criminal conduct."[55] The SRA had two primary purposes: to promote "honesty" in sentencing and to reduce sentencing disparity. The first of these was accomplished through the elimination of parole in the federal system. Henceforth, offenders would serve the prison sentence imposed upon them, apart from 54 days' "good time" per year after the first year, and that remains the law.[56] Reducing disparity would obviously be a more complex task and to this end, the original Commission was charged with drafting detailed guidelines centred on a two-dimensional grid. Along the vertical axis are 43 offence levels and along the horizontal axis are six criminal history categories. At the intersection of each is a permissible sentence range expressed in months with the higher value typically 25 per cent greater than the lower. Thus, in a case where the offence level is calculated at 28 and the offender has a criminal history score of 3, the guideline range is 97 to 121 months' imprisonment. Calculating the offence level remains a challenging task, as a glance at the hefty manual containing the Guidelines will indicate. Each offence has a so-called "base offence level" which, for example, is 20 in the case of robbery.[57] Upward adjustments must then be made for certain characteristics of the offence, such as the value of the property taken, the amount of drugs involved, the possession or use of a firearm or the infliction of personal injury, all depending on the particular offence involved, while downward departure is permissible for a small number of mitigating factors such as acceptance of responsibility. Each of these factors, in turn, has a specified numerical value. A robbery (20 points) in which a firearm was discharged (7 additional points), in which serious bodily injury was inflicted (4 additional points) and which resulted in the loss of a sum between $10,000 and $50,000 (1 additional point) would end up with an offence level of 32, though there might also be further enhancements for the offender's role in the criminal enterprise and other matters. Acceptance of responsibility would lead

---

[55]   28 USC § 991(b)(1)(B). On the background and drafting of the guidelines, see Breyer, "The Federal Sentencing Guidelines and the Key Compromises upon which they Rest" (1988) 17 Hofstra L.R. 1. (Breyer, now a Supreme Court Justice, was a member of the original Sentencing Commission).

[56]   *Barber v Thomas* 560 U.S. – (June 7, 2010).

[57]   Guidelines §2B3.1.

to a reduction of 2, leaving the ultimate offence level at 30. Assuming a criminal history score of 3 (and the calculation of that score is also quite complicated), the guideline sentence would be 121 to 151 months' imprisonment.[58] Some provision is made for non-custodial measures. The sentencing table or grid has four zones, A, B. C and D but generally speaking those offenders falling into zone D, which is by far the largest and encompasses guideline ranges of 15 to 21 months and upwards, face actual imprisonment.

By way of concrete example, one randomly-chosen case involving the receipt of child pornography illustrates the process of calculating a federal guideline sentence, even at a time when the guidelines themselves are purely advisory. The defendant in *United States v Raby*[59] was found in possession of 2,000 electronically-stored child pornography images, and he pleaded guilty. The base offence level was 22, but various enhancements had to be made including, for example, a two-level increase because the images involved pre-pubescent children, a five-level increase because the offence involved distribution, though for non-pecuniary gain, and a two-level increase because the offence involved the use of a computer. All of the enhancements brought the offence level to 40. He became entitled to a three-level decrease, principally for accepting responsibility, giving a final total of 37. As he had no criminal history, his guideline sentence was in the range of 210 to 262 months' imprisonment. The trial judge originally imposed 210 months, but following a reversal of that decision by the Court of Appeals, he re-sentenced the offender to 120 months. In brief terms, what this case illustrates is the complexity of guideline calculations, the rather arbitrary severity of the guideline sentences for certain offences such as those involving child pornography,[60] and the greatly increased discretion available to federal trial court judges in the wake of *Booker*.

Until the decision in *United States v Booker*,[61] the federal guidelines were mandatory in the sense that judges were obliged to follow them and in each case impose a sentence within the specified range.[62] Departure from the guidelines was permissible whenever there was a "circumstance of a kind, or to a degree, not adequately taken into consideration by the Sentencing Commission in formulating the guidelines that should result in a sentence different from that described."[63] Rather controversially, certain factors including race, sex, creed,

---

[58] These calculations are based on the *United States Sentencing Commission Guidelines Manual 2009*.

[59] 575 F. 3d 376 (4th Cir. 2009), later resentenced by the United States District Court for the Southern District of West Virginia: *http://wvsd.uscourts.gov*. See also *United States v Henderson*, Court of Appeals, Ninth Circuit, April 29, 2011, which has an excellent discussion of the evolution of child pornography sentencing guidelines.

[60] See also text accompanying fn.86 below.

[61] 543 U.S. 220 (2005).

[62] *United States v Booker* 543 U.S. 220 at 235 (2005) ("Booker's case illustrates the mandatory nature of the Guidelines").

[63] USC §3553(b).

national origin, socioeconomic hardship and economic circumstances may never provide a valid ground for departure. The SRA allowed the defendant to appeal an upward departure and the prosecution to appeal a downward departure. This contrasted sharply with the pre-guidelines era when, as already noted, merit-based appeals against sentence were virtually unknown in the federal system. In *Koon v United States*,[64] better known as the Rodney King case, the Supreme Court took a rather liberal approach towards guideline departures, holding that appeal courts owed trial courts a substantial level of deference and that, rather than embarking on *de novo* hearings, appeal courts should apply an abuse of discretion standard. Congress later moved to re-impose a more restrictive standard, but in the meantime trial courts had become much more adventurous in granting downward departures.[65]

One major dilemma facing those responsible for creating guidelines is whether to opt for charge-based or real offence sentencing. Under a charge-based or, more precisely, a conviction-based approach, sentence is determined solely or mainly according to the offence(s) of which the defendant has been convicted, and this is the approach adopted in guidelines systems of most states, including Minnesota. One consequence of strict adherence to charge-based sentencing is it reposes very extensive power in the prosecutor whose choice of charge, which is generally unreviewable, will effectively predetermine the sentence or, at the least, the sentence range. Real offence sentencing permits the judge to take account of a wide range of factors surrounding the commission of the offence including, in the case of the federal guidelines, uncharged and acquitted conduct.[66] The federal guidelines are so constructed that the offence of conviction determines the base value or starting point of the sentence, but the judge must then have regard to surrounding circumstances such as the possession or use of a firearm, the total value of the drugs involved, the total value of the property stolen and similar factors, and make the necessary sentence enhancements. In *United States v Watts*[67] a majority of the Supreme Court went so far as to uphold the practice of increasing sentence on account of conduct of which the defendant had been acquitted. Watts was convicted of possessing cocaine, but acquitted of using a firearm. Yet, the court was willing to hold that his sentence could be increased for having used a firearm. The majority reasoned, rather dubiously, that since acquittal simply meant that the jury was not

---

[64] 518 U.S. 81 (1993).

[65] Demleitner, Berman, Miller and Wright, *Sentencing Law and Policy: Cases, Statutes, and Guidelines* (New York: Aspen, New York, 2004), pp.162–164.

[66] Yellen, "Reforming the Federal Sentencing Guidelines' Misguided Approach to Real-Offence Sentencing" (2005) 58 Stanford L.R. 267 at 268 ("[R]eal offence sentencing is the use in sentencing of any facts beyond those necessarily found by a jury in reaching a guilty verdict or admitted by a defendant as part of a guilty plea. Real-offence sentencing information can concern the offence or the offender. It can relate to the harm caused by the offence, the defendant's culpability, or background information about the offender.").

[67] 519 U.S. 148 (1997). See also *Witte v United States* 515 U.S. 389 (1995).

convinced beyond a reasonable doubt of the defendant's guilt on a particular charge, a sentencing judge should not be precluded from reconsidering the matter under a preponderance of evidence standard. This practice of sentencing defendants for conduct of which they had not been convicted has been described as one of "the most unseemly aspects of the Guidelines."[68] Real offence sentencing, provided it is kept within reasonable limits, has its advantages and it exists to some extent in most systems, including our own. It means, for example, that courts can differentiate between offenders with different levels of involvement in the same criminal enterprise or between offenders convicted of the same offence committed in radically different circumstances. Otherwise, for example, two offenders convicted of robbery might have to receive the same or almost the same sentence despite vast differences in degrees of moral culpability.

The federal guidelines incorporated a very broad approach to real offence sentencing, as reflected in cases such as *Watts*, and this would eventually prove to be their undoing. Freddie Booker was found guilty by a jury of possessing 92.5 grams of crack cocaine with intent to distribute.[69] In light of this verdict and Booker's criminal history, the Guidelines mandated a sentence of 210 to 262 months' imprisonment. At the sentencing hearing, however, the trial judge concluded on a preponderance of evidence that Booker had an additional 566 grams of crack cocaine and that he was guilty of obstructing justice. On foot of these findings, the guideline sentence was 360 months to life, and Booker was in fact sentenced to 30 years' imprisonment. This was considerably higher than the 21 years and 10 months warranted by the jury verdict. The questions for the Supreme Court were whether this application of the Guidelines violated the Sixth Amendment right to jury trial and, if so, whether this should result in the invalidation of the Guidelines. A majority of the court answered the first question in the affirmative and this caused little surprise. After all, in *Apprendi v New Jersey*[70] the court had held: "Other than the fact of a prior conviction, any fact that increases the penalty for a crime beyond the prescribed statutory maximum must be submitted to a jury, and proved beyond a reasonable doubt." Even more to the point, in *Blakely v Washington*,[71] which involved the application of state guidelines rather similar to the federal ones, the court found a violation of the Sixth Amendment where the defendant had been sentenced to 90 months' imprisonment on foot of certain additional facts found by the judge although the jury verdict on its own would have mandated a sentence range of 49 to 53 months. In short, *Booker* held that the same considerations applied to the federal Guidelines. As to the appropriate remedy, a differently constituted majority, applying existing severability jurisprudence, held that the Guidelines should henceforth be treated as advisory and that certain statutory provisions

---

[68]   Yellen (fn.66 above), p.275.
[69]   *United States v Booker* 543 U.S. 220 (2005).
[70]   530 U.S. 466 at 490 (2000).
[71]   542 U.S. 296 (2004).

which declared them to be mandatory should accordingly be severed. Since then, appeal courts have been limited to deciding if sentences imposed by trial courts are "reasonable" under an abuse of discretion standard. A non-binding presumption of reasonableness may be applied by appeal courts to a sentence which has properly been calculated in accordance with the Guidelines.[72] The same standard governs review of sentences imposed outside the Guidelines, the Supreme Court having rejected the argument that extraordinary circumstances are required to justify a departure.[73] Significantly, however, the court has repeatedly held that not only are the Guidelines not binding on trial courts, they are not to be presumed reasonable at that level.[74] At the same time, it has held that a trial court's decision to depart from the guidelines attracts greatest respect when the court finds that a particular case is "outside the heartland" to which the Commission intended the relevant guideline to apply.[75] The Guidelines, after all are still advisory, not irrelevant. In *Kimbrough v United States*[76] the Supreme Court held that a district court, when sentencing for a crack cocaine offence, could depart from the Guidelines on the basis of a policy disagreement with them, and not simply on account of the sentence which Guidelines would yield in a particular case.

LESSONS FROM THE AMERICAN EXPERIENCE

Any sentencing reform exercise must be evaluated by reference to the objectives which it was designed to achieve and with due regard to the legal and political culture of the relevant jurisdiction. A broad brush approach towards the evaluation of American sentencing guideline systems runs the risk of over-generalisation and over-simplification. Disparity reduction remains a dominant purpose of most guideline systems. One of the animating principles of the North Carolina guidelines is that "(o)ffenders convicted of similar offences, who have similar prior records, should generally receive similar sentences." Other guideline systems have similar objectives. The pursuit of justice is, of course, a laudable and essential aim of any sentencing reform exercise but what the guidelines

---

[72] *Rita v United States* 551 U.S. 338 (2007). See Berman, "*Rita*, Reasoned Sentencing, and Resistance to Change" (2007) 85 Denver Univ. L.R. 7.

[73] *Gall v United States* 552 U.S. 38 (2007). An abuse of discretion standard essentially involves, first, asking if there has been any procedural error in the calculation of the guideline sentence and then, assuming no such error is found, considering if the sentence imposed is substantively reasonable.

[74] *Rita v United States* 551 U.S. 338 (2007); *Nelson v United States* 555 U.S. – (2009); Gertner, "Supporting Advisory Guidelines" (2009) 3 *Harvard Law and Policy Review* 261.

[75] *Kimbrough v United States* 552 U.S. 85, 109 (2007); *Pepper v United States* 562 U.S. – (2011), Breyer J.

[76] 552 U.S. 85 (2007). See also *Spears v United States* 555 U.S. 261 (2009) which reaffirms the same principle. On the application of this principle to child pornography offences, see *United States v Henderson,* Court of Appeals, Ninth Circuit, April 29, 2011.

movement often reminds us is that the concept of justice itself, in whatever context, is a deeply contested one and that, in any event, true justice can seldom be achieved through the application of rigid rules. Mandatory guidelines, especially when motivated principally by a desire to eliminate or reduce disparity, can seldom hope to achieve more than formal justice. To achieve any measure of success in this regard, they must often require sentencing judges to ignore factors which would traditionally have been considered relevant in order to achieve consistency of outcome. The federal guidelines, as already noted, prohibited judges from taking account of the basic human characteristics of an offender. This had, to be sure, a positive dimension in terms of prohibiting discrimination against offenders on the basis of race, gender and similar factors. But, taken together with other provisions of the guidelines and the enabling legislation, it also meant that judges were often prevented from fashioning sentences which reflected an offender's true culpability in light of his or her personal and background circumstances.

Perhaps the most obvious lesson to be drawn, particularly from the federal experience, is that abrupt transitions seldom work, especially when they attempt to replace largely unfettered discretion with rigid guidelines. Professor Dan Freed, for example, had long been one of the most influential sentencing scholars in the United States and a strong supporter of structured sentencing. As early as 1974, he was instrumental in convening a series of workshops at Yale Law School to examine Judge Frankel's proposal for establishing a sentencing commission. Indeed these workshops and seminars continued for more than two decades thereafter, and included meetings with members of the federal Sentencing Commission while they were drawing up the Guidelines. Yet, in a seminal article published in 1992, he expressed considerable disillusionment with the Guidelines and their operation. Guidelines, he argued, do not work unless they meet certain thresholds of quality and acceptability:

> "To achieve the requisite level of quality, a guidance system must contemplate multiple levels of discretion. It must leave ample room for departures from the guideline range so that judges can accommodate cases of greater and lesser seriousness. It must be developed by an institution that understands the complexity of criminal sentencing, that appreciates the wisdom, integrity and sense of justice that animates experienced judges, and that earns the respect of judges and practitioners."[77]

The title of a book later co-authored by another Yale Law School professor, Kate Stith, admirably summed up the central problem with the Guidelines—*Fear of Judging*.[78] The implementation of the Guidelines in November 1987 represented

---

[77] Freed, "Federal Sentencing in the Wake of Guidelines: Unacceptable Limits on the Discretion of Sentencers" (1992) 101 Yale L.J. 1681 at 1683.

[78] Footnote 13 above. See also, Gertner, "From Omnipotence to Impotence: American Judges and Sentencing" (2007) 4 Ohio State J. Crim. L. 523.

a rejection of virtually everything that had gone before in federal sentencing practice, without affording any opportunity for meaningful experimentation with less drastic measures than those mandated by the Guidelines. It is little wonder that they proved to be extremely unpopular with the vast majority of federal trial court judges and that all or part of the SRA was invalidated by no less than 200 district judges under the first two years of the its operation.[79] The challenges at that point were mostly based on separation of powers arguments and they were quickly rejected by the Supreme Court in *Mistretta v United States* in 1989.[80]

Another point which immediately strikes the foreign observer is that the vast patchwork of American sentencing reform over the past 30 years has done little to generate consistency on a nationwide level. Disparity levels may well have declined significantly within the federal system since the introduction of the Sentencing Guidelines in 1987. But this system, while covering the entire territory of the United States, deals with no more than a small percentage of the criminal cases disposed of annually by American courts. Some state guideline systems have also had a measure of success in reducing disparity and promoting so-called truth in sentencing. Significant variations can, however, be detected between states although this, as any American lawyer will immediately point out, is a factor of federalism. Subject to those provisions of the federal Constitution applicable to the states through the Fourteenth Amendment, states are under no obligation to enact identical laws or to follow identical practices whether in relation to sentencing or anything else. In fact, variations between states are usually seen as healthy and beneficial rather than the opposite. Yet, one cannot but be struck by some of the stark variations in penal policy among the states of the Union, and not just in relation to such fundamental issues as the retention of the death penalty or the imposition of life imprisonment without the possibility of parole (LWOP).[81] A study relating to the year 2000 found substantial differences in imprisonment rates, risk of imprisonment and duration of custody across the states.[82] Imprisonment rates varied from 128 per 100,000 of the population in Minnesota to 801 in Louisiana. Lengths of time served also varied significantly. The average time served at first release ranged from 18 months (in Missouri) to 73 months (in Ohio). After three decades of sentencing reform, it is surprising that the consequences of a conviction should depend so much on the jurisdiction in which the offender happens to have been tried. Morton Berger, a 57-year-old high school teacher, was convicted in Arizona on 20 counts of possessing child pornography. State law required that he receive 10 years' imprisonment on each count, and that all the sentences run consecutively, producing a total of 200 years to be served without the possibility of parole or other form of early release. This sentence was upheld by the Arizona Supreme

---

[79] Tonry (fn.9 above), p.140.
[80] 488 U.S. 361 (1989).
[81] *Graham v Florida* 560 U.S. – (2010) (Life without parole imposed on juvenile offender for a non-fatal offence violates the cruel and unusual punishment clause of the Eighth Amendment).
[82] Frost, "The Mismeasure of Punishment" (2008) 10 *Punishment and Society* 277.

Court, and the United States Supreme Court refused further review.[83] In a partly-dissenting judgment, Vice Chief Justice Berch of Arizona noted that the sentence far exceeded that imposed for similar crimes in other states and also exceeded the penalties regularly imposed in Arizona itself for many serious offences against the person, including homicide offences. Had Berger been tried in virtually any other state or within the federal system, he would have received a much more lenient sentence. In fact, the sentencing of child pornography offences under the federal guidelines has become controversial with some judges protesting that the recommended guideline sentence, which in many cases would run to six or seven years' imprisonment, is excessive.[84] In May 2010, a leading federal District Court judge in New York was reported to have twice thrown out the conviction of man found in possession of a large quantity of child pornography because such a conviction would have entailed a five-year prison sentence.[85] About the same time, the Court of Appeals for the Second Circuit quashed a 20-year sentence for one count of distributing child pornography because it found the sentence substantively unreasonable.[86] The contrast with Arizona's treatment of Morton Berger could not be more striking.

One of the more negative attributes of strong guidelines, such as those operating in the federal system, is that they significantly reduce the opportunity for moral reasoning at both trial court and appeal court levels. While it would be grossly unfair to make sweeping generalisations about the thousands of federal appeal court judgments on guideline departures that have been issued during the past quarter of a century or so, it is fair to say, and natural to expect, that most of them have been principally concerned with compliance. This was especially true during the pre-*Booker* era when the Guidelines were, for all practical purposes, mandatory and when a departure from the permitted guideline range, depending on its direction, furnished either the defence or prosecution with a ground of appeal. Even today, many appeal judgments focus largely on the recommended guideline range, though other factors must now be considered as well. This will hopefully change in the post-*Booker* era because the value of appeal court jurisprudence and the inclination of trial courts to abide

---

[83] *State of Arizona v Berger* 212 Ariz. 473, 143 P. 3d 378 (2006) (Supreme Court), 209 Ariz. 386, 103 P 3d 298 (2004) (Court of Appeals). The US Supreme Court denied certiorari in 2007.

[84] On federal sentencing for child pornography offences, see Exum, "Making the Punishment Fit the (Computer) Crime: Rebooting Notions of Possession for the Federal Sentencing of Child Pornography Offences" (2010) XVI Richmond J. Law and Technology 8, at *http://jolt. richmond.edu/v16i3/article8.pdf* [Last accessed August 22, 2011], and Efrati, "Judges Trim Jail Time for Child Porn", *The Wall Street Journal*, January 19, 2010. For a detailed account of federal sentencing for child pornography, see *United States v Henderson* Court of Appeals, Ninth Circuit, April 29, 2011.

[85] Sulzberger, "Defiant Judge Takes on Child Pornography Law", *New York Times,* May 21, 2010.

[86] *United States v Dorvee* 616 F. 3d 174 (2010). The court held that trial judges should "take seriously the discretion they possess in fashioning sentences ... [for child pornography offences], especially when dealing with an eccentric guidelines of highly unusual provenance". See Note, "*United States v Dorvee*" (2011) 124 Harvard L.R. 1082.

by it depend in no small measure on its moral persuasiveness. A bare assertion that a particular offence should ordinarily attract a specified range of punishment, or that a particular guideline departure was or was not legally permissible, is unlikely to have much impact beyond the confines of the case itself. The facts of any given case, including the personal circumstances of the offender, furnish an appeal court with a pedagogical opportunity to explain the legal and moral bases for ranking particular variations of a crime on the overall scale of gravity and for any adjustments that should be made for mitigating circumstances. Apart from being more credible and persuasive, judgments of this kind also promote and facilitate a continuing dialogue between appeal courts, trial courts, policymakers and academic commentators on salient aspects of sentencing policy. One of the flaws of mandatory sentencing guidelines and, to a lesser extent, of presumptive guidelines is that they purport to furnish the right answer to problems which rarely admit of definitive answers. Penal policy, whether at political or judicial level, is forever in the making as emerging patterns of crime and new insights into its causes and circumstances call for new directions in sentencing practice. Reasoned and persuasive appeal court judgments are vital to that developmental process.

It must, however, be stressed in conclusion that these criticisms are directed at restrictive guidelines which are essentially preoccupied with generating consistency at the expense of more individualised sentencing. Sentencing commissions, by contrast, can serve very useful purposes, particularly in collecting and analysing data and in monitoring sentencing practices. Leading American expert groups, including the American Law Institute which was responsible for the Model Penal Code (among many other initiatives), have stressed the importance of a sentencing commission to engage in research, planning and consensus building. The Constitution Project, a bipartisan, non-profit organisation which seeks to generate consensus on contentious legal issues, has adopted a set of principles for the reform of sentencing systems. One of these states:

> "Essential to the successful operation of a sentencing system is a sentencing commission or similar entity with the expertise and stature to study sentencing issues, gather data, and formulate proposed sentencing rules and amendments. The commission should continually assess the performance of sentencing rules and should periodically recommend modifications, which may include either upward or downward adjustments of sentences, based on its assessment. Commission processes should include transparency and fair administrative rulemaking procedures."[87]

---

[87] The Constitution Project, *Principles of the Design and Reform of Sentencing Systems: A Background Report* (2005), available at *www.constitutionproject.org/pdf/34.pdf* [Last accessed August 22, 2011]. See also New Jersey Commission to Review Criminal Sentencing, *Sentencing in the 21ˢᵗ Century and the Necessity of a Permanent Sentencing Commission in New Jersey* (2006), available at *www.sentencing.nj.gov*.

Some of the tasks enumerated in this principle seem to presuppose the existence of guidelines, but the broad thrust of it remains pertinent in any jurisdiction committed to developing and maintaining a rational and effective sentencing system. Sound policy formulation, whether it occurs within the legislative or judicial spheres, depends critically on the availability of detailed, reliable, up-to-date information on existing sentencing practices, projected prison population trends and related matters.[88] The title conferred on the entity responsible for these tasks is of little importance. What matters is that they should be discharged by an independent, competent and adequately-resourced body appointed for that purpose.

---

[88] The importance of this function was recognised by the United States Supreme Court in *Kimbrough v United States* 552 U.S. 85, 108–109 (2007) where it said that the United States Sentencing Commission "fills an important institutional role. It has the capacity courts lack to base its determination on empirical data and national experience, guided by a professional staff with appropriate expertise".

CHAPTER 7

SENTENCING INFORMATION SYSTEMS

Guideline systems vary a great deal in structure and purpose, but they all aspire to shape or influence future sentencing practice to some extent. Mandatory and presumptive guidelines demand high levels of compliance whereas voluntary guidelines leave judges with considerable levels of discretion. Sentencing information systems, on the other hand, being essentially descriptive rather than prescriptive, are intended to inform rather than direct. Their ultimate goal may be to generate more consistent or coherent sentencing by encouraging judges to have regard to past practice, but they seldom make any formal or explicit demand for adherence to that practice. While judges tend to resist the introduction of guidelines, and often with good reason, they are much more receptive to sentencing information systems. Guidelines curtail judicial discretion, sometimes quite substantially, but information systems are based on precedent, a concept with which judges and lawyers are comfortable and familiar. Previous sentencing practice does not, of course, constitute precedent in the conventional legal sense of the term, but it is heeded for reasons that are very similar to the customary justifications for observing formal precedent. The regular imposition of sentences that correspond with past practice in genuinely similar cases enhances the legitimacy and acceptability of the overall process. It also promotes fairness and predictability which are important qualities in public decision-making generally. Unwavering adherence to past practice, just like strict observance of formal precedent, also has its pitfalls, so it may be useful to begin with a brief review of the more salient aspects of precedent and its normative premises.

PRECEDENT AND ITS USES

Precedent has many technical aspects which are embodied in the general doctrine of stare decisis. Under this doctrine, the ratio decidendi of a judicial decision (or the "holding" in American parlance) is binding on later courts of equal or lower jurisdiction. Statements which do not form part of the *ratio* are classified as obiter dicta and, while not formally binding, often prove influential. The precise content of the *ratio* and the method by which it should be identified have proved to be contentious matters, among academic writers at least. Older treatises on jurisprudence, reflecting the positivist leanings of their authors, usually devoted considerable attention to this and other aspects of precedent. Austin, for example, described the *ratio* as consisting of "the general reasons or principles of a judicial decision"[1] while Salmond, in a similar vein, claimed that the *ratio* consisted of the underlying principle which forms the authoritative part of a judicial decision.[2] One of the more sustained analyses was provided by Goodhart in a contribution which provoked significant disagreement but which has also proved remarkably enduring.[3] He insisted on the primordial importance of identifying the material as opposed to the specific facts of a case, as indeed Austin had earlier done in slightly different language. In a typical tort case, for example, details as to identity, place, age, amount and similar matters would usually, though not invariably, be immaterial. According to Goodhart, the principle of a case is determined by identifying the judicial decision based on the material facts.[4]

Distilling the *ratio* obviously becomes more difficult in a case where several judgments are delivered and this, rather ironically, is most likely to happen in higher courts where the most authoritative precedents are developed.[5] Precedent operates both vertically and horizontally. Its vertical dimension is the more important in so far as a higher court decision is binding on lower courts even when, according to some views, the decision was reached *per incuriam*, and appears to display a material error.[6] A precedent established by a court of equal jurisdiction is also binding unless the later court is satisfied that the earlier decision is flawed because the authorities cited or submissions made were insufficient or misleading, or because the judge disregarded some important

---

[1]   Austin, *Lectures on Jurisprudence*, 5th edn, by Campbell (London: John Murray, 1885).

[2]   Salmond, *Jurisprudence*, 7th edn (London: Sweet and Maxwell, 1924), p.201.

[3]   Goodhart, "Determining the Ratio Decidendi of a Case" (1930) 40 Yale L.J. 161, reprinted in Goodhart, *Essays in Jurisprudence and the Common Law* (Cambridge: Cambridge University Press, 1931).

[4]   Goodhart (fn.3 above), p.182. This approach has been criticised by others including Stone, *Recent Trends in English Precedent* (Sydney: Associated General Publications Pty. Ltd., 1945), p.39. It also provided the backdrop to a sharp exchange of views in the *Modern Law Review* in the late 1950s: Montrose, "*Ratio Decidendi* and the House of Lords" (1957) 20 M.L.R. 124; Simpson, "The *Ratio Decidendi* of a Case" (1957) 20 M.L.R. 413; Montrose, "The *Ratio Decidendi* of a Case" (1957) 20 M.L.R. 587; Simpson, "The *Ratio Decidendi* of a Case" (1958) 21 M.L.R. 155; Goodhart, "The *Ratio Decidendi* of a Case" (1959) 22 M.L.R. 117. Leading texts on the topic include Cross and Harris, *Precedent in English Law*, 4th edn (Oxford: Clarendon Press, 1991); Goldstein, *Precedent in Law* (Oxford: Clarendon Press, 1987); Duxbury, *The Nature and Authority of Precedent* (Cambridge: Cambridge University Press, 2008). See also Abramowicz and Stearns, "Defining *Dicta*" (2005) 57 Stanford L.R. 953 which includes a detailed theoretical analysis of precedent, including a critique of Goodhart's proposal; Perry, "Judicial Obligation, Precedent and the Common Law" (1987) 7 O.J.L.S. 215.

[5]   In *Walsh v Curry* [1955] N.I. 112, for example, the Northern Ireland Court of Appeal attempted to find the *ratio* of *George Wimpey & Co. Ltd v British Overseas Airways Corporation* [1955] A.C. 169 where several speeches were delivered. See Montrose, "*Ratio Decidendi* and the House of Lords" (1957) 20 M.L.R. 124.

[6]   *People (DPP) v Geasley* [2009] IECCA 22, [2010] 1 I.L.R.M. 317 is an example of a case where an error in the precedent Court of Criminal Appeal decision was such that the trial judge was held to be justified in not following that decision.

aspect of the case or failed to abide by proper standards of adjudication.[7] Irrespective of the means by which it is identified, precedent seldom inhibits legal development to the extent that a purely abstract account of stare decisis might suggest. Courts routinely circumvent the strictures of precedent by distinguishing the case at hand from the earlier case, and this can be accomplished by identifying different material facts. In most common-law jurisdictions, the highest court is empowered to overrule its own precedents in certain circumstances. The Irish Supreme Court, while fundamentally committed to stare decisis, is prepared to overrule one of its own previous decisions which it clearly considers to be erroneous. But the court may not refuse to follow one of its precedents merely because it "inclines to a different conclusion" as to how the earlier case should have been decided.[8] Courts are bound solely by precedents established within the jurisdiction. Foreign precedents are often very useful but they are invariably treated as persuasive rather than binding.

More relevant for present purposes is the value of precedent as an organising legal principle. After all, by strictly and routinely adhering to precedent, a court might, to paraphrase Lord Justice Bowen, occasionally be compelled to sacrifice its better judgement upon the altar of authority.[9] Stability, consistency and coherence are undoubtedly important legal values, and all the more so when the applicable law must be distilled from a multitude of judicial decisions rather than from a statute or a code. Inherent in the notion of the proper administration of justice is the principle that a person should be able to receive correct legal advice rather than endure the uncertainty resulting from "the continual existence of inconsistent decisions of courts of equal jurisdiction."[10] By the same token, the common law derives its vitality from the maintenance of a delicate balance between continuity and change. Sensible adherence to precedent promotes stability and continuity, two vital common-law qualities; blind adherence produces fossilisation and injustice. The difficulty in striking a proper balance between certainty and flexibility, and the necessity for the law to respond promptly to changing social conditions has frankly been acknowledged by judges and commentators alike.[11] Most would probably agree that precedents "must often be stepping-stones rather than halting places."[12] The challenge is to

---

[7] *Irish Trust Bank Ltd v Central Bank of Ireland* [1976–1977] I.L.R.M. 50; *Anh v Browne* [2009] IEHC 29.
[8] *Mogul of Ireland v Tipperary (N.R.) C.C.* [1976] I.R. 260 at 272 (Henchy J.). The leading authorities on the matter are *Attorney General v Ryan's Car Hire Ltd* [1965] I.R. 642 and *O'Brien v Mirror Group Newspapers Ltd* [2001] 1 I.R. 1. See also *State (Quinn) v Ryan* [1965] I.R. 70, and *D.H. v Groarke* [2002] 3 I.R. 522. The United States Supreme Court has likewise held that while stare decisis applies to its own decisions, it is not an "inexorable command": *Planned Parenthood v Casey* 505 U.S. 833, 854 (1992). See also *Hutto v Davis* 454 U.S. 370, 375 (1982) which stressed the obligation of the lower federal courts to follow Supreme Court precedents.
[9] *Montagu v Earl of Sandwich* (1886) 32 Ch D 525 at 544.
[10] *Irish Trust Bank Ltd v Central Bank of Ireland* [1976–1977] I.L.R.M. 50 at 53 (Parke J.)
[11] Henchy, "Precedent in the Irish Supreme Court" (1962) 25 M.L.R. 544.
[12] *Birch Brothers v Brown* [1931] A.C. 605 at 631 (Lord Macmillan) quoted by Henchy (fn.11

decide when a superior court should lay down a new stepping stone rather than make do with those already in place.

Why then should existing precedents, however they are deduced or identified, be observed in the first place? Practitioners and scholars in many disciplines, including science and philosophy, draw heavily on their predecessors' work as a starting point for developing their own ideas. But they never feel bound to adopt ideas or research findings simply because they already exist or because they have been propounded by a particular authority.[13] In fact, what we value most in academic research is originality as opposed to an uncritical reaffirmation of existing knowledge. Why should law be any different? Schauer has identified three primary reasons for adhering to legal precedent: fairness in the sense that like cases should be treated alike, predictability and strengthened decision-making.[14] Keane C.J. has likewise referred to the "certainty, stability and predictability of law" on which the doctrine is grounded.[15] Decisions will undoubtedly become more predictable if they are made according to precedent, assuming the existence of substantial factual similarity between the instant case and the previous one, and this is not something that can readily be assumed in sentencing. Whether adherence to precedent generates fairness is a more contentious question. Admittedly, Schuaer was dealing with precedent in the sense of previously-established rules and principles of a reasonably general nature. These are to be found in sentencing as in all other areas of law; the principle that a guilty plea should ordinarily warrant a discount on the otherwise deserved sentence would be one such example. Decision-making can certainly be strengthened by having due regard to precedent as a source of information on how particular problems and issues were addressed in the past, and this in turn may provide inspiration as to how they should now be addressed. Consistency in decision-making may also promote public confidence in the legal system. Strict adherence to precedent might well, of course, have the opposite effect if the result clearly ran counter to current ideas and values.

Most sentencing principles derive from appeal court judgments but it is often difficult to identify the precise *ratio* in the case of a sentence appeal. *People (DPP) v Tiernan*, for example, is the leading Irish authority on sentencing for rape.[16] There, the Supreme Court reduced the prison term for a particularly violent rape from 21 years to 17 years, and did so mainly on the ground that insufficient credit had been given for the appellant's guilty plea. The legal significance of the judgment has little to do with the actual decision, except to

---

above), p.558. Lord Macmillan was, admittedly, referring to decisions on the progressive construction of statutes.

[13] Kronman, "Precedent and Tradition" (1990) 99 Yale L.J. 1029.

[14] Schauer, "Precedent" (1987) 39 Stanford L.R. 571, See the same author's *Thinking Like a Lawyer: A New Introduction to Legal Reasoning* (Cambridge, MA: Harvard University Press, 2009).

[15] *O'Brien v Mirror Group Newspapers Ltd* [2001] 1 I.R. 1.

[16] *People (DPP) v Tiernan* [1988] I.R. 250, [1989] I.R. 149

the extent that it might furnish a rough guide for sentencing similar cases in the future.[17] Rather it is important for certain statements in the majority judgment where it was said that rape ordinarily calls for an immediate and substantial term of imprisonment, that an early admission of responsibility followed by a guilty plea can be a significant mitigating factor (though this, admittedly, formed the principled basis for the ultimate decision), that neither the victim's previous sexual experience nor any suggestion that she might have exposed herself to the danger of being raped should be treated as mitigating factors, and that it was inappropriate for an appeal court to lay down any tariff or guideline sentences for particular offences. How many, if any, of these elements form part of the *ratio* is difficult to say and, in truth, it matters very little. They amount to clear statements of principle enunciated by the Supreme Court in a case which was solely and directly concerned with the appropriate sentence for a specific rape offence. As Atiyah remarks, the distinction between *ratio* and *dicta* is often "less important than the weight of the remarks in their context.[18] Fully considered *dicta* in the House of Lords are usually treated as more weighty than the *ratio* of a judge at first instance in the High Court."[19] This certainly holds true of many superior court sentencing judgments, including those which establish benchmarks as do many Court of Appeal judgments in England. Recommended benchmarks should probably be treated as *dicta* rather than as part of the *ratio*, but this seldom diminishes their status as a guide for future sentencing practice. The English Court of Appeal has generally held that while sentencing judges should pay close attention to the guidance offered by the court, a decision incorporating such guidance is not to be treated as a binding precedent. Indeed, the court has gone so far as to say that it is not bound by its own previous sentencing decisions in non-guideline cases.[20] The authorities in question predate the more structured guideline system introduced in England and Wales under the Criminal Justice Act 2003 and the Coroners and Justice Act 2009 but, even back then, guideline judgments were generally intended to be followed.[21]

---

[17] Note, however, the comments made in Ch.5 above about the possible anchoring effect of leading cases.

[18] Similar observations may be made about criminal appeal court decisions where the so-called proviso is applied—an appeal against conviction is dismissed because no miscarriage of justice has occurred. While that decision may form the *ratio* of the case, the true significance of the judgment will probably reside in the court's observations on the grounds on which the appeal was argued. See Cross and Harris (fn.4 above).

[19] Atiyah, *Law and Modern Society*, 2nd edn (Oxford: Oxford University Press, 1995), p.199.

[20] *R v Townsend* (1995) 16 Cr. App. R. (S.) 553 at 558; *R v Johnson* (1994) 15 Cr. App. R. (S) 827 at 830 (sentences should be broadly in line with guideline cases). See also critical comment by Thomas on *Townsend* at [1995] Crim. L.R. 182.

[21] Chapter 5 above. See, Wasik, "The Status and Authority of Sentencing Guidelines" (2007) 39 Bracton L.J. 9; Henham, "On the Philosophical and Theoretical Implications of Judicial Decision Support Systems" (2000) 14:3 *International Review of Law, Computers and Technology* 283 at 285 ("... sentencing principles postulate a normatively desirable course of action ... which is a reflection, not of the strict juridical application of a legal rule (legal

The role of precedent in sentencing must, in fact, be considered under two distinct headings. First, there are those situations where the conventional law of precedent operates, such as when a court must interpret a statutory provision or decide on the extent, if any, to which a common-law principle applies. If, for example, there is an authoritative superior court judgment to the effect that significant credit should always be granted for an early admission of guilt in a sex offence case, trial courts must observe this precedent just as they must apply a judicially-developed rule or principle in a tort case. Under the second heading are situations where trial courts, and perhaps appeal courts, have regard to earlier decisions which may be colloquially described as precedents, but which do not have the binding force of formal precedent. Previous trial court sentencing decisions clearly fall into this second category. The judges who made those decisions may be assumed to have applied the law, including any relevant binding precedents, but they were primarily engaged in an evaluative exercise— assessing the overall culpability of the offender and selecting an appropriate penalty. A survey of these earlier decisions, as a sentencing information system will often facilitate, may well be helpful in deciding on an appropriate penalty, but few would argue that any one of those decisions, or even a significant combination of them, should be treated as binding. Be that as it may, some of the comments already made about formal precedent are also applicable to sentencing precedents in the second, more colloquial sense. Judicial endeavours to craft sentences which are broadly reflective of past practice may well strengthen decision-making, thereby enhancing the legitimacy of the overall process. A sentence which is broadly in line with those previously imposed for similar offences will be more palatable to the individual offender and, indeed, to the public at large than one which merely seems to reflect the ideas or predilections of a particular judge. As against this, the drawbacks associated with strict adherence to formal precedent also apply to accumulated precedent derived from past sentencing practice. A formal precedent may not hold good for all time; it may often be more appropriately treated, in Lord Macmillan's phrase, as a stepping stone rather than a halting place.[22] The same holds true of past sentencing practice which, even if it displays some measure of consistency, cannot be treated as reflecting an intrinsically correct approach towards the sentencing of any given offence or towards sentencing in general. What it describes is not necessarily what might be prescribed after a thorough review of appropriate sentence ranges for commonly-prosecuted offences. Sentencing information systems do not, of course, purport to go beyond description. They are seldom, if ever, intended to achieve the more normative goals pursued by sentencing guideline systems. However, the availability of a reliable compendium

---

formalism), but the use of a sentencing decision to express what is, in reality, a matter of sentencing policy – in other words, the acceptable boundaries for the exercise of judicial discretion within the statutory framework of maximum sentences in particular types of cases" (internal citation omitted)).

[22] Footnote 12 above.

of past decisions is an indispensable foundation for the elaboration of a more normative approach, if that is desired.

A decision to develop a sentencing information system (or a case-based information system at any rate) clearly rests on certain assumptions about the value of precedent, whether in the narrow technical sense of stare decisis or in the broader sense of respecting the wisdom and authenticity of previous judicial decisions. It is tempting to associate recent interest in such systems with the revival of academic interest in historicism within the realm of constitutional theory.[23] The two phenomena may be entirely unrelated in origin, but they both reflect a belief or interest in the value of accumulated knowledge and experience. Sunstein, in particular, has provoked a renewed interest in "many minds" theory which in turn owes a good deal to Condorcet's jury theorem with its emphasis on the value of aggregated judgment and decision-making.[24] The resurgence of interest in Burkean traditionalism among political and constitutional theorists reflects a similar curiosity about the value of accumulated precedent.[25] Edmund Burke (1729–1797), often treated as the father of conservatism, famously championed the wisdom of the ages in his *Reflections on the Revolution in France* where he wrote:

> "We are afraid to put men to live and trade each on his own private stock of reason, because we suspect that this stock in each man is small, and that the individuals would do better to avail themselves of the general bank and capital of nations, and of ages. Many of our men of speculation, instead of exploding general prejudices, employ their sagacity to discover the latent wisdom that prevails in them."

He was not opposed to change based on reason provided it occurred gradually and organically rather through a sudden and fundamentally disruptive transition as exemplified by the French Revolution, the main impetus for his defence of tradition. A central tenet of his philosophy was that tradition and received wisdom were intrinsically superior to radical policy changes, whether these emerged from theoretical or speculative reflection on human nature (as in Locke) or as a result of legislative initiatives. Relying on the concept of prescriptive wisdom, he claimed that while individuals and multitudes acting

---

[23] Sunstein, *A Constitution of Many Minds: Why the Founding Document Doesn't Mean What It Meant Before* (Princeton, NJ: Princeton University Press, 2009); Vermeule, *Law and the Limits of Reason* (Oxford: Oxford University Press, 2009); Vermeule, "Many Minds Arguments in Legal Theory" (2009) 1 *Journal of Legal Analysis* 1.

[24] Sunstein, *Infotopia: How Many Minds Produce Knowledge* (New York: Oxford University Press, 2006); Austen-Smith and Banks, "Information Aggregation, Rationality, and the Condorcet Jury Theorem" (1996) 90:1 *American Political Science Review* 34.

[25] In his last published work, *The Morality of Consent* (New Haven: Yale University Press, 1975), Alexander Bickel devoted considerable attention to Burke's ideas. See also Kronman (fn.13 above); Kronman, "Alexander Bickel's Philosophy of Prudence" (1984) 94 Yale L.J. 1567.

without deliberation are foolish, "the species is wise, and, when time is given to it, as a species, it almost always acts right."[26] Two of Burke's contemporaries, Blackstone and Bentham, differed sharply over the comparative merits of common law and legislation. Blackstone's *Commentaries on the Laws of England* strongly championed the organic and evolutionary nature of the common law with all its intricacies, while Bentham advocated codified legislation which would set out the law in a manner accessible and comprehensible to all.[27] The common law is the ultimate diachronic institution, consisting as it does of rules and principles developed by "many minds" over many centuries. Some of these rules and principles have proved remarkably resilient, and have often been incorporated into legislation or, indeed, elevated to the status of constitutional principles. Many fair trial rights constitutionally protected in Ireland and elsewhere owe their origins to common-law precedents. Most rules and principles remaining within the sole province of the common law, apart from a few found to be incompatible with modern constitutional norms and therefore invalidated or abolished, continue to develop and evolve in response to prevailing social conditions. Consider, for example, the evolution of liability for negligence since the neighbour principle was first enunciated in *Donoghue v Stevenson*.[28] Others, such as the postal rule in contract,[29] have proved more stubborn but their rigours can be avoided by legislative exceptions or express contractual terms. In fact, the common law's most salient characteristic has been its capacity to adapt and innovate. Some of the great judicial names in the history of the common law—Coke, Hale, Mansfield, Cardozo—are remembered primarily as innovators.[30]

Sentencing information systems, particularly the Scottish and Irish models described below, may not have been consciously inspired by Burkean ideas but they do reflect a similar respect for the accumulated wisdom inherent in records of past practice. Their strength resides in the aggregation of knowledge. Individual decisions may be of limited value and could actually mislead unless accompanied by detailed information about the circumstances in which they

---

[26] Burke, *Speech on a Committee to Inquire into the State of the Representation of the Commons in Parliament* (1782) in Kramnick (ed.), *The Portable Edmund Burke* (New York: Penguin Books, 1999), pp.176–177. See Young, "Rediscovering Conservatism: Burkean Political Theory and Constitutional Interpretation" (1994) 72 North Carolina L.R. 619.

[27] Blackstone praised the common law as an "admirable system of maxims and unwritten customs" (*Commentaries*, Bk IV, p.375) while Bentham attacked it as a "fictitious composition which has no known person as its author" (*An Introduction to the Principles of Morals and Legislation*, edited by Burns and Hart (London: Athlone Press, 1970), p.8). Bentham strongly criticised other aspects of Blackstone's work in *A Comment on the Commentaries* which he wrote in 1774 but which remained unpublished until 1928. See Cross, "Blackstone v Bentham" (1976) 92 L.Q.R. 516; Posner, "Blackstone and Bentham" (1976) 19 *Journal of Law and Economics* 569–606; Oldham, "From Blackstone to Bentham: Common Law Versus Legislation in Eighteenth Century Britain" (1991) 89 Michigan L.R. 1637.

[28] [1932] A.C. 562.

[29] *Adams v Lindsell* (1818) B & Ald. 681.

[30] Strauss, "Common Law Constitutional Interpretation" (1996) 63 Univ. Chicago L.R. 877 at 888.

were made. But a large number of them taken together, and allowing for inevitable differences in approach and outcome, may be assumed to reflect a certain shared wisdom on the appropriate manner of dealing with recurring offence situations. Information systems work best when their users, and especially judicial users, are willing to take as much inspiration from Mansfield as from Blackstone or Burke. They must be ready to innovate where necessary; otherwise they may end up perpetuating a practice that is either inherently flawed or no longer appropriate. But with access to reliable data on past practice, they can make more informed choices when it comes to shaping future sentencing policy.

PENAL PURPOSE AND SYSTEM DESIGN

The kind of information needed to assist judges in their sentencing task must depend on the goals which they are expected to achieve. Most information systems aim to generate more consistent sentencing, at least to the extent of eliminating unwarranted disparity. This objective is most likely to be realised, theoretically at least, in a system where just deserts is the sole or principal justification for punishment or where proportionality is treated as the dominant distributive principle. When one or both of these conditions are present, courts and policy-makers can aspire to developing a sentencing jurisprudence which aims to treat like cases alike. Having access to an information system showing how similar cases have been treated in the past should assist judges in selecting sentences that are compatible with past practice. To that extent, the system should promote some degree of diachronic and inter-judge consistency. Suppose, however, that the principal goal of sentencing were crime reduction, and that judges were expected to select whatever measure seems most likely to dissuade the offender from further criminal conduct. Consistency, as conventionally understood, would not rank as a high priority within such a system where the focus would be on deterrence, incapacitation, reform or whichever combination of these utilitarian goals appeared most effective in promoting public safety. Scientific research findings might point to radically different sentences for two offenders convicted of similar offences. Having considered any available empirical evidence on the effectiveness of penal sanctions and the personal profiles of particular offenders, a judge might conclude that a lengthy custodial sentence was needed to prevent re-offending in one case whereas a treatment or community-based measure might adequately achieve the same goal in the other. Some might argue that this already happens in systems that are committed to individualised sentencing, as ours undoubtedly is. The difference, however, is that within our system proportionality remains the overarching distributive principle and, if nothing else, it imposes a ceiling on permissible levels of punishment by reference to offence gravity. Thus, a minor shoplifting offence cannot attract anything more than a modest sentence irrespective of the offender's criminal record or predicted recidivism. A system committed solely to crime reduction might not feel constrained by any such limit. The opposite would also hold true in the sense that a very lenient sentence might be considered appropriate for a serious offence committed by a person who is unlikely to re-offend.

The specific goals of sentencing will therefore shape the design and content of any decision-support system. The kind of information needed within a sentencing system primarily committed to risk reduction may differ quite profoundly from that needed within a system committed to just deserts or proportionality. A judge operating within the first of these must be furnished with appropriate tools for assessing the likelihood of recidivism together with relevant research findings on the most effective risk-reducing measures. Naturally enough, these findings will not always point in the same direction; social science research is constantly evolving and produces its share of professional disagreement. Close attention must also be paid to the particular environment in which the research was conducted. Legal, social, economic and organisational differences may result in a measure which has proved effective in one jurisdiction being far less successful in another. The success of probationary measures, for example, will often depend on intensity of supervision, the extent to which probationers are required to participate in treatment or training programmes and, crucially, the actual availability of such programmes. Crime reduction is, of course, a valid sentencing objective in most jurisdictions, but an official commitment to proportionality calls for much closer attention to sentencing equity. Similarly-situated offenders convicted of similar offences should not receive markedly different sentences.

The concept of evidence-based sentencing merits some consideration at this point because it may well become the orthodoxy of the future and, whether it does or not, a sentencing information system can easily accommodate criminological and other social science research findings on the effectiveness of sentencing measures. The value of evidence-led policy-making is progressively being recognised within political and research communities. By most conventional accounts, the concept of evidence-based practice originated in the field of medicine but did not gain prominence within the social sciences until the late 1990s.[31] Its guiding philosophy is that decisions should be based on reliable research findings as opposed to anecdote, intuition or ideology. Policy-makers are increasingly demanding evidence as to what does and does not work before making crucial choices. The research community has responded with increasingly sophisticated strategies for conducting empirical research and evaluating research findings. Within the American legal academy, empirical legal studies

---

[31] Hart, "Evidence-Based Assessment of Risk for Sexual Violence" (2009) 1 *Chapman Journal of Criminal Justice* 143 at 146 ("Evidence-based means an action or decision that was guided by, based on, or made after consulting a systematic review of relevant information in the form of observation, research, statistics, or well-validated theory." (internal citation omitted)).

seem set to challenge both the law and economics movement which tended to attract thinkers from the right, and critical legal studies which generally proved more attractive to those on the left.[32] Empirical research should, of course, be politically neutral, but experience has shown that this is not always the case. Research findings, when closely examined, often display evidence or traces of selection bias which may distort the accuracy and reliability of the conclusions. This, in turn, has led to the growth of a new discipline or approach which concentrates on systematic reviews or programme evaluation. The guiding principle of this approach is to concentrate on conclusions emerging from randomised field studies in the belief that the diversity of studies, provided each conforms with certain research standards, will reduce the possibility of selection and other forms of bias.[33] Two major internet-based initiatives have greatly facilitated this development: the Cochrane Collaboration[34] which deals with medical issues and the Campbell Collaboration[35] which is devoted to the social sciences. The former provides systematic reviews of the effects of various health care interventions. A review typically consists of a thorough analysis of carefully chosen empirical experiments which have already been published or otherwise made available in order to draw conclusions about the existing state of medical knowledge on the effectiveness of particular interventions. The Campbell collaboration aims to do the same for the social sciences, including many aspects of criminal justice. Both organisations make their findings available free of charge on the internet.

In so far as sentencing is concerned, evidence-based practice is most strongly advocated by those who believe that sentences should be tailored primarily to promote public safety which, in turn, is best achieved by reducing the risk of recidivism.[36] Judge Michael Marcus, a trial judge in the State of Oregon, who has written extensively on the topic,[37] as well as maintaining a personal website

---

[32] The strong growth of empirical legal studies is reflected in the existence of the Society for Empirical Legal Studies (SELS) and the *Journal of Empirical Legal Studies*, published since 2004 and which, according to a recent report, now accepts less than one in ten of the papers submitted to it. See "Follow the Numbers" (Autumn 2008) *The Law School* (NYU Law School alumni magazine) at 30.

[33] Sherman, "Misleading Evidence and Evidence-led Policy: Making Social Science more Experimental" (2003) 589 *Annals of the American Academy of Political and Social Sciences* 6.

[34] *www.cochrane.org.*

[35] *www.campbellcollaboration.org.*

[36] This has recently been advocated by the influential American organisation, the Pew Centre on the States in its report, *Arming the Courts with Research: 10 Evidence-Based Sentencing Initiatives to Control Crime and Reduce Costs* (2009) available at *www.pewpublicsafety.org.*

[37] Judge Marcus has set out his arguments for evidence-based sentencing in several articles including: "Sentencing in the Temple of Denunciation: Criminal Justice's Weakest Link" (2004) 1 Ohio State J. Crim, L. 671; "Comments on the Model Penal Code: Sentencing Preliminary Draft 1" (2003) 30 Am. J. Crim. L. 136 ("Any improvement in criminal sentencing must make crime reduction the primary focus of sentencing" (p.150); "... those who make policy and individual decisions about sentences [should] be provided with the best information available, so as to determine which dispositions are most effective in preventing the recidivist criminal

entitled "Smart Sentencing: Sentencing for Public Safety and Crime Reduction", is the best-known judicial advocate of this approach. He insists that the information tendered to judges at sentencing hearings should include all available data on the effectiveness of various measures in dealing with an offence and/or offender of the category being sentenced. In fact, the State of Oregon now requires that 75 per cent of its corrections funding be spent on evidence-based programmes. Experimental criminology, now something of a growth area, also emphasises the importance of selecting measures which have proved empirically effective when deciding on criminal justice policies in areas such as policing, prosecution and sentencing. Systematic reviews of empirical evidence are seen as the best means currently available for evaluating effective responses to crime, especially in areas such as policing, restorative justice, treatment programmes and sentencing.[38]

In common with most other utilitarian goals, crime reduction produces its share of moral and empirical problems. Measures chosen for their effectiveness may not invariably be more punitive than those chosen for retributive or deterrent purposes. As it happens, a major study by Sherman and Strang shows that restorative justice may be more effective than conventional criminal justice measures in preventing or reducing the repetition of certain kinds of crime.[39] But it is surely as likely that research would occasionally point to a lengthy prison sentence as the most effective crime-reduction strategy even where it might be grossly disproportionate to the offence of conviction. This is a serious moral difficulty as it raises the spectre of preventive detention which we believe to be repugnant to our constitutional norms.[40] Some advocates of evidence-based sentencing would of course respond that it is just as likely to produce more lenient sentences provided it is applied across the board to all offence categories. Judge Marcus, for example, accepts proportionality as one of the limits within which an evidence-based approach to sentencing should operate, though it is not entirely clear how this would work out in practice. In a comprehensive critique of evidence-based sentencing, Etienne notes that it is "only mildly interested in retributive notions of just deserts."[41] She also expresses the valid concern that this approach to sentencing could create further disparity by favouring better-

---

behaviour of which offenders" (p.169)); "*Blakely, Booker* and the Future of Sentencing" (2005) 17 Fed. Sen. Rep. 243; "Conversations on Evidence-Based Sentencing" (2009) 1 *Chapman Journal of Criminal Justice* 61. See also Wolff, "Missouri's Information-Based Discretionary Sentencing System" (2006) 4 Ohio State J. Crim. Law 95.

[38] Sherman, "Evidence and Liberty: The Promise of Experimental Criminology" (2009) 9 *Criminology and Criminal Justice* 5.

[39] Sherman and Strang, *Restorative Justice: the Evidence* (London: Smith Institute, 2007).

[40] Robinson, "Punishing Dangerousness: Cloaking Preventative Detention as Criminal Justice" (2001) 114 Harv. L.R. 1429; Robinson, *Distributive Principles of Criminal Law* (Oxford: Oxford University Press, 2008), Ch.6.

[41] Etienne, "Legal and Practical Implications of Evidence-Based Sentencing by Judges" (2009) 1 *Chapman Journal of Criminal Justice* 43 at 45–46.

off defendants who can furnish the sentencing court with favourable empirical evidence and identify suitable community-based programmes in which they are willing to participate, perhaps at their own cost.[42] Intertwined with all of this is the empirical problem of how much reliance we can place upon science. Social science research is forever making new discoveries and challenging existing assumptions. That is one of its great strengths but also a quality which calls for circumspection when relying on its results as a basis for decision-making. It would surely compound the injustice if offenders were incarcerated for disproportionately long periods on foot of research findings which were subsequently contradicted. Until recently at least, it was accepted that most predictive instruments were prone to a high margin of error. Actuarial models of prediction are generally considered superior to unstructured clinical judgment, and there are some indications that those models are becoming more sophisticated and reliable.[43] To be fair, many proponents of evidence-based decision-making acknowledge this point and they accept the need for large scale randomised trials to produce reliable data.[44] In a widely-quoted editorial in the *British Medical Journal*, the authors wrote:

> "Good doctors use both individual clinical expertise and the best available external evidence, and neither alone is enough. Without clinical expertise, practice risks becoming tyrannised by evidence, for even excellent external evidence may be inapplicable to or inappropriate for an individual patient. Without current best evidence, practice risks becoming rapidly out of date, to the detriment of patients".[45]

This observation is highly germane to sentencing as well. Discretion, if it is to be exercised in a principled and effective manner, should certainly be informed by relevant empirical information as well as by governing legal principles. After all, rehabilitation and deterrence remain valid sentencing objectives subject to the limiting principle of proportionality. Reliable information on the rehabilitative or dissuasive impact of various sentencing dispositions is certainly desirable in so far as it can reliably be obtained. In fact, Hogarth, who pioneered the idea of computer-assisted sentencing, envisaged the development of a system which would provide judges with information about the probabilities of reconviction

---

[42] Etienne (fn.41 above) at 52 ("The beneficiaries at sentencing will be white collar, American-born, English-speaking, privileged, connected, and wealthy defendants with strong community ties").

[43] Andrews, Bonta and Wormith, "The Recent Past and Near Future of Risk and/or Need Assessment" (2006) 52 *Crime and Delinquency* 7.

[44] Bird, "Prescribing sentence: time for evidence-based justice" (2004) 364 *The Lancet* 1457; Atkins, Siegel and Slutsky, "Making Policy when the Evidence is in Dispute" (2005) 24 *Health Affairs* 102.

[45] Sackett et al., "Evidence-Based Medicine: What It Is and What It Isn't" (January 1996) 312 *British Medical Journal* 71.

associated with the various options available.[46] But judgement and experience are equally indispensable. Scientific data, no matter how sophisticated, can never replace an individualised judicial assessment of the offender who is present in court, taking account of all that is known about the offender's record and the circumstances of the offence. Such data can, of course, help in deciding on the most appropriate measure to adopt, but no more than that.

In any event, the essential point being made here is that the kind of general information required by sentencing judges must be determined by the penal purposes which they are expected to achieve. A sentencing system grounded on a policy of just deserts or which has adopted proportionality as its dominant distributive principle will call for one kind of information bank. A system animated predominantly or exclusively by a policy of public protection and crime reduction will require another. This is not to deny that a database for the former system, of which Ireland's would be reasonably typical because of its adherence to proportionality, might not also include relevant research findings. In fact, it will later be argued that it should. But the overriding objective in a system like ours must be to furnish judges with reliable and accessible information on formal sentencing rules and principles as set out in statutes and appeal court jurisprudence, and on the past sentencing practice of the relevant trial courts.

SENTENCING INFORMATION SYSTEMS: A BRIEF HISTORY

The idea of a sentencing information system as a means of promoting more coherent sentencing practices is sometimes traced back to an address delivered by Norval Morris in 1953 to an Australian law conference.[47] While Morris undoubtedly stressed the need for more and better information for judges on the manner in which sentences were implemented, including information on the reality of prison life and on the effectiveness of various forms of punishment, he referred only briefly to the idea of a sentencing information system as we generally understand that concept today. Overall, his address represents an important milestone in the development of sentencing scholarship. Morris, who later moved to the United States and came to be regarded as one of the leading criminal justice scholars of the twentieth century, was clearly thinking about sentencing in a more profound and creative way than most of his contemporaries. He drew attention to several British and American studies which had showed significant levels of inter-judge disparity in sentencing convicted offenders, and concluded by suggesting:

---

[46] Hogarth, *Sentencing as a Human Process* (Toronto: Toronto University Press, 1971), p.392. See also Doob and Park, "Computerised Sentencing Information for Judges: An Aid to the Sentencing Process" (1987) 30 *Criminal Law Quarterly* 54.

[47] Morris, "Sentencing Convicted Criminals" (1953) 27 *Australian Law Journal* 186 (address delivered to Eighth Legal Convention of the Law Council of Australia).

"More information of current sentencing practice and the effects of different punishments is essential, and this should be of two kinds: statistics in each state regarding the sentences imposed by different courts (related at least to the crimes committed, to the ages of the criminals sentenced and to their criminal records), so that individual judges and magistrates may be able to see clearly where they stand in relation to their brethren; and follow-up studies of the later histories of samples of convicted criminals, so that the effectiveness of different punishments for different types of criminals may be gauged and enlightened rather than fortuitous individualization of punishment become possible."[48]

This recommendation, if implemented, would provide a valuable database for sentencing judges, particularly in a federal system like Australia where considerable disparity might exist between, as well as within, individual states. The first part of the recommendation approximates to a modern version of a sentencing information system by concentrating on judicial sentencing practices. The second, no less important, would aim to furnish information on the effectiveness of various measures for different categories of offender, a more resource-intensive exercise. The printed version of Morris's address in the *Australian Law Journal* is followed by a summary of contributions from other participants. One of these, Mr Justice Ligertwood, referred to a system in place in his own jurisdiction of South Australia. He said that in the South Australia Supreme Court which dealt with all non-minor offences and which sentenced 40 to 50 offenders a month, the judges kept a sentence book "which went back to time immemorial". Before imposing sentence, a judge would consult the book in order to be as consistent as possible, not only with his own previous sentencing practice, but also with that of his colleagues.[49] This, we may assume, represented a sort of sentencing information system in a pre-computer age. The advent of computer-based technology clearly opened up new possibilities for the collection and analysis of sentencing data, an idea that began to be explored from the early 1970s onwards.[50]

The first documented efforts to develop a large scale sentencing information system were made in Canada. Doob and Park developed a system which operated for several years in four Canadian provinces. Having secured financial assistance from both government and foundation sources, they constructed a computerised database on existing sentencing practices for a reasonably wide range of commonly prosecuted offences. Several meetings were held with judges and eventually a standard form consisting of one page only was devised for the collection of data. Judges themselves or, in some cases, court staff working under judicial supervision were charged with completing those forms

---

[48] Morris (fn.47 above), p.200.
[49] (1953) 57 *Australian Law Journal* 205.
[50] See, in particular, Hogarth (fn.46 above).

which, in turn, were used to input data to the computer system. Among the many logistical problems to be surmounted was the question of how to deal with previous convictions. Eventually, rather than opt for a detailed list of previous convictions, they opted for a simple formula whereby previous record would be described as: "None, inconsequential", "Some, but not serious" and "Substantial". Judgments and case summaries of the various courts of appeal were also included. This was a system which appeared to hold considerable promise, and cost very little, yet it did not eventually work out largely because judges lost interest in it. They appeared to attach greater significance to appeal court judgements which were mostly available from other sources in any event, but they showed little interest in the sentencing practices of their own trial court colleagues.[51] A separate system which operated in British Columbia from 1987 to 1992 had extensive data on trial court sentencing outcomes, decisions of the Court of Appeal and other relevant information. That, too, was abandoned for want of judicial interest and also on account of cost.

Scotland's sentencing information system probably remains the most sophisticated case-based system yet developed and also the best documented.[52] Based on an initiative by the senior judiciary, it was constructed from court archival material on sentences passed by the High Court during the period 1989 to 2003. In all, more than 13,000 cases, including 1,000 appeal court decisions were analysed.[53] The results were presented in such a way as to permit the end user to interrogate the system at various levels. For any of the offences covered, the user could view a bar chart illustrating the range of sentences imposed and could then elicit more specific information according to the presence or absence of various factors and eventually view narrative descriptions of individual cases. Appeal court decisions were also available in full text. The Scottish system was created retrospectively from existing information and on the basis of a taxonomy developed with future judicial users. The researchers were fortunate in having access to such detailed records. It was envisaged that court staff would be trained to collect and record data on an ongoing basis in order to keep the system operative and up-to-date. As matters now stand, the Scottish system seems to

---

[51] Doob, *Sentencing Aids: Final Report to the Donner Canadian Foundation* (Centre of Criminology, University of Toronto, 1990).

[52] Tata, Wilson and Hutton, "Representations of Knowledge and Discretionary Decision Making" (1996) 2 *Journal of Information Law and Technology: http://www2.warwick.ac.uk/fac/soc/law/elj/jilt/1996_2/tata* [Last accessed August 23, 2011]; Hutton and Tata, "Sentencing Reform by Self-Regulation: Present and Future Prospects of the Sentencing Information System for Scotland's High Court Justiciary" (2000) 6 *Scottish Journal of Criminology* 37; Tata and Hutton, "Beyond the Technology of Quick Fixes" (2003) 16:1 Fed. Sent. Rep. 67; Tata, "Sentencing as Craftwork" (2007) 16 *Social & Legal Studies* 425; Tata, "Sentencing and penal decision-making: Is Scotland losing its distinctiveness?" in Croall, Mooney and Munro (eds), *Criminal Justice in Scotland* (Cullompton: Willan Publishing, 2010), p.195, pp.210–211.

[53] Tata et al., *A Sentencing Information System for the High Court of Justiciary of Scotland: Report of the First Phase of Implementation and Enhancement* (Centre for Sentencing Research, University of Strathclyde, 2002).

have suffered much the same fate as its Canadian predecessors, though part of the blame for this must be attributed to the virtual absence of quality control and the little training provided to users. Despite their initial enthusiasm, few judges now appear to use it, although this could well change in the future. One peculiar feature of that system was that access was restricted solely to judges. This, in turn, meant that lawyers could not incorporate information from the system into their submissions and this may well have contributed to its present fate. However, the fact remains that the Scottish system was groundbreaking. Its creators had to grapple with some very fundamental problems about the nature of sentencing decision-making in general, and the published academic research resulting from the exercise has been highly illuminating for those wishing the follow the same path in other jurisdictions.[54] One major problem facing anyone who attempts to develop such a system is how to treat multiple convictions. Sentencing guideline judgments and academic treatises on sentencing often proceed on the assumption, which has little basis in reality, that courts typically sentence offenders for one offence at a time. Nothing could be further from the truth. Trouble, according to the old proverb, may always come in threes but offences of conviction can sometimes come in even higher quantities. The Scottish system adopted a principal offence approach whereby cases are classified both according to the most serious offence of conviction and also a more novel whole offence approach. The two exist side-by-side but complement one another.

Decision-support systems developed in two Australian jurisdictions, Victoria and New South Wales, also provide excellent models for a viable sentencing information system. Each of these jurisdictions has specialist bodies devoted to the study and analysis of sentencing practice, the Sentencing Advisory Council in Victoria, and the Judicial Commission as well as the Sentencing Council in New South Wales. None of them appears to have constructed a searchable database of trial court sentencing practice similar to the Scottish system, but all provide a great deal of information and research findings on the general operation of the sentencing systems within their respective jurisdictions. Victoria's Sentencing Advisory Council is an independent statutory body created in 2004.[55] It has a council of nine to 12 members and significant number of specialist support staff. It produces statistical reports on sentencing practice as well as reports on various contentious aspects of sentencing, a relatively recent example being a document on sentence indication and specified sentence discounts.[56] The Judicial Commission of New South Wales was established by the Judicial Officers Act

---

[54] See, in particular, the publications cited in fn.52 above.

[55] Freiberg, "The Victorian Sentencing Advisory Council: Incorporating Community Views into the Sentencing Process" in Freiberg and Gelb (eds), *Penal Populism, Sentencing Councils and Sentencing Policy* (Cullompton: Willan Publishing, 2008), Ch.11.

[56] Sentencing Advisory Council, *Sentence Indication and Specified Sentence Discounts: Final Report* (2007), available at *www.sentencingcouncil.vic.gov.au*.

1986 and one of its stated purposes is to the assist the courts in achieving consistency in sentencing.[57] It continues to produce an enormous amount of very useful information, much of which is of great comparative value in other common-law jurisdictions. Its online service Judicial Information Research System (JIRS) includes legislation, case law, sentencing principles and statistical information. A subset of this overall system, the Sentencing Information System (SIS), is available on subscription only. Among its more valuable services are bench books which are regularly updated with information about recent decisions and research monographs on specific sentencing topics.[58] The Sentencing Council of New South Wales was established in 2003 with the specific purpose of advising the Attorney General on sentencing and related matters. It has a more diverse membership than the Judicial Commission as it includes victim representatives and representatives of the general community. As well as publishing annual reports on sentencing trends and practices, it also publishes detailed reports on specific sentencing issues including fines, suspended sentences and similar matters.[59]

Ireland has recently completed a pilot project on the establishment of a sentencing information system (ISIS) which aims to combine the best features of the Scottish and Australian models.[60] It includes a searchable database of trial court sentencing decisions, much like Scotland's, as well as statistical information, appeal court judgments and other information somewhat similar to that provided by the Judicial Commission of New South Wales. The project was sponsored by the Courts Service and was supervised by a steering committee, consisting mainly of senior judges. In terms of constructing a database of trial court sentencing practice, it started with one major disadvantage compared to Scotland in that it did not have access to records from which a reliable data set could be constructed. This was simply because sufficiently detailed records did not exist. However, this also proved to be something of an advantage in so far as it meant that records had to be compiled prospectively. This was done by selecting a number of Circuit Court venues, mainly in Dublin (but later including Cork and Limerick) into which researchers were sent to collect data. A similar exercise, though of much shorter duration, was carried out in some

---

[57] Potas et al., "Informing the Discretion: The Sentencing Information System of the Judicial Commission of New South Wales" (1998) 6 *International Journal of Law and Information Technology* 99; Abadee, "The New South Wales Sentencing Council" in Freiberg and Gelb (eds), (fn.55 above), Ch.9.

[58] See, for example, *Sentencing Robbery Offenders since the Henry Guideline Judgment* Research Monograph 30 (2007).

[59] See the Council's website at *www.lawlink.nsw.gov.au/sentencingcouncil*, and Abadee, "The NSW Sentencing Council" paper prepared for the Victorian Sentencing Advisory Council Conference, July 2006, and available on that website.

[60] Conroy and Gunning, "The Irish Sentencing Information System (ISIS); A Practical Guide to a Practical Tool" [2009] *Judicial Studies Institute Journal* 37. The pilot itself may be viewed at *www.irishsentencing.ie*.

Dublin District Courts and yielded about 120 cases. All of the researchers were recently qualified barristers who already had some experience of criminal practice. They were provided with a questionnaire or template designed by the steering committee to collect as much relevant data as possible on all sentencing decisions made by the courts in question. During the early stages of the pilot study, the researchers provided a great deal of valuable feedback on the adequacy of the existing templates which were then adjusted, as the need arose, to accommodate various issues which had not previously been foreseen. Once a final template was agreed, it proved to be very effective in collecting relevant data. The initial collection phase began early in 2007 and was completed by the end of 2009 by which time the database had 440 Circuit Court cases involving more than 700 sentences. Because the data was collected specifically for the purpose of constructing an information system, detailed information is available on each case in regard to the offender, the victim, the offence, previous convictions and sentences, bail status at the time of the offence, sentence imposed and so forth. The system can be interrogated at various levels, like the Scottish system, to the point at which users will be able to view the specific data on individual cases. It is envisaged that the system will be publicly available, as the results of the pilot project now are. Offender identities are not revealed; otherwise, the system might have run counter to data protection legislation and might have had the further undesirable consequence of allowing jurors or potential jurors in the future to check if persons currently on trial had previous criminal records. Under Irish law, a jury may not, save in very exceptional circumstances, be made aware of an accused person's previous criminal record. The Irish system also aims to include appeal court judgments, statistical information and other relevant material as it develops over the years. Assuming that it continues to receive a reasonable level of financial and institution support, this system has the capacity to be a world leader in so far as it encompasses the best features of both the Scottish and Australian models. It has the advantage of being confined to a relatively small jurisdiction which happens to have a courts service with high levels of technological expertise. In these circumstances, maintaining the trial court sentencing database, which will probably be the most cost-intensive component of the system, should be entirely feasible. The cost of developing the pilot project was, by any reasonable standards, miniscule. Indeed, it is interesting to contrast the situations in Ireland and the state of Victoria which have broadly similar populations (4.5 million in one and 5.5 million in the other). Yet, the Victorian Sentencing Advisory Council had an income of almost 2 million Australian dollars from public funds in 2009.[61]

---

[61] *Sentencing Advisory Council: Annual Report 2008–2009* (Melbourne, 2009).

CONTENT, DESIGN AND MAINTENANCE

From this brief survey of the various sentencing information systems developed over the past few decades, we can identify a few basic models. The case-based model as first developed in Canada and more fully in Scotland aims to provide systematic information on past trial court sentencing practice by allowing users to identify sentences previously imposed for a range of offences. Users can interrogate case-based systems from a menu of offence or offender characteristics in a way which allows them to retrieve information at varying levels of generality or specificity. They might merely want, for example, to view the range of sentences imposed for manslaughter over a given period or they may (and probably will) want to go further and view the salient characteristics of the cases in which particular levels of punishment were imposed. Other models are essentially data driven in the sense that they provide more general statistical information on recent sentencing practice. The information is general only in the sense that it does not describe the outcomes of specific cases although it may be quite specific in its presentation and analysis of existing sentencing patterns. Other models are also possible. An information system might, for example, consist of a systematic presentation of appeal court judgments, perhaps incorporating some foreign jurisprudence for comparative purposes. It could also concentrate on presenting policy documents and academic writings, or it might be more prescriptive in nature by recommending benchmarks or guidelines of some description. Each of these models creates its own set of conceptual and logistical problems. From a developmental perspective, a system devoted mainly or exclusively to appeal court judgments should be the least difficult to devise and construct. All written judgments originate nowadays in electronic form, if only in the elementary sense that they are typed and stored on a word processor, so it should be easy to make them searchable by reference to offence, sentence, defendant's name, date of delivery and so forth. An excellent model is available on the website of the English Sentencing Council which includes, amongst other things, a compendium of guideline judgments issued by the Court of Appeal (Criminal Division). The compendium is divided into broad categories, such as sex offences and drug offences, with more specific sub-categories where links to the relevant judgments can be found.[62]

Maintenance is undoubtedly the biggest challenge facing most sentencing information systems. Institutional and financial support may readily be available when the project is first mooted and throughout the early stages of development, but the utility of any information system, irrespective of its content and design, will always depend on its currency. A database consisting solely of appeal court judgments, which is probably the least complicated form of information system, would not only be inadequate but positively misleading unless all new judgments, especially those effecting any changes or developments in the law,

---

[62] *www.sentencingcouncil.org.uk.*

were added as soon as possible. The same holds true of case-based systems and statistical databases of the Australian variety which need not perhaps be updated with the same degree of urgency as collections of appeal court judgments, but which may also mislead unless they reflect current sentencing trends. In recent years, for example, changing social attitudes have led to heavier sentences being imposed in many countries for certain road traffic, corruption and child pornography offences. An information system which was out of date by a few years would fail to reflect contemporary sentencing practice in these areas. The ease with which a case-based or data-based system can be maintained depends to a great extent on the presence or absence of an institutional culture of record-keeping. Unless the raw data is consistently and accurately recorded, there is little point in creating sophisticated systems for storage, analysis and retrieval. There is no one ideal recipe for the effective collection of data because so much depends on the roles assigned to different court officials, the amount of relevant data that may conveniently be gleaned from other documentation and, of course, the amount of data which it is desired to collect. The pilot scheme conducted in Ireland in 2007–2009 probably represented the most thorough data collection exercise undertaken in any jurisdiction to date, because it was based on a template specifically designed to cater for the information needs of the intended users. Yet, financial constraints, if nothing else, will render it practically impossible to continue this exercise indefinitely, especially if it is to be extended to all courts, or even to all Circuit Courts which deal with the vast bulk of serious criminal cases. Other data collection models will have to be explored, though it should be possible to devise an effective alternative. Regard must obviously be had to the time and opportunity available to judges and other court personnel to complete the relevant forms. It is telling, for example, that when Doob and his colleagues were developing an information system in Canada in the 1980s, they agreed that it would be unrealistic to expect a busy trial court judge to spend more than one minute completing the form for routine cases.[63] The form consisted of single page in checklist format. Obviously, the more detailed the information collected, the more valuable the resulting database will be, but those responsible for managing the system may ultimately have to cut their cloth according to the measure of what can reasonably be expected from those responsible for compiling the raw data. In 2008, the Gage Working Group commissioned a month-long data collection exercise in ten Crown Court Centres in England and Wales, though the survey was confined to four offences.[64] Each judge was required to complete a 10-page form (preferably in electronic form though a hard copy option was also available) for each adult offender sentenced in a case where the principal offence was among the four being surveyed. There was an estimated survey return rate of 52 per cent,

---

[63] Doob and Park (fn.46 above), p.61.
[64] Sentencing Commission Working Group, *Sentencing Guidelines in England and Wales: An Evolutionary Approach* and its addendum, *Crown Court Sentencing Survey* (London, 2008). The four offences were: assault and other offences against the person; sexual assault and sexual assault of a child under 13; robbery; burglary of a dwelling or non-dwelling.

with more than 320 returns. Understandably, however, judges commented on the time-consuming nature of the exercise and some indicated that they were unable to deal with as many cases as normal because of the time needed to complete the forms. The Working Group had originally estimated that it would take 10 to 15 minutes to complete the survey, though this was probably optimistic in light of the range of questions to be answered. The Working Group's report acknowledged the burden that such an exercise, if be routinely carried out, would place on the court system and accepted that additional resources would be necessary. It did, however, note that such exercises are routinely carried out by American judges with the assistance of court officials.[65]

Assuming that sufficient quantity of relevant and reliable data can be collected, an effective structure must then be put in place to manage that data, to analyse it and present the results in an appropriate format. This in turn requires an independent research or information unit dedicated to that purpose. At the time of writing, the Irish Government has just produced the heads of a bill providing for the creation of a judicial council. This will be an independent statutory body with its own structure and resources. Among its primary functions will be the provision of continuing education and professional development for judges, the preparation of bench books and the dissemination of information on sentencing. Once established, the Judicial Council would be the perfect home for a sentencing information system like that now developed in pilot form. Within that kind of permanent structure, the system could be developed and adapted to meet the ongoing needs of the courts.

DATA AND NARRATIVE

Before terms like "computer science" and "information technology" came into vogue, we had "data processing". Mention of data processing today may conjure up images of large mainframe computers with punch cards and the like, but the much more accessible and sophisticated computer technology we now enjoy is still largely devoted to the collection, storage, retrieval and analysis of data, although it also has a much wider potential. The digitalisation of printed books for internet publication is one example, and probably not a very impressive one by current standards, of how computer technology has moved well beyond data processing in the traditional sense. Case-based sentencing information systems are clearly data-driven because they entail the collection and electronic storage of certain key pieces of information about decided cases, with appropriate mechanisms for convenient retrieval and consultation by intended users. Data in this sense is often contrasted with narrative. Lev Manovich, a leading theorist of digital media, has described the contrast in these terms:

---

[65] Sentencing Commission Working Group, *Sentencing Guidelines in England and Wales* (London, 2008), paras 5.4 and 5.5 and *Crown Court Sentencing Survey* (London, 2008), Chs 2 and 3.

"As a cultural form, database represents the world as a list of items and it refuses to order this list. In contrast, a narrative creates a cause-and-effect trajectory of seemingly unordered items (events). Therefore, database and narrative are natural enemies. Competing for the same territory of human culture, each claims an exclusive right to make meaning out of the world."[66]

Data and narrative already co-existed, even in the realm of case law, long before the advent of computer technology. Digests used to be the principal tool for case retrieval on a subject or topic basis. A lawyer seeking relevant authorities on, say, the defence of provocation would consult case digests which were typically published at five- or ten-year intervals. Digested cases were first classified under broad headings such as "criminal law" and then under more detailed headings such as (for example) "defences" and "provocation". An entry for a specific case might consist of no more than the *ratio* or it might also include a very short account of the facts. To discover the full narrative, one had to consult the court judgment. Narrative is essentially about connection and meaning. Within the social sciences, where narrative is increasingly valued as a form of qualitative research, it has been described as a discourse "with a clear sequential order that connects events in a meaningful way for a definite audience and thus [offers] insights about the world and/or people's experiences".[67]

A sentencing system committed to individualisation and proportionality demands narrative precedents, not necessarily to the exclusion of statistical data but certainly in addition to it. Judges and lawyers working within such a system need narrative accounts which connect the very basic facts about the offence of conviction and the offender's previous convictions, with the sentence ultimately imposed. Otherwise, the relevance and value of particular precedents, whether in the form of appeal court judgments or examples of past sentencing practice, will be difficult to evaluate. The best sentencing information systems therefore will incorporate both data and narrative. The Scottish system achieved this goal by allowing for the progressive interrogation of the database to a point where outline details of specific cases could be obtained. Another model, close to the Australian systems mentioned earlier, would provide statistical data on sentencing practices coupled with a comprehensive and accessible database of appeal court judgments. Ideally, an information system should incorporate all of these elements though the feasibility of doing so will obviously depend on the level of resources committed to the exercise. One serious limitation of appeal

---

[66] Manovich, *The Language of New Media* (Cambridge, Mass.: MIT Press, 2001), p.225. See also Aas, *Sentencing in the Age of Information: From Faust to Macintosh* (London: Glasshouse Press, 2005), pp.82 et seq.

[67] Hinchman and Hinchman, "Introduction" in Hinchman and Hinchman (eds), *Memory, Identity, Community: the Idea of Narrative in the Social Sciences* (Albany, NY: State University of New York Press, 1997), p.xvi. See also Elliott, *Using Narrative in Social Research: Qualitative and Quantitative Approaches* (London: Sage Publications, 2005).

court judgments, which is also reflected in much of the sentencing scholarship built around them, is that they tend to focus on single offences or on specific factors associated with certain kinds of offences or certain categories of offender. American-style guidelines, and grid-based guidelines in particular, go much further in this regard by prescribing the precise weight to be attributed to particular factors such as the amount of drugs involved or the offender's role in the overall criminal enterprise. These approaches fail to reflect the complexity of the task faced by most sentencing judges on a day-to-day basis. More often than not, the offender will have been convicted of more than one offence and, irrespective of the number of offences involved, the judge must usually take (and will usually want to take) a holistic view of the offender's culpability and personal circumstances. In these circumstances, an information system based, partly at least, on narratives of past practice is likely to be far more useful than the more atomistic or fragmented approach reflected in many guideline systems.[68]

Data collection and retention practices must nowadays comply with national and international rules which are primarily designed to protect personal privacy.[69] Ethnic data has become a particularly sensitive issue, and this is obviously a matter to which operators of sentencing information systems must have regard. Certain ethnic groups, and the Roma in particular, have claimed that data can be manipulated in order to create or reinforce popular assumptions about such matters as their propensity to engage in criminal activities, begging and so forth. Opinion seems divided, at international level at least, over the collection of ethnic data.[70] Those in favour of collection claim that in the absence of reliable empirical information it will be difficult to advance reasoned arguments for measures to counter discrimination and promote greater social integration. Others argue that ethnic data, particularly in the area of criminal justice, can be used (or more often abused) to the detriment of certain marginalised groups. Selective data on the tendency of certain groups to engage in begging, for example, may promote negative and distorted stereotypes unless counterbalanced with further data on background social and economic circumstances. This does not necessarily imply that information about national or ethnic origin should be excluded from published sentencing data. But it does

---

[68] Miller, "A Map of Sentencing and a Compass for Judges: Sentencing Information Systems, Transparency, and the Next Generation of Reform" (2005) 105 Columbia L.R. 1351 at 1379 ("An SIS offers the possibility of suggesting narratives flexible enough to account for variations in key facts and the range of seriousness reflected in the distribution of sentences actually imposed").

[69] e.g. Convention for the Protection of Individuals with regard to Automatic Processing of Personal Data (1981) CETS No. 108 (entered into force in 1985 and now ratified by 42 countries).

[70] Council of Europe, *Roma and Statistics* MG-S-ROM (2000) 13; Project on Ethnic Relations, *Roma and Statistics* (Princeton, New Jersey, 2000); Simon, *"Ethnic" Statistics and Data Protection in the Council of Europe Countries: Study Report* (Council of Europe, Strasbourg, 2007); *The Situation of Roma in Europe and Relevant Activities in the Council of Europe* (Parliamentary Assembly, Council of Europe, 2010).

require that the collection and presentation of data should comply with certain ethical principles such as those applicable to European Community statistics. A regulation adopted in 1997 lists those principles as impartiality, reliability, relevance, cost effectiveness, statistical confidentiality and transparency.[71] The use made of ethnic statistics should obviously be subject to equivalent standards.

A TENTATIVE EVALUATION

Viewed from a historical perspective, sentencing information systems are still in their infancy, so any conclusions as to their usefulness and effectiveness must necessarily be tentative. Programme evaluation in any sphere of public administration usually begins with an identification of the purposes which the programme was designed to serve, so that appropriate performance indicators can be agreed accordingly. Sentencing information systems, as noted, may have a variety of overlapping purposes. They may be intended to generate more consistent sentencing (however, that is to be defined), or merely to assist judges in discharging their sentencing function without necessarily obliging them to work towards the elimination of inter-judge disparity, or they might be designed primarily to allow for the collection, and possibly the dissemination, of detailed and reliable data on existing sentencing practice. These various aims are not, of course, mutually exclusive and may eventually have a cumulative impact. For instance, the availability of reliable information on existing practice may prompt or facilitate the introduction of other measures more explicitly designed to structure judicial discretion.

Most sentencing information systems are intended as decision-support systems rather than expert systems.[72] The main difference between the two is that expert systems are designed to replace or imitate human decision-makers by, for example, solving mathematical problems, whereas decision-support systems are designed to assist and inform human decision-making.[73] There can be little doubt about the practical utility and value of the kind of information

---

[71] EC Regulation on Community Statistics (No. 322/97 of 17 February 1997) OJ L 052, 22.2.97, p.1. See also Guidelines Concerning Computerized Personal Data Files, adopted by United Nations General Assembly on December 14, 1990.

[72] On the use of decision-support systems in sentencing and related areas, see Schild, "Criminal Sentencing and Intelligent Decision Support" (1998) 6 *Artificial Intelligence and Law* 151; Lovegrove, "Statistical Information Systems as a Means to Consistency and Rationality in Sentencing" (1999) 7 *International Journal of Law and Information Technology* 31; Henham, "On the Philosophical and Theoretical Implications of Judicial Decision Support Systems" (2000) 14:3 *International Review of Law, Computers and Technology* 283; Hall et al., "Supporting Discretionary Decision-Making with Information Technology: A Case Study in the Criminal Sentencing Jurisdiction" (2005) 1 *University of Ottawa Law and Technology Journal* 1.

[73] Hutton, "Sentencing, Rationality and Human Technology" (1995) 22:4 *Journal of Law and Society* 549; Susskind, *Expert Systems in Law* (Oxford: Oxford University Press, 1987), and Susskind, *The Future of Law* (Oxford: Oxford University Press, 1996), pp.120 et seq.

provided by the Australian sentencing information model—appeal court judgments, statistical surveys and analyses, research reports and so forth. Courts already draw upon these sources quite extensively; in fact they have no option but to follow binding precedents contained in appeal court judgments. Irish courts may not make much use of statistical material—the same is largely true of courts in other common-law jurisdictions—but this is due in some measure at least to the absence of reliable statistical data. The Court of Criminal Appeal has occasionally sought or been presented with data on the sentencing of particular offences, but the material submitted has seldom been sufficiently detailed to offer much meaningful assistance.

Systems based on the Scottish model, or incorporating such a component, may be greeted with more scepticism. Experience seems to show, after all, that those judges for whom searchable databases of trial court sentencing decisions were designed seldom make much use of them. However, before there is any rush to judgement on this point, a few important considerations must be borne in mind. First, the experience in question is very limited, being largely confined to the short-lived Canadian experiments and, apparently, the Scottish system, although that may prove more resilient in the longer term, particularly if political efforts are made to introduce formal sentencing guidelines. Secondly, there is no reason why the success of a system should be evaluated solely by reference to its use by trial judges. They certainly form an important constituency of user, but by no means the only one. Responsibility for drawing a court's attention to all relevant legal authorities and other pertinent information rests unambiguously with counsel (or solicitors, as the case may be) appearing for the various parties. The Scottish system was accessible solely to judges which, in turn, meant that counsel could not draw upon the database when formulating their submissions. Apart from everything else, such an arrangement runs counter to the fundamental principle of justice that a judge or other public decision-maker should not reach a decision on the basis of information of which the parties are unaware or which they have no opportunity to challenge. This was one reason why the Steering Committee charged with developing the Irish system decided at the outset that the system, once operative, would be publicly accessible to all.

When assessing the need for a comprehensive database of past sentencing practice, regard must also be had to existing information sources, or the lack of them, in the particular jurisdiction concerned. The provision of detailed and reliable information on sentencing practice facilitates professional research and serves to enhance public accountability. Some jurisdictions are already well served with detailed, up-to-date official data on the operation of their criminal justice systems, but others are not. In Ireland right now, rational debate about sentencing policy, and the extent to which it may be in need of reform, is virtually impossible because of the information vacuum in which it must unfold. This knowledge deficit has existed since the foundation of the State, and possibly earlier, but its impact has been particularly noticeable in recent years with repeated public demands that "something be done" about judicial sentencing practices. Precisely what needs to be made right is seldom clear because of uncertainty as to what, if anything, is wrong. Available statistical information is at best skeletal and seldom sufficient to make an informed assessment of the manner in which most categories of offence and offender are currently sentenced. In these circumstances, the case for establishing a sentencing information system seems unanswerable. Sentencing is always a matter of considerable, and very legitimate, public concern. The manner in which courts discharge their sentencing function may impinge heavily on public safety, not to mention the public purse. The public do indeed have a right to know but, more importantly, they have a right to know the truth, something which can only emerge from the routine collection, analysis and dissemination of reliable information on the sentences ultimately imposed in those criminal cases, with all of their attendant complexities, which have resulted in conviction.

Nobody expects that judges will invariably consult a sentencing information system, where it exists, before deciding on each and every sentence which they are called upon to impose. Time constraints alone, especially in courts of summary jurisdiction, would rule out such a routine practice. Moreover, some trial judges have such extensive experience in sentencing commonly-prosecuted offences that they are already well aware of going penalty rates. Cases will, however, arise where a judge, even an experienced one, can benefit from information about sentences previously imposed in similar or analogous cases. This might happen where a case had some unusual combination of facts or where the offender's circumstances seemed in some respect unique. A judge who is undecided as to whether to impose a fairly short prison sentence or a suspended sentence in, say, a manslaughter case would surely find it useful to investigate the circumstances in which similar sentences were previously imposed. He or she (as well as counsel) will obviously want to consult relevant appeal court judgments as well, but that merely confirms the wisdom of having an information system which is as comprehensive as possible in terms of content. In other jurisdictions which have experimented with sentencing information systems, judges have sometimes remarked that they find information about past sentencing practice most helpful when dealing with an uncommon offence. Rather paradoxically, of course, that is when the database is least likely to be helpful, in its early stages of development at any rate. But that situation also illustrates the need for a further component which any sentencing information system can easily accommodate, and that is a series of working papers or briefing documents on sentencing particular offences or certain categories of offender. An experienced Circuit Court judge in this country probably needs little assistance when it comes to sentencing a routine burglary offence but the same might not hold true when it came, for example, to sentencing a perjury offence (particularly since this is a common-law offence with no statutory maximum sentence). Here it would be useful to have a briefing document distilling such principles as can be identified from existing Irish authorities and from the case law of other jurisdictions with a similar offence and broadly similar sentencing principles. The same might be said of sentencing for manslaughter following a successful plea of diminished responsibility which has only recently been introduced here.[74] Again, it should be recalled that any such documents, like all other components of the information system, would be publicly available to everyone.

A final point worth making in this regard, and one that is often overlooked, is that Irish courts are generally badly served in terms of accessible information services. Decision-support systems, of which sentencing information systems are but one example, have never been technology-dependent. The nineteenth-century predecessors of today's District Court judges and practitioners had the immense benefit of the various *Justices of the Peace*, compiled by authors such as O'Connor, Molloy and Humphreys.[75] These works generally included the text of all statutes likely to be applied in courts of summary jurisdiction together with case digests and professional commentary. They were truly decision-support systems although that expression was happily unknown at the time. Indeed many of us still find them useful today. There has, of course, been a welcome upsurge over the past few decades in the amount of secondary legal literature being published, and this is very valuable in itself. But the idea of furnishing a compendium of information tailored to the needs of a particular court or the exercise of a particular jurisdiction seems to have disappeared with the *Justices of the Peace*. The ever-expanding reach of the criminal law, the proliferation of criminal offences, and the growing complexity of criminal procedure all militate against the possibility of regularly producing up-to-date, paper-based compendia equivalent to the old *Justices of the Peace*. Nor would such a publishing venture be commercially viable in a small jurisdiction. But it is here that computer-based technology comes into its own. Advances in information technology now permit the collection and analysis of data in ways that are accessible and helpful to ultimate users who, in the case of sentencing data, are most likely to be judges, advocates and policy-makers. It can also go much further by combining with this data all relevant text-based sources which, as noted earlier, are nowadays all produced in electronic format to begin with.

Susskind has drawn a useful distinction in this context between automation and innovation.[76] Automation occurs when existing processes, such as with-

---

[74] Criminal Law (Insanity) Act 2006.

[75] Sir James O'Connor's *The Irish Justice of the Peace,* first published in Dublin in 1911 ran to almost 1,400 pages. A second edition appeared in 1915 followed in 1925 by a criminal case digest compiled by George Gavan Duffy. Constantine Molloy's *The Justice of the Peace for Ireland* was published in Dublin in 1890 with some later editions by R.M. Hennessy, while Henry Humphrey's *The Justice of the Peace for Ireland* first appeared in 1863 with several later editions the last of which appears to be the ninth, by Sandford, published in 1897. The genre had a much longer history dating back to Dalton's *The Countrey Justice* (*sic*) (London, 1677) and possibly earlier. Indeed, *Stone's Justices' Manual*, covering English law, which began in the mid-nineteenth century, continues to be published annually in three volumes.

[76] Susskind, *The Future of Law: Facing the Challenges of Information Technology* (Oxford: Oxford University Press, 1998), pp.49–50.

drawing money from a bank account, are performed through the use of technology in place of traditional methods. We now use "hole in the wall" cash dispensers rather than going into a bank, filling out a form and getting the money from a cashier. The same may be said of accessing legal information where computer-based technology has so far concentrated on automating existing services. We can now read law reports online instead of consulting the paper sources, but the reports remain essentially the same format, content, structure and presentation. However, as Susskind also remarks, we can reap much greater benefits from technology by using it to innovate rather than just automate. To take an example far removed from sentencing, all of the legislation, case law and perhaps some precedents relating to probate and succession can probably be found nowadays in electronic form. In all likelihood, however, they are located in much the same formats and categories as existed in the pre-computer age—the cases in online case law services, the statutes on a government-sponsored legislation website and so forth. A more creative approach would be to have a single website including all relevant cases, statutes, precedents, commentary and advice presented in such a way as to serve the needs of different users. Such services may, of course, already exist and, if so, they provide a good example of innovation. They can obviously co-exist with the more conventional automated versions of the original documents.

Sentencing information systems provide a tremendous opportunity to exploit the innovative potential of information technology. The very idea of providing a searchable database of past sentencing practice, as developed in Scotland, was highly innovative in itself. The same information could conceivably be presented in traditional paper-based format, but it would be nowhere near as accessible or user-friendly as the electronic version. However, as shown earlier in this chapter and as the Australian models so well illustrate, an information system can be greatly enriched through the addition of further material including case law, statistical data, specially commissioned reports, and academic commentary from a variety of disciplines. Moreover, all of this information can be presented in a coherent and unified manner on a single website. By means of hypertext and other linking devices, users can explore many different kinds and sources of information on the same topic in a manner which would have scarcely been feasible if they were relying exclusively on paper-based sources. The system currently being piloted in Ireland aims to do all of this when fully developed. As well as proving useful for local users, it may also operate, in the same spirit as Justice Brandeis saw the individual American states,[77] as a kind of laboratory in which a very interesting experiment is being conducted and from which other countries may draw some useful lessons and insights.

---

[77] *New State Ice Co v Liebmann* 285 U.S. 262, 311 (1932) ("It is one of the happy incidents of the federal system that a single courageous State may, if its citizens choose, serve as a laboratory; and try novel social and economic experiments without risk to the rest of the country").

CHAPTER 8

THE CHOICE OF PENALTY

When selecting a sentence, a judge must first decide on the type of penalty to be imposed and then determine the appropriate amount of that penalty. Additional matters, such as the imposition of a disqualification or other ancillary order, may also arise for consideration, but what matters most, especially for the offender, is whether immediate custody is to be ordered. Because imprisonment is available for most offences other than very minor ones, it will naturally suggest itself as a possible sanction for any offence of a medium-to-high level of gravity. In such circumstances, the critical issue at the first stage of the decision-making process is whether the custody threshold has been reached. The notion of a custody threshold has occasionally received some judicial attention, mainly, as it happens, in relation to child pornography offences, but few efforts have been made to develop general principles, standards or criteria to assist trial courts in deciding when the threshold has been reached. In structural terms, the present sentencing system leaves enormous scope for the avoidance of immediate custody. Most offences, apart from those at the upper and lower ends of the scale of gravity, are punishable with imprisonment *or* a fine or both.[1] The maximum fine and term of imprisonment are usually set out in the statute creating the relevant offence or in an amending provision. Significantly, however, very few statutory provisions require that prison be chosen in preference to a fine. Furthermore, courts are almost invariably empowered to suspend a term of imprisonment or to employ some other measure such as probationary super-vision or community service. The number of offences carrying mandatory or mandatory minimum prison sentences remains statistically minuscule which, in turn, means that courts have a wide discretion to use non-custodial sanctions when minded to do so. In fact, a number of studies have shown that the increased prison population in England and Wales is largely, though not entirely, attributable to sentencing practices rather than an increase in crime levels or the number of cases processed by the courts.[2] The pattern may not be so pronounced in Ireland.

---

[1] The offence of blasphemy introduced in the Defamation Act 2009 s.36 is unusual because, although stated to be an indictable offence, it is punishable solely with a maximum fine of €25,000. This arrangement was, of course, influenced by the political and religious sensitivities surrounding the introduction of the offence which is necessitated by Art.40.6 of the Constitution of Ireland.

[2] See, for example, Hough, Jacobson and Millie, *The Decision to Imprison: Sentencing and the Prison Population* (London: Prison Reform Trust, 2003). The Carter Report concluded that increased sentence severity in England and Wales was due to a number of factors, including

Of the sentenced prisoners in custody here in December 2009, 38 per cent were serving sentences of five years or longer, compared to 30 per cent in 2001. At least some of this increase is attributable to the lengthy sentences required for drug-dealing offences, but that is a result of political rather than judicial decision-making.

We may start with the assumption that imprisonment is a legitimate form of punishment for some offenders. Arguments in favour of prison abolition have never been particularly persuasive and are unlikely to attract much support in the foreseeable future.[3] The challenge is to identify those circumstances in which imprisonment is both appropriate and necessary. This formulation of the issue may, of course, be criticised for appearing to assume the centrality of imprisonment within the sentencing system, thereby relegating other sanctions to the mere status of alternatives to custody. There is some force in that argument which will be further explored below, but the fact remains that for most offences of any appreciable level of gravity, the "in/out" question is central to the sentencing decision. Does the offender deserve to go directly to prison or should he remain at liberty, conditionally or otherwise? This is the most difficult question faced by sentencing judges on a daily basis. How they answer it may have profound implications for offenders and their families, victims and society at large. The judicial choice of penalty is shaped by several factors, the most obvious one being the level of sentencing discretion conferred upon the courts by statute. Legislators are constitutionally entitled to prescribe mandatory or mandatory minimum prison sentences for serious offences provided they have due regard to the requirements of rationality and proportionality.[4] Aside from that, the nature and severity of a penalty is strongly determined by prevailing cultural and political sensibilities.[5] This may be the least tangible of factors influencing sentence but it is in many ways the most fundamental, as any cross-cultural survey of penal practices will quickly reveal. An offence that typically attracts capital punishment or mutilation in one country may attract no more than a relatively short prison sentence or a community-based measure in another. A serial offender convicted of multiple fraud or sex offences may receive a cumulative sentence running to hundreds of years (not unusual in parts of the

---

legislative and guideline changes, the influence of media comment, political pressure and, interestingly, a decline in judicial confidence in the efficacy of fines (Carter, *Managing Offenders: Reducing Crime* (London: Government Strategy Unit, 2003)).

[3] On the abolitionist case, see Mathiesen, *The Politics of Abolition* (London: Martin Robertson, 1974); Mathiesen, "The Politics of Abolition" (1986) 10 *Contemporary Crises* 81; Ryan and Sim, "Campaigning for and campaigning against prisons: excavating and reaffirming the case for prison abolition" in Jewkes (ed.), *Handbook on Prisons* (Cullompton: Willan Publishing, 2007); Feest and Bettina, "Abolitionismus: Einige Antworten auf oft gestellte Fragen" (2008) 40 *Kriminologisches Journal* 6.

[4] Chapter 4 above.

[5] Garland, *Punishment and Modern Society* (Oxford: Clarendon Press, 1990); Garland, "Sociological Perspectives on Punishment" in Tonry (ed.), *Crime and Justice: A Review of Research* Vol.14 (Chicago: University of Chicago Press, 1991), p.115.

United States) in one jurisdiction but a much shorter or, at any rate, less-than-life sentence in another.[6] These variations are best explained in terms of legal and moral values. Ordering a large number of custodial sentences to run consecutively rather than concurrently, thereby producing an aggregate prison term far exceeding the offender's natural life expectancy, is theoretically defensible. So, for that matter, is the more pragmatic (and merciful) approach favoured in this and other jurisdictions of tailoring a cumulative sentence so that the offender is left with some realistic prospect of eventually regaining his liberty. Opinions will vary about the respective merits of these approaches but ultimately it boils down to a question of prevailing legal values, and the same holds true when it comes to selecting an appropriate penalty for an offence which is punishable with a high maximum sentence such as life imprisonment.

Decisions to imprison are also influenced by the range and, equally importantly, the credibility of available alternatives to custody. In so-called cusp cases, meaning those where custody, while possibly merited, may be avoided without committing an error of principle, judges will naturally be concerned to ensure that any non-custodial measure chosen will serve whatever goal or combination of goals seems appropriate in the circumstances. Their capacity to craft suitable non-custodial sentences in these circumstances depends on the range of options which the political branches of government have chosen to introduce and sustain with sufficient funding. In Ireland at present the main options, aside from suspended prison sentences, are fines, probation orders and community service orders. Probation is meant to serve rehabilitative or therapeutic goals and to reduce the risk of re-offending. Fines and community service can serve a broader range of penal purposes including retribution and deterrence, and they are generally adequate for most offences of low-to-medium levels of gravity. The more serious the offence, the more difficult it becomes to identify a non-custodial penalty which reflects the gravity of the crime, whatever about the personal circumstances of the offender. Heavy fines are possible for many serious offences and recent reforms made by the Fines Act 2010 add to the credibility of the fine as a response to many offences apart from those at the upper reaches of the scale of gravity. Community Service is explicitly intended as an alternative to imprisonment and may not be imposed unless the court is satisfied that the offence of conviction is one for which imprisonment would be appropriate.[7] Yet, the upper limit of 240 hours clearly restricts the range of cases

---

[6] In 2001, Thomas Reedy was sentenced by a United States Federal District Court to a total of 1,335 years' imprisonment for large-scale distribution of child pornography, a sentence later reduced to 180 years: *United States v Reedy* 304 F 3d 358 (2005). This prosecution formed the background to several international police investigations into child pornography, including Operation Amethyst in Ireland in 2002. The 150 years' imprisonment imposed on Bernie Madoff in 2009 by a United States federal court following his guilty plea to charges connected with the operation of a Ponzi scheme which defrauded investors of billions of dollars, is an another well-known example of a longer-than-life sentence (*New York Times*, June 29, 2009).

[7] Criminal Justice (Community Service) Act 1983 s.2; *Foley v Murphy* [2005] 3 I.R. 574.

in which community service will be considered an adequate punishment.[8] More onerous options could be developed, but Irish governments have so far shown little inclination in this regard. These might include some type of combination order equivalent to that introduced in England and Wales in 1991 which, in its original form, allowed for the making of an order which included probationary supervision as well as community service (though subject to a maximum of 100 hours, as opposed to 240 hours in a stand-alone community service order).[9] This arrangement has now been radically overhauled, largely as a result of recommendations made in the Halliday Report.[10] The Criminal Justice Act 2003 introduced a "community sentence" which, as the name suggests, is a non-custodial order but which may entail a substantial array of requirements, up to 12 in all.[11] These include an unpaid work requirement—community service in effect—subject to a maximum of 300 hours, an activity requirement (usually served in a rehabilitation centre of some kind), a prohibited activity requirement, a curfew requirement, a mental health treatment order, a drug or alcohol rehabilitation order, and an attendance centre order. Such an order may not be imposed unless the court is satisfied that the offence of conviction or the combination of that offence and other associated offences is sufficiently serious to warrant it, a requirement clearly intended to ensure, as far as possible, that it is not used where a more lenient measure will suffice.[12] More demanding community-based measures like these certainly have their attraction and, in principle at least, should be effective in diverting more offenders from custody. Two reservations must, however, be entered. First, there is no point in introducing such a measure unless it is accompanied by a clear and binding commitment to provide adequate resources to whichever body is to be responsible for its implementation, and that will probably be the Probation Service. Secondly, careful attention must be paid to the consequences of a breach, bearing in mind that the more complex and demanding the order in any one case, the greater the likelihood of a breach. This under-scores once again the signal importance of ensuring that a combination order is not made in any case where a less onerous measure might suffice. Otherwise, some offenders may end up being imprisoned for the breach of an order even though the original offence might have been well below the custody threshold.

Community-based penalties must be credible as well as effective. No sentencing arrangement can survive very long in teeth of sustained public

---

[8] On community service generally, see Pease, "Community Service Orders" in Tonry and Morris (eds), *Crime and Justice: An Annual Review of Research* Vol. 6 (Chicago: University of Chicago Press, 1985), p.51; Mair, "Community Penalties in England and Wales" (1998) 10 Fed. Sent. Rep. 263.

[9] Criminal Justice Act 1991 s.11. See Mair (fn.8 above).

[10] Halliday, J., *Making Punishments Work: Report of a Review of the Sentencing Framework for England and Wales* (London: Home Office, 2001).

[11] For a detailed account, see Ashworth, *Sentencing and Criminal Justice*, 5th edn (Cambridge: Cambridge University Press, 2010), pp.338–357; *Blackstone's Criminal Practice 2010* (Oxford: Oxford University Press, 2009), Section E8.

[12] Criminal Justice Act 2003 s.148(1).

opposition or disdain. The sentencing option itself—probation, community service or whatever—may well survive, but the circumstances in which it is used may arouse intense public disapproval. As noted earlier, the role of public opinion in sentencing is a complex one.[13] Judges should not allow public emotion to determine or influence the sentences imposed in specific cases. Were they to do so, as they have repeatedly recognised, they would be frustrating the entire constitutional purpose of assigning the sentencing task to an independent, disinterested and impartial judiciary. As against this, they must avoid acting in such a way as to erode public confidence in the justice system, something that may well occur if sentences are routinely or consistently seen to be inadequate or inappropriate, even by those who take the trouble to look behind popular media portrayals of sentencing practices. Research in this area has generally shown that members of the public underestimate the severity of judicial sentencing practices, but it also shows that the more information respondents are given, the closer their preferred sentences become to those actually imposed. Public attitudes toward the conditional sentence introduced in Canada in 1996 exemplify this phenomenon. Conditional sentences are effectively prison sentences served in the community, which seems rather contradictory, but the underlying idea is that while offenders avoid going to prison, they remain subject to a range of conditions, some of which may impose severe restrictions on their liberty of movement and lifestyle choices.[14] Research carried out some years after their introduction showed that very few considered conditional sentences an adequate punishment for certain offences, such as sexual assault. But when respondents were informed of the true nature and full implications of the sentence, public support increased significantly.[15] Similar findings have been recorded elsewhere, showing that support for non-custodial measures is heavily dependent on the quality of information given to respondents about the nature of those measures and their impact on offenders.[16] Meanwhile, research has also shown that judges tend to regard imprisonment as being in an entirely different league from community-based sanctions. This strong judicial perception of qualitative difference made it unlikely that any community-based measure would be treated as a viable alternative to immediate custody once a decision to imprison had been reached. The furthest that some judges in one particular study were prepared to go was treat electronic monitoring as a possible alternative to a short term of imprisonment.[17]

---

[13]   Chapter 1 above.

[14]   *R v Proulx* [2000] 1 S.C.R. 61.

[15]   Sanders and Roberts, "Public Attitudes Towards Conditional Sentencing: Results of a National Survey" (2000) 32 *Canadian Journal of Behavioural Science* 199–207.

[16]   Hutton, "What do the Scottish Public Think about Sentencing and Punishment?"(2003) 9 *The Scottish Journal of Criminal Justice Studies* 41.

[17]   Millie, Tombs and Hough, "Borderline Sentencing: A Comparison of Sentencers' Decision Making in England and Wales, and Scotland" (2007) 7 *Criminology and Criminal Justice* 243, 252.

Much of the research and commentary on alternatives to imprisonment has concentrated on the question of equivalency by trying to identify community-based measures that might plausibly be regarded as having roughly the same punitive impact as a given term of custody. Leading advocates of intermediate sanctions have accepted the importance of penal equivalence when it comes to fostering public confidence in a less prison-oriented system.[18] More targeted research has shown, however, that public acceptance depends very much on the nature of the crime. One Canadian study revealed that while members of the public were willing to accept monetary penalties, provided they were set at appropriate levels, as sufficient for certain kinds of crime, and property offences in particular, they were unwilling to accept such penalties as an adequate response to offences against the person.[19] Imprisonment may carry heavier social costs, but a fine, no matter how large, failed to reflect the cultural importance attached to personal autonomy and security. Similar views would probably prevail in most other Western countries and are, indeed, reflected in existing sentencing practices. Violent offences against the person ordinarily attract custodial penalties and it is seldom argued that the law should provide otherwise. In reality therefore, the debate about the use of non-custodial measures is largely confined to non-violent offences (apart perhaps from minor assaults).

THE CUSTODY THRESHOLD

The establishment of agreed custody thresholds is an essential precondition for the development of a coherent sentencing system. Some variation in sentencing practice is a price worth paying for genuine judicial independence and for a healthy level of sentencing discretion. But the injustice of a system where similarly-situated offenders convicted of similar offences receive punishments that are markedly different in both nature and quantum cannot be ignored. Much has been written *around* the topic of custody thresholds and on the various alternatives to custody, but judges, appeal courts and scholars have been noticeably reluctant to suggest practical principles for determining appropriate thresholds.[20] Any such principles must necessarily be expressed in fairly general terms but, unless they are to prove entirely useless, they must also establish reasonably specific criteria for identifying those cases where immediate

---

[18] Morris and Tonry, *Between Prison and Probation: Intermediate Punishments in a Rational Sentencing System* (Oxford: Oxford University Press, 1990), p.100.

[19] Marinos, "Equivalency and Interchangeability: The Unexamined Complexities of Reforming the Fine" (1997) 39 *Canadian Journal of Criminology* 27; Doob and Marinos, "Reconceptualizing Punishment: Understanding the Limitations on the Use of Intermediate Punishments" (1995) 2 Univ. Chicago Law School Roundtable 413.

[20] One notable exception is Wasik, "What Guides Sentencing Decisions?" in Bottoms, Rex and Robinson (eds), *Alternatives to Imprisonment: Options for an Insecure Society* (Cullompton: Willan, 2004), Ch.12.

imprisonment is justified. Most sentencers and policy-makers probably agree, on a rhetorical level if nothing else, that imprisonment should be a sanction of last resort. This principle is enshrined in legislation in several common-law jurisdictions, but is also treated as part of the common law.[21] The Crimes (Sentencing Procedure) Act 1999 of New South Wales, for example, provides:

> A court must not sentence an offender to imprisonment unless it is satisfied, having considered all possible alternatives, that no penalty other than imprisonment is appropriate.[22]

General exhortations of this kind have some value, not least because they explicitly require judges to consider and eliminate all other options before selecting imprisonment, although they seldom provide any detailed guidance on when exactly imprisonment is the only appropriate sanction. The facts also show that the enactment of such a measure provides no guarantee that imprisonment will be more sparingly used. New Zealand affords an instructive example in this regard as it has a general population about the same size as Ireland's. The legal systems of the two countries have much in common as have the general sentencing principles recognised and applied by their courts. New Zealand formally introduced a last resort principle in 2002 with a statutory provision to the effect that a sentencing court should always have regard to the desirability of keeping offenders within the community as far as that is practicable and consonant with the safety of the community.[23] A court must not impose a prison sentence unless satisfied that the statutory purposes of sentence cannot be achieved by any other means.[24] Yet, New Zealand's prison population has more than doubled since 1992. It now stands at approximately 9,000 with an imprisonment rate of 200 per 100,000 of the population, about twice Ireland's present rate. The same pattern is evident in Australia (overall) and Canada which have imprisonment rates of 134 and 117 respectively,[25] which goes to show that a bare statement of the last resort principle, whether by way of legislation or judicial pronouncement, may be of little value in itself.

---

[21] Judicial Commission of New South Wales, *Sentencng Bench Book* §3–300, available at *www.judcom.nsw.gov.au*.

[22] Section 5(1). There is a similar provision in the Commonwealth Crimes Act 1914 s.17A. See Edney and Bagaric, *Australian Sentencing: Principles and Practice* (Cambridge: Cambridge University Press, 2007), pp.297–298. Other Australian states have a similar provision. See, for example, *Duncan v R* (1983) 47 A L.R. 746 (Western Australia). The Canadian Criminal Code s.718.2(d) and (e), provides that an offender should not be deprived of liberty where less restrictive alternatives may be appropriate, and all other sanctions that may be reasonable in the circumstances should first be considered.

[23] Sentencing Act 2002 s.16(1).

[24] Section 16(2).

[25] These figures are based on the most recent information available in the World Prison Brief published by King's College London, available at *www.kcl.ac.uk/depsta/law/research/icps/worldbrief/* [Last accessed, December 28, 2010].

Closer to home, efforts made in England and Wales at different times over the past 30 years to curtail the use of imprisonment cast further light on the problems associated with last resort policies. The Criminal Justice Act 1982 was intended to curtail the use of custody when dealing with young offenders. It provided that when sentencing a person under 21 years of age, a court should not impose a custodial sentence:

> ... unless it is of the opinion that no other method of dealing with him is appropriate because it appears to the court that he is unable or unwilling to respond to non-custodial penalties or because a custodial sentence is necessary for the protection of the public or because the offence was so serious that a non-custodial sentence cannot be justified.[26]

This seems to have worked, for a time at least, in the sense that there was a considerable reduction in the number of young offenders sentenced to custody during the next decade or so. The Criminal Justice Act 1991 introduced a rather similar provision for offenders generally, providing:

> [T]he court shall not pass a custodial sentence on the offender unless it is of the opinion: (a) that the offence, or the combination of the offence and one other offence associated with it, was so serious that only such a sentence can be justified for the offence; or (b) where the offence is a violent or sexual offence, that only such a sentence would be adequate to protect the public from serious harm from him.[27]

The attempt made in this subsection to confine sentencers to considering the offence of conviction and one other associated offence proved to be one of the more controversial aspects of the entire statute which was quickly amended to allow for more previous convictions to be considered.[28]

It took the English Court of Appeal quite some time to offer any interpretation of s.1(4) of the Criminal Justice Act 1982 and even then, it was only on the prompting of a *Criminal Law Review* editorial.[29] In *R v Bradbourn*,[30] the court, per Lawton L.J., said that the author of the editorial "may not appreciate that this Court and other courts can recognise an elephant when they see one, but

---

[26] Criminal Justice Act 1982 s.1(4).

[27] Criminal Justice Act 1991 s.1(2). The equivalent provision now in force (the Powers of Criminal Courts (Sentencing) Act 2000 s.79) is substantially similar save that it allows for a custodial sentence where the offence of conviction "or the combination of the offence and one or more offences associated it with it, was so serious that only such a sentence could be justified for the offence." A judge who, having had regard to this provision, nonetheless imposes a custodial sentence must explain in open court the reason for doing so.

[28] Criminal Justice Act 1993 s.66.

[29] [1985] Crim L.R. 257.

[30] (1985) 7 Cr. App. R. (S.) 180 at 183.

may not find it necessary to define it." He then proceeded rather reluctantly to offer a general test in relation to the custody threshold for young offenders in light of the 1982 Act. According to this test, the offence had to be one of a kind which "would make right thinking members of the public, knowing all the facts, feel that justice had not been done by the passing of any sentence other than a custodial one." Following the enactment of the Criminal Justice Act 1991, the Court of Appeal adopted the same test in relation to the custody threshold for all offenders.[31] Ashworth and von Hirsch later dismissed this "right-thinking people" test as "vacuous" and proposed instead a "living-standard" criterion.[32] In 1998, a differently-constituted Court of Appeal abandoned the *Bradbourn* test and replaced it with a more credible one based on culpability and harm, while candidly accepting that there is no bright line separating those cases where custody is justified and those where it is not. It held that offender-related factors, such as acceptance of responsibility, could be taken into account in borderline cases.[33]

Other criteria for identifying the custody threshold have been suggested from time to time by academic writers and professional bodies. Morris and Tonry, writing in an American context, have suggested that imprisonment should not be imposed unless one or more of the following conditions are fulfilled:

> "Any lesser punishment would depreciate the seriousness of the crime or crimes committed;
>
> Imprisonment is necessary for deterrence, general or special;
>
> Other less restrictive sanctions have been frequently used or recently applied to this offender."[34]

This formula had already been proposed by Morris in a previous work[35] and was inspired by certain provisions of the Model Penal Code and the American Bar Association's *Criminal Justice Standards*. The current version of those *Standards* makes broadly similar recommendations in respect of sentences of total confinement:

> "(a) A sentencing court should prefer sanctions not involving total confinement in the absence of affirmative reasons to the contrary. A court may select a sanction of total confinement in a particular case if the court determines that:

---

[31] *R v Cox* [1993] 1 W.L.R. 188, (1993) 96 Cr. App. R. 452, (1993) 14 Cr. App. R. (S.) 479.

[32] Ashworth and von Hirsch, "Recognising Elephants: the Problem of the Custodial Threshold" [1997] Crim L.R. 187; Von Hirsch and Jareborg, "Gauging Criminal Harm: A Living-Standard Analysis" (1991) 11 *Oxford Journal of Legal Studies* 1.

[33] *R v Howells* [1999] 1 W.L.R. 307, [1999] 1 All E.R. 50, [1999] 1 Cr. App. R. 98, [1999] 1 Cr. App. R. (S.) 335.

[34] Morris and Tonry, *Between Prison and Probation: Intermediate Punishments in a Rational Sentencing System* (Oxford: Oxford University Press, 1990), p.13

[35] Morris, *The Future of Imprisonment* (Chicago: University of Chicago Press, 1974).

> (i) the offender caused or threatened serious bodily harm in the commis-
> sion of the offence,
>
> (ii) other types of sanctions imposed upon the offender for prior offences
> were ineffective to induce the offender to avoid serious criminal
> conduct,
>
> (iii) the offender was convicted of an offence for which the sanction of
> total confinement is necessary so as not to depreciate unduly the
> seriousness of the offence and thereby foster disrespect for the law, or
>
> (iv) confinement for a very brief period is necessary to impress upon
> the offender that the conduct underlying the offence of conviction
> is unlawful and could have resulted in a longer term of total
> confinement.
>
> (b) A sentencing court should not select a sanction of total confinement because
> of community hostility to the offender or because of the offender's apparent
> need for rehabilitation or treatment."[36]

Offence gravity forms the common denominator of most proposed formulations.
Culpability and harm are generally accepted as the primary ingredients of
gravity. Harm in itself would be a thoroughly unreliable indicator of gravity
because a person may cause a great deal more harm than he intended or, through
some form of diminished capacity, may not have fully appreciated the likely
consequences of his conduct. By the same token, a person may happen to cause
less harm that he intended or risked. Culpability, on the other hand, is concerned
with the offender's subjective blameworthiness, and can be measured in the first
instance according to the mental element which accompanied, or appears to have
accompanied, the conduct constituting the offence. A person who acts with the
intention of causing certain harm is generally more blameworthy than one who
acts recklessly or negligently. In so-called conduct crimes, knowledge may be
just as blameworthy as intention in result crimes. Thus, a person who engages
in a sexual act with another person, knowing that the other person is not
consenting to it, is acting with a high degree of culpability. Once the basic level
of culpability has been established—and it may well be apparent from the
verdict—regard must then be had to the presence of any aggravating or
mitigating factors which may increase or reduce the offender's overall blameworthiness. Thus far, of course, we are describing no more than the standard
criteria for assessing culpability, irrespective of the nature of the offence. What
matters most, when seeking to identify custody thresholds, is the nature of the
harm which the offender knowingly inflicted, intended to cause or risked
causing, as the case may be. Harm and culpability are therefore inextricably
linked for this purpose.

---

[36] ABA, *Criminal Justice Standards: Sentencing,* Standard 18–6.4 (1994), available at
www.abanet.org/crimjust/standards/home.html [Last accessed September 27, 2011]. On the
origin and influence of the *Standards,* see Marcus, "The Making of the ABA Criminal Justice
Standards: Forty Years of Excellence" (2009) 23:4 *Criminal Justice* 10.

What kind of culpable harm, then, should be sufficient to bring the offender above the custody threshold? At the outset, we may as well accept, in the words of the English Court of Appeal, that this is "one of the most elusive problems of criminal sentencing".[37] A person who acted with the intention of causing serious personal injury to another, and who accomplished that aim, would normally be considered deserving of imprisonment, while one who stole a small quantity of goods, worth no more than a few Euro, would not. Both have violated constitutionally-protected rights—bodily integrity and private property respectively. The first, however, has infringed a more fundamental right, because bodily integrity ranks superior to property on any hierarchy of rights, and moreover he has done so grievously. One approach, therefore, towards the assessment of culpable harm is to ask how fundamental a right has been violated or endangered. The criminal law is concerned, not only to prevent and punish harms that have actually materialised, but also to punish harms that have been attempted or risked, a concern that is reflected in the existence of inchoate, preparatory and possession offences. Conduct such as attempted murder or solicitation to murder which endangers a fundamental right is properly treated as worthy of severe censure. It is equally true that not all highly culpable conduct causes direct or immediate injury to identified individuals. Many crimes, such as drug-dealing, are treated seriously because of their injurious impact on the community in general, although in the longer term they will probably harm particular individuals as well. Then there is conduct, such as cruelty to animals, which is criminalised, not because it violates human rights, but because it offends our collective sense of decency and morality.

Scaling criminal harm is fraught with difficulty as those charged with drafting sentencing guidelines have repeatedly learned, but a few general propositions must surely attract broad support. First, on any hierarchy of protected rights and interests, life and bodily integrity rank highest. Nothing can compensate for loss of life, and it may be very difficult, if not impossible, genuinely to compensate a victim left seriously incapacitated following a criminal act. Bodily integrity is violated by any non-fatal offence against the person such as assault, endangerment or sexual violence. Personal dignity and autonomy are also increasingly recognised as important interests worthy of strong legal protection. These interests are typically violated, not through the infliction of physical injury in the conventional sense, but through conduct which demeans or degrades the victim. Those who take indecent photographs of children (or adults, for that matter) and then publish them or transmit them over the internet are usually sentenced quite severely because their conduct has violated a basic right to personal dignity. In *R v McCann*,[38] for example, the appellant, a serving police officer at the time of the offence, was convicted of voyeurism for having secretly

---

[37] *R v Howells* [1999] 1 W.L.R. 307 at 310, [1999] 1 All E.R. 50, [1999] 1 Cr. App. R. 98, [1999] 1 Cr. App. R. (S.) 335.

[38] [2007] 1 Cr. App. R. (S.) 4 (p.20). He was convicted under s.67(4) of the Sexual Offences Act 2003.

installed a surveillance camera in a neighbour's bathroom, although there was no evidence of pictures or videos having been made or distributed. He was sentenced to six months' imprisonment, and it was argued on appeal that this was not a suitable case for imprisonment. The Court of Appeal disagreed, having regard to the breach of trust involved, the appellant's occupation at the time, victim impact, the lack of possible credit for a guilty plea and the calculated nature of the offence. It did, however, reduce the sentence by half.

Personal liberty, in the sense of freedom from physical restraint, also ranks high on any hierarchy of rights, and is violated through kidnapping, involuntary detention or captivity, consciously wrongful arrest and similar conduct. Under Irish law, false imprisonment carries a maximum sentence of life imprisonment.[39] John Locke, writing in the late seventeenth century, defined the "civil interest" as "life, liberty, health and indolency of the body, and the possession of outward things."[40] Private property, although it ordinarily ranks next after life, liberty and bodily integrity, is more contentious in ideological terms, but for sentencing purposes the important question is not whether the law should protect private property as an institution, but rather the degree of hardship or harm caused by the offence. The gravity of property offences committed against individuals cannot be assessed solely by reference to the amount taken but also, and often more importantly, according to the suffering or hardship which the deprivation imposed on the victim. A small sum of money stolen from an impoverished person may cause much more hardship and reflect a great deal more callousness on the part of the offender than the theft of a much larger sum from, say, a financial institution. This is not to suggest that theft from institutions should be treated lightly, especially where the offence places the very existence of an institution in jeopardy or when it has serious repercussions for the entire financial sector and, consequently, for the community at large. Broad offence categories such as crimes against the person and against property, while having some utility for the purpose of identifying custody thresholds, often fail to reflect the lack of fit between formal legal definitions and the reality of the criminal conduct itself. Robbery, for example, may formally be classified as a property crime, but by definition it entails the use of force and, in many cases, involves the infliction of severe violence.[41] Residential burglary may seem to be quintessentially a non-violent property crime, assuming that nobody has been physically hurt during the commission of the offence. Yet, research has shown that what victims of burglary resent most is not so much the loss of property but rather the sense of intrusion into their private space and the prolonged experience

---

[39]   Non-Fatal Offences Against the Person Act 1997 s.15.
[40]   Locke, *A Letter Concerning Toleration* (1689). A century later, the Virginia Declaration of Independence (1776) declared as inherent and imprescriptible rights "the enjoyment of life and liberty, with the means of acquiring and possessing property, and pursuing and obtaining happiness and safety." The Constitution of Ireland protects private property both as an institution (Art.43) and as a personal right (Art.40.3).
[41]   Criminal Justice (Theft and Fraud Offences) Act 2001 s.14.

of insecurity and anxiety that often follows. It can cause lasting psychological damage and have a particularly severe impact on people living alone.[42] The same holds true of theft which may be minor in nature but which, even in the absence of personal violence or intrusion into a dwelling, may cause great inconvenience and distress. This would hold true, for example, of the theft of a passport from a tourist, or of the theft of keys, credit cards and other essential personal belongings. Care must therefore be taken not to be over prescriptive in linking custody thresholds to legal offence classifications. When deciding if the threshold has been reached when sentencing mid-range offences, courts can only have regard to the nature of the particular offence and its impact on the victim in order to determine if the case, viewed in its totality, is so serious that a non-custodial penalty would be manifestly inadequate to mark its gravity.

Aside from the major crime categories just mentioned, there is still a wide spectrum of offending which may fall above or below the custody threshold depending on the circumstances. Vandalism, causing damage to the environment and public order offences are often difficult to locate on any scale of harm because they do not always violate the rights of any readily identifiable individual and also because they vary enormously in nature and impact. The same holds true of drug offences which may vary from possession for personal use to wholesale distribution which, in various ways, may wreak havoc on entire communities. Again, it is impossible to prescribe any detailed rules or criteria for identifying custody thresholds, but drawing upon the principles suggested by the American Bar Association and other bodies, the dominant consideration should be whether the offence and its intended impact were such that any sanction other than imprisonment would fail to reflect the gravity of the offence.[43] By way of further qualification, a court should be obliged to consider and decide if any other sanction could adequately fulfil the purpose(s) which the sentence is designed to advance. The range of available alternatives will obviously have a significant bearing on the frequency with which imprisonment is imposed in these circumstances.

The fact that an offence, by its nature, ordinarily surpasses the custody threshold does not mean that everyone convicted of it must be imprisoned. Serious offences involving fundamental rights violations may carry a broad presumption of custody, but no more than that, as the English Court of Appeal stressed in *R v Cox*,[44] a leading authority on the last resort principle under the Criminal Justice Act 1991. There, the court concluded that the offence was sufficiently serious to warrant a prison sentence but ultimately, having regard to mitigating factors, principally the offender's age and antecedents, it substituted

---

[42] Maguire, "The Impact of Burglary Upon Victims" (1980) 20 Brit. J. Crim. 261; Grabosky, *Burglary Prevention* (Canberra: Australian Institute of Criminology, 1995). Leading English guideline judgments on sentencing for burglary include *R v McInerney* [2003] 1 Cr. App. R. 36 (p.627), [2003] 2 Cr. App. R. (S.) 39 (p.240).

[43] Page 193 above.

[44] [1993] 1 W.L.R. 188, (1993) 96 Cr. App. R. 452, (1993) 14 Cr. App. R. (S.) 479.

a sentence of probation.[45] The same principle is, of course, reflected in leading Irish authorities on rape and related offences which must *ordinarily* attract an immediate and substantial custodial term. But it has always been recognised that exceptional cases may arise where something less, including a non-custodial measure, may be more appropriate.[46] What brings an offence over the custody threshold is the normal or typical gravity of the relevant conduct. In any system committed to individualised sentencing, the presumption of custody may always be displaced by offender-related considerations. A number of surveys among judges in other common-law jurisdictions have shown that offender-related factors are highly influential in this regard. Respondents in one such study indicated that the offence, as it appeared on paper, would often seem to make imprisonment inevitable, but the evidence and submissions offered at the sentencing hearing might then convince the judge that a non-custodial penalty would be a more appropriate response in light of the offender's character and circumstances.[47]

Rather problematically, however, a failure on the part of the offender to respond to previous non-custodial measures is often treated as a further indication that the last resort has been reached. This is reflected in the criteria proposed by Morris and Tonry and by the ABA, quoted earlier. Persistent minor offenders undoubtedly cause serious problems for sentencing courts which must balance the requirements of proportionality and public protection. Shoplifting, road traffic and public order offences might not ordinarily exceed the custody threshold unless they were of a particularly serious nature. Yet, when a court is faced with sentencing a person convicted of stealing a small quantity of goods from a shop and that person has numerous previous convictions for similar offences, it will often be left in something of a quandary. The offence of conviction, taken on its own, might adequately be punished with a fine or other non-custodial measure, but the offender's previous record may strongly indicate a lack of willingness to desist from further offending. Does a short prison sentence serve any purpose in these circumstances? It may have some value as a public signal that the courts take repeat offending of this nature seriously and that they are prepared to respond accordingly. This, in itself, is an important consideration. Whether it will have any dissuasive impact is much more debatable, and will depend very much on the circumstances of the individual offender. Some offenders may find the experience of imprisonment, even for a short period, so harsh or traumatic that they will make a determined effort to avoid it in the future—hopefully by refraining from crime. Others may be undeterred, which underscores the truth of the argument that while previous

---

[45] As Wasik (fn.20 above), p.291 remarks, since the decision in *Cox*, "offence seriousness may propel the offender over the custody threshold for an immediate custodial sentence, while personal mitigation may have the effect of pulling him back ...".

[46] *People (DPP) v Tiernan* [1988] I.R. 250, [1989] I.L.R.M. 149.

[47] See, in particular, Hough, Jacobson and Millie (fn.2 above).

non-custodial penalties may not have worked, there is little reason to believe that imprisonment will work either. There seems to be little doubt but that most judges are strongly influenced by the offender's previous record when sentencing so-called cusp cases. Other influential factors typically include the presence or absence of remorse, the degree to which the offender seems determined to refrain from further offending, the presence or absence of family or community ties and employment prospects. The nature of the offence itself is often much less significant than the record, attitude and circumstances of the offender.[48] One study, for example, showed judges inclined to view offenders as either "redeemable" or "irredeemable". Those in the former category were likely to be spared imprisonment, while those in the latter category were not.[49]

Even if a short prison sentence were justified in these circumstances on utilitarian grounds, it might well be a disproportionately severe response to the instant offence. This, in turn, raises the old and difficult question of whether previous convictions should be treated as an aggravating factor capable of increasing a sentence beyond the level that might have been deserved by the offence of conviction.[50] Suffice it to say for present purposes that there are at least three possible responses to this problem. One is to adopt a flat-rate approach which ignores previous record, which may be either good or bad, as in the case of administrative fines and fixed penalty systems which are now becoming quite prevalent for road traffic and public order offences. Another would be to treat at least some previous convictions, perhaps those for similar misconduct, as an aggravating factor which would justify an increase in the otherwise deserved punishment. This is the approach reflected in many American guideline systems where the permissible punishment range is found at the intersection of the value attached to the offence of conviction and the offender's criminal record score.[51] The third approach, often described as progressive loss of mitigation, allows some degree of mitigation for the absence of previous convictions, but the more convictions the offender accumulates the less mitigation he becomes entitled to, until eventually he is entitled to none. Despite occasional indications to the contrary, this appears to be the policy now favoured in Ireland. It also happens to be the approach most consistent with proportionality which holds that a sentence should reflect, first of all, the gravity of the offence and then the personal circumstances of the offender. Courts wishing to treat previous convictions as an aggravating factor must therefore interpret personal circumstances as including criminal record, and also face up

---

[48] Hough, Jacobson and Millie (fn.2 above); Millie, Tombs and Hough (fn.17 above); Maguire, "Consistency in Sentencing" [2010] 2 *Judicial Studies Institute Journal* 14.

[49] Tombs and Jagger, "Denying Responsibility: Sentencers' Accounts of their Decisions to Imprison" (2006) 46 Brit. J. Crim. 803 at 815.

[50] Roberts and von Hirsch (eds), *Previous Convictions at Sentencing: Theoretical and Applied Perspectives* (Oxford: Hart Publishing, 2010), an excellent collection of essays on this topic.

[51] Chapter 6 above.

to the reality that they are retrospectively imposing further punishment for previously sentenced offences.

SHORT PRISON SENTENCES

The vast majority of those sentenced to custody in Ireland receive short prison terms. There were almost 11,000 committals under sentence in 2009 but more than half of these (5,750) were for less than three months. In fact, the number of sentences less than three months imposed in 2009 increased by 63 per cent over the 2008 figure. Sentences in the three to six months and six to 12 months categories also increased significantly over the same period.[52] Road traffic offences appear to account for most of the very short sentences, and again 2009 saw very significant increases in this regard. The number of committals for those offences rose from 2,254 in 2008 to 3,601 in 2009, an increase of 60 per cent. More than 70 per cent of those sentences were for three months or less. Statistics such as these might suggest that short-term prisoners account for a high proportion of the prison population at any one time, yet the opposite appears to be the case. A snapshot of the prison population on December 4, 2009 revealed that there were only 49 offenders in custody serving sentences less than three months. Longer-term prisoners, by contrast, accounted for most of the total inmate population which stood at 4,040 on that date.[53] Three-quarters were serving sentences of two years or longer. The biggest group, accounting for 54 per cent of the sentenced population, were serving sentences of three to ten years. Offenders sentenced to short terms proceed through the system very quickly and most are probably granted early release long before they would ordinarily qualify for remission. A similar pattern emerges in relation to those imprisoned for non-payment of fines. Close on 5,000 people were committed to prison for this reason in 2009, almost double the figure for the previous year. Yet, on December 4, 2009 there were only 25 people in prison for non-payment of fines.

The speed with which short-term prisoners progress through the system, especially when further accelerated by temporary release, raises serious questions about the wisdom of imposing very short custodial sentences in the first place. The number of committals involving such sentences may appear unacceptably high, but two points should be noted in this regard. According to Court Service statistics, less than 2 per cent of road traffic offenders were sentenced to imprisonment or detention in 2009, in sharp contrast to the 37 per cent who had the charges struck out and the 30 per cent who were fined.

---

[52] 1,561 sentences varying from six to 12 months were imposed in 2009 compared with 1,404 in 2008 (an increase of 11 per cent). 1,905 sentences varying from three to six months were imposed in 2009 compared with 1,494 in 2008 (an increase of 28 per cent). All of this information is drawn from the Irish Prison Service, *Annual Report 2009.*

[53] This figure included 602 remand prisoners and 20 detainees under immigration law.

Secondly, the District Court often finds itself dealing with repeat road traffic offenders, including some caught driving while disqualified. Stern measures are clearly justified in such cases, if only on grounds of public safety. To allow court orders to be flouted or disobeyed with virtual impunity or undue leniency would ill serve the community at large. One can therefore understand the view, often expressed by judges in these circumstances, that a point has been reached where nothing less than imprisonment will be adequate by way of punishment or deterrence. As against this, short prison sentences seldom produce any obvious benefits. They amount, at most, to a short suspension of the offender's freedom. In some cases, this may have severe collateral consequences such as loss of employment and family hardship. In others, it may have no ostensible effect apart from briefly exposing the offender to the culture and experience of imprisonment. An assessment of the effectiveness of short prison systems by a Scottish working group some years ago ranked them in accordance with their capacity to achieve conventional penal goals. Not surprisingly, they were ranked high as punishment but low when it came to incapacitation, deterrence, rehabilitation and reparation.[54] This seems intuitively correct. Apart possibly from some instances of business or white-collar crime, a prison sentence, whether long or short, will generally destroy any opportunity to make reparation. Indeed, for many repeat offenders, a very short prison sentence may not, in subjective terms, rank high even as punishment.[55]

Several other jurisdictions are trying to grapple with large numbers of short-term prisoners, and the problem is by no means new.[56] Recent reports have highlighted the problem in both Scotland and England and Wales. A Green paper published in 2010 revealed that two thirds of custodial sentences passed each year in England and Wales are for six months or less, and many are for just a matter of weeks.[57] According to a National Audit Office report published shortly before that, 35,700 offenders received sentences of three months or less in 2008. Short-sentenced offenders (meaning those sentenced to less than 12 months) had, on average, 16 previous convictions. Theft and violence were the most common offences leading to such sentences, while motoring offences accounted for about 10 per cent.[58] The Halliday Report stated quite bluntly that "one of the most important deficiencies in the present framework is the lack of utility in short prison sentences ... the sentence used for large numbers of persistent

---

[54] *Short-Term Prison Sentences: Report to the Criminal Justice Forum* (Edinburgh: Scottish Executive, 2001), p.5.

[55] Kolber, "The Subjective Experience of Punishment" (2009) 109 Columbia L.R. 182.

[56] Mannheim, "Comparative Sentencing Practice" (1958) 23 *Law and Contemporary Problems* 557. Following an analysis of prison statistics from several Western European countries, he noted (p.582) the large number of short prison sentences imposed in many of those countries.

[57] Ministry of Justice, *Breaking the Cycle: Effective Punishment, Rehabilitation and Sentencing of Offenders* (London: Stationery Office, 2010), Ch.4.

[58] Comptroller and Auditor General, *Managing Offenders on Short Custodial Sentences* (London: The Stationery Office, 2010), Pt 1.

offenders with multiple problems and high risks of reoffending ... A more effective recipe for failure could hardly be conceived."[59] A similar pattern has been evident in Scotland where 83 per cent of prison sentences in 2005–2006 were for six months or less, and almost 60 per cent were for 90 days or less.[60] One valuable observation made by the Scottish Prisons Commission is that snapshots of the prison population showing no more than a small number of short-term prisoners in custody on a given day are misleading because they fail to reveal the extent to which these prisoners contribute to reception rates which are, of course, highly significant in terms of prison administration.[61] Another common phenomenon is the high rate of recidivism among recently-released short term prisoners. In England and Wales, 60 per cent of short-term prisoners were convicted of another offence within one year of release.[62] Most countries experiencing this problem claim to be committed to addressing it, usually by a combination of better crime prevention strategies and more reliance on community-based measures.

One approach has been to make the imposition of short prison sentences subject to strict statutory conditions. The German Criminal Code (s.47), for instance, provides:

> The court shall not impose a term of imprisonment of less than six months unless special circumstances exist, either in the offence or the person of the offender, that strictly require the imposition of imprisonment either for the purpose of reform of the offender or for reasons of general deterrence.

Scotland has recently introduced a statutory provision prohibiting a court from passing a prison sentence of three months or less except where it is satisfied that "no other method of dealing with the person is appropriate."[63] A court imposing such a sentence must state and record its reasons for concluding that no other measure would be appropriate. The manner in which this provision is implemented over the coming years will make an interesting case study, particularly as it is applied to repeat offenders. Judges subject to provisions of this kind can readily develop standard formulae to justify short prisons sentences by referring to the number of previous convictions or the offender's persistent failure to respond positively to non-custodial measures. Short prison sentences are also proving problematic in other European countries including Denmark and Italy. An Italian law passed in 2010 requires that prison sentences of less than 12 months should ordinarily be served by way of house arrest, and this appears to have been

---

[59] Halliday (fn.10 above), para.3.1.
[60] Scottish Prisons Commission, *Scotland's Choice: Report of the Scottish Prisons Commission 2008* (Edinburgh, 2008), p.13.
[61] Footnote 60 above.
[62] Comptroller and Auditor General (fn.58 above), p.15.
[63] Criminal Justice and Licensing (Scotland) Act 2010 s.17.

motivated solely by a concern to reduce the prison population.[64] Sentence implementation procedures vary from one country to another but in France, for example, a *juge de l'application des peines*, a judge responsible for supervising the execution of sentences, can transform a prison sentence to another measure such as electronic monitoring.[65] In common-law countries, the sentence imposed by the trial court stands, unless it is varied on appeal. Legislation recently introduced in Ireland requiring courts to consider community service instead of short prison sentences is clearly in line with measures being introduced elsewhere in Europe but, without wishing to be fatalistic about it, one cannot be confident about its effectiveness in diverting low-level offenders (and repeat offenders in particular) from custody.[66]

There is no easy solution to the problem of short sentences. A complete ban on the imposition of such sentences (which might be defined as sentences of three or six months or less) would scarcely be politically feasible, and might not be objectively justifiable in any event. Apart from the possibility of judicial circumvention through the imposition of sentences slightly above the specified threshold, short sentences may serve a useful purpose in certain cases. Those jurisdictions, such as Germany and Scotland, which require that short prison sentences be reserved for cases where no other measure is considered appropriate clearly believe that there are actually some circumstances in which such sentences are warranted. The problem is that they fail to indicate what those circumstances might be. A short sentence should not, obviously, be imposed except in cases which fall above the custody threshold and the key question is whether a case should ever be so classified if the offence of conviction is not, in itself, sufficiently serious to warrant some term of imprisonment. It is suggested that in a sentencing system with proportionality as its overarching distributive principle, this question should be answered in the negative. Taking the offender's previous record into account for this purpose amounts in effect to double punishment—this is one of the standard objections to treating previous convictions as an aggravating factor. Once defensible criteria have been agreed as to the exceptional circumstances in which short prison sentences are appropriate, it is then essential to ensure that those sentences are actually served, less any standard remission or parole arrangements which happen to be in place. At a time of prison overcrowding, short-term prisoners are likely to be released after serving no more than a very small portion of their sentences. This can lead, and in this country has been known to lead, to a situation in which offenders refuse to consent to community service knowing that they will have to endure no more than a very short spell in prison as a result. This state of affairs scarcely does much to instil confidence in the fairness or effectiveness of the sentencing system as a whole.

---

[64]   Law of November 26, 2010, n. 199 (*Gazzetta Ufficiale N. 281 del 1 Dicembre 2010*).
[65]   Page 225 below.
[66]   Criminal Justice (Community Service) (Amendment) Act 2011.

ALTERNATIVES TO IMMEDIATE IMPRISONMENT

Use of the expression "alternatives to imprisonment" often meets with the objection that it presupposes imprisonment as the normal or presumed punishment for criminal offences. Terms such as "community sanctions" are preferred because they implicitly acknowledge the validity and worth of non-custodial measures in their own right. Reference is made here to alternatives to immediate imprisonment in order to embrace measures such as the suspended sentence which is formally a custodial measure although it may never result in actual custody if the recipient observes the conditions specified by the court. However they are characterised, alternatives to custody have been treated with some degree of ambivalence in recent decades. They have been welcomed and generally supported for their capacity to spare offenders the experience of imprisonment and to prevent prison overcrowding. But they have also been treated with some caution and scepticism for their so-called net-widening capacity. Social theorists, in particular, have criticised the extended use of community-based sanctions for their capacity to widen the net of social control.[67] According to this argument, the increased availability and use of supervisory measures such as community service, intensive probation and electronic monitoring, leads to more and more people being made subject to various forms of state control and surveillance.[68] Seen in this light, community sanctions operate as "add-ons" to existing imprisonment practices.[69] This might not be a bad thing if all of those subject to supervisory measures would otherwise be imprisoned. Critics have argued, however, that these measures are often used interchangeably rather than as genuine alternatives to imprisonment. Offenders who might previously have been dealt with by way of a fine or discharge are given community service or intensive probation orders as those measures become available. There is, of course, the counter-argument that some offenders may benefit more in the longer term from a supervisory measure than from a once-off penalty such as a fine. The critics are on stronger ground when they point to the capacity of some community-based measures to increase the chances of eventual imprisonment. Violations of the terms of a community sanction are often punishable with imprisonment, and the more intense the level of surveillance required by a community sanction, the greater the risk of a technical violation.[70]

---

[67] McMahon, "'Net-Widening': Vagaries in the Use of a Concept" (1990) 30 Brit. J. Crim. 121; Cohen, *Visions of Social Control* (Cambridge: Polity Press, 1985); Vass and Weston, "Probation Day Centres as an Alternative to Custody" (1990) 30 Brit. J. Crim. 189.

[68] On this notion of the dispersal of discipline, see Rodger, "Social Work as Social Control Re-examined: Beyond the Dispersal of Discipline Thesis" (1988) 22 *Sociology* 563.

[69] McMahon (fn.67 above), p.123.

[70] Tonry and Lynch, "Intermediate Sanctions" in Tonry (ed.), *Crime and Justice: A Review of Research* Vol. 20 (Chicago: Chicago University Press, 1996), p.99 at p.101.

Fines are, of course, the most commonly-used criminal sanction in Ireland and many other countries. They are perfectly adequate for the vast majority of minor offences and also for the increasing number of regulatory offences attracting fixed penalties.[71] In 2009, more than 73,000 offenders were fined in the District Court in respect of the main categories of offences dealt with by that court, compared to 12,400 who received a prison sentence and 15,000 who received a community service order or an order under the Probation of Offenders Act 1907.[72] The proportion of offenders convicted in the higher courts who were eventually fined is much smaller, and so are the actual numbers. Fines become more effective for retributive and deterrence purposes when they can be judicially tailored to reflect offenders' means, something which day fine and unit fine systems, though they do not exist in Ireland, can best achieve. What matters most, when it comes to keeping more offenders within the community rather than sending them to prison, is the availability of viable and effective intermediate sanctions. These are mostly non-pecuniary measures which are punitive to some degree, if only in the sense of imposing limited restrictions on a person's liberty, though they may also incorporate some rehabilitative or therapeutic elements. It is the availability and use of these sanctions which give rise to the debate about net-widening and interchangeability. The best way of avoiding unnecessary use of such measures is to establish something similar to the approach adopted in the English Criminal Justice Act 1991 which required courts to consider specifically if, in any given case, a particular level of sanction (as opposed to a more lenient one) was actually required on proportionality grounds. This is one area where general guidelines, from whatever source, would be most useful.

Assuming that problems of over-use and inappropriate use can effectively be addressed, the next question is whether the range of available intermediate sanctions is adequate to facilitate their use for a reasonably wide variety of offences. As noted earlier, non-custodial penalties of all kinds arouse some degree of public scepticism when applied to anything other than minor offences. Ireland's present menu of intermediate sanctions is, to put it mildly, rather minimal, consisting mainly of probationary supervision and community service. The possibility of introducing additional options such as electronic monitoring and periodic or intermittent detention should at least be investigated, though it must be said that periodic detention poses its share of logistical problems and is suitable for no more than a narrow range of offenders. It exists in several Australian and continental European jurisdictions, and provision has also been made for it in England and Wales under the Criminal Justice Act 2003 (s.183).[73]

---

[71] Bottoms, "Neglected Features of Contemporary Penal Systems" in Garland and Young (eds), *The Power to Punish* (London: Heinemann, 1983), p.166.

[72] Courts Service, *Annual Report 2009* (Dublin, 2010).

[73] New South Wales Sentencing Council, *Review of Periodic Detention* (Sydney, 2007). On the principles and procedure governing the use of periodic detention in New South Wales, see *R v Douar* [2005] NSWCCA 455 at [69]–[72] and *R v Zamagias* [2002] NSWCCA 17.

A recent Australian report claims that the significance of this measure is dwindling, partly because of the increased use of electronic monitoring and partly also because of a shortage of prison space.[74] It is potentially suitable as a response to some serious road traffic and white-collar offences in the sense that it would leave offenders free to continue working while serving a very definite punishment in the form of imprisonment for a number of days each week for the duration of the sentence. Home detention and electronic monitoring probably hold more promise as they do not require the allocation of institutional space but can still have a reasonably strong punitive impact because of the restrictions which they impose on an offender's liberty.[75] Consideration should also be given to the creation of combination orders, similar to those now existing in England and Wales,[76] which would permit the imposition of more onerous community-based measures on certain offenders. This is one area of sentencing law which has never received any sustained attention in Ireland and, given the rapidly growing prison population, the time is now ripe for a thorough review of alternative sanctioning systems. There can be no guarantee that the creation of a wider range of alternatives than now exist would lead to any dramatic reduction in the prevalence of short prison sentences. We have already seen that England and Wales, for all its innovations in the area of community-based sentences, still has a serious problem with short prison sentences.[77] One positive consequence, however, is that courts would have fewer excuses for imposing short custodial sentences in borderline cases and they could be more legitimately required to justify their decisions whenever they did so.

ASSISTANCE AND DESISTANCE

Legal and political discourse on repeat offenders tends to concentrate on the notion of persistence and on the optimum methods of responding to it. In fact, the debate at judicial and political levels often boils down to the crude question of whether previous convictions should be treated as an aggravating factor or as a ground for denying mitigation. This is certainly an important question within our existing sentencing framework but it risks diverting attention from what is arguably a more important question in policy terms: that of how to generate higher levels of desistance from crime. Desistance has become an important area of criminological research in recent times.[78] Traditionally, criminologists concentrated largely on the onset of delinquency and the beginning of criminal

---

[74] New South Wales Sentencing Council (fn.73 above), p.15.

[75] On electronic monitoring generally, see Nellis, "Surveillance and Confinement: Explaining and Undestanding the Experience of Electronically Monitored Curfews" (2009) 1 *European Journal of Probation* 41.

[76] Page 188 above.

[77] Page 201 above.

[78] Kazemian, "Desistance from Crime: Theoretical, Empirical, Methodological, and Policy

careers, but they have become increasingly aware that many of those who engage in crime in their teenage years eventually desist and lead largely law-abiding lives. The so-called age-crime curve is well recognised in the international literature. Male offending tends to peak at about 18 years of age, after which it sharply declines. By the age of 25, most offenders will have given up on crime, although a certain number persist and continue to offend well into their later years.[79] Various theories have been proposed to explain why, in most cases, offending is limited to the adolescent years while, in others, it persists for much longer. Moffitt, for example, in a well-known article on the topic puts forward this hypothesis:

> "At the crossroad of young adulthood, adolescence-limited and life-course-persistent delinquents go different ways. This happens because the developmental histories and personal traits of adolescence-limiteds allow them the option of exploring new life pathways. The histories and traits of life-course-persisents have foreclosed their options, entrenching them in the anti-social path".[80]

This seems plausible enough, but the real challenge is to devise a set of effective interventions to address the problems of those who seem likely to persist. For quite some time, researchers were discouraged from embarking on this enterprise because of the "nothing works" philosophy which held sway in correctional thinking from the early 1970s onwards.[81] The other major challenge is to understand desistance rates and patterns among more seasoned adult offenders who already have considerable experience of imprisonment. The high rate of recidivism among released prisons provides very little ground for believing that "prison works", a phrase forever associated with Michael Howard during his time as British Home Secretary.[82] Maturing with age is only one factor which leads to desistance. Developing social bonds, through stable relationships, employment and so forth, has also emerged as an important influence. Then, there is the phenomenon sometimes termed "narrative", which may well be the most important of all, as it traces the process by which some

Considerations" (2007) 23 *Journal of Contemporary Criminal Justice* 5 (which has a useful survey of the literature on the topic).

[79] Barclay, "The Peak Age of Known Offending by Males" (1990) 28 *Home Office Research Bulletin* 20; Farrington, "Human Development and Criminal Careers" in Maguire, Morgan and Reiner (eds), *The Oxford Handbook of Criminology*, 2nd edn (Oxford: Clarendon Press, 1997), p.511; Gadd and Farrall, "Criminal Careers, Desistance and Subjectivity" (2004) 8 *Theoretical Criminology* 123.

[80] Moffitt, "Adolescence-Limited and Life-Course-Persistent Antisocial Behaviour: A Developmental Taxonomy" (1993) 100 *Psychological Review* 674.

[81] Martinson, "What Works? Questions and Answers about Prison Reform" (1974) 10 *The Public Interest* 22; Allen, *The Decline of the Rehabilitative Ideal: Penal Policy and Social Purpose* (New Haven, CT: Yale University Press, 1981).

[82] Burnett and Maruna, "So 'Prison Works', Does It? The Criminal Careers of 130 Men Released from Prison under Home Secretary, Michael Howard" (2004) 43 *The Howard Journal of Criminal Justice* 390.

offenders decide at a certain point to re-envision themselves as ex-offenders who are determined to desist from further crime. As McNeill writes:

> "Thus, desistance resides somewhere in the interfaces between developing personal maturity, changing social bonds associated with certain life transitions, and the individual subjective narrative constructions which offenders build around these key events and changes. It is not just the events and changes that matter; it is what these events and changes *mean* to the people involved."[83]

Attitudinal change and a re-orientation of self-image therefore seem highly significant in the desistance process. Research has also shown that this change is most likely to occur when there is somebody else willing to show confidence in the offender's capacity to reform. One of the leading research studies on this topic concluded that "with the help of some outside force, somebody who 'believed in' the ex-offender, the narrator is able to accomplish what he or she was 'always meant to do' …".[84]

There is clearly much more work to be done in Ireland and elsewhere to gain a better understanding of desistance and the factors contributing to it. But it is relevant in the present context for two reasons. First, existing research points quite clearly to the importance of effective probation practice in encouraging desistance. Various paradigms of probation, including treatment, assistance, and control models, have been proposed and implemented in other countries in recent decades.[85] Ireland retains on its statute books, through inertia more than anything else, the Probation of Offenders Act 1907 which imposes on probation officers a duty to "advise, assist, and befriend" the offender and, where necessary, to endeavour to find him suitable employment.[86] This provision survives largely because there has never been a general review of the statute law governing probation but, rather ironically, it reflects precisely the kind of approach towards probation practice which modern desistance studies would seem to support. Resources may therefore be much better deployed in developing and extending probation services with a view to encouraging desistance rather than devoting more them to the expansion of custodial facilities. The second and related reason for referring to desistance in the present context is that, in the event that a decision were taken to introduce combination orders of the kind mentioned earlier, care should be taken to preserve the integrity of probation as a measure

---

[83] McNeill, "A Desistance Paradigm for Offender Management" (2006) 6 *Criminology and Criminal Justice* 38 at 47. See also McNeill, "What Works and What's Just?" (2009) 1 *European Journal of Probation* 21.

[84] Maruna, *Making Good* (Washington, DC: American Psychological Association, 2001), p.87.

[85] McNeill (fn.83 above); Bottoms and McWilliams, "A Non-Treatment Paradigm for Probation Practice" (1979) 9 *British Journal of Social Work* 160; Raynor and Vanstone, "Probation Practice: Effectiveness and the Non-Treatment Paradigm" (1994) 24 *British Journal of Social Work* 387.

[86] Section 4(d).

designed to assist offenders rather than allow it to be subsumed into the armoury of penal or control-oriented sanctions.

THE AMOUNT OF PUNISHMENT

This chapter has concentrated on the issues surrounding the kind of penalty to be selected when courts have a choice in the matter. Deciding how much of the chosen penalty should be imposed on individual offenders is a different, but equally important, question. This is essentially a matter to be determined according to judicially-developed principles and benchmarks as recommended elsewhere in this book. In Chapter 5, we noted the limitations of the present appeals system as an effective mechanism for elaborating sentencing guidance, and in Chapter 10 a proposal will be advanced as to how policy- and decision-making functions should be allocated between courts and other agencies. While guidance on the quantum of punishment is desirable in respect of all kinds of penalty, it is particularly vital in the case of imprisonment which is the most severe and intrusive penalty for offenders and the most expensive, in monetary terms, for society. The length of custodial sentences has two dimensions: the term of custody which a court should impose by way of a proportionate penalty, and the amount of that term which the offender should be required to serve before being eligible for release by way of remission, parole or both. The latter issue is addressed in the next chapter. The appropriate length of judicially-imposed sentences clearly requires more detailed attention than it has so far received from the courts and other official agencies. As in the case of alternatives to imprisonment, it is an issue fraught with tensions and policy contradictions. People may generally agree that prison should be avoided where possible and that custodial sentences should be no longer than strictly necessary (whatever that may mean). Any indication, however, that sentence levels for certain kinds of offences, such as sex offences, may be reduced will inevitably lead to strong objections.

Proportionality can never afford anything more than a rough guide to the right starting point in any case. In the absence of guidelines, it is impossible to say how much punishment is enough for any particular offence. This is not to suggest that a guideline penalty would necessarily be correct or universally acceptable, but it would at least function as an articulated standard which might be periodically revised or, at least, debated. Periods of imprisonment are judicially chosen, and publicly evaluated, largely in a notional or intuitive fashion. We seldom, for example, pause to consider the units of time by which we should measure custodial terms. In common-law countries, at any rate, prison sentences are usually expressed (and imagined) in large units of time—years for most serious offences, months for less serious ones. The prison sentences recommended in the Magistrates' Court Guidelines for England and Wales, for example, are mostly expressed in months, except for a few offences such as failure to surrender to bail for which the recommended sentences are expressed in days. David Rothman once remarked that in an age when most human activities are performed and imagined in progressively shorter time units (and this is especially true in the field of communications), we still think of imprisonment in pre-industrial units of time.[87] Might the judicial evaluation and public perception of sentence severity be different if custodial terms were expressed in days rather than years? A sentence of seven or ten years' imprisonment for a serious offence will sometimes be criticised as too lenient. Would the public reaction be different if the same sentence were expressed as a term of 2,500 days or 3,650 days? Judges who impose prison sentences and their critics in the wider community generally have one thing in common: they have never experienced imprisonment and cannot therefore realistically imagine the impact of any given period of total confinement in a penal institution. Suppose, for example, that a policy decision were taken, perhaps in response to severe prison overcrowding, that a year would be shaved off every prison sentence longer than, say, four years. This would be in addition to any ordinary entitlement to early release. Would society become any less safe as a result? Would a potential offender be less deterred by an anticipated five-year as opposed to a six-year prison term? These are questions which deserve serious and honest consideration in a much-needed policy review of the length of prison sentences imposed in this country. Shorter prison sentences might well prove much more publicly acceptable than we imagine once their rationale and impact are properly explained.[88]

---

[87]   Rothman, "Doing Time: Days, Months and Years in the Criminal Justice System" (1978) 19 *International Journal of Comparative Sociology* 130.

[88]   Doob, "Transforming the Punishment Environment: Understanding Public Views of What Should be Accomplished at Sentencing" (2000) 42 *Canadian Journal of Criminology* 323–340.

CHAPTER 9

EARLY RELEASE FROM PRISON

A coherent system of judicial sentencing has limited value unless accompanied by a fair and rational system for determining the actual length of time to be served by those sentenced to immediate imprisonment. Courts, after all, merely pronounce sentence. It falls to other state actors to determine the extent to which and, within limits, the manner in which any particular sentence is actually implemented. This distinction between judicial word and executive deed is a vitally important characteristic of the sentencing process.[1] Very few prisoners, if any, remain in custody for the entire duration of their sentences. Almost all are granted some form of early release whether by way of executive clemency, standard remission or parole. This holds true of most countries although, as might be expected, there are considerable variations in the generosity of early release provisions and the procedures by which they operate. Early release of sentenced prisoners may be difficult to justify in theoretical terms. If a particular sentence is judicially chosen to give effect to a policy of just deserts, deterrence or incapacitation, it should in principle be served in its totality if the original purpose is not to be frustrated. Early release is much more easily reconciled with a policy of rehabilitation. A prison sentence judicially imposed in order to provide the offender with a rehabilitative opportunity may legitimately be ended once he seems fit to be released back into the community. Courts rarely tie themselves to any one moral justification for punishment, unless compelled to do so by legislation. Irish courts generally treat all of the traditional justifications —just deserts, deterrence, rehabilitation and incapacitation—as legitimate considerations. The weight to be attributed to any one of them will depend on the nature and circumstances of the case. However, proportionality is the dominant distributive principle of punishment in Ireland. Again, this is not easily reconcilable with early release from prison. If a trial judge or an appeal court decides that, say, five years' imprisonment is a proportionate sentence taking account of all relevant factors, it seems contradictory to allow the executive branch of government or one of its agencies to decide later on that the offender should serve no more than two or three years.

Yet, the grant of early release and other executive reductions of punishment have always been motivated by a different ethic from that pursued by judicial sentencing authorities. Clemency and mercy are well recognised as having some role to play in the criminal justice system, although opinions vary as to whether

---

[1] Cover, "Violence and the Word" (1986) 95 Yale L.J. 1601.

they should remain within the sole preserve of the executive branch or be allowed to influence the judicial choice of sentence as well.[2] There have, of course, been some spirited debates over whether clemency has any role whatever in the system, as exemplified by the heated exchange between Albert Camus and François Mauriac over the treatment of collaborators in post-War France, but eventually even Camus came to accept the futility of punishment for its own sake.[3] The need for clemency is obviously greatest when courts are either obliged or inclined to impose harsh sentences which fail to reflect varying degrees of individual culpability and other personal circumstances. We have already noted the vibrant and essential role of the prerogative of mercy in the eighteenth and early nineteenth centuries when so many offences carried the death penalty.[4] Executive reduction of prison sentences, whether through commutation, remission or some form of parole, may also be motivated by more immediate or practical considerations such as the prevention of overcrowding, preparing prisoners for reintegration back into the community or the futility of detaining certain prisoners beyond a point at which their continued custody serves no ostensible purpose. What matters most is that the rules governing early release should be rational and purposeful, and applied in a fair, even-handed and reasonably predictable manner.

REMISSION

Two distinct forms of remission exist in Irish law: special remission and standard remission. Under Art.13.6 of the Constitution, the President is vested with the right of pardon and the power to commute or remit any punishment imposed by a criminal court, with the qualification that this power may also be conferred on other authorities. Pursuant to this qualification, the Criminal Justice Act 1951 conferred upon the Government the power to commute or remit any criminal punishment in whole or in part, subject to such conditions as it thinks proper. The Government may by order delegate any power conferred upon it in this regard to the Minister for Justice.[5] Commutation involves changing punishment from one form to another. While the death penalty remained the mandatory sentence for murder, it was frequently commuted by executive order to life imprisonment or a fixed-term of imprisonment.[6] Remission involves the

---

[2] Tasioulas, "Mercy" (2003) 103 *Proceedings of the Aristotelian Society* 101; O'Malley, *Sentencing Law and Practice*, 2nd edn (Dublin: Thomson Round Hall, 2006), p.106.

[3] Dunn, "Albert Camus and the Dubious Politics of Mercy" in English and Skelly (eds), *Ideas Matter: Essays in Honour of Conor Cruise O'Brien* (Dublin: Poolbeg Press, 1998), Ch.26.

[4] Chapter 4 above.

[5] Criminal Justice Act 1951 s.23 as amended by the Criminal Justice (Miscellaneous Provisions) Act 1997 s.17. See *Callan v Ireland* [2011] IEHC 190 for a valuable analysis of remission and commutation.

[6] Replying to a parliamentary question in 1963, the Minister for Justice said that from 1925 to

reduction of punishment and can, of course, apply to all forms of punishment including fines.[7] Once a prison sentence is remitted, it comes to an end. This would have been the general understanding of executive remission as it existed in common-law jurisdictions when the present Constitution was adopted in 1937.[8] With the abolition of the death penalty and the introduction of temporary release, the need for special remission of prison sentences declined, but it remains a useful reserve power to terminate an offender's liability to further punishment in exceptional circumstances. Special remission might also occasionally be used to facilitate so-called amnesty arrangements where a group of prisoners are released for political or other reasons. In 1946, 24 Republican prisoners, including Brendan Behan, were released by Government decision. This may have been an exercise in special remission although since they were all serving sentences of penal servitude, they could have been released on licence in any event.[9] The papal visit of 1979 was marked with the release of 76 prisoners, most serving short sentences for minor offences, although their release was delayed until the Pope had left the country, a decision which showed little confidence in the rehabilitative impact of custody.[10] The prerogative of mercy, as it was then known, was also exercised by the Government under the Free State Constitution of 1922 and was then understood to include a power to grant release in order to correct a perceived miscarriage of justice, such as where a jury verdict appeared to be unsupported by the evidence. Government decisions in 1932 to release Charles Dullea,[11] sentenced to three years' penal servitude for rape offences, and Hyman Levison sentenced to the same term for an abortion offence, caused considerable political controversy when it transpired that the Minister had recommended release for this reason.[12] Today, redress in such cases would probably be sought by way of a renewed appeal to the Court of Criminal Appeal under the Criminal Procedure Act 1993.

1962 inclusive, 317 people were charged with murder (though 120 of these charges were in the period 1925 to 1927), 68 were convicted and 27 (40 per cent of those convicted) were executed. Details of the prison terms served by those whose death sentences were commuted were also provided. The longest term served was 17 years and 2 months by a person convicted in 1925. Three served less than a year, but most served somewhere between two and 12 years (205 *Dáil Debates*, Col.324 (October 24, 1963). A similar pattern was observable in England and Wales. The Royal Commission, which reported in 1953, found that 45 per cent of those sentenced to death between 1900 and 1949 were reprieved.

[7] *Brennan v Minister for Justice* [1995] 1 I.R. 612, [1995] 2 I.L.R.M. 206.

[8] *Re Royal Prerogative of Mercy upon Deportation Proceedings* [1933] S.C.R. 269, [1933] 2 D.L.R. 269.

[9] "Government Frees 24 Internees", *Irish Times,* December 19, 1946.

[10] *Irish Times*, September 29, 1979.

[11] The surname is variously reported as "Dullea" and "Dunlea".

[12] 44 *Dáil Debates*, Col.541 (October 27, 1932). Levison's appeal had been dismissed by the Court of Criminal Appeal ([1932] I.R. 158) though, admittedly on the basis that the court could not re-examine questions of fact decided by the jury. Subsequently, at its first session, the newly-established Medical Registration Council declined to remove Dr Levison's name from the Register of Medical Practitioners (*Irish Times,* July 13, 1932).

For more than a century, most prisoners serving determinate sentences have been entitled to some level of standard remission, a practice which may be traced back to the ticket of leave system operated in the nineteenth century as an incentive to good conduct for those sentenced to transportation.[13] The Prisons (Ireland) Act 1907, adopting the language of the Prison Act 1898 which applied to England only, permitted the making of rules to enable prisoners "by special industry and good conduct" to earn remission so that upon release their sentence would be deemed to have expired. While originally intended as a mechanism for controlling inmate behaviour, and it still serves that purpose to some extent, it later became more valuable as a means of controlling the size of the prison population.[14] In more recent times, the Prison Rules 1947 provided that a prisoner sentenced to one month or longer could by industry and good conduct earn remission amounting to no more than one-quarter of his sentence.[15] This arrangement has been carried over into the present Rules adopted in 2007 but with the proviso that the Minister may increase remission to one-third "where a prisoner has shown further good conduct by engaging in authorised structured activity and the Minister is satisfied that, as a result, the prisoner is less likely to re-offend and will be better able to reintegrate into the community."[16] For all practical purposes, therefore, standard remission is a right which may be lost in whole or in part through bad behaviour while in prison, rather than a privilege to be earned.[17] There have been some recent suggestions that remission should have to be earned through more positive conduct, such as participation in treatment or training programmes, but so far those suggestions have been unaccompanied by any analysis of their likely impact on the prison population.

PAROLE

Parole is a convenient term to describe a variety of arrangements for granting early or temporary release to prisoners before the formal expiry of their sentence.[18] Some countries have highly structured parole systems so that prisoners can ordinarily expect to be released at a certain point in their sentence, in much the same way that an Irish prisoner can expect release at the three-quarters mark

---

[13] Cavadino and Dignan, *The Penal System: An Introduction*, 4th edn (London: Sage Publications, 2007), p.288.

[14] Cavadino and Dignan (fn.13 above), p.288.

[15] Rules for the Government of Prisons (Stat. R. & Ords, 320/1947), r.38(1). See *State (Carney) v Governor of Portlaoise Prison* [1957] I.R. 25.

[16] Prison Rules 2007 (S.I. No. 252 of 2007) r.59(1).

[17] On the method by which remission is computed, see *Harris v Delahunt* [2008] IEHC 152.

[18] On the history of parole, see Bottomley, "Parole in Transition: A Comparative Study of Origins, Developments, and Prospects for the 1990s" in Tonry and Morris (eds), *Crime and Justice: A Review of Research* Vol. 12 (Chicago: University of Chicago Press, 1990), p.319, and *The Parole System in England and Wales: Report of the Review Committee* (the Carlisle Report) Cm 532 (London: HMSO, 1988), Ch.2.

through the standard remission system. Others have more discretionary and less predictable systems under which early release is granted on a case-by-case basis by prison authorities, the executive branch of government or, in some countries, by way of judicial decision. Unlike remission, the grant of parole does not bring the sentence to an end. Release on parole may be for a defined period and the currency of the sentence may even be suspended for that period or, in any event, a breach of parole conditions may lead to the offender being returned to prison to serve out the remainder of the original sentence.[19] When considering early release under Irish law, it is important to draw a distinction between the constitutional power vested in the executive branch of government to remit a sentence, thereby bringing it to an end, and the statutory power vested in the Minister for Justice and Law Reform to grant temporary release. The first of these powers has already been discussed and it is equivalent in many respects to the prerogative of clemency historically vested in the Crown. The ministerial power to grant temporary release is the nearest we have to a parole system though, as we shall see, it is supplemented nowadays by the work of an advisory body known as the Parole Board. That power was introduced by the Criminal Justice Act 1960 which, in its original form, simply permitted the Minister to make rules "providing for the temporary release, subject to such conditions (if any) as may be imposed in each particular case, of persons serving a sentence of penal servitude or imprisonment, or of detention in Saint Patrick's Institution."[20] This has now been replaced by a more elaborate provision but one which does not effect any radical structural change. The decision to grant temporary release remains vested in the Minister.[21] Furthermore, the new provision continues to refer to "temporary" rather than "early" release or parole.

The new legislation specifies a range of purposes for which temporary release may be granted, and these include preparing the prisoner for full release, assisting in the prevention or detection of offences, health or humanitarian grounds, and ensuring the good government of the prison. Release may also be granted where the Minister is satisfied that the prisoner is sufficiently rehabilitated to be capable of reintegration into society. Factors which the Minister must take into account include the nature and gravity of the offence for which the sentence is being served, the portion of the sentence actually served, and any implications which the release might have for public safety. The rather minimalist arrangements for early release in the Criminal Justice Act 1960 contrast sharply with the more detailed and formal parole arrangements introduced in England in 1967. Prison overcrowding was scarcely an issue in Ireland in 1960; in fact, the

---

[19] The Criminal Justice Act 1960 s.5 provides that the currency of a sentence may be suspended while the person is on release. This is a statutory power entirely separate from the constitutional powers of remission and commutation: *Kinahan v Minister for Justice and Law Reform* [2001] 4 I.R. 454.

[20] Criminal Justice Act 1960 s.2(1).

[21] Criminal Justice (Temporary Release of Prisoners) Act 2003, supplemented by Prisoners (Temporary Release) Rules (S.I. No. 680 of 2004).

prison population at the time was at a historic low, with an average daily population of 400 or so. Temporary release was introduced to deal with a particular legal problem which then came to light. It transpired that while the Government, acting through the Minister for Justice, was empowered to grant release to a serving prisoner, that release was strictly speaking remission which meant that the released person was not legally obliged to return to prison. Some mechanism was therefore needed to permit the Minister to allow a prisoner out of custody for a short period because of a family bereavement or illness, or some similar reason. This apparently explains why temporary release was introduced at that time.[22] No doubt, it was a perfectly adequate arrangement in an era of low crime rates and a very low prison population. Longer-term prisoners, such as the few serving life sentences, could be dealt with by way of commutation or remission under the Criminal Justice Act 1951.

In 1989, a non-statutory Sentence Review Group was established to advise the Minister for Justice on the administration of long prison sentences, defined as sentences of seven years or more. This was replaced in 2001 with a body known as the Parole Board, though this too was established administratively and has never been placed on a statutory footing. Its function, like that of its predecessor, is to provide advice to the Minister on the administration of prison sentences, but only in respect of those prisoners serving eight years or longer. A case must first be referred to the Board by the Minister. According to its most recent report, the Board normally reviews individual cases at the half-way mark of a sentence, or after seven years, whichever comes first.[23] This means, in effect, that no prisoner is eligible to have his case reviewed until he has served at least four years. Other prisoners may, of course, be granted temporary release—as many short-term prisoners currently are—but this is accomplished by way of a ministerial decision without advice from the Parole Board. The limitations of this system will be discussed later but this outline serves to illustrate the minimal efforts made at political level in this country to establish an effective parole system.

The English parole system has undergone many changes since it was first established in 1967, but some of its features, past and present, are worth noting for the purpose of suggesting a new model of early release in this country. In keeping with the practice of the time, the provisions of the Criminal Justice Act 1967 introducing parole in Britain were drafted with great economy.[24] They simply established a Parole Board to advise the Secretary of State (the Home Secretary) with regard to the release on licence of persons whose cases had been referred to it by the Secretary. A prisoner, other than a life prisoner, who had served one-third of his sentence or 12 months, whichever expired later, might be released on licence following a favourable recommendation from the Board.

---

[22]   See statement of Minister for Justice (Mr Traynor), 52 *Seanad Debates*, Col.1999 (July 13, 1960).

[23]   Parole Board, *Annual Report 2008* (Dublin, 2009), p.7.

[24]   Criminal Justice Act 1967 ss.59–64. This part of the Act also applied to Scotland.

This meant that parole applied solely to prisoners serving 18 months or more.[25] Life prisoners might also be released on licence following a recommendation from the Board though obviously, on account of the indeterminate nature of that sentence, there was no fixed point at which lifers became eligible for release. In fact, the Home Secretary had a statutory power to release life prisoners on licence since 1948,[26] but now a Parole Board recommendation was required. The number of cases dealt with by the Board during its early years was much higher than expected, so that in 1972 Local Review Committees were introduced and they were entitled to make direct recommendations in some cases without going through the Parole Board. A major review of the system was carried out in the late 1980s by a committee chaired by Lord Carlisle.[27] One notable and commendable feature of this report was that it proposed a standard criterion to govern release decisions. This was to be "an evaluation of the risk to the public of the person committing a serious offence at a time when he would otherwise be in prison" which in turn was to be set against "the benefit both to him and the public of his being released from prison back into the community under a degree of supervision which might assist his rehabilitation and thereby lessen the risk of his re-offending in the future."[28] Granted, this formulation leaves a great deal of room for interpretation because of its concern to balance public safety and offender rehabilitation, but at least it excludes any possibility of the offender being effectively re-sentenced as a result of parole authorities having regard to the gravity of the offence of conviction. Various procedural reforms were also recommended and most of these were incorporated in the Criminal Justice Act 1991.[29] The distinction between remission and parole was abolished and replaced with a unified release system under which a short-term prisoner (one serving less than four years) was automatically entitled to release after serving half his sentence. Those sentenced to less than 12 months were released unconditionally at the half-way mark, while those serving 12 months or more but less than four years were released on licence at the half-way mark and remained under probationary supervision until the licence expired, which was usually at the three-quarters point of the original sentence. Offenders in both categories remained "at risk" in the sense that they could be returned to prison if they were convicted of a further imprisonable offence before the end of the original sentence, or failed to abide by the terms of their licence as the case might be. Long-term prisoners (those serving four years or more) could also be released once they had served half their sentences, provided the Parole Board

---

[25] West, "Parole in England: An Introductory Explanation" in West (ed.), *The Future of Parole* (London: Duckworth, 1972), Ch.1.

[26] Criminal Justice Act 1948 s.57.

[27] *The Parole System in England and Wales: Report of the Review Committee* Cm 352 (the Carlisle Report) (London: HMSO, 1988).

[28] Carlisle Report (fn.27 above), para.321. See Hood and Shute, "Parole Criteria, Parole Decisions and the Prison Population: Evaluating the Impact of the Criminal Justice Act 1991" [1996] Crim. L.R. 77.

[29] The parole provisions are contained in Pt II of the Act, ss.32–51.

so recommended. Otherwise, they were entitled to be released on licence once they had served two-thirds of their sentences. They, too, were "at risk" in the sense already described until the expiry of the original sentence. Special arrangements were also made for those serving discretionary life sentences. The system has been further amended by the Criminal Justice Act 2003 which, in keeping with the recommendations of the Halliday Report,[30] was designed to simplify existing parole arrangements. The most notable feature of the present system, for comparative purposes, is that, with some exceptions, a fixed-term prisoner serving 12 months or longer must be released on licence at the half-way point of the sentence.[31] Special arrangements apply to life sentence prisoners.[32]

Several aspects of the present Irish system combine to make it arbitrary and unsatisfactory. Although the Criminal Justice (Temporary Release of Prisoners) Act 2003 purports to set out in detail those matters which the Minister must consider when deciding on the grant of temporary release, it still leaves the decision entirely in the Minister's hands. While he must have regard to any report submitted by a prison governor, a probation officer, a member of the Gardaí or another person who might be considered to be of assistance, he is not obliged to seek or obtain a professional report on the suitability of any particular prisoner for release. Parole Board recommendations will probably be available for prisoners serving eight years or longer, a group that accounts for no more than a small proportion of the prison population at any one time. But the Parole Board system, as we shall see, has its own deficiencies. For the vast majority of prisoners, temporary release is available only on an ad hoc discretionary basis and, in the present climate with an ever-expanding prison population in the midst of an economic crisis, it is probably used predominantly as a means of controlling that population. On June 1, 2010, according to Departmental figures, there were about 4,200 prisoners in custody and a further 968 on temporary release. This means that almost one-fifth of those supposed to be serving custodial sentences were on release, more than twice as many as would ordinarily be on release in the absence of overcrowding. Having so many on release is not necessarily objectionable in itself, provided they have been selected on a rational basis and are given whatever assistance and supervision is needed to encourage them to desist from further crime and to reintegrate back into the community.[33]

Another arbitrary aspect of the system is that temporary release is denied by statute to prisoners serving sentences for selected offences. This is a pattern which began with the Criminal Justice Act 1990 (s.5) in respect of those

---

[30]   Halliday, *Making Punishments Work: Report of a Review of the Sentencing Framework for England and Wales* (London: Home Office, 2001).

[31]   Criminal Justice Act 2003 s.244.

[32]   Page 223 below.

[33]   There is little information publicly available on the profile of those prisoners on temporary release at any given time. It may be, for example, that most of them are either serving very short sentences or in prison for failure to pay fines, in which case the problem may be far less serious than the statistics would suggest.

sentenced to minimum terms of 40 years' imprisonment for murders that were hitherto capital (such as the murder of a member of the Gardaí while acting the course of duty).[34] Persons convicted of this offence are not entitled to special remission or commutation under the Criminal Justice Act 1951 or to temporary release under the Criminal Justice Act 1960 although they are entitled to standard remission on whatever minimum period they have been ordered to serve. Temporary release prior to qualification for remission may be granted in exceptional cases but only for a grave reason of a humanitarian nature and then only for such limited period as is necessary for that reason. Similar restrictions have since been imposed on the release of those sentenced to minimum periods for section 15A and section 15B drug offences and for certain firearms offences.[35] This is a classic example of democracy and distrust. The legislative branch of government has imposed a significant restraint on the capacity of its executive counterpart to exercise powers which are ordinarily within its exclusive remit. Ironically, of course, all of the legislation in question was drafted and sponsored by the Government itself, so it effectively amounts to a series of self-imposed executive restraints. One practical consequence of this arrangement in so far as drug offenders are concerned is that they now account for a significant portion of the longer-term prison population. Of the 2,500 prisoners serving sentences of two years or more and who were in custody on December 4, 2009, 687 (27 per cent) were drug offenders and 420 of these were serving sentences of five years or more. The Prisons Act 2007 (s.39) confers a general power on the Minister to grant release to prisoners for specified periods on compassionate grounds or for the purpose of social rehabilitation. This seems to apply to all prisoners, irrespective of the offence.

A Right or a Privilege?

Viewed in abstract terms, parole might be treated as a right or a privilege. As a right, it would be subject to the principles of legality; its availability and operation would be specified and governed by law; and decisions in specific cases, even if made by an executive authority, would be subject to judicial supervision or review. If it is merely a privilege, it will attract less formal legal protection and will operate on a largely discretionary basis. Temporary release in Ireland and parole in Britain have been treated from the beginning as administrative rather than judicial processes, an arrangement made possible by the classification of both forms of release as a privilege rather than a right. This was made clear by the English Parole Board at an early stage of its existence[36] and is also reflected in one of the leading Irish judicial statements on the matter:

---

[34] The same applies to those convicted of treason and to anyone sentenced to a minimum 20-year period for an attempted murder under the Act.
[35] Page 101 et seq. above.
[36] *Annual Report of Parole Board* (of England and Wales) (London: HMSO, 1975), para.13.

"The temporary release is a privilege or concession to which a person in custody has no right and indeed it has never been argued, so far as I am aware that he should be heard in relation to any consideration given to the exercise of such a concession in his favour. That being so, it seems to me that the only right of the applicant or any other person in custody is to enjoy such temporary release as may be granted to him for whatever period is allowed and subject to such conditions as are attached to it. The fact that the release may be renewed on a number of occasions and not renewed subsequently does not confer any additional or new right on the prisoner."[37]

Later courts, including the Supreme Court, have repeatedly endorsed this understanding of temporary release as an aspect of sentence implementation and therefore exclusively within the remit of the executive branch.[38] One consequence of classifying parole as a privilege is that most prisoners can never predict their likely release date and, when granted release for a defined period, they cannot be certain that it will be renewed. All that prisoners who are serving determinate sentences can know with any degree of certainty is the date on which they will be released if they qualify for full remission, an advantage denied to those serving life sentences. This state of affairs is scarcely conducive to efforts being made by either the prisoner or the prison authorities to engage in meaningful preparation for release. Another consequence of treating temporary release as a privilege is that there is limited scope for judicial supervision of the process, except to the extent of insisting on the observance of constitutional justice in revocation decisions. Release decisions will not be reviewed in the absence of evidence that they have been made capriciously, arbitrarily or unjustly.[39] The High Court held, for example, that a prisoner was not entitled to legal representation before the former Sentence Review Group, although it did accept that he was entitled to the disclosure of certain documentation.[40] It has also refused to hold that a person appearing before the Parole Board is entitled to legal aid for that purpose.[41] These

---

[37]   *Ryan v Governor of Limerick Prison* [1988] I.R. 198 at 200.

[38]   *Murray v Ireland* [1991] I.L.R.M. 465 at 472 (temporary release is "a matter which under the constitutional doctrine of the separation of powers rests entirely with the executive"); *People (DPP) v Tiernan* [1988] I.R. 250 at 256, [1989] I.L.R.M. 149 at 153 (temporary release is an executive power); *Dowling v Minister for Justice, Equality and Law Reform* [2003] 2 I.R. 535 at 543 ("… temporary release decisions are entirely within the discretion of the [Minister] acting in the exercise of executive clemency on behalf of the State"); *Lynch and Whelan v Minister for Justice, Equality and Law Reform* [2010] IESC 34. On the question of whether remission and commutation should be treated as judicial or executive in nature, see *State (O) v O'Brien* [1973] I.R. 50 and *Brennan v Minister for Justice* [1995] 1 I.R. 612, [1995] 2 I.L.R.M. 206. By present-day standards, however, the preferred classification should not diminish the need for procedural fairness, rationality and transparency in the exercise of these powers.

[39]   *Murray v Ireland* [1991] I.L.R.M. 465 at 473; *Kinahan v Minister for Justice and Law Reform* [2001] 4 I.R. 454 at 459.

[40]   *Barry v Sentence Review Group* [2001] 4 I.R. 167.

[41]   *Grogan v Parole Board* [2008] IEHC 204.

determinations flow essentially from the entirely discretionary nature of temporary release and the purely advisory role of the Parole Board and its predecessor.

The characterisation of parole or any other form of early release as a privilege within the gift of the executive should not, however, be a cause for either judicial or executive complacency. Prisoners may not have a formal right to liberty before the legal expiry of their sentence, but they have a strong interest in liberty which is too important to be left at the mercy of an arbitrary decision-making process. The need for enhanced procedural protections was among the key governing principles identified by the Carlisle Committee which, while recognising that parole was formally a privilege, proceeded to say:

> "The parole decision is more narrowly focused than the original sentencing decision and we do not think it necessary for identical procedures and safeguards to apply in each case. But we do believe that the structure and procedures for decision-making in parole cases need to take much more account than now of the fact that questions of freedom and custody are at stake. Our view that a parole system for long-term prisoners should be justified on a basis of assessment of risk reinforces the need for these safeguards, given the difficulty of making assessments of that sort."[42]

The legal quality of parole was intensely debated by the American Law Institute while it was drafting the Model Penal Code in the late 1950s. Professor Herbert Wechsler, one of its leading architects, suggested three possible approaches: (1) to treat parole as normal and require reasons for not granting release; (2) to treat retention as normal and seek reasons for granting parole; and (3) to merely state the considerations which a parole authority should take into account.[43] The Model Penal Code eventually reflected a combination of the first and third of these. It provided that every prisoner should be paroled at the earliest possible date and that release should be not be deferred except for one of four specified reasons including, predictably, a risk that the prisoner might not observe parole conditions, or that release at a particular point would depreciate the seriousness of the crime or promote disrespect for the law.[44] The right–privilege dichotomy remains at the heart of parole policy.

ANIMATING VALUES

No system of early release, no matter how it is characterised, can operate satisfactorily unless it is guided by one or more clearly-stated purposes and unless it operates in accordance with the tenets of natural justice and procedural

---

[42] Footnote 27 above, para.251.
[43] Quoted in Shea, "Parole Philosophy in England and America" in West (fn.25 above) at 73.
[44] Model Penal Code s.305.9(1).

fairness. The guiding purpose of early release must obviously shape the decision-making process. One obvious purpose might be to ensure that offenders are not detained in custody beyond the point at which they will no longer pose any discernible risk to the community if released. If this were the sole criterion, it might lead to some prisoners being released almost immediately after committal, irrespective of the nature or gravity of the offence. Consider the case of an elderly person who has been convicted of a child sexual abuse offence committed decades earlier and who has not, by all credible accounts, re-offended in the meantime. All of the indications, including the best professional opinion, may be that there is virtually no risk that he will re-offend in the future. Such a person might qualify for a suspended sentence, but if he is sentenced to a term of immediate imprisonment because of the gravity of the offences, he will be expected to serve some reasonable portion of it. His immediate release, irrespective of risk or the lack of it, would not be publicly acceptable unless there were exceptional mitigating factors such as extreme infirmity or ill-health. Judicial decisions to imprison are usually guided by considerations of desert, deterrence or incapacitation, or some combination of these. Grants of early release may well be within the exclusive constitutional competence of the Executive but they are not intended to set judicial sentencing decisions, or the animating purposes of those decisions, entirely at nought. Ideally, therefore, and as reflected in the rules and practices of other jurisdictions, there should be some mechanism for identifying the absolute minimum period which a sentenced prisoner is ordinarily required to serve before being eligible for release. We must also recognise that under our constitutional scheme, the Executive may remit a sentence at any time and it is important that it should retain this power to deal with exceptionally deserving cases. But our concern here is with the general run of cases where no such need arises.

From its very beginning, usually identified as a rehabilitation-based initiative adopted at the Elmira Reformatory for young offenders in New York in the late nineteenth century, modern parole policy has suffered from the lack of a clear consensus as to its dominant purpose.[45] While there may have been an enduring rhetorical commitment to a reformative or rehabilitative objective, institutional and managerial considerations have tended to predominate. Parole has been valued most as an incentive for serving prisoners to abide by prison discipline, as a safety valve to relieve prison overcrowding and, in more straightforward economic terms, as a means of avoiding the cost of providing additional prison space. None of those objectives is directly related to rehabilitation or to the risk of re-offending following release. Institutional behaviour has often been a strong factor influencing parole decisions. Yet, a prisoner's good behaviour might be no more than a deliberate strategy to secure early release in order to continue a

---

[45] Bottomley, *Decisions in the Penal Process* (London: Martin Robertson, 1973), Ch.5.
[46] Wilcox, "Parole: Principles and Practice" (1929) 20 *Journal of American Institute of Law and Criminology* 345 at 348.

life of crime.[46] Parole policies, at a minimum, should be directed at reducing overall levels of crime. To succeed in this regard, they must form part of a much broader set of therapeutic and risk reduction strategies. The process must begin in prison itself with appropriate programmes of training, work experience and treatment, depending on individual needs and deficiencies. It must then continue during a later period of parole supervision when released prisoners are encouraged and assisted to settle back into the community and desist from further criminal activity. The supervision element is crucially important to the success of any parole arrangement. Several studies have shown the positive and therapeutic benefits of the relationship between released prisoners and probation staff, particularly in the case of prisoners who have served long terms of custody and who may have few remaining ties in the community as a result.[47] Unfortunately, when parole is used principally as a means of coping with prison overcrowding the rehabilitative element is often either forgotten or relegated in the overall scheme of managerial priorities.

Once a system for establishing non-parole periods has been devised by, for example, adopting one of the models considered under the next heading, we can begin to think more clearly about an acceptable rationale for early release. By most modern standards, the dominant consideration should be to avoid detaining prisoners for any longer than is necessary for public safety once they have completed the "punitive" component of their sentence. The New Zealand Parole Act 2002, for example, sets out a number of guiding principles for early release decisions, the first of which is that the paramount consideration should be the safety of the community.[48] A further, related, principle is that "offenders must not be detained any longer than is consistent with the safety of the community, and that they must not be subject to release conditions that are more onerous, or last longer, than is consistent with the safety of the community."[49] The New Zealand Court of Appeal has held that considerations of general deterrence, while relevant at the sentencing stage, are not relevant to parole decision-making.[50] In a similar vein, the Council of Europe Recommendation on Conditional Release (Parole) has as its first general principle that release, "should aim at assisting prisoners to make a transition from life in prison to a law-abiding life in the community through post-release conditions and supervision that promote this end and contribute to public safety and the reduction of crime in the community".[51]

---

[47] See, for example, Appleton, *Life after Life Imprisonment* (Oxford: Oxford University Press, 2010). In *R (Smith and West) v Parole Board* [2005] UKHL 1 at [25], Lord Bingham said: "It is accordingly very desirable that the process of transition should be professionally supervised, to maximise the chances of the ex-prisoner's successful reintegration into the community and minimise the chances of his relapse into criminal activity."

[48] Section 7(1).

[49] Section 7(2).

[50] *Reid v New Zealand Parole Board* [2006] NZCA 232.

[51] Recommendation 22 of 2003 of Committee of Ministers of Council of Europe on Conditional Release (Parole), para.3.

To this end, it also recommends that parole should be available to all prisoners, including life prisoners. What early release decisions should not involve is an exercise in re-sentencing. The amount of deserved punishment is decided in each case by the sentencing court, with or without adjustment on appeal. For a parole authority later to reassess the term which a prisoner should serve by way of punishment for the offence would amount to a usurpation of the judicial function. It would scarcely be compatible with the fundamental constitutional principle that the selection of sentence, where there is a selection to be made, is exclusively a judicial task.[52] Yet, it seems that the Irish Parole Board sometimes takes this factor into account as reflected in the following extract from the Chairman's introduction to the 2007 *Annual Report*:

> "In coming to its decision as to what it will recommend to the Minister, the Board takes into consideration many issues. First and foremost there is the gravity of the crime and the circumstances under which it is committed.
>
> Then there is the prisoner's attitude to that crime. Is remorse shown? Is acknowledgment of wrongdoing shown or do circumstances exist that would satisfy the Board that the prisoner no longer represents a threat to the public if granted temporary release?
>
> A further issue must be the public abhorrence of the general public of the crime that was committed and the sufficient part of the prisoner's sentence which must be served in custody to allay this."

Arguably, only one of these factors is properly within the jurisdiction of a non-judicial parole authority and that is whether the prisoner any longer represents a threat to the public. Assessment of the gravity of the crime and the circumstances of its commission as well as "public abhorrence" (however that is to be defined and assessed) are quintessentially matters for the sentencing court. As already noted, one of the key recommendations of the Carlisle Committee in England and Wales was that the parole board should concentrate exclusively on the risk of a prisoner committing a serious offence if released. It was adamant that the board should not engage in "resentencing" by considering the seriousness of the offence and aggravating circumstances.[53] The parole system as it operated until then had often been criticised on this ground.[54] Apart from the obvious constitutional difficulty, allowing a parole authority to consider the aggravating features of the offence may lead to the offender being doubly punished, as those factors will (or should) have been taken into account by the trial court in deciding on sentence length. For an executive agency to determine the punishment which an offender deserves to undergo would surely violate the

---

[52] *Deaton v Attorney General and Revenue Commissioners* [1963] I.R. 170.

[53] Footnote 27 above.

[54] Ashworth, *Sentencing and Penal Policy* (London: Weidenfeld & Nicolson, 1983); Hood, "Tolerance and the Tariff" in Baldwin and Bottomley (eds), *Criminal Justice: Selected Readings* (London: Martin Roberston, 1978).

separation of powers mandated by the Constitution.[55] The Irish Parole Board might possibly defend its approach by pointing to the absence of specified or standard non-parole periods in this jurisdiction. But, as against that, it may be argued that the confinement of eligibility for release to those who have served at least half of a long sentence should be treated as the de facto equivalent to a non-parole period.

Once the purposes of parole have been agreed, they should be implemented in a fair and transparent manner. This, in turn, raises the question of whether parole decisions should be made by a court or by an administrative agency. Several European countries commit all or most decisions on the implementation of sentence, including the grant of early or temporary release, to special judicial officers or tribunals such as the *juge de l'application des peines* in France who decides on the early release of prisoners serving sentences of less than 10 years, but with less than three years left to serve. Another court decides on cases falling outside of that judge's jurisdiction. All first-instance decisions may be appealed to a three-judge appeal court (*chambre de l'application des peines*).[56] A *juge de l'application des peines* can transform a sentence of less than two years to some other measure such as electronic monitoring or community service. Belgium likewise has a *tribunal de l'application des peines* which deals with prisoners serving sentences longer than three years. The *tribunal* consists of judge and two assessors. The relevant law sets out the minimum periods which prisoners must serve before becoming eligible for conditional release.[57] Common-law countries have generally committed the implementation of sentence to the executive branch of government, acting through, or with the advice of, a specialised body such as a parole board. Opinions vary as to the relative merits of the judicial and administrative models, but what matters ultimately is the quality of the decision-making process rather than the structure within which it unfolds. In either case, the decision-making body should have access to the expertise necessary to evaluate the risk posed by individual prisoners if released, and have the time and resources necessary to consider applications and, where appropriate, to prescribe release conditions. Crucially, also, it should be insulated from transient public

---

[55] *Grogan v Parole Board* [2008] IEHC 204 per McMahon J. ("When the prisoner is entrusted to the executive, the executive is obliged to carry out the sentence of the court. It cannot look behind the sentence or question its fairness, for to do so would disturb the delicate balance struck by the separation of powers enshrined in the Constitution … The [Parole] Board is not there to determine the innocence or guilt of the applicant, much less to second guess the sentence imposed by the court.")

[56] Herzog-Evans, *Droit de l'éxecution des peines*, 3rd edn (Paris: Dalloz, 2007); Herzog-Evans, "French Post Custody Law (2000–2009): From Equitable Trial to the Religion of Control" (2009) 1 *European Journal of Probation* 97; Reuflet, "France" in Padfield, van Zyl Smit and Dünkel (eds), *Release from Prison: European Policy and Practice* (Cullompton: Willan Publishing, 2010), Ch.7.

[57] Loi du 17 mai 2006 instaurant les tribunaux de l'application des peines. For a critical account, see Beyens and Scheirs, "Les juges belges face à l'(in)éxecution des peines" (2010) 34 *Déviance et Societé* 401.

and political pressure (while obviously having public safety as a foremost consideration) and be so constituted and organised as to be able to make its decisions impartially and objectively. On the face of it, a judicial body seems better equipped than a political one to fulfil all of these criteria. But an administrative or executive authority, such as a parole board, may be equally effective provided it has the necessary levels of institutional and decisional independence.[58] In one respect it may be superior to a judicial parole authority by virtue of the diversity of expertise which it can bring to the performance of its functions. Ideally, a parole authority should comprise experts drawn from the fields of psychology, psychiatry, criminology, law, probation practice and other relevant disciplines. It may include some community representatives as well. Provided its members have adequate security of tenure and are not beholden to any external entity, political or otherwise, they can develop sound practices and accumulate considerable institutional wisdom as time goes on.[59] Implementation courts may also be assumed to have access to appropriate expertise and could, of course, develop the same qualities as those of a well-functioning parole board. But just as trial court judges may vary, as they undoubtedly do, in selecting sentence, so implementation judges may develop their own ideas and practices over time in relation to dealing with applications from serving prisoners for release and other benefits.

MODELS OF EARLY RELEASE

Wherever the possibility of early release exists, those sentenced to imprisonment should be able to identify with some certainty the date on which they will become eligible for release. This need not entail any guarantee of actual release prior to the legal expiry of sentence, but it provides prisoners with an incentive to fulfil whatever conditions are likely to influence release decisions. The Council of Europe Recommendation states in this regard:

> "When starting to serve their sentence, prisoners should know either when they become eligible for release by virtue of having served a minimum period

---

[58] On these concepts of independence, see p.255 below.

[59] It is significant, for example, that while art.5(4) of the European Convention on Human Rights guarantees to everyone deprived of their liberty following arrest or detention the right to have the legality of the detention speedily determined by a "court", the European Court of Human Rights has held that the court in question need not be "a court of law of the classic kind" but could, for example, be a parole board which had the requisite decision-making power as well as the necessary levels of independence and impartiality: *Weeks v United Kingdom* (1987) 10 E.H.R.R. 293. In relation to discretionary life prisoners, however, the European Court found a breach of art.5(4) because the Parole Board had a purely advisory rather than a decision-making role in relation to their release on licence: *Thynne, Wilson and Gunnell v United Kingdom* (1990) 13 E.H.R.R. 666. The situation was remedied by the Criminal Justice Act 1991 (s.34).

(defined in absolute terms and/or by reference to a proportion of the sentence) and the criteria that will be applied to determine whether they will be granted release ('discretionary release system') or when they become entitled to release as of right by virtue of having served a fixed period defined in absolute terms and/or by reference to a proportion of the sentence ('mandatory release system')."[60]

Various models are available for determining non-parole periods and eligibility for release. The first is an entirely discretionary system under which prisoners are released whenever, and for whatever reason, the relevant authority deems fit. The present Irish system is largely discretionary because, apart from those serving sentences long enough to warrant consideration by the Parole Board and those sentenced for certain drug and firearm offences, most prisoners are released when, or if, the Minister so decides. This arrangement has a number of drawbacks, one being the lack of predictability which is now regarded as a highly desirable aspect of early release provisions. Flowing from this is the related disadvantage that neither the prisoner nor the prison service can prepare in any meaningful way for the prisoner's eventual return to the outside community. Furthermore, when the ultimate authority to release is vested in a political branch of government or an elected official, some prisoners will be at a greater disadvantage than others. While sentencing decisions, by virtue of their public nature, often attract considerable media attention, the release of prisoners seldom attracts any. Most prisoners are released unnoticed. But there will always be a few who, because of the nature of the crime, the identity of the victim, or their own notoriety, remain the subject of media interest throughout their terms of imprisonment. Any elected official who decides to release such a prisoner may become the target of intense public or media-led criticism.[61] One need only recall the public furore that erupted in this country in summer 2010 when a serious sex offender was released on the completion of a lengthy determinate sentence. Although he had served his entire sentence, less remission, right down to the last minute, or so it seems, there was a general feeling, fuelled as always by some sections of the media, that he should not be at large.[62] Any Minister or

---

[60] Recommendation 22 of 2003 of Committee of Ministers of Council of Europe on Conditional Release (Parole), para.5.

[61] The introduction of a judicial release system in Belgium, the *tribunal de l'application des peines* described earlier, resulted largely from the controversy surrounding the Dutroux case. In 2002, Marc Dutroux was convicted of killing and sexually abusing several young girls in 1995 while he was on parole from a lengthy prison sentence for sexual offences committed against other young girls. This obviously led to a great deal of public criticism about the operation of the system under which he was released. As it happens, at the time of writing, a new controversy has erupted over a decision of the new *tribunal* to grant conditional release to Dutroux's former partner, Michelle Martin, who was arrested in 1996 and sentenced to 30 years' imprisonment in 2004 for her role in the crimes. (*Le Figaro*, May 11, 2011).

[62] This was the case of Larry Murphy who was released in August 2010 after serving the entirety of a sentence, less standard remission, imposed for rape and attempted murder.

other elected official with the power to detain that particular offender further or to rescind the release decision would have been placed under unbearable pressure to keep him in custody. When such an offender is subject to a life sentence, his chances of release are greatly diminished even if, by all reasonable standards, he is actually fit for release. Cases such as these illustrate the desirability of assigning release decisions to an independent body with adequate security of tenure and charged with making decisions in accordance with prescribed criteria and reliable evidence.

A second possibility would be to alter current sentencing practice so as to require judges when imposing a prison sentence (at least when it reaches a certain length) to stipulate a non-parole period. This is a common practice in Australia, although the system varies from one state to another.[63] Typically, a judge is required to set a non-parole period when imposing a prison sentence of any appreciable duration, although the requirement may be dispensed with in exceptional cases. One advantage of this kind of arrangement is that it removes or reduces the conflict that inevitably arises in traditional parole arrangements where sentence is imposed to advance one set of goals and later terminated (conditionally at any rate) to advance another. Parole authorities need not therefore yield to the temptation to re-sentence the offender by having regard to offence seriousness when deciding on release. The non-parole period set by the sentencing court may be assumed to reflect the court's assessment of the gravity of the offence as well as the offender's circumstances. Dissatisfaction with the length of a non-parole period could also be the subject of a defence or prosecution appeal. At first sight, it might seem contradictory that a court should first specify a sentence which it considers appropriate in light of all the circumstances of a case and then prescribe a shorter period to be served. Essentially, however, the court would be deciding that the case called for a prison term during which the offender should be liable to be held in custody. The non-parole period would have to be served subject to the executive entitlement to grant remission or commutation in exceptional circumstances. During the remaining period, the offender would be released subject to conditions and, hopefully, supervision or, for that matter, detained in prison if the relevant authorities did not consider it safe to release him. This particular strategy has some merit, particularly in relation to longer sentences, but it may not be feasible to require that each and every prison sentence should have a specified non-parole period.

The third possibility is to have a standardised parole system like that introduced in England and Wales in 1991.[64] Under this arrangement, prisoners become entitled to release or, more likely, eligible for consideration for parole after serving a defined portion of their sentence. Non-parole periods may be

---

[63]   Edney and Bagaric, *Australian Sentencing; Principles and Practice* (Cambridge: Cambridge University Press, 2007), p.314 et seq.

[64]   Page 217 above.

expected to vary according to the length of the original sentence, the nature of the offence of conviction or both. In New Zealand, for example, a person sentenced to more than 24 months' imprisonment ordinarily becomes eligible for parole after serving one-third of the sentence or such minimum period as may have been specified by the court. The non-parole period attaching to a life sentence is ordinarily 10 years.[65] Standardised systems have the virtue of administrative efficiency in so far as they relieve parole authorities of the duty to consider each case individually, an obviously important consideration in countries with large prison populations. The periods which prisoners are statutorily required to serve will presumably reflect legislative assessments of the appropriate tariff. There are, of course, some practical disadvantages. One is the possibility that courts may increase the length of sentences generally in order to counteract the impact of early release, especially in cases where release becomes an absolute entitlement once a defined portion of the sentence has been served. Legislation should therefore include a specific prohibition on taking parole entitlement into account when sentence is being selected. Another problem is that where standard parole entitlements are established by statute, and there is no realistic alternative, they will always be vulnerable to alterations and restrictions as a result of public pressure and political posturing in response to isolated incidents such as a serious crime committed by a person following early release from prison. The history of bail reform in this country illustrates the willingness of legislators to make abrupt legal changes in response to such incidents and usually without regard to the bigger picture in terms of patterns of offending by those on remand or parole.

Standard non-parole periods bear some resemblance to part-suspended sentences, save that they are predetermined by statute rather than being judicially decided on a case-by-case basis.[66] The legitimacy, effectiveness and public acceptability of such a system will depend to a large extent on a factor already mentioned, and that is the degree of supervision offered to prisoners following their release. At a time when parole is viewed predominantly as a means of controlling prison populations, the supervisory element is at risk of being forgotten or downplayed. Early release of prisoners convicted of serious crimes may understandably cause some degree of public disquiet. Yet all such prisoners, apart from those serving life sentences, are virtually guaranteed release once they have served three-quarters of their sentence. The question therefore is whether public safety is better served by releasing prisoners back into the community without any supervision once they have served all of their sentences less remission, or by releasing some of them at any earlier point but subjecting them to professional supervision for a certain period of time thereafter. Supervision might last until the time at which the entire sentence would have expired or, more likely, until the date on which the offender would

---

[65] Parole Act 2002 s.84.
[66] Bottomley, "The Pitfalls of Automatic Parole", *The Times*, August 21, 1981.

have qualified for release with remission. The intensity of the supervision necessary in any given case will depend on the personal circumstances and characteristics of the offender, but in any case it will allow for appropriate steps, including parole revocation, to be taken where the offender commits a further offence or behaves in a manner which gives cause for concern.

As the law now stands, sex offenders may be subject to post-release supervision following their release from prison, the length and terms of the supervision being determined by the sentencing court.[67] This is entirely different from parole supervision as it takes effect on whatever date the prisoner is released, and many sex offenders serve their full prison terms less remission. The problem with this approach, especially if it were applied across the board to all long-term prisoners, is that it may lead to large numbers of prisoners remaining in prison for longer than necessary. Parole does, after all, have an important institutional dimension in that it frees up prison space and provides a strong incentive to prisoners to abide by prison discipline and take advantage of treatment and training programmes to prepare for eventual release. This is not to say that parole policies should be entirely driven by prison economics—the estimated risk to public safety posed by individual applicants for parole must always be the dominant consideration—but other things being equal, the institutional value of parole must not be overlooked. Viewed in this light, it makes little sense to detain some prisoners unnecessarily when better long-term results may well be achieved through supervised early release. Such an arrangement need not interfere with the existing law regarding the post-release supervision of sex offenders. Some of these offenders may simply be unsuitable for release on parole at any time before they qualify for release with remission. Nobody suggests that parole, once introduced, must automatically be granted to everyone, but there must be a rational and coherent process for determining eligibility for release accompanied by transparent criteria for assessing individual cases.

STEPS TOWARDS REFORM

The purpose and structure of parole arrangements are inextricably linked to the nature and purpose of imprisonment. A prison sentence may legitimately be imposed for retributive, deterrent or incapacitative purposes, but it does not follow that the regime within which it is served should be so tailored as to intensify the punishment experience. It has long been held, if not always enthusiastically accepted, that offenders are imprisoned as punishment, not *for* punishment.[68] In other words, the deprivation of liberty is sufficient punishment

---

[67] Sex Offenders Act 2001 Pt 5.

[68] The phrase is usually attributed to Alexander Paterson (1884–1947), a British Commissioner of Prisons ("Men are sent to prison as a punishment, not *for* punishment").

in itself. Whatever the original judicial purpose in imposing sentence, the prison regime should be humane and conducive towards eventual social reintegration. After all, the International Covenant on Civil and Political Rights, which Ireland has ratified, provides that "the penitentiary system shall comprise the treatment of prisoners the essential aim of which shall be their reformation and social rehabilitation."[69] The European Prison Rules likewise state: "All detention shall be managed so as to facilitate the reintegration into free society of persons who have been deprived of their liberty".[70] National and European courts have also been placing increased emphasis on the importance of social reintegration and preparation for release.[71] Parole in the form of supervised release clearly has an important role in that overall process of reintegration. Early release in its various forms is an integral part of the overall sentencing process. In Ireland, unlike many other common-law countries nowadays, prisoners serving determinate sentences can still expect to be granted standard remission. Additionally, they can expect to be considered for, and possibly granted, parole-type release before qualifying for remission.[72]

The failure to place the present Irish Parole Board on a statutory footing has been subject to persistent criticism, mainly from the political parties now in Government. To the extent that it might guarantee the Board's independence and effectiveness, a statutory foundation would indeed be desirable and, for reasons to be outlined, may well become essential, if the process is to conform with the requirements of the European Convention on Human Rights. But the most immediate necessity is a thorough review of the purpose of parole, its relationship to the sentencing system and the most appropriate mechanism for ensuring that early release procedures operate fairly and rationally. A specialist review body should be established for this purpose. In fact, much of the groundwork has already been done by similar bodies in other jurisdictions such as the Carlisle Committee in England and Wales and, more recently, JUSTICE (the British Section of the International Commission of Jurists) in its report, *A New Parole System for England and Wales*.[73] While their views and recommendations need not, of course, be accepted uncritically, they do provide a penetrating analysis of the development and purposes of parole arrangements (Carlisle) and of the values that should animate a modern parole system (JUSTICE).

One matter of crucial importance is the relationship between a parole board and the executive branch of government. The ready judicial acceptance of

---

[69] Article 10(3).

[70] Recommendation of Committee of Ministers of Council of Europe adopted on January 11, 2006, principle 6.

[71] *Dickson v United Kingdom* (2007) 44 E.H.R.R. 21 at [28]; *R (Smith and West) v Parole Board* [2005] UKHL at [25].

[72] See remarks to this effect by Lord Phillips in *R (Black) v Secretary of State for Justice* [2009] 1 A.C. 949, [2009] 2 W.L.R. 282, [2009] 4 All E.R. 1 at [16], although there he was referring to the statutory regime in England and Wales at the time.

[73] London: JUSTICE, 2009.

temporary release as a privilege to be granted at ministerial discretion should not obscure the reality that early release (however it is described or classified) can amount in reality to a sentencing decision. Release, especially in the form of parole, brings the operative part of a prison sentence to an end even if, in contrast to remission, it leaves the offender liable to recall either indefinitely in the case of a life sentence or, in other cases, until the sentence legally expires. A person who abides by the release conditions can ordinarily expect to remain at liberty. Just as it would be unthinkable nowadays that any person or body other than a judge should be permitted to determine sentence following conviction, so it should be accepted that early release decisions ought to be made by an independent, court-like body. The fact that the privilege theory of early release has survived virtually unchallenged until now does not mean that it remains valid, or consistent with current human rights values and the rule of law. In *Stafford v United Kingdom*,[74] the European Court of Human Rights found the respondent state in violation of art.5 of the European Convention because it continued to detain the applicant without adequate justification during the post-tariff period. The judgment is of interest in the present context because the court changed its mind on the question of whether the mandatory life sentence in England and Wales was in a different category from the discretionary life sentence. It had previously decided that the two sentences were different,[75] but in *Stafford* it accepted that, in so far as tariff-fixing was concerned, there was no difference between the two forms of life sentence under English law. The court stressed the importance of interpreting the Convention in a manner which reflected emerging consensus on the human rights standards to be achieved. It said that a failure on its part "to maintain a dynamic and evolutive approach would risk rendering it a bar to reform or improvement."[76]

Leaving a prisoner's eligibility for early release, or his entitlement to it, entirely at the mercy of the executive branch of government is scarcely compatible with modern human rights and rule of law values, all the more so in the case of those prisoners (the vast majority of Irish prisoners) who do not even qualify for consideration by the present Parole Board. Qualities such as predictability, openness and accountability, which should be the hallmarks of a system amounting to de facto sentencing, are noticeable for their absence when release decisions are entirely at the discretion of the executive. In *R (Brooke) v Parole Board*[77] the Court of Appeal decided that the English Parole Board, which by then had become, in effect, a judicial body charged with deciding if prisoners could safely be released, did not, objectively speaking, have the requisite level of independence because it was too close to the sponsoring Government department and because members of the board did not have

---

[74] (2002) 35 E.H.R.R. 32.
[75] *Wynne v United Kingdom* (1994) 19 E.H.R.R. 333.
[76] (2002) 35 E.H.R.R. 32 at para.68.
[77] [2008] 1 W.L.R. 1950, [2008] 3 All E.R. 289.

adequate security of tenure. For instance, it found that the power vested in the Secretary of State to terminate the appointment of a member of the Board if satisfied that the member had failed to perform his duties in a satisfactory manner was incompatible with the level of independence which should attach, and be seen to attach, to a judicial body. This, however, was in a context where the role of the Parole Board had changed quite radically from being an advisory body to one which was charged with deciding on prisoner release. Formerly, the Board was advising the Secretary of State. Now, the Secretary was merely a party to proceedings before the Board to which he was entitled to make recommendations and submissions.

One of the ironies of the present Irish situation is that because it has remained more or less static for the past half-century during which temporary release has been treated as a privilege, it has escaped judicial censure at home and in Europe. This is in stark contrast to the English system which has operated a tariff system for life prisoners for many years and which has found itself in constant tension with the European Convention on Human Rights as a result. While the history of the tariff is long and complex,[78] it will suffice for present purposes to say that until the Criminal Justice Act 2003 came into force, the Home Secretary fixed a tariff for those serving mandatory life sentences. The tariff was meant to reflect the custodial term deemed necessary for punitive and deterrent purposes. Once that term had been served, the prisoner became eligible for release on licence. In 2002, the House of Lords declared that this tariff-fixing function was, in reality, a sentencing exercise and that the statutory provision authorising the Home Secretary to set it was accordingly incompatible with art.6 of the European Convention on Human Rights.[79] This decision was effectively endorsed by the European Court of Human Rights in *Easterbrook v United Kingdom* decided a short time later.[80] Both courts stressed that sentencing is part of the trial process (indeed, Lord Bingham invoked *Deaton*[81] in this regard) and as such must be exercised by an independent and impartial tribunal in accordance with art.6 of the European Convention. Once the fixing of a tariff was treated as a sentencing exercise—and both courts accepted that it should be so treated—it was clearly

---

[78] It is set out with characteristic clarity by Lord Bingham in *R (Anderson) v Secretary of State for the Home Department* [2003] 1 A.C. 837, [2008] 3 W.L.R. 1800, [2002] 4 All E.R. 1089, [2003] 1 Cr. App. R. 32.

[79] *Anderson* (fn.78 above). This had been presaged by the European Court's decision in *Stafford v United Kingdom* (2002) 35 E.H.R.R. 32 (p.1121) to the effect that there was no meaningful difference between mandatory and discretionary life sentences in so far as tariff-setting was concerned, and it had already held that the tariff for those serving discretionary life sentences should be set by a body independent of the executive (*Thynne, Wilson and Gunnell v United Kingdom* (1990) 13 E.H.R.R. 666). See also, Padfield, *Beyond the Tariff: Human Rights and the Release of Life Sentence Prisoners* (Cullompton: Willan, 2002).

[80] *Easterbrook v United Kingdom* (2003) 37 E.H.R.R. 40.

[81] *Deaton v Attorney General and Revenue Commissioners* [1963] I.R. 170. See Ch.4 above.

[82] The situation was remedied in England and Wales by the Criminal Justice Act 2003 (s.269) which provides that the court which passes a mandatory life sentence should specify the term

one which should be discharged by a tribunal with the requisite level of independence and impartiality.[82] Some might argue that these principles are not directly relevant in Ireland which never adopted a tariff system for either life sentence prisoners or any others. But there is a strong counter-argument to be made that whichever body decides on the release of a life sentence or long-term prisoner is, in effect, determining the operative length of that person's custodial term. Right now, the decision is made on an entirely discretionary basis by the executive branch of government. The fact that temporary release, as opposed to release on continuing licence, is the only formal basis for executive release in Ireland does not remove the need for more objective and transparent procedures. As the European Court has repeatedly held, what matters is the substance and reality of a procedure as opposed to its legal form or nomenclature. In that light, it is difficult to regard the present Irish system as being compatible with the evolving requirements of justice in the administration as well as in the imposition of sentence.

The Irish parole system therefore needs to be reformed in a number of respects. First, a decision must be made as to the preferred model for deciding on entitlement to parole. Even with a relatively small prison population, compared to that of England and Wales, it may not be feasible to require a Parole Board decision on each and every prisoner who is applying or potentially eligible for early release. Some standardised form of parole may be necessary for shorter-term prisoners, either in addition to or instead of the present standard remission system. But there will still be many cases including, obviously, life-sentence prisoners where a more individualised assessment is required. If the grant of early release, however it is characterised, amounts to a de facto sentencing decision, it should bear the same essential hallmarks as judicial sentencing. This need not entail transferring release decisions to a law court, but it does require, at a minimum, that the responsible body should be independent in the performance of its functions. This, in turn, requires that it has adequate security of tenure, that its decisions are made in accordance with clear statutory criteria and, needless to say, that it is shielded from political interference. Members of the parole authority should be required to act judicially in the sense of giving a fair and adequate hearing to all interested parties and giving reasoned decisions once they have considered all the relevant evidence. The authority's decisions should be subject to judicial review on the usual grounds, such as a failure to observe the principles of natural and constitutional justice or a want of reasonableness. There is nothing particularly radical about these proposals; they merely demand that decisions on the early release of prisoners should be made according to the standards already expected of public bodies charged with making determinations which affect the rights and liabilities of citizens and others. Nor are these proposals intended to detract in any way from the

---

to be served. See Ward and Davies, *The Criminal Justice Act 2003: A Practitioner's Guide* (Bristol: Jordans, 2004), p.218 et seq.

dedication and objectivity which members of the existing non-statutory Parole Board bring to the exercise of their functions. What is being suggested instead is that the entire underlying structure is in need of reform in order to bring it into harmony with present-day constitutional and human rights values.

Writing more than a half-century ago, a member of a Californian parole board described one form of parole then existing as operating "[like] the orchardist who watches the colour and the fuzz on his peaches and picks them at just the right time."[83] This presupposes that some person or group has the experience and expertise to identify the precise point at which a prisoner may safely be released. A parole authority should have adequate expertise for this purpose. For instance, at the time of writing, the English Parole Board has 255 members including 100 judges, 30 psychiatrists, 10 psychologists, 15 probation personnel and 100 independent members. According to the website of the Irish Department of Justice,[84] our Parole Board has 11 members consisting of a chairperson (though the person in question, who was a solicitor, is recently deceased), one consultant psychiatrist, an official from the Department of Justice, the Director of the Probation Service, an official from the Prison Service and six community members. In a country of this size, the overall complement of the Board may be reasonably adequate but the balance of the membership should be redressed in order to introduce more professional expertise and it should preferably include one or more judicial members as well. Community members should be appointed following a transparent and objective recruitment process and be selected by an independent expert body.

---

[83] Finsley, "Who Gets Parole?" (1953) 17:3 *Federal Probation* 26.
[84] Consulted in mid-May 2011.

CHAPTER 10

STRUCTURED SENTENCING: POLICIES, PRINCIPLES AND DECISIONS

Judicial sentencing practices are expected to embody four primary qualities: legality, fairness, effectiveness and consistency. Legality, at least when narrowly construed, creates few difficulties as courts seldom stray beyond their formal jurisdiction when selecting sentence. Reconciling the remaining three qualities is a much more difficult challenge, as many countries have discovered in their efforts to structure or curtail judicial sentencing discretion. It is probably fair to say that none of them can yet claim to have achieved the perfect balance. Fairness, effectiveness and consistency may occasionally point in the same direction, but they are just as likely to produce conflicting results when applied to specific cases. A modest fine may be a fair punishment for a minor traffic offence but it will rarely be an effective deterrent. A mandatory prison sentence for such an offence might well deter but it would also, by our standards, be manifestly unfair. Once a consistency requirement is added to the mix, sentence selection becomes all the more difficult. Consistency and effectiveness may indeed be compatible. A mandatory 30-day prison sentence for everyone convicted of illegal parking would surely meet the demands of consistency and effectiveness, but it would just as surely be unfair. However obvious the tension between fairness, effectiveness and consistency, it is often brushed aside by policy-makers, legislators and, indeed, by some academic commentators who claim that a fundamental review of the entire sentencing process could produce a system embracing all of these qualities. It is a belief reflected in European legislation such as the Framework Decision on combating racism and xenophobia which requires the prohibited conduct to be punished with "effective, proportionate and dissuasive criminal penalties", and stipulates maximum penalties of "at least between 1 and 3 years of imprisonment".[1] The legislators clearly believed that a custodial sentence within this range, flexible though it may be, would satisfy all of the expressed penal purposes. Consistency is not mentioned, as this is a matter for member states to address within their general sentencing systems. But there is a clear assumption that effectiveness, proportionality and deterrence can easily be reconciled.

Concern about the effectiveness of penalties has been somewhat eclipsed in recent times by the preoccupation with legal strategies for eliminating

---

[1] Council Framework Decision 2008/913/JHA of 28 November 2008 on combating certain forms and expressions of racism and xenophobia by means of criminal law, art.3.

unwarranted disparity. Achieving consistency of approach obviously remains an important goal of any sentencing system but it should not be allowed to divert attention from the need to devise constructive sentencing arrangements that hold some promise of producing worthwhile results, in addition to being fair and equitable. It seems to be an unfortunate reality that measures designed to increase consistency often have the effect of producing more and longer prison sentences.[2] To aim for effective sentencing need not entail the abandonment of justice-based distributive criteria. Proportionality can still prevail as the dominant distributive principle, provided it is interpreted as permitting courts to fashion sentences that are designed to reduce the risk of recidivism or to act as a deterrent to others. This may sometimes result in measures which appear lenient when viewed from a rigid just deserts perspective although it should never, of course, result in punishment exceeding that which is deemed commensurate with the gravity of the offence and the personal circumstances of the offender. The concept of effectiveness in a sentencing context is, admittedly, an elusive one but it is essentially concerned with risk reduction. This, in turn, need not entail the adoption of an actuarial approach under which offenders are sentenced by reference to the class or category to which they are assigned through some risk assessment exercise.[3] The emergence of so-called problem-solving courts such as drug courts, although they have received mixed reviews, has shown that it is possible to adopt an individualised approach to the disposition of offenders while simultaneously taking concrete steps to assist them in coping with addiction and other problems.[4] An important function of a sentencing information unit of the kind recommended later in this chapter would be to monitor (and perhaps commission) research findings on the effectiveness of various measures in assisting offenders to become more socially integrated or in dissuading them from persisting in criminal activities. Courts would then be in a better position to select penalties and other measures which, without being excessive in punitive terms, seem best suited for particular offenders.

Sentencing reform, if it is to have any hope of success, must be compatible with the broader legal culture within which it is intended to operate. It must be respectful of the wisdom that has accumulated over time on the issues that confront lawyers and judges on a daily basis and it must reflect, as much as possible, the values and aspirations of the broader community. The last-mentioned requirement is, of course, highly problematic. The "community", a

---

[2] See, for example, the comments of some sentencing judges to this effect in relation to judicial training in Hough, Jacobson and Millie, *The Decision to Imprison: Sentencing and the Prison Population* (London: Prison Reform Trust, 2003), pp.27–28.

[3] On the concept of actuarial justice, see Feeley and Simon, "The New Penology: Notes on the Emerging Strategy of Corrections and its Implications" (1992) 30 *Criminology* 449.

[4] For a variety of perspectives on drug courts, see Burke, "Just What Made Drug Courts Successful (Nov/Dec 2010) 94 *Judicature* 119; Marlowe, deMatteo and Festinger, "A Sober Assessment of Drug Courts" (2003) 16 Fed. Sent. Rep. 153; Justice Policy Institute, *Addicted to Courts: How a Growing Dependence on Drug Courts Impacts People and Communities* (Washington DC, 2011).

rather overworked term, has many different constituencies which, in the present context, include the judiciary and the legal profession, the media, victim support groups, civil liberties and penal reform organisations, political parties and that most amorphous of groups, the general public. No reform proposal, whether in relation to sentencing or anything else, will command the support of all of these constituencies or of their individual members. However, to revert to a recurring theme in this book, the community's response will depend on how well it is informed about both the reality of existing practices and the implications of any proposed reforms. That is why any data or information produced by the various research units proposed in this chapter should be available to the general public and presented in a manner which will facilitate a broad general understanding of the issues covered. Abrupt policy shifts which are at odds with existing legal and social culture seldom work. If it is to be genuinely acceptable, change must not only be grounded on convincing evidence, it must also be gradual and capable of incorporation into existing legal frameworks.

RECONCILING PENAL PURPOSES

A sentencing reform programme should ideally be underpinned by a strong consensus on the purpose of criminal punishment. Individual theorists may argue tenaciously in favour of their preferred purpose, which may be retributive or utilitarian, but courts and legislators are seldom willing to pin their colours to the mast of any particular moral justification. Britain's Criminal Justice Act 1991 represented something of an exception to this pattern by providing that terms of imprisonment and other penal measures should, with some exceptions, be commensurate with the gravity of the offence and any associated offences. The just deserts philosophy reflected in these provisions failed to gain any secure foothold as a result of various judicial decisions and legislative amendments which followed quickly thereafter and which permitted or required sentencers to take account of factors other than the seriousness of the offence of conviction.[5] In any event, it was decisively abandoned in the Criminal Justice Act 2003 which provides that a court must have regard to five stated purposes of sentencing: the punishment of offenders, the reduction of crime (including reduction by deterrence), the reform and rehabilitation of offenders, the protection of the public, and reparation by offenders to persons affected by their offences.[6] Sentencing statutes in other common-law countries frequently include a similar menu of penal purposes. The Canadian Criminal Code lists six acceptable purposes including denunciation, deterrence, rehabilitation, reparation

---

[5] In *R v Cunningham* [1993] 1 W.L.R. 183, (1993) 96 Cr. App. R. 422, (1993) 14 Cr. App. R. (S.) 444, the Court of Appeal interpreted "commensurate with the seriousness of the offence" to mean commensurate with the level of punishment and deterrence which the seriousness of the offence requires.

[6] Criminal Justice Act 2003 s.142.

and separating the offender from society.[7] Separately, it states as a fundamental principle that a sentence must be proportionate to the gravity of the offence and the personal responsibility of the offender.[8] In Australia, Victoria's Sentencing Act 1991 lists six purposes as the only ones for which sentence may be imposed, but they include all the traditional punishment goals.[9] New Zealand's Sentencing Act 2002 adopts a similar approach. Statutory statements of sentencing purposes in this form are of little practical value as they merely reflect pre-existing law and fail to offer any guidance as to when one purpose should take precedence over the others. Ashworth has criticised the British Criminal Justice Act 2003 as appearing to embody the worst kind of "pick-and-mix" sentencing, and the same may be said of the various Commonwealth statutes just mentioned.[10] They may have some value in terms of excluding impermissible purposes, such as responding to the prevalence of crime in a particular locality, something which became an issue during the debates leading to the British Criminal Justice Act 2003, but that is a rather negligible benefit.[11]

Some might argue that the adoption of proportionality as an overarching sentencing principle obviates the need to decide upon a single purpose of punishment or to establish a hierarchy among a list of acceptable purposes. While occasionally fulfilling this function in practice, proportionality is essentially a distributive principle. It indicates in broad terms the amount of punishment appropriate in a specific case but it fails to tell us why the punishment is merited in the first place. Granted, it is often difficult to distinguish between proportionality as a distributive principle and just deserts as a moral justification. Both require that punishment be calibrated to the offender's culpability which, in turn, must be assessed by reference to the gravity of the offence and the responsibility of the offender. Some versions of proportionality, such as that favoured by the Irish courts, also require that account be taken of the personal circumstances of the offender at the time of sentence but this, too, can be accommodated within a reasonably enlightened version of just deserts. The problem with this line of argument is that a jurisdiction which endorses proportionality as the dominant distributive principle may also acknowledge the validity of more utilitarian penal purposes such as deterrence or rehabilitation. This happens to be true of Ireland as well. In these circumstances, one can only assume that proportionality is intended to operate as kind of limiting principle, similar to Norval Morris's idea of limiting retributivism, which allows courts to adopt the penal purpose of their choice provided it does not lead to the

---

[7] Section 718.

[8] Section 718.1.

[9] On similar legislation in other Australian states, see Mackenzie and Stobbs, *Principles of Sentencing* (Annandale, NSW: Federation Press, 2010), p.43.

[10] Ashworth, *Sentencing and Criminal Justice*, 5th edn (Cambridge: Cambridge University Press, 2010), p.77.

[11] Ward and Davies, *The Criminal Justice Act 2003: A Practitioner's Guide* (Bristol: Jordans, 2004), p.165.

imposition of a disproportionately severe sentence.[12] Viewed in this light, proportionality, rather than pointing to a specific penalty as the only appropriate one, permits a certain penalty range in any given case. When selecting a penalty from within that range, a judge may be guided by whichever penal purpose seems most fitting in the circumstances. General deterrence might be the most appropriate purpose in one case, rehabilitation in another. This brings us back a full circle to the question of how the accepted purposes of punishment should be ranked, either generally or in specified circumstances.

Hart's conceptual distinction between the general justifying aim of criminal punishment as an institution and the rationale for imposing punishment in individual cases is now well accepted.[13] Rawls had earlier drawn a very similar distinction between justifying a practice as a system of rules and justifying particular actions taken according to those rules.[14] The criminal law, including the various punishments which it authorises, is fundamentally intended to deter people from engaging in injurious conduct. That is its general aim. But it does not follow that every sentence imposed for a specific breach of that law must be motivated by a deterrence rationale, or by any other utilitarian purpose for that matter. In fact, just deserts and other versions of retributivism have emerged in recent decades as the favoured rationale for allocating punishment. Nowhere is the divide between theory and practice more pronounced than in sentencing policy. Most theoretical arguments flow from an invincible conviction that there is only one morally defensible rationale for criminal punishment. Sometimes, though not always, proponents of such arguments try to show how a viable sentencing system might be constructed on the basis of their preferred rationale. Courts and legislators (as reflected in the various British and Commonwealth statutory provisions mentioned earlier) prefer a more eclectic approach and, from a practical standpoint, that is also the right approach. Given the ever-expanding reach of the criminal law and the range of circumstances in which different sorts of crime may be committed, it is only fitting that courts should be empowered to pursue different penal purposes depending on the nature of the offence or the offender. At the same time, it is also widely accepted that one of the main causes of sentencing disparity is a lack of consensus among judges as to the penal purposes which they should try to advance in different circumstances. The hybrid approach has much to commend it as long it is accompanied by guiding principles. To attempt to set out those principles in legislation would scarcely be practicable because of the many variables to be taken into account. They could obviously be incorporated in guidelines where they exist, but in a jurisdiction committed to retaining a common-law approach they can be

---

[12] Morris, *Madness and the Criminal Law* (Chicago: University of Chicago Press, 1982), Ch.5.
[13] Hart, *Punishment and Responsibility: Essays in the Philosophy of Law*, 2nd edn with introduction by Gardner (Oxford: Oxford University Press, 2008), Ch.1.
[14] Rawls, "Two Concepts of Rules" (1955) 64 *Philosophical Review* 3.

developed quite effectively by appeal courts. In fact, courts are becoming more willing to indicate, on an offence-specific basis, the purposes which sentencing should aim to achieve. Canadian and New Zealand courts, for example, have stressed the importance of deterrence in sentencing drink driving offences causing death or serious injury and in commercial drug-dealing.[15] In Ireland, the Central Criminal Court has adopted a similar approach towards the sentencing of competition offences and, by implication, to other forms of economic crime.[16] However, to discharge this task effectively, an appeal court needs the support of an advisory body or information unit which can furnish it with a broader range of data and advice than might ordinarily be expected from legal submissions.

ALLOCATION OF DECISION-MAKING COMPETENCE

All three branches of government have important roles in the sentencing system. Legislators must create an appropriate legal framework by specifying the sentencing options available to the courts, the maximum sentences attaching to specific offences and certain other general rules. The executive branch of government must ensure, amongst other things, that adequate administrative structures and resources are available for the implementation of judicially-imposed sentences. Selection of sentence, where there is a selection to be made, is exclusively a judicial task.[17] This, however, represents no more than a large-scale map of the system as it exists in most common-law jurisdictions. The critical question, however, in an era where sentencing is becoming ever more complicated is precisely how sentencing policy should be devised and implemented. Reliance on the general constitutional framework is no longer sufficient. Sentencing law in statutory form must, of course, be made by the legislature; courts must continue to sentence individual offenders; and the executive will remain responsible for sentence implementation though not necessarily with the level of discretion which it currently exercises.[18] But important questions remain about the content of the rules and principles which trial courts are required to follow and how that content should be decided. For the first 75 years or so after independence in this country, the legislature rarely interfered in the sentencing process except to establish or revise the maximum penalties for particular offences. Granted, there were some significant statutory and constitutional developments such as the progressive abolition of the death penalty[19] and the introduction of community service as an alternative to

---

[15] *R v McVeigh* (1985) 145 C.C.C. (3d) 145; *R v Ramage* (2008) 53 C.R. (6th) 342, upheld in *R v Ramage* 2010 ONCA 488 (drink driving); *R v Terewi* [1999] 3 N.Z.L.R. 62 (commercial drug-dealing).

[16] *People (DPP) v Duffy* [2009] 3 I.R. 613, [2009] 2 I.L.R.M. 301.

[17] *Deaton v Attorney General and Revenue Commissioners* [1963] I.R. 170.

[18] Chapter 9 above.

[19] Criminal Justice Act 1964; Criminal Justice Act 1990; Constitution of Ireland Art.15.5.2 (inserted by amendment in 2002).

imprisonment,[20] but they were few and far between. A marked change of policy has been discernible since 1999 when presumptive minimum sentences were introduced for drug-dealing offences, later supplemented by similar sentences for certain firearms offences and genuinely mandatory minimum sentences for repeat offenders, and these are just the more significant developments.[21] The most problematic aspect of these measures is that they were introduced in an empirical vacuum. The implicit rationale for presumptive and mandatory minimum sentences is that courts cannot be trusted to impose adequate or condign punishments for the offences to which they apply. Yet, the minimum sentences introduced here from 1999 onwards were unsupported by any reliable evidence about existing sentencing practices, although there was no shortage of misleading media comment on the matter.

Mandatory and presumptive minimum sentences tend to be introduced on a selective, arbitrary and spasmodic basis, usually because of pressure from individuals or organisations. When those exerting pressure can claim some degree of moral superiority because of a collective feeling of vulnerability or particular experiences of victimisation, their demands are politically difficult to resist. This is not to deny that there may be legitimate cause for concern about the prevalence of certain kinds of crime or about apparent inconsistency in the sentencing of those who are eventually apprehended and convicted. There may indeed be problems in this regard, but minimum sentences are rarely the solution if only because, as we have already seen, they may create more disparity than they remove.[22] Two recent developments in Ireland illustrate the phenomenon under discussion, and many other examples could be cited as well. At its annual conference in 2010, the Garda Representative Association called for the introduction of a mandatory 12-year prison sentence for the offence of assaulting a member of the Gardaí. How the proponents of the motion decided on 12 years as opposed to any other fixed period remains unclear. Assaults on members of the police and others providing front-line services must, of course, be treated with the utmost seriousness; nobody committed to the maintenance of a safe and orderly society could possibly argue otherwise. It is difficult to imagine circumstances in which a serious assault on a member of the police would merit anything other than a substantial prison sentence, and the same holds true of assaults on others providing essential and life-saving services such as fire-fighters and ambulance crews. But it is equally difficult to argue that any assault, irrespective of its gravity, should automatically merit 12 years' imprisonment just because it happens to be committed against a member of a particular occupational group. In so far the proposal has any credibility, we must assume that when eventually examined more thoroughly it would allow for more graded sentencing arrangements corresponding to the various levels of assault. A more

---

[20]   Criminal Justice (Community Service) Act 1983.
[21]   The various minimum sentences are described at pp.101 et seq. above.
[22]   Chapter 4 above.

fundamental objection to the proposal is that, as reported in the media at any rate, it was unaccompanied by any analysis of existing sentencing practices for assaults committed against members of the Gardaí. Aside from that, there is the ever-present question of whether a crude mandatory sentence of the kind proposed would be constitutionally acceptable, even by the rather restrictive standard of review recently adumbrated by the Supreme Court.[23]

The second example relates to residential burglaries in which elderly persons living alone are seriously and sometimes fatally injured. Again, one need hardly stress the inherent gravity of this offence which is often carefully planned and ruthlessly executed. The injuries deliberately inflicted on victims may be tantamount to torture, even in the strict legal sense of the term.[24] Victims and their families are understandably angered as well as traumatised by the feral nature of such assaults, and all the more so when the perpetrators remain undetected. A few such cases in recent years—at least one of which led to the death of an elderly person—have produced calls for mandatory sentences for aggravated residential burglaries of this kind. In October 2009 it was reported that the Minister for Justice, Equality and Law Reform, in response to a number of such incidents, had requested the Attorney General to refer the matter to the Law Reform Commission. The same report indicated that the Minister believed existing penalties for burglaries of this kind to be inadequate.[25] Credit is due to the Minister for referring the matter to the Commission, which has yet to report, rather than rush ahead with legislation introducing minimum penalties similar to those already in place for drug and firearms offences. Hopefully the Commission will try to identify existing sentencing practices before deciding whether it should recommend any reforms. But the underlying assumption that mandatory sentences are, or may be, the answer remains objectionable. Changes in judicial sentencing practices may, indeed, be necessary but these are best accomplished through the adoption of revised sentencing principles. These should be preceded by a thorough investigation of the salient characteristics of aggravated burglary offences and offenders, the factors which should influence sentence, and the levels of sentence which are most likely to further the goals of desert and deterrence in particular circumstances. In very serious cases, burglary is unlikely to be the sole charge; defendants may face homicide or serious assault charges as well. Given that a conviction on any one of these would almost inevitably result in a heavy sentence in any event, the case for requiring a mandatory minimum for a burglary conviction becomes all the weaker. The background to the leading case of *People (DPP) v Conroy (No.2)*[26]

---

[23] *Lynch and Whelan v Minister for Justice, Equality and Law Reform* [2010] IESC 34, discussed at p.91 above.

[24] The Criminal Justice (United Nations Convention Against Torture) Act 2000 s.1 defines torture as the intentional infliction of severe pain or suffering, whether physical or mental, for certain purposes.

[25] Brady, "Minimum Sentences for Burglary to be Examined", *Irish Independent*, October 13, 2009.

is instructive in this regard. A gang of four men had attacked the elderly occupants of two houses in the course of the same day. In the second house, two elderly brothers were seriously assaulted. One of them died almost immediately while the other died some weeks later. No charges were brought in respect of the latter death. Of the four defendants, one was convicted of murder and two others, having pleaded guilty to manslaughter, were each sentenced to nine years' imprisonment. (Both were aged 18 years at the time of the offences and this appears to have influenced the level of sentence.) The defendant in this appeal was tried for murder twice and convicted once, but that conviction was quashed on a point of law by the Supreme Court. He then pleaded guilty to manslaughter for which he received life imprisonment and also to burglary (arising from the incident in the first house) for which he received a concurrent term of 12 years' imprisonment. While refusing to hold that a life sentence was invariably wrong in principle following a guilty plea to manslaughter, the Supreme Court held that, on the facts, a 17-year sentence would have been appropriate in this case. In light of the time the appellant had already spent in custody, a sentence of 14 years effective from the date of the appeal decision was imposed. While this judgment was not intended as a guideline—it was handed down on the same day as *People (DPP) v Tiernan*[27] in which the court had eschewed the general notion of issuing guidelines—it illustrates the courts' willingness to impose and uphold severe sentences for aggravated residential burglaries and for injuries inflicted on victims in the course of those burglaries.

What these episodes, as well as our experience of sentencing reform at home and abroad over the past decade or so, clearly demonstrate is that the creation of an effective and coherent sentencing system calls for different levels of decision-making. Certain fundamental matters must be decided as a matter of political policy; judicial sentencing practices should be guided by a mixture of rules and principles which may be devised by bodies other than courts; and individual sentencing decisions must remain exclusively with the courts. As a first step, therefore, we must acknowledge the functional differences between policies, rules, principles and decisions. Secondly, we must identify the institutions that are most competent, in both constitutional and practical terms, to devise policies, principles and rules which, unlike decisions in specific cases, are general norms intended to guide, without invariably determining, the manner in which individual cases are sentenced. Most, though admittedly not all, of those who have devoted serious thought to the matter would agree that justice demands a system of individualised sentencing which permits all the relevant circumstances of both offence and offender to be taken into account. In other words, the selection of sentence should remain exclusively a judicial task. Acceptance of this principle need not, however, entail the conclusion that the development of principles, let alone policies, should also be left to the courts. It

---

[26] [1989] I.R. 160, [1989] I.L.R.M. 139.
[27] [1988] I.R. 250, [1989] I.L.R.M. 149.

never follows that those who charged with implementing rules should also make the rules, though it is equally true that those who are charged with making certain decisions on a regular and frequent basis are in a stronger position than most to evaluate the effectiveness of the rules they are applying and to recommend reforms.[28]

POLICY FORMULATION

It is axiomatic, if only on democratic and constitutional grounds, that rules, in the sense of positive laws, should be made by the legislature. What matters most for present purposes is the content of those rules and the process by which that content should be decided. Criminal justice reform in recent times has tended to be reflexive rather than reflective. Many aspects of criminal procedure and sentencing have been altered because of a perceived or proclaimed need to respond urgently to some particular event whether it be the commission of a serious crime or the collapse of an important criminal case. Closely connected with this is the growing tendency to treat the criminal law as a form of memorial. This pattern is now well entrenched in the United States where several state and federal statutes dealing with the sentencing of sex offenders or the provision of public information about their identity and whereabouts are named after victims of fatal assaults or disappearances. Examples include Megan's Law (New Jersey), Jessica's Law (Florida), the Adam Smith Child Protection and Safety Act, the Sexual Offender (Jacob Wetterling) Act and many others. Nobody could reasonably or humanely object to these public measures being named after innocent young victims of brutal and tragic crimes. The danger, from a policy perspective, is that laws hastily enacted in response to those crimes will be either unproductive or counterproductive, as illustrated by another American statute, the Anti-Drug Abuse Act 1986. In June 1986, Len Bias, a star basketball player and a student at the University of Maryland died at the age of 23 following a cocaine overdose. Within a few months, and with an eye to the approaching mid-term elections, Congress passed the Anti-Drug Abuse Act which infamously introduced the 100:1 ratio for crack and powder cocaine. As described earlier, this had socially catastrophic results and the entire episode should provide a stark warning of the dangers of hasty and opportunistic political responses to isolated events, however tragic those events may be.[29]

Sentencing policy is therefore uniquely vulnerable to short-lived moral panics over isolated incidents which may be entirely unrepresentative of general patterns of criminal behaviour, law enforcement or sentencing practice, as the

---

[28] Chapter 3 above.

[29] Chapter 4 above. On the political background to the Anti-Drug Abuse Act, see Baum, *Smoke and Mirrors: The War Against Drugs and the Politics of Failure* (New York: Little, Brown and Co., 1996), p.225.

case may be. This vulnerability is further intensified by a common tendency to blame the sentencing system for problems that are entirely outside of its control. The growing incidence of gangland crime, and gangland murder in particular, has often been blamed on unduly lenient or inconsistent sentencing. Yet, the real problem in most gangland cases is not the leniency or inconsistency of punishment but insufficiency of evidence to support a criminal charge in the first place. If convicted, a gangland murderer, like all other murderers, will receive life imprisonment. At the other end of the spectrum, courts are sometimes blamed, entirely illogically, for the release of prisoners long before they have completed the full term of their sentence. This, of course, is entirely a matter for the executive branch of government. Yet when the public clamour grows loud enough, it is difficult for politicians to resist calls for change, and more punitive sentencing measures will often appear to be the most obvious response. It has, after all, a number of attractions. It can be accomplished straightaway with little parliamentary opposition and general public approval, and readily demonstrates an apparent willingness to be tough on crime. Secondly, revised sentencing arrangements, whether in the form of mandatory minimums or increased maximum sentences, have a "buy now, pay later" element because their full human, financial and institutional implications will not materialise until long after their introduction. This further underscores the need for systems which will allow perceived deficiencies in the criminal law or in sentencing practice to be objectively investigated and evaluated prior to any formal legislative or policy decisions being taken.

A fair measure of agreement is possible in regard to those matters which are most appropriately governed by legislative rules as opposed to general principles. It would be widely accepted, for example, that the legislature should decide on which forms of conduct should be criminalised and on the maximum penalties that should attach to the offences covering that conduct.[30] The legislature should also decide on the range of sentencing options available to the courts, if only because the funding necessary to support those options must come from the public purse. It is also entitled to enact general rules indicating the order of preference which courts should adopt when choosing among available sanctions. It may stipulate, for example, that imprisonment should be a sanction of last resort or that community-based measures should ordinarily be considered preferable to short prison sentences. This is not intended to be an exhaustive list of sentencing-related matters properly within the competence of the political branches of government, but it is scarcely a controversial one. Irrespective, however, of their content and scope, legislative and political decisions should be grounded on a rational assessment of the need for any proposed measures and of their future implications. One major advantage enjoyed by the political branches is that they can carry out or commission

---

[30] Under the Constitution of Ireland, in any event, the sole and exclusive power to make laws is vested in the Oireachtas (the legislature): Art.15.2.1.

research on policy proposals in a way which the judicial branch ordinarily cannot. Irish criminal justice legislation, particularly in recent times, has sadly been characterised by the absence of evidence-based justification. On a more positive note, the review of community service scheme completed in 2009 was a remarkably worthwhile and productive exercise which provided badly-needed information on the scheme's operation.[31] When the Government came to introduce amending legislation designed to encourage more extensive use of community service orders instead of short prison sentences, it was able to draw on this research to show that community service is generally under-used and that judges vary considerably in their willingness to use it.[32]

Effective policy development requires the existence of a dedicated unit charged with maintaining an overview of the criminal justice system and its various components, and with formulating proposals for new programmes and initiatives. Ideally this unit should operate at a remove from the Government, while being responsive to governmental needs in terms of information, data analysis and policy recommendations. The Economic and Social Research Institute (ESRI) might provide a useful model in this regard though a criminal justice policy unit could operate on a much more modest scale. Alternatively, and especially on account of the limited resources likely to be available for the foreseeable future, a dedicated research unit within the Department of Justice might be equally effective, provided it had the managerial independence and resources necessary to discharge its functions effectively. The Irish Youth Justice Service, located within the Department of Justice, seems to work quite well. The entity being proposed here would have a broader remit and concentrate largely on adult crime. Ireland has seriously lagged behind most other Western countries in promoting empirical research on criminal justice issues. Throughout much of the history of the State, levels of crime and imprisonment were low compared with those of many neighbouring jurisdictions, with the result that there seemed to be no obvious need for research and analysis.[33] It is only in recent years that criminology has gained a foothold as an academic discipline in third-level institutions. Demographic changes over the past 10 or 15 years, coupled with significant growth in the number of recorded serious offences and, within the past few years, a dramatic rise in the prison population all point to the need for careful, expert and independent evaluations of existing laws and practices, and for new thinking on how recurring and emerging problems might best be

---

[31] Department of Justice, Equality and Law Reform, *Value for Money and Policy Review of the Community Service Scheme* (Dublin, 2009).

[32] Criminal Justice (Community Service) (Amendment) Bill 2010, Regulatory Impact Analysis, available at *www.justice.ie*. The Bill became law in summer 2011.

[33] In England and Wales, by contrast, the Home Office Research Unit was first established in 1957 to engage in a long-term research programme, particularly in relation to the treatment of offenders. See Nuttall, "The Home Office and Random Allocation Experiments" (2003) 27 *Evaluation Review* 267 (which has some particularly valuable insights on criminal justice research in general).

addressed.[34] We did, admittedly, have a body called the Crime Council which lasted from 1999 until its abolition, for budgetary reasons, in 2008, but its output was not remarkably impressive. It is now time to start afresh by establishing a new entity dedicated to criminal justice policy research which will pursue a structured agenda designed to inform legislative and executive initiatives. Its output might also be of considerable value to a sentencing information unit within the courts system.[35] Meanwhile, academic criminology should be fostered and encouraged, if only to ensure that analyses and proposals emanating from state bodies, including the suggested criminal justice policy unit, can be subjected to ongoing critical evaluation.[36]

PRINCIPLES

The jurisdictional competence to develop policies and principles has been the subject of much academic and judicial debate. One of the better known and more respected judicial contributions is that of Lord Scarman in *McLoughlin v O'Brian*[37] where he was adamant that policy was a matter for parliament while courts are entitled to assume responsibility for the formation and development of principle. As he said in this regard:

> "The distinguishing feature of the common law is this judicial development and formation of principle. Policy considerations will have to be weighed: but the objective of the judges is the formulation of principle. And, if principle inexorably requires a decision which entails a degree of policy risk, the court's function is to adjudicate according to principle, leaving policy curtailment to the judgment of Parliament. Here lies the true role of the two law-making institutions in our constitution. By concentrating on principle the judges can keep the common law alive, flexible and consistent, and can keep the legal system clear of policy problems which neither they, nor the forensic process which it is their duty to operate, are equipped to resolve. If principle leads to results which are thought to be socially unacceptable, Parliament can legislate to draw a line or map out a new path."[38]

---

[34] On the achievements of the English Advisory Council for the Treatment of Offenders (ACTO) and the Advisory Council on the Penal System (ACPS), which between them lasted from the late 1940s to the late 1970s, see Radzinowicz, *Adventures in Criminology* (London: Routledge, 1999), Ch.13. See also Hood, "Some Reflections on the Role of Criminology in Public Policy" [1987] Crim L.R. 527.

[35] Chapter 5 above and p.254 below.

[36] Cottee, "Sir Leon's Shadow" (2005) 9 *Theoretical Criminology* 203 (on the impact of Home Office funding on academic research in England and Wales).

[37] [1983] 1 A.C. 410, [1982] 2 W.L.R. 982, [1982] 2 All E.R. 298.

[38] [1983] 1 A.C. 410 at 430.

Principles are not always easily distinguishable from policies, except that they operate at a somewhat lower level of abstraction. They are perhaps more readily distinguishable from rules which are more specific and generally apply in an "all-or-nothing" manner. It remains difficult to improve upon Roscoe Pound's definitions of those concepts. Rules, he says, are "precepts attaching a definite detailed consequence to a definite, detailed state of facts" while principles are "authoritative starting points for legal reasoning, employed continually and legitimately where cases are not covered or are not fully covered by rules in the narrower sense."[39] As he also says, the application of a principle does not entail any specific consequence, because a principle is a "starting point from which to proceed according to the received technique."[40] Due in no small measure to Dworkin's influence, few would now deny that principles are part of the law just as much as rules and that they may just as legitimately be invoked by judges in order to inform the exercise of their discretion or as an aid to choosing between competing rules.[41]

Sentencing decisions are made predominantly by reference to principles rather than rules. As long as courts observe the limits imposed by statutory maximum sentences and a few residual rules requiring, for example, that consecutive sentences be imposed in certain circumstances, they are generally free to choose the nature and amount of the penalty they deem most appropriate. Mandatory penalties, as we have seen, produce more than their share of injustice and are seldom effective as deterrent or incapacitative measures.[42] Other statutory provisions may attempt to shape the exercise of discretion in general terms by setting out the permissible goals of punishment, indicating the circumstances in which certain forms of punishment are presumptively appropriate, or imposing restraints on the use of short prison sentences. But no statutory code, no matter how detailed, can realistically be expected to cater prospectively for the entire range of factors and circumstances which may arise in specific cases. Some guideline systems, such as the United States federal guidelines, have attempted to do just that, but often at the expense of producing new forms of disparity and unduly severe sentences. Principles, which are norms operating at a higher level of generality than rules, provide a more effective means of structuring judicial sentencing discretion. When sufficiently developed, they cabin the use of discretion without eliminating it and, more importantly, they permit exceptions and departures when the need arises. The development of principle is an ongoing process so that, over time, courts can elaborate upon existing precedents to take account of novel offence- or offender-related factors and similar matters.

---

[39] Pound, "Hierarchy of Sources and Forms in Different Systems of Law" (1933) 7 Tulane L.R. 475 at 482–483. The remaining normative categories which he describes are "conceptions", "doctrines" and "standards".

[40] Pound (fn.39 above), p.483.

[41] Dworkin, *Taking Rights Seriously* (Cambridge, MA: Harvard University Press, 1978), esp. Chs 1 and 2.

[42] Chapter 4 above.

Discretionary decision-making, irrespective of the subject matter, always arouses some degree of public suspicion, particularly where it is seen to produce apparently inconsistent outcomes. Sometimes, of course, the suspicion is well justified; the decisions in question may have been made without reference to any guiding norm, and may simply reflect the personal views or preferences of the decision-maker. To meet the demands of justice and to command a reasonable measure of public confidence, discretionary decisions must be genuinely explicable by reference to settled principles, and departures from accepted standards or benchmarks must be capable of rational explanation.[43]

The limited capacity of appeal court jurisprudence to deliver a coherent set of sentencing principles has already been discussed.[44] As the authors of the revised Model Penal Code sentencing provisions have written in an American context:

> "An inescapable difficulty, in any sentencing policy that incorporates moral intuitions or constraints, is that people of good faith often disagree about what justice demands in particular cases. Systemwide benchmarks for the determination of proportionate sanctions provide a useful starting point for reasoned case-specific analysis in the criminal courtrooms"[45]

The same holds true of any jurisdiction which is committed to maintaining a healthy degree of judicial sentencing discretion, and it was to this end that a recommendation was made in Chapter 5 for the creation of a sentencing information unit within the Irish court system. Such a unit could work in perfect harmony with the criminal justice policy unit recommended earlier in this chapter. The policy unit's remit would extend far beyond judicial sentencing, as it would undertake research on a wide range of criminal justice issues, including the treatment of offenders. A sentencing information unit would, of course, draw on the fruits of that research in framing proposals specifically in the area of sentencing. But its essential purpose would be to enhance the capacity of appeal courts to develop a coherent body of sentencing jurisprudence which, in turn, would offer concrete guidance to trial courts and provide a more reliable set of criteria than now exist for evaluating trial court sentencing decisions that are challenged on appeal.

The District Court

District Court sentencing poses particular problems and challenges which are not easily resolved. This is the court in which almost all criminal cases begin and it is also where most of them end. In 2009, the Central Criminal Court

---

[43] Chapter 3 above.
[44] Chapter 5 above.
[45] Model Penal Code: Sentencing, Commentary on Art. 1 (p.10).

disposed of 108 cases (mostly murders and serious sexual offences), the Circuit Criminal Court dealt with about 3,500 cases (6,105 offences involving 3,489 defendants), while the District Court disposed of 521,058 offences, about 30,000 less than the previous year but still an indication of the vast criminal workload of that court. The Circuit Court imposed almost 2,000 prison sentences, while the District Court imposed prison sentences on more than 12,000 defendants.[46] Granted, most of the Circuit Court sentences would have been quite long—more than half were in the two- to five-year bracket—while District Court sentences are much shorter. We know, for example, that 7,655 committals to prison in 2009 involved sentences of less than six months.[47] Any critique or review of District Court sentencing practice must take account of that court's workload and the relatively few resources committed to it. During the past 40 years, the number of High Court judges has increased fivefold, but the number of District Court judges has not even doubled. The maximum number of judges of that court was set at 34 in 1961 whereas there are now only 64, including the President.[48] Yet, its civil and criminal jurisdiction has increased considerably in both extent and complexity during that period. In fact, by European standards, Irish courts are generally under-resourced. According to the European Commission for the Efficiency of Justice (CEPEJ), Ireland had the lowest ratio of professional judges, measured in terms of full-time equivalents, per 100,000 of the population in any of the countries listed. Ireland had a ratio of 3.1, reflecting the fact that we have less than 150 judges for a general population of 4.5 million.[49] Most countries had ratios between 15 and 25. These statistics must obviously be treated with some caution because of organisational differences. The Irish figure refers solely to judges appointed to the law courts in accordance with the Constitution, whereas the equivalent figures for some continental countries may include members of administrative tribunals. Even so, it appears that our courts are generally under-resourced in term of both judicial complement and support staff. Furthermore, all of our judges are full-time office-holders. We do not have the legal option of appointing lay or part-time judges, equivalent to magistrates and recorders in England and Wales, in order to ease workloads or deal with case backlogs.

Strictly speaking, there is only one District Court, just as there is only one Circuit Court.[50] However, both courts are organised on a regional basis, and most districts and circuits have one or more judges permanently assigned to them. Once assigned, judges have few formal opportunities for interaction and consultation with their colleagues. This factor, coupled with the extraordinary

---

[46] Courts Service, *Annual Report 2009* (Dublin, 2010).
[47] Irish Prison Service, *Annual Report 2009* (Dublin, 2010).
[48] Courts (Supplemental Provisions) Act 1961 s.28; Civil Law (Miscellaneous Provisions) Act 2008 s.32.
[49] CEPEJ, *European Judicial Systems* (Strasbourg: Council of Europe Publishing, 2008). The data relate to 2006.
[50] Courts (Establishment and Constitution) Act 1961 ss.4 and 5.

volume and variety of offences processed entirely in the District Court, strongly suggests the need for more formal sentencing standards in that court than may be necessary in the higher courts. One obvious desideratum is an agreed and enforceable set of standards for identifying custody thresholds. The problems associated with establishing such a threshold have already been discussed,[51] but they are particularly acute in the District Court where many defendants will already have lengthy criminal records, consisting mostly of minor offences. Judges may vary considerably in the weight they attribute to previous convictions when identifying an appropriate sentence, just as they may differ over the most suitable sentence for a first-time offender convicted of a reasonably serious offence, such as an assault causing harm, or a combination of road traffic offences.[52] These and other considerations point to the need for a set of guidelines or standards specially designed for the District Court. The Magistrates' Court Sentencing Guidelines in England and Wales represent one possible approach although they are probably more detailed and prescriptive than would be feasible or desirable in this country at present.[53] Ideally, standards, guidelines or tariffs should be agreed in the first instance by judges of the District Court acting collectively. Whatever system they agree upon should be given a reasonable chance to work, but if it proves ineffective or is routinely ignored, it may have to be replaced by a more prescriptive set of standards authorised by legislation. Legislation has recently been enacted which obliges courts to consider community service an option where a prison sentence of 12 months or less might otherwise be appropriate.[54] Similar measures have been enacted in other jurisdictions, but they all leave enormous discretion to trial courts to decide the appropriate form of sentence in any case.[55] This is clearly one area where clear guidance is necessary as to circumstances in which one kind of sentence rather than another should be imposed. Otherwise, the statutory purpose of encouraging the use of non-custodial penalties may be largely frustrated. Even a checklist of conditions to be fulfilled before a sentence of immediate custody should be imposed would be a useful beginning.

---

[51] Chapter 8 above.

[52] Similar observations were made of English magistrates' courts, at least before the formal institution of the Magistrates' Court Sentencing Guidelines. See, for example, Ashworth, "Criminal Justice and the Criminal Process" (1988) 28 Brit. J. Crim. 111 at 114 ("Discretion without guidance remains the predominant feature of magistrates' court sentencing, since Court of Appeal judgments have little relevance there"). See also Hood's classic study, *Sentencing in Magistrates' Courts* (London: Stevens, 1962).

[53] The present Magistrates' Court Sentencing Guidelines were adopted by the Sentencing Guidelines Council in 2008 and now operate under the aegis of the Sentencing Council: *www.sentencingcouncil.org.uk*.

[54] Criminal Justice (Community Service) (Amendment) Act 2011.

[55] Page 200 et seq. above.

DECISIONS

For both constitutional and sound policy reasons, the selection of penalty in specific cases must remain exclusively a judicial function. The Supreme Court has held that the choice of sentence, where there is a choice to be made, must not be allocated to, or appropriated by, any branch of government except the judiciary.[56] Mandatory and mandatory minimum sentences introduced by statute obviously remove or curtail judicial sentencing discretion but, for reasons outlined elsewhere in this book, structured judicial discretion is the most effective means of delivering a just sentencing system.[57] No other system can achieve an adequate balance between the necessity to impose a condign punishment for the offence of conviction and the need to give due consideration to the personal circumstances of the particular offender. Judicial sentencing is most commonly criticised for producing inconsistent outcomes, and the criticism is often well justified. It is defended here, not just as a matter of constitutional necessity, but also on the basis that, if the recommendations made earlier in this chapter and in Chapter 5 are implemented, it will be more firmly guided by well-established principles and informed by evidence-based policy decisions. There is no perfect balance between principled and individualised sentencing. Some systems tend to be unduly preoccupied with following pre-established guidelines or benchmarks while others tend to veer too far in favour of individualisation. The Irish system undoubtedly falls into the latter category, though this is certainly the lesser of the two evils. Justice is always preferable to consistency, and the more courts are obliged to comply with formal sentencing norms, the greater the risk of injustice in individual cases. By the same token, justice entails more than the obligation or opportunity to fashion an appropriate penalty in each case. It also calls for consistency of approach in order to ensure that similarly situated offenders do not receive dissimilar punishments.[58] This still leaves considerable scope for individualising punishment provided all judges apply the same decision-making criteria in terms of ascertaining and weighing relevant factors, and in identifying those cases that call for exceptional measures. Thus the importance of generating settled principles and benchmarks against which the facts of individual cases can be assessed.

One potential weakness in the scheme being recommended here is that principles and benchmarks, whether developed by appeal courts or other authorities, cannot guarantee even the limited degree of consistency or coherence for which we are aiming. Appeal courts have a limited capacity to correct aberrational sentencing practices, if only for want of opportunity.

---

[56]   *Deaton v Attorney General and Revenue Commissioners* [1963] I.R. 170.

[57]   Chapter 3 above.

[58]   *Pepper v United States* 562 U.S. – (2011), Breyer J. (concurring) ("A just sentencing system seeks not only to treat different cases differently but also to treat like cases alike. Fairness requires sentencing uniformity as well as efforts to recognise relevant sentencing differences").

Defence appeals to the Court of Criminal Appeal are most likely to involve heavy sentences or, at any rate, sentences that are considered excessive in light of the overall circumstances of the case. Prosecution appeals against unduly lenient sentences are intended to be the exception rather than the rule.[59] The court's case load combined with the limited time and resources available to it means that it cannot realistically be expected to deliver considered judgments in anything more than a small proportion of decided appeals. The situation with District Court appeals is even less satisfactory, because the Circuit Court, which hears those appeals, rarely, if ever, delivers written sentencing judgments or decisions, and it does not appear to have any formal means of delivering feedback to the District Court.[60] Official statistics are distinctly unenlightening in terms of identifying the outcome of District Court appeals. Trial courts therefore need more specific guidance than is currently available and that is best delivered by comprehensive guideline judgments, which may eventually include quantitative benchmarks, based on a reliable data generated in the manner recommended earlier.[61] They would also, of course, have access (like everyone else) to documentation provided by a sentencing advisory or information unit. Trial courts have an important role in developing sentencing principles because they, after all, deal directly with a much wider range of cases than will ever come before appeal courts. Recorded reasons given by trial courts for their sentencing decisions are therefore indispensable for promoting the development of principled discretion. There has recently been a good deal of ill-informed criticism of trial judges for failing to give reasons for their sentences. In fact, in the higher criminal courts, reasons are given and recorded on transcript. There is, admittedly, a problem at District Court level where the case load is such that it would be impractical to give detailed reasons in every case. However, a useful compromise would be to require judges of that court to give reasons for imposing custodial sentences. It may be added parenthetically that the problem of compliance is by no means confined to semi-structured sentencing systems. A recurring criticism of many guideline systems is that they lack any mechanism for the systematic investigation of the extent to which established guidelines or benchmarks are applied by the courts.

At the same time, there is little point in embarking on a sentencing reform programme which does not incorporate some procedure for monitoring compliance with established principles and benchmarks. Because of the historic information deficit in the Irish criminal justice system, there has never been anything more than skeletal data on recorded crime, the prison population and the operation of probation and parole schemes. In fact, it was only with the creation of the Courts Service in 1998 that statistical information on the disposal of cases by the various criminal courts began to be published. When the

---

[59]   Page 117 above.
[60]   Chapter 5 above.
[61]   Page 129 et seq. above.

Working Group on the Jurisdiction of the Courts was established in 2002, it commissioned empirical research on the operation of the criminal courts. As the researchers who conducted the investigation noted in their report: "Just as the [courts] system has not been subjected to any critical review since its inception, so too it has lacked the empirical foundation on which such a review might be conducted."[62] The same information deficit became painfully obvious when work began on the Irish Sentencing Information System described in Chapter 7. In the absence of a bank of knowledge on previous sentencing practice, it became necessary to collect information prospectively by sending researchers into selected courts to collect detailed data on a case-by-case basis. That exercise may, however, point the way forward for the more consistent generation of raw data. On-site collection of sentencing data by specially-commissioned researchers on anything other than a pilot basis is scarcely feasible, if only on financial grounds. Efficient systems must therefore be developed to track cases through the criminal justice system so as to generate reliable data on the decisions taken at various points along the continuum from the initial detection or reporting of offences to their final disposal. This would naturally include sentencing data sufficiently detailed to allow for later analysis according to standard variables, including the offences for which sentences were imposed and the courts in which they were passed. Judges might have some reservations about such a system if it appeared to operate in a "Big Brother" fashion. However, the entire purpose would be to collect sufficient information to draw conclusions about general patterns of sentencing rather than to monitor the performance of individual sentencing judges. When the Irish Sentencing Information System was being designed, care was taken to ensure that the identities of sentencing judges were not revealed. This was done to forestall the possibility of unsupported conclusions being drawn about the performance of individual judges without due attention being paid to material differences in the cases being sentenced. The more systematic collection of data being recommended here should likewise be organised so as to focus attention on general sentencing patterns rather than on individual practice. But it will be impossible to assess the need for more specific sentencing principles and benchmarks unless there is a steady flow of reliable information on prevailing trial court practice.

JUDICIAL INDEPENDENCE

Any proposal for structuring judicial sentencing discretion is liable to meet with the objection that it may be incompatible with the principle of judicial independence which is, of course, a constitutional imperative in this and many

---

[62] Jackson and Doran, *A Study of the Jurisdiction of the Criminal Courts in Ireland*, Appendix V of the *Report of the Working Group on the Jurisdiction of the Courts* (Dublin: Stationery Office, 2003).

other countries. Article 35.2 of the Irish Constitution provides that all judges shall be independent in the exercise of their judicial functions and shall be subject only to the Constitution and the laws. In the United Kingdom, the Constitutional Reform Act 2005 (s.3) requires the Lord Chancellor and other ministers to uphold the continued independence of the judiciary.[63] While judicial independence is rarely defined in constitutions or statutes, it is well accepted to have two primary dimensions: institutional independence and decisional independence. Those concepts were analysed in some detail in a series of Canadian Supreme Court decisions in the 1980s and 1990s which dealt, in one way or another, with the control of judicial salaries. In one of these, *R v Beauregard*,[64] Dickson C.J. said:

> "Historically, the generally accepted core of the principle of judicial independence has been the complete liberty of individual judges to hear and decide the cases that come before them: no outsider—be it government, pressure group, individual or even another judge—should interfere in fact, or attempt to interfere, with the way in which a judge conducts his or her case and makes his or her decision. This core continues to be central to the principle of judicial independence."

This, as he noted, is the essence of decisional independence. Institutional independence, in the sense of freedom from collective control or influence by other branches of government is nowadays of equal importance. Judicial independence does not exist for the benefit of judges themselves but rather to promote and maintain public confidence in the administration of justice and to uphold the rule of law.[65] What matters for this purpose is the freedom to decide each case impartially, reasonably and, importantly, in accordance with law. This quality of judicial independence is consistently enumerated in the various declarations adopted over the years by international association and conferences. The so-called Latimer House principles adopted by Commonwealth Heads of Government in 2003, which have received widespread approval, refer to the judicial function as interpreting and applying national constitutions and legislation, consistent with applicable international law.[66]

---

[63] Section 3(5) provides more specifically: "The Lord Chancellor and other Ministers of the Crown must not seek to influence particular judicial decisions through any special access to the judiciary."

[64] [1986] 2 S.C.R. 56 at [11]. See also *R v Valente* [1985] 2 S.C.R. 673; and *Reference re Remuneration of Provincial Judges* [1997] 3 S.C.R. 3.

[65] *Reference re Remuneration of Provincial Judges* [1997] 3 S.C.R. 3 at [10].

[66] *Commonwealth (Latimer House) Principles on the Three Branches of Government* endorsed by Commonwealth Heads of Government, Abuja, Nigeria, 2003. See also address by Lord Phillips, President of United Kingdom Supreme Court on "Judicial Independence and Accountability: A View from the Supreme Court" delivered at University College London in

None of these authorities or declarations gives any indication that the formulation of sentencing policy should be the sole preserve of the judiciary. The essence of the judicial function, according to all of them, is to interpret and apply the law rather than make it. Independence is preserved as long as judges discharge their duties "without fear or favour, affection or ill-will towards any man" (in the words of the declaration prescribed by Art.34.5 of the Irish Constitution), and are permitted to do so.[67] The *Deaton* principle, described earlier, which requires that the selection of sentence, when there is a selection to be made, must remain exclusively a judicial task, is perfectly compatible with this principle.[68] It reflects the requirement that decisions in individual cases should be made by properly-appointed judges acting independently and impartially. Sentencing principles and, where they exist, guidelines are in the form of general directives binding on the courts, and may therefore be created by the legislature or an agency specially created for that purpose. After all, there has never been any challenge to the constitutional legitimacy of certain general statutory rules governing the sentencing process in this country, such as the requirement that consecutive prison sentences be imposed for offences committed while on bail.[69] The same would hold true of a more extensive legislative or executive initiative to establish more prescriptive norms for judicial sentencing. Having said this, there can be nothing unconstitutional about appeal courts embarking on the same exercise; the elaboration of principle is, after all, one of the main functions of senior appeal courts within common-law systems. (The legislature would still retain the upper hand in the sense of being able to alter by statute a judicially-developed principle with which it did not agree, provided the alteration did not conflict with any substantive constitutional norm.) The system which has been suggested in this chapter, therefore, should not pose any constitutional difficulty as it leaves the elaboration of sentencing principles and benchmarks to the judiciary in the first place. The legislature could nonetheless, if it were so minded, assume responsibility for this task as long as it did not attempt to influence the sentencing decision in any specific case and provided the prescribed rules and principles were reasonable, proportionate and non-discriminatory. However, for the reasons set out earlier in this book, and particularly in Chapters 2 and 3, this is a task more appropriately left to the judicial branch of government. All depends ultimately on the willingness of appeal courts to adopt a more dynamic approach towards the development of principles and benchmarks.

February 2011, and available at *www.ucl.ac.uk/constitution-unit/events/judicial-independence-events/launch* [Last accessed August 24, 2011].

[67] Ashworth, "Sentencing and the Constitution" (1990) 1 King's College L.J. 29 (although dealing with English law, the main constitutional arguments made in this article would be equally applicable in Ireland).

[68] *Deaton v Attorney General and Revenue Commissioners* [1963] I.R. 170.

[69] Criminal Justice Act 1984 s.11 as amended by Criminal Justice Act 2007 s.22.

BIBLIOGRAPHY

Aas, K.F., *Sentencing in the Age of Information: from Faust to Macintosh* (London: Glasshouse Press, 2005)

Abadee, A., "The New South Wales Sentencing Council" in Freiberg and Gelb (eds), *Penal Populism, Sentencing Councils and Sentencing Policy*, Ch.9

Abramowicz, M. and Stearns, M., "Defining *Dicta*" (2005) 57 Stanford L.R. 953–1094

Adelman, L. and Deitrich, J., "Marvin Frankel's Mistakes and the Need to Rethink Federal Sentencing" (2008) 13 *Berkeley Journal of Criminal Law* 239–260

Aebi, M. and Delgrande, N., *Council of Europe Annual Penal Statistics Space I: Survey 2007* (Strasbourg: Council of Europe, 2009)

Alfini, J.J., "Centennial Reflections on Roscoe Pound's 1906 Address to the American Bar Association: Fanning the Spark that Kindled the White Flame of Progress" (2007) 48 South Texas L.R. 849–852

Allen, F.A., *The Decline of the Rehabilitative Ideal: Penal Policy and Social Purpose* (New Haven, CT: Yale University Press, 1981)

Alschuler, A.W., "Sentencing Reform and Prosecutorial Power: A Critique of Recent Proposals for 'Fixed' and 'Presumptive' Sentencing" (1978) 126 Univ. Pennsylvania L.R. 550–577

American Law Institute, *Model Penal Code Sentencing*, Tentative Draft 1 (Philadelphia, 2007)

Amnesty International, *Death Sentences and Executions in 2008* (London: Amnesty International Publications, 2009)

Amnesty International, *Hanging by a Thread: Mental Health and the Death Penalty in Japan* (London: Amnesty International Publications, 2009)

Anderson, J.M., Kling, J.R. and Stith, K., "Measuring Interjudge Sentencing Disparity: Before and After the Federal Sentencing Guidelines" (1999) 42 *Journal of Law and Economics* 271–307

Andrews, D.A., Bonta, J. and Wormith, S., "The Recent Past and Near Future of Risk and/or Need Assessment" (2006) 52 *Crime and Delinquency* 7–27

Anon, "The Indeterminate Sentence" (1911) 108 *Atlantic Monthly* 320–322

Aristotle, *Ethics* trans. by J.A.K. Thomson (London: Penguin Books, 1976)

Appleton, C., *Life after Life Imprisonment* (Oxford: Oxford University Press, 2010)

Armstrong, S. and McAra, L. (eds), *Perspectives on Punishment: The Contours of Control* (Oxford: Oxford University Press, 2006)

Ashworth, A., *Sentencing and Penal Policy* (London: Weidenfeld and Nicolson, 1983)

Ashworth, A., "Criminal Justice and the Criminal Process" (1988) 28 Brit. J. Crim. 111–123

Ashworth, A., "Sentencing and the Constitution" (1990) 1 King's College L.J. 29

Ashworth, A., "Sentencing Reform Structures" in M. Tonry (ed.), *Crime and Justice: A Review of Research*, Vol. 16 (Chicago: University of Chicago Press, 1992), pp.181–241

Ashworth, A., "Conceptions of Overcriminalization" (2008) 5 *Ohio State Journal of Criminal Law* 407–425

Ashworth, A., "English Sentencing Guidelines in their Public and Political Context" in A. Freiberg and K. Gelb, *Penal Populism, Sentencing Councils and Sentencing Policy*, Ch.8

Ashworth, A., *Sentencing and Criminal Justice*, 5th edn (Cambridge: Cambridge University Press, 2010)

Ashworth, A., Genders, E., Mansfield, G., Peay, J. and Player, E., *Sentencing in the Crown Court: Report of an Exploratory Study*, Occasional Paper No.10 (University of Oxford: Centre for Criminological Research, 1984)

Ashworth, A. and Hough, M., "Sentencing and the Climate of Public Opinion" [1996] Crim. L.R. 776–787

Ashworth, A. and von Hirsch, A., "Recognising Elephants: the Problem of the Custody Threshold" [1997] Crim L.R. 187–200

Ashworth, A., von Hirsch, A, and Roberts, J., *Principled Sentencing: Readings on Theory and Policy*, 3rd edn (Oxford: Hart Publishing, 2009)

Ashworth, A. and Wasik, M., "Ten Years of the Sentencing Advisory Panel" in *Annual Report of the Sentencing Guidelines Council and the Sentencing Advisory Panel 2009/2010* (London, 2010)

Atiyah, P.S., *Pragmatism and Theory in English Law* (London: Stevens, 1987)

Atiyah, P.S., *Law and Modern Society*, 2nd edn (Oxford: Oxford University Press, 1995)

Atkins, D., Siegel, J. and Slutsky, J., "Making Policy when the Evidence is in Dispute" (2005) 24 *Health Affairs* 102–113

Austen-Smith, D. and Banks, J.S., "Information Aggregation, Rationality, and the Condorcet Jury Theorem" (1996) 90:1 *American Political Science Review* 34–45

Austin, A., *Criminal Justice Trends: Key Legislative Changes in Sentencing Policy 2000-2010* (New York: Vera Institute, 2010)

Austin, J., *Lectures on Jurisprudence*, 5th edn by R. Campbell (London: John Murray, 1885)

Australian Institute of Criminology, *Criminal Justice on the Spot: Infringement Penalties in Victoria* (Canberra, Australia, 1995)

Bagaric, M., "Home Truths about Home Detention" (2002) 66 J. Crim. L. 425–444

Baker, J.H., *An Introduction to English Legal History*, 2nd edn (London: Butterworths, 1979)

Barclay, G., "The Peak Age of Known Offending by Males", *Home Office Research Bulletin*, No. 28 (London, 1990), 20–23

Barkow, R.E. and O'Neill, K.M., "Delegating Punitive Power: The Political Economy of Sentencing Commission and Guideline Formation" (2006) 84 Texas L.R. 1973–2022

Barrett, B.S., "Sentencing Guidelines: Recommendations for Sentencing Reform" (1992) 57 Missouri L.R. 1077–1116

Bartlett, P. and Wright, D. (eds), *Outside the Walls of the Asylum: the History of Care in the Community 1750-2000* (London: Athlone Press, 1999)

Baum, D., *Smoke and Mirrors: The War on Drugs and the Politics of Failure* (New York: Little, Brown and Company, 1996)

Beale, S.S. "What's Law Got to Do with It? The Political, Social, Psychological and other Non-Legal Factors Influencing the Development of (Federal) Criminal Law" (1997) 1 Buffalo Crim. L.R. 23–66

Beattie, J.M., *Crime and the Courts in England 1660-1800* (Princeton, NJ: Princeton University Press, 1986)

Beck, A.J. and Greenfeld, L.A., *Violent Offenders in State Prison: Sentences and Time Served* (Washington, DC: Department of Justice, 1995)

Bellamy, J. *Criminal Law and Society in Late Medieval and Tudor England* (New York: St. Martin's Inc., 1984)

Bentham, J., *An Introduction to the Principles of Morals and Legislation* ed. by J.H. Burns and H.L.A. Hart (London: Athlone Press, 1970)

Berman, D.A., "Reconceptualizing Sentencing" [2005] *University of Chicago Legal Forum* 1–53

Berman, D.A., "Distinguishing Offence Conduct and Offender Characteristics in Modern Sentencing Reforms" (2005) 58 Stanford L.R. 277–291

Berman, D.A., "*Rita*, Reasoned Sentencing, and Resistance to Change" (2007) 85 Denver Univ. L.R. 7–26

Berman, D.A., "The Enduring (and Again Timely) Wisdom of the Original *MPC* Sentencing Provisions" (2009) 61 Florida L.R. 709–725

Berman, D.A. and Bibas, S., "Making Sentencing Sensible" (2006) 4 *Ohio State Journal of Criminal Law* 37–72

Berman, D.A. and Chanenson, S., "The Real (Sentencing) World: State Sentencing in the Post-*Blakely* Era" (2006) 4 *Ohio State Journal of Criminal Law* 27–35

Bessette, J.M., "Deliberative Democracy: The Majority Principle in Republican Government" in R.A. Goldwin and W.A. Schambra (eds), *How Democratic is the Constitution?* (Washington, DC: American Enterprise Institute, 1980), pp.102–116

Beyens, K., Françoise, C. and Scheirs, V., "Les juges belges face à l'(in)execution des peines" (2010) 34 *Déviance et Societé* 401–424

Bibas, S., "Plea Bargaining outside the Shadow of Trial" (2004) 117 Harvard L.R. 2464–2547

Bickel, A.M., *The Morality of Consent* (New Haven: Yale University Press, 1975)

Bingham, T., "The Judges: Active or Passive" (2006) 139 *Proceedings of the British Academy* 55–72

Bingham, T., "The Rule of Law" (2007) Cambridge L.J. 67–85

Bingham, T., *The Rule of Law* (London: Allen Lane, 2010)

Bird, S.M., "Prescribing Sentence: Time for Evidence-Based Justice" (2004) 364 *The Lancet* 1457–1459

Bjerk, D., "Making the Crime Fit the Penalty: The Role of Prosecutorial Discretion under Mandatory Minimum Sentencing" (2005) 48 *Journal of Law and Economics* 591–625

Blackstone, W., *Commentaries on the Law of England,* Book 4, facsimile of first edition (1765) (Chicago: University of Chicago Press, 1979)

Bottomley, A.K., *Decisions in the Penal Process* (London: Martin Robertson, 1973)

Bottomley, A.K. "The Pitfalls of Automatic Parole", *The Times,* August 21, 1981.

Bottomley, A.K., "Parole in Transition: A Comparative Study of Origins, Developments, and Prospects for the 1990s" in M. Tonry and N. Morris, *Crime and Justice: A Review of Research,* Vol. 12 (Chicago: University of Chicago Press, 1990), pp.319–374

Bottoms, A.E., "Neglected Features of Contemporary Penal Systems" in D. Garland and P. Young (eds), *The Power to Punish* (London: Heinemann, 1982), pp.166–202

Bottoms, A. and McWilliams, W., "A Non-Treatment Paradigm for Probation Practice" (1979) 9 *British Journal of Social Work* 160–201

Bottoms, A., Rex, S., and Robinson, G. (eds), *Alternatives to Prison: Options for an Insecure Society* (Cullompton: Willan Publishing, 2004)

Boulanger, C. and Sarat, A., "Putting Culture into the Picture" in Sarat, A. and Boulanger, C., *The Cultural Lives of Capital Punishment* (Stanford: Stanford University Press, 2005)

Braithwaite, J. and Pettit, P., *Not Just Deserts: A Republican Theory of Criminal Justice* (Oxford: Clarendon Press, 1992)

Breyer, S., "The Federal Sentencing Guidelines and the Key Compromises upon Which They Rest" (1988) 17 Hofstra L.R. 1–50

Broad, J., "Whigs and Deer-Stealers in Other Guises: A Return to the Origins of the Black Act" (May 1988) 119 *Past and Present* 56–72

Brody, S., *The Effectiveness of Sentencing* Home Office Research Study No. 35 (London: HMSO, 1976)

Burke, K.S., "Just What Made Drug Courts Successful?" (Nov./Dec. 2010) 94 *Judicature* 119

Burnett, R. and Maruna, S., "So 'Prison Works', Does It? The Criminal Careers of 130 Men Released from Prison under Home Secretary, Michael Howard" (2004) 43 *Howard Journal* 390–404

Burton, S.J., "Particularism, Discretion and the Rule of Law" in Shapiro (ed.), *The Rule of Law,* NOMOS XXXVI (New York: New York University Press, 1994)

Byrne Hessick, C. and Hessick, F.A., "Recognizing Constitutional Rights at Sentencing" (2011) 99 California L.R. 47–94

Carlen, P., Review of Pratt, *Punishment and Civilisation: Penal Tolerance and Intolerance in Modern Society* (London: Sage, 2002) in (2003) 5 *Punishment and Society* 487–490

Cavadino, M. and Dignan, J., *The Penal System: An Introduction*, 4th edn (London: Sage Publications, 2007)

Chanenson, S.L., "The Next Era of Sentencing Reform" (2005) 54 Emory L.J. 377–460

Christie, G.C., "An Essay on Discretion" [1986] Duke L.J. 747–778

Clark, T.C., "A Tribute to Roscoe Pound" (1964) 78 Harvard L.R. 1–3

Clarkson, C.M.V. and Morgan, R. (eds), *The Politics of Sentencing Reform* (Oxford: Clarendon Press, 1995)

Cohen, S., *Visions of Social Control: Crime, Punishment and Classification* (Cambridge: Polity Press, 1985)

Cole, D., "Can Our Shameful Prisons be Reformed?" *New York Review of Books,* November 19, 2009

Conroy, B. and Gunning, P.G., "The Irish Sentencing Information System (ISIS): A Practical Guide to a Practical Tool" [2009] *Judicial Studies Institute Journal* 37–53

Cooper, J., "The Sentencing Guidelines Council – A Practical Perspective" [2008] Crim. L.R. 277–286

Cottee, S., "Sir Leon's Shadow" (2005) 9 *Theoretical Criminology* 203–225

Cox, E., *The Principles of Punishment* (London: Law Times Office, 1877)

Craig, P., "Formal and Substantive Conceptions of the Rule of Law: An Analytical Framework" [1997] *Public Law* 467–487

Cross, A.L., "The English Criminal Law and Benefit of Clergy during the Eighteenth and Early Nineteenth Centuries" (1917) 22 *American Historical Review* 544–565

Cross, R., "Blackstone v Bentham" (1976) 92 L.Q.R. 516–527

Cross, R. and Harris, J.W., *Precedent in English Law*, 4th edn (Oxford: Clarendon Press, 1991)

Cruickshanks, E. and Erskine-Hill, H., "The Waltham Black Act and Jacobitism" (1985) 24 *Journal of British Studies* 358–365

Crutcher, N., "Mandatory Minimum Penalties of Imprisonment: An Historical Analysis" (2001) 44 *Criminal Law Quarterly* 279–308

Davis, K.C., *Discretionary Justice: A Preliminary Inquiry* (Baton Rouge: Louisiana State University Press, 1969)

Davis, K.C., *Police Discretion* (St. Paul, Minn.: West Publishing Ltd., 1975)

Dawson, R.O., "The Decision to Grant or Deny Parole: A Study of Parole Criteria in Law and Practice" [1966] Washington Univ. L.Q. 243–303

de Keijser, J.W. and Elffers, H., "Cross-Jurisdictional Differences in Punitive Public Attitudes?" (2009) 15 *European Journal on Criminal Policy and Research* 47–62

de Vere, R.S., "Discretion in Penalties" (1911) 27 L.Q.R. 317–325

Delgrande, M.F. and Aebi, N., "European Prisons: Stability or Changes?" (November 2009) 8:3 *Criminology in Europe* (Newsletter of the European Society of Criminology) 1, 17–19

Demleitner, N.V., Berman, D.A., Miller, M.L. and Wright, R.F., *Sentencing Law and Policy: Cases, Statutes, and Guidelines* (New York: Aspen Publishers, 2004), with updates

Department of Justice, Equality and Law Reform, *Value for Money and Policy Review of the Community Service Scheme* (Dublin, 2009)

Diamond. S.S. and Zeisel, H., "Sentencing Councils: A Study of Sentence Disparity and its Reduction" (1975) 43 Univ. Chicago L.R. 109–149

Dicey, A.V., *Introduction to the Study of the Law of the Constitution*, 10th edn (London: Macmillan, 1959)

Doob, A.N., *Sentencing Aids: Final Report to the Donner Canadian Foundation* (University of Toronto: Centre for Criminology, 1990)

Doob, A.N., "The United States Sentencing Commission Guidelines: If you do not know where you are going, you might not get there." in Clarkson and Morgan (eds), *The Politics of Sentencing Reform*, Ch.8

Doob, A.N., "Transforming the Punishment Environment: Understanding Public Views of What Should be Accomplished at Sentencing" (2000) 42 *Canadian Journal of Criminology* 323–340

Doob A.N. and Cesaroni, C., "The Political Attractiveness of Mandatory Minimum Sentences" (2001) 39 Osgoode Hall L.J. 287–304

Doob, A.N. and Marinos, V., "Reconceptualizing Punishment: Understanding the Limitations on the Uses of Intermediate Punishments" (1995) 2 Univ. Chicago Law School Roundtable 413–433

Doob, A.N. and Park, N.W., "Computerized Sentencing Information for Judges: An Aid to the Sentencing Process" (1987) 30 *Criminal Law Quarterly* 54–72

Dunn, J., *Setting the People Free: The Story of Democracy* (London: Atlantic Books, 2006)

Dunn, S., "Albert Camus and the Dubious Politics of Mercy" in R. English and J.M. Skelly, *Ideas Matter: Essays in Honour of Conor Cruise O'Brien* (Dublin: Poolbeg Press, 1998), Ch.26

Duxbury, N., *The Nature and Authority of Precedent* (Cambridge: Cambridge University Press, 2008)

Dworkin, R., "The Model of Rules" (1967) 35 Univ. of Chicago L.R. 14–46

Dworkin, R., *Taking Rights Seriously* (Cambridge, MA: Harvard University Press, 1978)

Dworkin, R., *A Matter of Principle* (Cambridge, MA: Harvard University Press, 1985)

Edney, R, and Bagaric, M., *Australian Sentencing: Principles and Practice* (Cambridge: Cambridge University Press, 2007)

Efrati, A., "Judges Trim Jail Time for Child Porn", *The Wall Street Journal,* January 19, 2010

Elliot, J., *Using Narrative in Social Research; Qualitative and Quantitative Approaches* (London: Sage Publications, 2005)

Elster, J. (ed.), *Deliberative Democracy* (Cambridge: Cambridge University Press, 1998)

Emmerson, B., Ashworth, A. and Macdonald, A., *Human Rights and Criminal Justice*, 2nd edn (London: Sweet & Maxwell, 2007)

Englich, B., Mussweiler, T. and Strack, F., "Playing the Dice with Criminal Sentences: the influence of Irrelevant Anchors on Experts' Judicial Decision Making" (2006) 32 *Personality and Social Psychology Bulletin* 188–200

Etienne, M., "Legal and Practical Implications of Evidence-Based Sentencing by Judges" (2009) 1 *Chapman Journal of Criminal Justice* 43–60

European Commission for the Efficiency of Justice (CEPEJ), *European Judicial Systems, Edition 2008* (Strasbourg: Council of Europe Publishing, 2008)

Exum, J.J., "Making the Punishment Fit the (Computer) Crime: Rebooting Notions of Possession for the Federal Sentencing of Child Pornography Offences" (2010) XVI Richmond J. Law & Technology 8

Fallon, R.H., *Implementing the Constitution* (Cambridge, MA: Harvard University Press, 2001)

Farrall, S. and Maruna, S., "Desistance-Focused Criminal Justice Policy Research" (2004) 43 *The Howard Journal* 358–367

Farrington, D.P., "Human Development and Criminal Careers" in M. Maguire, R. Morgan and R. Reiner (eds), *The Oxford Handbook of Criminology*, 2nd edn (Oxford: Clarendon Press, 1997)

Farrington, D.P. and Burrows, J.N., "Did Shoplifting Really Decrease?" (1993) 33 Brit. J. Crim. 57–69

Feeley, M.M. and Simon, J., "The New Penology: Notes on the Emerging Strategy of Corrections and its Implications" (1992) 30 *Criminology* 449–474

Feest, J. and Bettina, P., "Abolitionismus: Einige Antworten auf oft gestellte Fragen" (2008) 40 *Kriminologisches Journal* 6–20

Field, S., and Tata, C., "Connecting Legal and Social Justice in Neo-Liberal World? The Construction and Use of Pre-Sentence Reports" (2010) 12 *Punishment and Society* 235–238

Finley, M.I., *Democracy Ancient and Modern.* 2nd edn (London: Hogarth Press, 1985)

Finnane, M., "Asylums, Families and the State" (Autumn 1985) *History Workshop* No. 20, 134–148

Finsley, F. "Who Get's Parole" (1953) 17:3 *Federal Probation* 26–29

Flaxman, K.N., "The Hidden Dangers of Sentencing Guidelines" (1979) 7 Hofstra L.R. 259–280

Fleet, E., "Sentencing the Criminal – A Judicial Responsibility" (1986) 9 *American Journal of Trial Advocacy* 369–376

Floud, J. and Young, W., *Dangerousness and Criminal Justice* (London: Heinemann, 1981)

Fogel, D., *We Are the Living Proof: The Justice Model for Corrections* (Cincinnati: Anderson, 1975)

Foucault, M., *Madness and Civilization: A History of Insanity in the Age of Reason,* trans by R. Howard (London: Tavistock Publications, 1967)

Fox, R. and Freiberg, A., *Sentencing: State and Federal Law in Victoria*, 2nd edn (Oxford: Oxford University Press, 1999)

Frase, R.S., "Sentencing Principles in Theory and Practice" (1997) 22 *Crime and Justice: A Review of Research* 363–433

Frase, R.S., "Sentencing Guidelines in Minnesota, Other States and the Federal Courts: A Twenty-Year Retrospective" (1999) 12:2 Fed. Sent. Rep. 69–82

Frase, R.S., "Is Guided Discretion Sufficient? Overview of State Sentencing Guidelines" (2000) 44 St Louis Univ. L.J. 425–449

Frase, R.S., "State Sentencing Guidelines: Diversity, Consensus and Unresolved Policy Issues" (2005) 105 Columbia L.R. 1190–1232

Frase, R.S., "Sentencing Guidelines in Minnesota, 1978–2003" in M. Tonry (ed.), *Crime and Justice: A Review of Research,* Vol. 32 (Chicago: University of Chicago Press, 2005) 131–219

Freed, D.J., "Federal Sentencing in the Wake of Guidelines: Unacceptable Limits on the Discretion of Sentencers" (1992) 101 Yale L.J. 1681–1754

Freiberg, A., "The Victorian Sentencing Advisory Council: Incorporating Community Views into the Sentencing Process" in Freiberg and Gelb (eds), *Penal Populism, Sentencing Councils and Sentencing Policy*, Ch.11

Freiberg, A. and Gelb, K. (eds), *Penal Populism, Sentencing Councils and Sentencing Policy* (Cullompton, Devon: Willan Publishing, 2008)

Friedman, D.D. "Making Sense of English Law Enforcement in the Eighteenth Century" (1995) 2 *University of Chicago Law School Roundtable* 475–505

Friedman, B., "The Politics of Judicial Review" (2005) 84 Texas L.R. 257–337

Friedman, L.M., *Crime and Punishment in American History* (New York: BasicBooks, 1993)

Frost, N.A., "The Mismeasure of Punishment: Alternative Measures of Punitiveness and their (Substantial) Consequences" (2008) 10 *Punishment and Society* 277–300

Gabel, L.C., *Benefit of Clergy in England in the Later Middle Ages* (New York: Octagon Books, 1969, first published 1929)

Gabor, T. and Crutcher, N., *Mandatory Minimum Penalties: Their Effects on Crime, Sentencing Disparities and Justice System Expenditures* (Department of Justice, Ottawa: Research and Justice Division, 2002)

Gadd, D. and Maruna, S., "Criminal Careers, desistance and subjectivity: Interpreting Men's Narratives of Change" (2004) 8 *Theoretical Criminology* 123–156

Galinsky, A.D. and Mussweiler, T., "First Offers as Anchors: The Role of Perspective-Taking and Negotiator Focus" (2001) 81:6 *Journal of Personality and Social Psychology* 657–669

Gallie, W.B., "Essentially Contested Concepts" (1956) 56 *Proceedings of the Aristotelian Society* 167–198

Galligan, D.J., "The Nature and Function of Policies within Discretionary Power" [1976] *Public Law* 332–357

Garland, D., *Punishment and Modern Society* (Oxford: Clarendon Press, 1990)

Garland, D., "Sociological Perspectives on Punishment" in M. Tonry (ed.), *Crime and Justice: A Review of Research,* Vol. 14 (Chicago: University of Chicago Press, 1991), pp.115–165

Gatrell, V.A.C., "Crime, Authority and the Policeman State" in F.M.L. Thompson (ed.), *Cambridge Social History of Britain 1750-1950* (Cambridge: Cambridge University Press, 1990), Vol. 3, pp.243–257

Gertner, N., "From Omnipotence to Impotence: American Judges and Sentencing" (2007) 4 Ohio State J. Crim. L. 523–539

Gertner, N., "Supporting Advisory Guidelines" (2009) 3 *Harvard Law and Policy Review* 261–281

Giffard, C. and Muntingh, L., *The Effect of Sentencing on the Size of the South African Prison Population* (Newlands, SA: Open Society for South Africa, 2006)

Glazebrook, P. (ed.), *Reshaping the Criminal Law; Essays in Honour of Glanville Williams* (London: Stevens & Co., 1978)

Goldstein, H., "Police Discretion; The Ideal versus the Real" (1963) 23 *Public Administration Review* 140–148

Goldstein, J., "Police Discretion Not to Invoke the Criminal Process: Low Visibility Decisions in the Administration of Justice" (1960) 69 Yale L.J. 543–594

Goodhart, A.L., "Determining the Ratio Decidendi of a Case" (1930) 40 Yale L.J. 161–183, reprinted in Goodhart, A.L., *Essays in Jurisprudence and the Common Law* (Cambridge: Cambridge University Press, 1931)

Goodhart, A.L., "The *Ratio Decidendi* of a Case" (1959) 22 M.L.R. 117–124

Grabosky, P.N., *Burglary Prevention* (Canberra: Australian Institute of Criminology, 1995)

Grainger, B., "Hard Times and Automation: Should Computers Assist Judges in Sentencing Decisions?" (1984) 26 *Canadian Journal of Criminology* 231–233

Greaves, C.S., *The Criminal Law Consolidation and Amendment Acts of the 24 and 25 Vict. With Notes and Observations* (London: V. & R. Stevens & Sons; H. Sweet, and W. Maxwell, 1861)

Green, D.A., "Public Opinion versus Public Judgment about Crime: Correcting the 'Comedy of Errors'" (2006) 46 Brit. J. Crim. 131–154

Greenawalt, K., "Discretion and Judicial Decision: The Elusive Quest for the Fetters that Bind Judges" (1975) 75 Columbia L.R. 359–399

Greer, D., "A Security against Illegality? The Reservation of Crown Cases in Nineteenth Century Ireland" in Dawson, N. (ed.), *Reflections on Law and History: Irish Legal History Society Discourses and Other Papers, 2000-2005* (Dublin: Four Courts Press/The Irish Legal History Society, 2006), pp.163-202

Gurthrie, C., Rachlinski, J.J., and Wistrich, A.J., "Blinking on the Bench: How Judges Decide Cases" (2007) 93 Cornell L.R. 1–43

Hall, M.J.J., Calabro, D., Sourdin, T,, Stranieri, A., and Zeleznikow, J., "Supporting Discretionary Decision-Making with Information Technology: A Case Study in the Criminal Sentencing Jurisdiction" (2005) 2 *University of Ottawa Law and Technology Journal* 1–36

Halliday, J., *Making Punishments Work: Report of a Review of the Sentencing Framework for England and Wales* (London: Home Office, 2001)

Hammond, K.R., *Human Judgment and Social Policy* (Oxford: Oxford University Press, 1996)

Hansen, M.H., *The Athenian Democracy in the Age of Demosthenes: Structure, Principles, and Ideology,* trans. by J.A. Crook (Oxford: Basil Blackwell, 1991)

Harcourt, B.E., "From the Asylum to the Prison: Rethinking the Incarceration Revolution" (2006) 84 Texas L.R. 1751–1786

Hart, H.L.A., *Punishment and Responsibility: Essays in the Philosophy of Law*, 2nd edn with introduction by J. Gardner (Oxford; Oxford University Press, 2008)

Hart, H.M., "The Supreme Court 1958 Term – Foreword: The Time Chart of the Justices" (1959) 73 Harv. L.R. 84–125

Hart, H.M. and Sachs, A.M., *The Legal Process: Basic Problems in the Making and Application of Law* (unpublished edn, 1952)

Hart, S., "Evidence-Based Assessment of Risk for Sexual Violence" (2009) 1 *Chapman Journal of Criminal Justice* 143–165

Hawkins, K. (ed.), *The Uses of Discretion* (Oxford: Clarendon Press, 1994)

Hay, D., "Crime and Justice in Eighteenth- and Nineteenth-Century England" in N. Morris and M. Tonry (eds), *Crime and Justice: An Annual Review of Research* Vol. 2 (Chicago: University of Chicago Press, 1980), pp.45–84

Hay, D., Linebaugh, P., Rule, J.G., Thompson, E.P., Winslow, C., *Albion's Fatal Tree: Crime and Society in Eighteenth-Century England* (London: Penguin Books, 1977)

Heclo, H., "Hyperdemocracy" (1999) 23 *Wilson Quarterly* 62–71

Henchy, S., "Precedent in the Irish Supreme Court" (1962) 25 M.L.R. 544–558

Henham, R., "Back to the Future on Sentencing: The 1996 White Paper" (1996) 59:6 M.L.R. 861–875

Henham, R., "On the Philosophical and Theoretical Implications of Judicial Decision Support Systems" (2000) 14 *International Journal of Law, Computers and Technology* 283–296

Herzog-Evans, M., *Droit de l'éxecution des peines*, 3rd edn (Paris: Dalloz, 2007)

Herzog-Evans, M., "French Post Custody Law (2000-2009): From Equitable Trial to the Religion of Control" (2009) 1:2 *European Journal of Probation* 97–111

Hilson, C., "Judicial Review, Policies and the Fettering of Discretion" [2002] *Public Law* 111–129

Himmerlfarb, G., "Reflections on Burke's 'Reflections'" (February 2009), *The New Criterion* 4–10

Hinchman, L.P. and Hinchman, S.K. (eds), *Memory, Identity, Community: the Idea of Narrative in the Human Sciences* (Albany, NY: State University of New York Press, 1997)

Hoffman, P.B. and DeGostin, L.K., "Parole Decision-Making: Structuring Discretion" (1974) 38:4 *Federal Probation* 7–15

Hogarth, J., *Sentencing as a Human Process* (Toronto: Toronto University Press, 1971)

Holdsworth, W., *Some Makers of English Law* (Cambridge: Cambridge University Press, 1938)

Holmes, O.W., "The Path of the Law" (1897) 10 Harvard L.R. 457–478

Hood, R., *Sentencing in Magistrates' Courts* (London: Stevens, 1962)

Hood, R., "Tolerance and the Tariff" in J. Baldwin and A.K. Bottomley (eds), *Criminal Justice: Selected Readings* (London: Martin Robertson, 1978), pp.296–307

Hood, R., "Some Reflections on the Role of Criminology in Public Policy" [1987] Crim L.R. 527–538

Hood, R. and Shute, S., "Parole Criteria, Parole Decisions and the Prison Population: Evaluating the Impact of the Criminal Justice Act 1991" [1996] Crim L.R. 77–87

Hornby, D.B., "Speaking in Sentences" (Winter 2011) 14 *Green Bag* 2d, 147–161

Hough, M., Jacobson, J. and Millie, A., *The Decision to Imprison: Sentencing and the Prison Population* (London: Prison Reform Trust, 2003)

Hudson, B. and Bramhall, G., "Assessing the 'Other': Constructions of 'Asianness' in Risk Assessments by Probation Officers" (2005) 45 Brit. J. Crim. 721–740

Hutcheson, J.C. "The Judgment Intuitive; The Function of the 'Hunch' in Judicial Decision" (1929) 14 Cornell L.R. 274–288

Hutton, N., "Sentencing, Rationality and Human Technology" (1995) 22 *Journal of Law and Society* 549–570

Hutton, N., "What do the Scottish Public Think about Sentencing and Punishment?" (2003) 9 *The Scottish Journal of Criminal Justice Studies* 41–53

Hutton, N., "Sentencing as a Social Practice" in Armstrong and McAra, *Perspectives on Punishment: The Contours of Control,* Ch.9

Hutton, N., Tata, C. and Wilson, J.N., "Sentencing and Information Technology: Incidental Reform" (1995) 2 *International Journal of Law and Information Technology* 255–286

Irish Prison Service, *Annual Reports,* available at *www.irishprisons.ie*

Jackson, J.D. and Doran, S., *A Study of the Jurisdiction of the Criminal Courts in Ireland,* Appendix V of the Report of *Report of Working Group on the Jurisdiction of the Courts: The Criminal Jurisdiction of the Courts* (Dublin: Stationery Office, 2003)

Jackson, R.H., "Serving the Administration of Criminal Justice" (1953) 17:4 *Federal Probation* 3–7

Jackson, R.H., "Criminal Justice: the Vital Problem of the Future" (August 1953) 39 *ABA Journal* 743–746

Jackson, R.M., *Enforcing the Law*, rev. edn (Harmondsworth: Penguin Books, 1972)

Jenkins, D., "From Unwritten to Written: Transformation in the British Common-Law Constitution" (2003) 36 Vanderbilt J. Transnational L. 863–960

Johnson, D., "Trial by Jury in Ireland 1860-1914" (1996) 17 *The Journal of Legal History* 270–293

Jolowicz, H.F. and Nicholas, B., *Historical Introduction to the Study of Roman Law*, 3rd edn (Cambridge: Cambridge University Press, 1972)

JUSTICE, *A New Parole System for England and Wales* (London: JUSTICE, 2009)

Justice Policy Initiative, *Addicted to Courts: How a Growing Dependence on Drug Courts Impacts People and Communities* (Washington, DC, 2011)

Kadish, S.H., "Legal Norm and Discretion in the Police and Sentencing Processes" (1962) 75 Harvard L.R. 904–931

Kazemian, L., "Desistance from Crime: Theoretical, Empirical, Methodological, and Policy Considerations" (2007) 23 *Journal of Contemporary Criminal Justice* 5–27

Kennedy, E.M., "Introduction" (to Symposium on Sentencing, Part 1) (1979) 7 Hofsra L.R. 1–9

King, P., "Decision-Makers and Decision-Making in the English Criminal Law, 1750-1800" (1984) 27 *The Historical Journal* 25–58

King, P., *Crime, Justice and Discretion in England 1740-1820* (Oxford: Oxford University Press, 2000)

Kirby, M., "'Judicial Activism'? A Riposte to the Counter-Reformation" (2005) 11 Otago L.R. 1–16

Kissinger, H.A., "Domestic Structure and Foreign Policy" (1966) 95:2 *Daedalus* 503–529

Kittrie, N.N. and Zenoff, E.H., *Sanctions, Sentencing, and Corrections: Law, Policy, and Practice* (Mineola, NY: The Foundation Press, Inc., 1981)

Kolber, A.J., "The Subjective Experience of Punishment" (2009) 109 Columbia L.R. 182–236

Koriyama, Y. and Szentes, B., "A Resurrection of the Condorcet Jury Theorem" (2009) 4 *Theoretical Economics* 227–252

Kramnick, I. (ed.), *The Portable Edmund Burke* (New York: Penguin Books, 1999)

Kress, J.M., Wilkins, L.T. and Gottfredson, D.M., "Is the End of Judicial Sentencing in Sight?" (1976) 60 *Judicature* 216–222

Kronman, A.T., "Alexander Bickel's Philosophy of Prudence" (1984) 94 Yale L.J. 1567–1616

Kronman, A.T., "Living In the Law" (1987) 54 Univ. Chicago L.R. 835–876

Kronman, A.T., "Precedent and Tradition" (1990) 99 Yale L.J. 1029–1068

Kubista, N.J., "'Substantial and Compelling Circumstances'; Sentencing of Rapists under the Mandatory Minimum Sentencing Scheme" (2005) 18 *South African Journal of Criminal Justice* 77–86

Kutak, R.J. and Gottschalk, J.M., "In Search of a Rational Sentence: A Return to the Concept of Appellate Review" (1974) 53 Nebraska L.R. 463–520

Labbe, R.M., "Appellate Review of Sentences: Penology on the Judicial Doorstep" (1977) 68 *Journal of Criminal Law and Criminology* 122–134

LaFave, W.R., *Arrest: the Decision to Take the Suspect into Custody* (Boston: Little Brown, 1956)

Langbein, J.H., "Shaping the Eighteenth-Century Criminal Trial: A View from the Ryder Sources" (1983) 50 Univ. of Chicago L.R. 1–136

Langbein, J.H. "*Albion's* Fatal Flaws" (1983) 98:1 *Past and Present* 96–120

Lanzoni, S., "The Asylum in Context; An Essay Review" (2005) 60:4 *Journal of the History of Medicine and Allied Sciences* 499–505

Lasker, M.E., "Presumption Against Incarceration" (1979) 7 Hofstra L.R. 407–416

Law Reform Commission of Western Australia, *Review of the Law of Homicide: Final Report* (Perth, 2007)

Leiter, B., "Positivism, Formalism, Realism" (1999) 99 Columbia L.R. 1138–1164

Levin, R.M., "The Administrative Law Legacy of Kenneth Culp Davis" (2005) 42 San Diego L.R. 315–347

Levit, N., "Practically Unreasonable – A Critique of Practical Reason: A Review of the *Problems of Jurisprudence* by Richard Posner" (1991) 85 Northwestern Univ. L.R. 494–518

Liang, B., Lu, H., Miethe, T.D. and Zhang, L., "Sources of Variation in Pro-Death Penalty Attitudes in China" (2006) 46 Brit. J. Crim. 119–130

Lipton, D.S., Martinson, R. and Wilks, J., *The Effectiveness of Correctional Treatment: A Survey of Treatment Evaluation Studies* (New York: Praeger, 1975)

List. C. and Goodin, R.E., "Epistemic Democracy: Genealizing the Condorcet Jury Theorem" (2001) 9:3 *Journal of Political Philosophy* 277–306

Locke, J., *Two Treatises of Government* rev. edn by P. Laslett (Cambridge: Cambridge University Press, 1963)

Lovegrove, A., "Statistical Information Systems as a Means to Consistency and Rationality in Sentencing" (1999) 7 *International Journal of Law and Information Technology* 31–72

Luna, E., "Misguided Guidelines: A Critique of Federal Sentencing" in G. Healy (ed.), *Go Directly to Jail: The Criminalization of Almost Everything* (Washington, DC: Cato Institute, 2004), Ch.6

Lynch, G.E., "Revising the Model Penal Code: Keeping it Real" (2003) 1 *Ohio State Journal of Criminal Law* 219–239

Lynch, G.E., "Letting Guidelines be Guidelines (and Judges be Judges)" *Ohio State Journal of Criminal Law: Views from the Field* (January 2008), at *http://osjcl. blogspot.com* [Last accessed September 15, 2011]

McDowell, R.B., "The Irish Courts of Law 1801-1914" (1957) 10 *Irish Historical Studies* 363–391

McMahon, M., "'Net-Widening': Vagaries in the Use of a Concept" (1990) 30 Brit. J. Crim. 121–149

McNeill, F., "A Desistance Paradigm for Offender Management" (2006) 6 *Criminology and Criminal Justice* 39–62

McNeill, F., "What Works and What's Just?" (2009) 1 *European Journal of Probation* 21–40

Mackay, J.P.H. (Lord Mackay of Clashfern), "Can Judges Change the Law?" (1987) 73 *Proceedings of the British Academy* 285–308

Mackenzie, G. and Stobbs, N., *Principles of Sentencing* (Annandale, NSW: Federation Press, 2010)

Mackenzie, M.M., *Plato on Punishment* (Berkeley: University of California Press, 1981)

Macedo, S., "The Rule of Law, Justice, and the Politics of Moderation in I. Shapiro (ed.), *The Rule of Law*, NOMOS XXXVI (New York: New York University Press, 1994), Ch.7

Maguire, M., "The Impact of Burglary upon Victims" (1980) Brit. J. Crim. 261–275

Maguire, N., "Consistency in Sentencing" [2010] 2 *Judicial Studies Institute Journal* 14–54

Mair, G., "Community Penalties in England and Wales" (1998) 10:5 Fed. Sent. Rep. 263–267

Malcolm, E., "'Ireland's Crowded Madhouses': the Institutional Confinement of the Insane in Nineteenth- and Twentieth-Century Ireland" in Porter and Wright (eds), *The Confinement of the Insane: International Perspectives 1800-1965*, pp.315–333

Mannheim, H., "Comparative Sentencing Practice" (1958) 23 *Law and Contemporary Problems* 557–582

Manovich, L., *The Language of New Media* (Cambridge, Mass.: MIT Press, 2001)

Marcus, M., "The Making of the ABA Criminal Justice Standards: Forty Years of Excellence" (2009) 23:4 *Criminal Justice* 10–15

Marcus, M.H. "Comments on the Model Penal Code: Sentencing Preliminary Draft No 1" (2003) 30 Am. J. Crim. L. 135–169

Marcus, M.H., "Sentencing in the Temple of Denunciation: Criminal Justice's Weakest Link" (2004) 1 Ohio State J. Crim. L. 671–681

Marcus, M.H., "*Blakely, Booker* and the Future of Sentencing" (2005) 17 Fed. Sent. Rep. 243–248

Marcus, M.H., "Conversations on Evidence-Based Sentencing" (2009) 1 *Chapman Journal of Criminal Justice* 61–126

Marinos, V., "Equivalency and Interchangeability: The Unexamined Complexities of Reforming the Fine" (1997) 39 *Canadian Journal of Criminology* 27–50

Marlowe, D.B., deMatteo, D.S. and Festinger, D.S., "A Sober Assessment of Drug Courts" (2003) 16 Fed. Sent. Rep. 153–157

Marques, C.S., "Anthony Kronman on the Virtue of Practical Wisdom" (2002) 15 *Ratio Juris* 328–340

Martinson, R., "What Works? Questions and Answers about Prison Reform" (1974) 10 *The Public Interest* 22–54

Martinson, R., "New Findings, New Views: A Note of Caution regarding Sentencing Reform" (1979) 7 Hofstra L.R. 243–258

Maruna, S., *Making Good* (Washington, DC: American Psychological Association, 2001)

Mathiesen, T., *The Politics of Abolition* (London: Martin Robertson, 1974)

Mathiesen, T., "The Politics of Abolition" (1986) 10 *Contemporary Crises* 81–94

May, T., "On Raz and the Obligation to Obey the Law" (1997) 16 *Law and Philosophy* 19–36

Mayr, E., "When is Historiography Whiggish?" (1990) 51:2 *Journal of the History of Ideas* 301–309

Miethe, T.D., "Charging and Plea Bargaining Practices under Determinate Sentencing: An Investigation of the Hydraulic Displacement of Discretion" (1987) 78 *Journal of Criminal Law and Criminology* 155–176

Miethe, T.D. and Lu, H., *Punishment; A Comparative Historical Perspective* (Cambridge: Cambridge University Press, 2005)

Miller, M.L., "Sentencing Reform 'Reform' through Sentencing Information Systems" in M. Tonry (ed.), *The Future of Imprisonment* (Oxford: Oxford University Press, 2004), pp.121–153

Miller, M.L., "A Map of Sentencing and a Compass for Judges: Sentencing Information Systems, Transparency, and the Next Generation of Reform" (2005) 105 Columbia L.R. 1351–1395

Miller, M. and Freed, D.J., "Editors' Observations: The Chasm between the Judiciary and Congress over Mandatory Minimum Sentences" (1993) 6:2 *Federal Sentencing Reporter* 59–62

Millie, A., Tombs, J. and Hough, M., "Borderline Sentencing: A Comparison of Sentencers' Decision Making in England and Wales, and Scotland" (2007) 7 *Criminology and Criminal Justice* 243–267

Moffitt, T.E., "Adolescence-Limited and Life-Course-Persistent Antisocial Behaviour: A Developmental Theory" (1993) 100 *Psychological Review* 674–701

Montrose, J.L, "*Ratio Decidendi* and the House of Lords" (1957) 20 M.L.R. 124–130

Montrose, J.L., "The *Ratio Decidendi* of a Case" (1957) 20 M.L.R. 587–595

Morris, N., "Sentencing Convicted Criminals" (1953) 27 *Australian Law Journal* 186–208

Morris, N., *Madness and the Criminal Law* (Chicago: University of Chicago Press, 1982)

Morris, N. and Tonry, M., *Between Prison and Probation: Intermediate Punishments in a Rational Sentencing System* (Oxford: Oxford University Press, 1990)

Mueller, G.O.W., "Penology on Appeal: Appellate Review of Legal but Excessive Sentences" (1962) 15 Vanderbilt L.R. 671–697

Mueller, G.O.W. and Le Poole, F., "Appellate Review of Legal but Excessive Sentences: A Comparative Study" (1968) 21 Vanderbilt L.R. 411–432

Munro, C. and Wasik, M. (eds), *Sentencing, Judicial Discretion and Training* (London: Sweet & Maxwell, 1992)

Nagel, S.S. "Discretion and the Criminal Justice System: Analyzing, Channeling, Reducing, and Controlling It" (1982) 31 Emory L.J. 603–633

Nellis, M., "Surveillance and Confinement: Explaining and Understanding the Experience of Electronically Monitored Curfews" (2009) 1 *European Journal of Probation* 41–65

Neuborne, B., "Of Sausage Factories and Syllogism Machines: Formalism, Realism and Exclusionary Selection Techniques" (1992) 67 N.Y.U. L. Rev. 419–449

New South Wales Sentencing Council, *Review of Periodic Detention* (Sydney, 2007)

Newman, D.J., *Conviction: The Determination of Guilt or Innocence without Trial* (Boston: Little Brown, 1966)

Nilsen, E.S., "Indecent Standards: The Case of *U.S. versus Weldon Angelos*" (2006) 11 Roger Williams Univ. L.R. 537–563

Note, "Appellate Modification of Excessive Sentence" (1960) 46 Iowa L.R. 159–166

Note, "*United States v Dorvee*" (2011) 124 Harvard L.R. 1082–1089

Nuttall, C., "The Home Office and Random Allocation Experiments" (2003) 27 *Evaluation Review* 267–289

O'Donovan, M. and Redpath, J., *The Impact of Minimum Sentencing in South Africa* (Newlands, SA: Open Society for South Africa, 2006)

Oldham, J., "From Blackstone to Bentham: Common Law Versus Legislation in Eighteenth-Century Britain" (1991) 89 Michigan L.R. 1637–1660

Oliss, P., "Mandatory Minimum Sentencing: Discretion, the Safety Valve, and the Sentencing Guidelines" (1995) 63 Univ. Cincinnati L.R. 1851–1892

O'Hear, M.M., "The Original Intent of Uniformity in Federal Sentencing" (2006) 74 Univ. Cincinnati L.R. 749–817

O'Hear, M.M., "The Beginning of the End for Life without Parole?" (2010) 23:1 Fed. Sent. Rep. 1–9

O'Malley, T., "Sentencing Murderers: The Case for Relocating Discretion" (1995) 5 I.C.L.J. 31–66

O'Malley, T., "The Power to Punish: Reflections on *Deaton v AG* (1963) in E. O'Dell (ed.), *Leading Cases of the Twentieth Century* (Dublin: Round Hall Sweet and Maxwell, 2000), pp.196–207

O'Malley, T., *Sentencing Law and Practice*, 2nd edn (Dublin: Thomson Round Hall, 2006)

O'Malley, T., *The Criminal Process* (Dublin: Round Hall, 2009)

O'Malley, T., "Ireland" in Padfield, van Zyl Smit and Dünkel (eds), *Release from Prison: European Policy and Practice*, Ch.10

O'Malley, T., "Sentencing Recidivist Sex Offenders: A Challenge for Proportionality" in I. Bacik and L. Heffernan (eds), *Criminal Law and Procedure: Current Issues and Emerging Trends* (Dublin: Firstlaw, 2009), pp.106–133

Padfield, N., *Beyond the Tariff: Human Rights and the Release of Life Sentence Prisoners* (Cullompton: Willan Publishing, 2002)

Padfield, N., van Zyl Smit, D. and Dünkel, F., *Release from Prison: European Policy and Practice* (Cullompton, Devon: Willan Publishing, 2010)

Palys, T.S. and Divorski, S., "Explaining Sentence Disparity" (1986) 28:4 *Canadian Journal of Criminology* 347–362

Partridge, A. and Eldridge, W.B., *The Second Circuit Sentencing Study: A Report to the Judges and Justices of the Second Circuit* (Washington, DC: Federal Judicial Centre, 1974)

Pease, K., "Community Service Orders" in M. Tonry and N. Morris (eds), *Crime and Justice: An Annual Review of Research* Vol. 6 (Chicago: University of Chicago Press, 1985), pp.51–94

Perry, S.R., "Judicial Obligation, Precedent and the Common Law" (1987) 7 O.J.L.S. 215–257

Pew Centre on the States, *Arming the Courts with Research: 10 Evidence-Based Sentencing Initiatives to Control Crime and Reduce Costs* (May 2009) available at: *www.pewpublicsafety.org.*

Polanksy, R.M., "'Phronesis' on Tour: Cultural Adaptability of Aristotelian Ethical Notions" (2000) 10 *Kennedy Institute of Ethics Journal* 323–336

Porter, N.D., *The State of Sentencing 2010: Developments in Policy and Practice* (Washington, DC: The Sentencing Project, 2011)

Porter, R. and Wright, D. (eds), *The Confinement of the Insane: International Perspectives 1800–1965* (Cambridge: Cambridge University Press, 2003).

Posner, R.A., "Blackstone and Bentham" (1976) 19 *Journal of Law and Economics* 569–606

Posner, R., *The Problems of Jurisprudence* (Cambridge, MA: Harvard University Press, 1990)

Posner, R., *How Judges Think* (Cambridge, MA: Harvard University Press, 2008)

Potas, I., Ash, D., Sagi, M., Cumines, S. and Marsic, N., "Informing the Discretion: The Sentencing Information System of the Judicial Commision of New South Wales" (1998) 6 *International Journal of Law and Information Technology* 99–124

Pound, R., "Mechanical Jurisprudence" (1908) 8 Columbia L.R. 605–623

Pound, R., "Hierarchy of Sources and Forms in Different Systems of Law" (1933) 7 Tulane L.R. 475–487

Pound, R., "The Causes of Unpopular Dissatisfaction with the Administration of Justice" (2007) 48 South Texas L.R. 853–870 (paper delivered to American Bar Association in 1906)

Powell, H.J., "'Cardozo's Foot': The Chancellor's Conscience and Constructive Trusts" (1993) 56 *Law and Contemporary Problems* 7–27

Priest, G.L., "The Common Law Process and the Selection of Efficient Rules" (1977) 6 J. Legal Stud. 65–82

Prior, P.M., "Murder and Madness: Gender and the Use of the Insanity Defence in Nineteenth-Century Ireland" (2005) 9:4 *New Hibernia Review* 19–36

Radin, M., "The Theory of Judicial Decision: or How Judges Think" (1925) 11 Am. B.A.J. 357–362

Radzinowicz, L., "The Waltham Black Act: A Study of the Legislative Attitude towards Crime in the Eighteenth Century" (1945) 9 Cambridge L.J. 56–81

Radzinowicz, L., *Adventures in Criminology* (London: Routledge, 1999)

Radzinowicz, L. and Hood, R., *The Emergence of Penal Policy in Edwardian and Victorian England,* Vol. 5 of *A History of English Criminal Law and its Administration from 1759* (Oxford: Clarendon Press, 1990)

Radzinowicz, L. and Hood, R., "Judicial Discretion and Sentencing Standards: Victorian Attempts to Solve a Perennial Problem" (1979) 127 Univ. Pennsylvania L.R. 1288–1349

Rawls, J., "Two Concepts of Rules" (1955) 64 *The Philosophical Review* 3–32

Rawls, J., *A Theory of Justice* (Oxford: Oxford University Press, 1972)

Raz, J., *The Concept of a Legal System*, 2nd edn (Oxford: Oxford University Press, 1980)

Raz, J., *The Authority of Law: Essays on Law and Morality*, 2nd edn (Oxford: Oxford University Press, 2009)

Reich, C.A., "The New Property" (1964) 73 Yale L.J. 733–787

Reisman, W.M. and Schreiber, A.M., *Jurisprudence: Understanding and Shaping Law: Cases, Readings, Commentary* (New Haven, CT: New Haven Press, 1987)

Reisman W.M., *Folded Lies: Bribery, Crusades, and Reforms* (New York: The Free Press, 1979)

Reitz, K.R., "Modeling Discretion in American Sentencing Systems" (1998) 20 *Law & Policy* 389–428

Reitz, K.R., "Sentencing Guideline Systems and Sentence Appeals: A Comparison of Federal and State Experiences" (1997) 91 Northwestern Univ. L.R. 1441–1506

Remington, F.J. and Rosenblum, V.G., "The Criminal Law and the Legislative Process" [1960] *University of Illinois Law Forum* 481–499

Report of Review Committee, *The Parole System in England and Wales* (Carlisle Report) Cm 532 (London: HMSO, 1988)

Roach, K., "Searching for *Smith*: The Constitutionality of Mandatory Sentences" (2001) 39 Osgoode Hall L.J. 367–412

Roach, K., "Conditional Sentences, Restorative Justice, Net-Widening and Aboriginal Offenders" in *The Changing Face of Conditional Sentencing: Symposium Proceedings* (Ottawa: Department of Justice, 2000), pp.25–37

Roach, K., *Criminal Law*, 4th edn (Toronto: Irwin Law, 2009)

Roberts, J.V., "Discovering the Sphinx: Conditional Sentencing after the Supreme Court Judgement in *R v Proulx*" in *The Changing Face of Conditional Sentencing: Symposium Proceedings* (Ottawa: Department of Justice, 2000), pp.39–52

Roberts, J.V. and Hough, M.J., *Changing Attitudes to Punishment: Public Opinion, Crime and Justice* (Cullompton: Willan Publishing, 2002)

Roberts, J.V. and M.J. Hough, *Understanding Public Attitudes to Criminal Justice* (Maidenhead: Open University Press, 2005)

Roberts, J.V., "Mandatory Minimum Sentences of Imprisonment: Exploring the Consequences for the Sentencing Process" (2001) 39 Osgoode Hall L.J. 305–327

Roberts, J.V., "Aggravating and Mitigating Factors at Sentencing: Towards Greater Consistency of Application" [2008] Crim L.R. 264–276

Roberts, J.V., Crutcher, N. and Verbrugge, P., "Public Attitudes to Sentencing in Canada: Exploring Recent Findings" (2007) 49 *Canadian Journal of Criminology and Criminal Justice* 75–107

Roberts, J.V. and Manson, A., *The Future of Conditional Sentencing: Perspectives of Appellate Judges* (Ottawa: Department of Justice, 2004)

Roberts, J.V. and von Hirsch, A. (eds), *Previous Convictions at Sentencing: Theoretical and Applied Perspectives* (Oxford: Hart Publishing, 2010)

Robinson, P.H., "Punishing Dangerousness: Cloaking Preventive Detention as Dangerousness" (2001) 114 Harv. L.R. 1429–1456

Robinson, P., *Distributive Principles of Criminal Law* (Oxford: Oxford University Press, 2008)

Robson, G., "The Sentencing Advisory Panel: An Under-valued Institution" *Criminal Law and Justice Weekly,* August 15, 2009.

Rodger, J.J., "Social Work as Social Control Re-examined: Beyond the Dispersal of Discipline Thesis" (1988) 22 *Sociology* 563–581

Rogers, P., "The Waltham Blacks and the Black Act" (1974) 17:3 *The Historical Journal* 465–486

Rosenberg, M., "Judicial Discretion of the Trial Court, Viewed from Above" (1971) 22 Syracuse L.R. 635–667

Roth, S.M., "South African Mandatory Minimum Sentencing: Reform Required" (2008) 17 *Minnesota Journal of International Law* 155–182

Rothman, D.J., "Doing Time: Days, Months and Years in the Criminal Justice System" (1978) 19 *International Journal of Comparative Sociology* 130–138

Ruby, C.C., "Range of Sentence" (1985) 28 *Criminal Law Quarterly* 447–453

Rumgay, J., "Custodial Decision Making in a Magistrates' Court: Court Culture and Immediate Situational Factors" (1995) 35 Brit. J. Criminol. 201–217

Rundell, O.S., "The Chancellor's Foot: the Nature of Equity" (1958) Univ. Kansas City L.R. 71–85

Russell, N. and Morgan, R., *Sentencing of Domestic Burglary* Research Report 1 (London: Sentencing Advisory Panel, 2001)

Ryan, M. and Sim, J., "Campaigning for and campaigning against prisons: excavating and reaffirming the case for prison abolition" in Y. Jewkes, *Handbook on Prisons* (Cullompton: Willan Publishing, Cullompton, 2007), Ch.30

Sabol, W.J., West, H.C. and Cooper, M., *Prisoners in 2008,* Bureau of Justice Statistics Bulletin (Washington, DC: US Department of Justice, 2009)

Salmond, J.W., *Jurisprudence*, 7th edn (London: Sweet and Maxwell, 1924)

Sanders, T. and Roberts, J.V., "Public Attitudes Toward Conditional Sentencing: Results of a National Survey" (2000) 32 *Canadian Journal of Behavioural Science* 199–207

Savelsberg, J.J., "Law That Does Not Fit Society: Sentencing Guidelines as a Neoclassical Reaction to the Dilemmas of Substantivized Law" (1992) 97:5 *American Journal of Sociology* 1346–1381

Sawyer, J.K., "'Benefit of Clergy' in Maryland and Virginia" (1990) 34 *American Journal of Legal History* 49–68

Schauer, F., "Precedent" (1987) 39 Stanford L.R. 571–605

Schauer, F., *Thinking Like a Lawyer: A New Introduction to Legal Reasoning* (Cambridge, MA: Harvard University Press, 2009)

Schild, U.J., "Criminal Sentencing and Intelligent Decision Support" (1998) 6 *Artificial Intelligence and the Law* 151–202

Schild, U.J., "Statistical Information Systems for Sentencing: The Israeli Approach" (2000) 14 *International Review of Law, Computers and Technology* 317–324

Schneider, C.E., "Discretion and Rules: A Lawyer's View" in K. Hawkins (ed.), *The Uses of Discretion* (Oxford: Clarendon Press, 1994), Ch.2

Schulhofer, S.J., "Rethinking Mandatory Minimums" (1993) 28 Wake Forest L.R. 199–222

Scott, R.W., "Inter-Judge Sentencing Disparity after *Booker*: A First Look" (2010) 63 Stanford L.R. 1–66

Scull, A., "A Convenient Place to Get Rid of Inconvenient People: the Victorian Lunatic Asylum" in A.D. King (ed.), *Buildings and Society; Essays on the Social Development of the Built Environment* (London: Routledge & Kegan Paul, 1980), pp.19–31

Scull, A., *The Most Solitary of Afflictions: Madness and Society in Britain 1700-1900* (New Haven: Yale University Press, 1993)

Sentencing Advisory Council of Victoria, *Maximum Penalties: Principles and Purposes* (Melbourne, 2010)

Sentencing Commission for Scotland, *The Scope to Improve Consistency in Sentencing* (2006)

Sentencing Commission Working Group, *Sentencing Guidelines in England and Wales: An Evolutionary Approach* (the Gage Report) (London, 2008)

Sentencing Guidelines Council and Sentencing Advisory Panel, *Annual Report 2009/2010* (London, 2010)

Shapiro, M., *Courts: A Comparative and Political Analysis* (Chicago: University of Chicago Press, 1986)

Sharpe, J.A., *Judicial Punishment in England* (London: Faber and Faber, 1990)

Shea, E., "Parole Philosophy in England and America" in D.J. West, *The Future of Parole* (London: Duckworth, 1972), Ch.5

Sherman, L.W., "Misleading Evidence and Evidence-led Policy: Making Social Sciences More Experimental" (2003) 589 *Annals of American Academy of Political and Social Sciences* 6–19

Sherman, L., "Evidence and Liberty: The Promise of Experimental Criminology" (2009) 9 *Criminology and Criminal Justice* 5–28

Sherwin, E., "Restitution and Equity: An Analysis of the Principles of Unjust Enrichment" (2001) 79 Texas L.R. 2083–2113

Shute, S., "The Place of Public Opinion in Sentencing Law" [1998] Crim. L.R. 465–477

Shute, S., "Punishing Murderers: Release Procedures and the 'tariff' 1953-2004" [2004] Crim. L.R. 160–182

Siegel, N.S., "The Virtue of Judicial Statesmanship" (2008) 86 Texas L.R. 959–1032

Simon, P., *"Ethnic" Statistics and Data Protection in the Council of Europe Countries: Study Report* (Strasbourg: Council of Europe, 2007)

Simpson, A.W.B., "The *Ratio Decidendi* of a Case" (1957) 20 M.L.R. 413–415

Simpson, A.W.B., "Legal Iconoclasts and Legal Ideals" (1990) 58 Univ. Cincinnati L.R. 819–844

Singer, J.W., "The Player and the Cards: Nihilism and Legal Theory" (1984) 94 Yale L.J. 1–69

Slobogin, C., "Introduction to the Symposium on the Model Penal Code's Sentencing Proposals" (2009) 61 Florida L.R. 665–682

Smith, K., "Criminal Law" in *The Oxford History of the Laws of England*, Vol. XIII (Oxford: Oxford University Press, 2010), pp.3–143

Sobeloff, S.E., "A Recommendation for Appellate Review of Criminal Sentences" (1954) 21 Brooklyn L.R. 2–11

Solum, L.B., "Equity and the Rule of Law" in I. Shapiro (ed.), *The Rule of Law, NOMOS XXXVI* (New York: New York University Press, 1994), Ch.6

Spiller, P., *Cox and Crime* (Institute of Criminology, University of Cambridge, 1985)

Steinmetz, C.R., "Power of Appellate Court to Modify Sentences on Appeal" (1933) 9 Wisconsin L.R. 172–177

Stephen, J.F., "Variations in the Punishment of Crime" (1885) 17 *The Nineteenth Century* 755–776

Stewart, F. and Freiberg, A., "Provocation in Sentencing: A Culpability-Based Framework" (2008) 19 *Current Issues in Criminal Justice* 283–308

Stith, K. and Cabranes, J.A., *Fear of Judging: Sentencing Guidelines in the Federal Courts* (Chicago: University of Chicago Press, 1998)

Strauss, D.A., "Common Law Constitutional Interpretation" (1996) 63 Univ. Chicago L.R. 877–935

Sunstein, C.R., *Infotopia: How Many Minds Produce Knowledge* (New York: Oxford University Press, 2006)

Sunstein, C.R., *A Constitution of Many Minds: Why the Founding Document Doesn't Mean What It Meant Before* (Princeton, NJ: Princeton University Press, 2009)

Susskind, R., *Expert Systems in Law: A Jurisprudential Inquiry* (Oxford: Clarendon Press, 1987)

Susskind, R., *The Future of Law: Facing the Challenges of Information Technology* (Oxford: Clarendon Press, 1996)

Szasz, T.S., *The Manufacture of Madness* (London: Routledge & Kegan Paul, 1971)

Szasz, T.S., *The Myth of Mental Illness* rev. ed. (London: Perennial Library, 1974)

Sze, V.S., "A Tale of Three Strikes: Slogan Triumphs over Substance as our Bumper-Sticker Mentality Comes Home to Roost" (1995) 28 Loyola of Los Angeles L.R. 1047–1098

Tamanaha, B.Z., *On the Rule of Law: History, Politics, Theory* (Cambridge: Cambridge University Press, 2004)

Tasioulas, J., "Mercy" (2003) 103 *Proceedings of the Aristotelian Society* 101–132

Tata C., "Sentencing as Craftwork and the Binary Epistemologies of the Discretionary Decision Process" (2007) 16 *Social & Legal Studies* 425–447

Tata, C., "Sentencing and penal decision-making: Is Scotland losing its distinctiveness?" in H. Croall, G. Mooney and M. Munro (eds), *Criminal Justice in Scotland* (Cullompton, Devon: Willan Publishing, 2010), pp.195–215

Tata, C., "A Sense of Justice: The Role of Pre-Sentence Reports in the Production (and Disruption) of Guilt and Guilty Pleas" (2010) 12 *Punishment and Society* 239–261

Tata, C. and Hutton, N., "What 'Rules' in Sentencing? Consistency and Disparity in the Absence of 'Rules'" (1998) 26 *International Journal of the Sociology of Law* 339–364

Tata, C. and Hutton, N., "Beyond the Technology of Quick Fixes: Will the Judiciary Act to Protect Itself and Shore Up Judicial Independence? Recent Experience from Scotland" (2003) 16:1 Fed. Sent. Rep. 67–75

Tata, C., Hutton, N., Wilson, J.N., Paterson, A. and Hughson, I.D. *A Sentencing Information System for the High Court of Justiciary of Scotland: Report of the Study of the First Phase of Implementation* (Glasgow: University of Strathclyde, 2002)

Tata, C. and Hutton, N. (eds), *Sentencing and Society: International Perspectives* (Aldershot, Hampshire: Ashgate Publishing, 2002)

Tata, C., Wilson, J.N. and Hutton, N., "Representations of Knowledge and Discretionary Decision-Making by Decision-Support Systems: the Case of Judicial Sentencing" (1996) 2 *Journal of Information Law & Technology*, available at *http://www2. warwick.ac.uk/fac/soc/law/elj/jilt/1996_2/tata* [Last accessed September 30, 2011].

Terblanche, S., *Research on the Sentencing Framework Bill* (Newlands, SA: Open Society for South Africa, 2008)

Terblanche, S. and Mackenzie, G., "Mandatory Sentences in South Africa: Lessons for Australia" (2008) 41 *The Australian and New Zealand Journal of Criminology* 402–420

Terblanche, S. and Roberts, J.V., "Sentencing in South Africa: Lacking in Principle but Delivering Justice" (2005) 18 *South African Journal of Criminal Justice* 187–202

Thomas, D.A., "Appellate Review of Sentences and the Development of Sentencing Policy: The English Experience" (1968) 20 Alabama L.R. 193–226

Thomas, D.A., *Constraints on Judgment: The Search for Structured Discretion in Sentencing, 1860-1910* (Cambridge: Institute of Criminology, 1979)

Thomas, D.A., "The Role of the Court of Appeal in the English Sentencing System" (1998) 10:5 Fed. Sent. Rep. 259–262

Thompson, E.P., *Whigs and Hunters: The Origin of the Black Act* (London: Allen Lane, 1975)

Thucydides, *History of the Peloponnesian War,* trans. by R. Warner (London: Penguin Books, 1972)

Tidmarsh, J., "Pound's Century, and Ours" (2006) 81 Notre Dame L.R. 513–590

Tombs, J. and Jagger, E., "Denying Responsibility: Sentencers' Accounts of their Decisions to Imprison" (2006) 46 Brit. J. Crim. 803–821

Tomes, N., "A 'Torrent of Abuse': Crimes of Violence between Working-Class Men and Women in London, 1840-1875" (1978) 11 *Journal of Social History* 328–345

Tonry, M.H., "The Sentencing Commission in Sentencing Reform" (1979) 7 Hofstra L.R. 315–353

Tonry, M., "Structuring Sentencing" in M. Tonry and N. Morris (eds), *Crime and Justice: A Review of Research* Vol. 10 (Chicago: University of Chicago Press, 1988), pp.267–337

Tonry, M., "Mandatory Penalties" in M. Tonry (ed.), *Crime and Justice: A Review of Research* Vol. 16 (Chicago: University of Chicago Press, 1992), pp.243–273

Tonry, M., "Judges and Sentencing Policy – the American Experience" in Munro and Wasik (eds), *Sentencing, Judicial Discretion and Training* (London: Sweet & Maxwell, 1992)

Tonry, M., *Sentencing Matters* (Oxford: Oxford University Press, 1996)

Tonry, M., *Thinking about Crime: Sense and Sensibility in American Penal Culture* (Oxford: Oxford University Press, 2004)

Tonry, M. (ed.), *The Future of Imprisonment* (Oxford: Oxford University Press, 2004)

Tonry, M., "The Mostly Unintended Effects of Mandatory Penalties: Two Centuries of Consistent Findings" in M. Tonry (ed.), *Crime and Justice: A Review of Research* Vol. 38 (Chicago: University of Chicago Press, 2009), pp.65–114

Tonry, M. and Lynch, M., "Intermediate Sanctions" in M. Tonry (ed.), *Crime and Justice: A Review of Research* Vol. 20 (Chicago: University of Chicago Press, 1996), pp.99–144

Tonry, M. and Morris, N., "Sentencing Reform in America" in Glazebrook, *Reshaping the Criminal Law; Essays in Honour of Glanville Williams* (London: Stevens & Co., 1978), pp.434–448

Townshend, C., *Political Violence in Ireland: Government and Resistance since 1848* (Oxford: Clarendon Press, 1983)

Twentieth Century Fund Task Force on Criminal Sentencing, *Fair and Certain Punishment* (New York: McGraw-Hill, 1976)

Tyler, H.R., "Sentencing Guidelines: Control of Discretion in Federal Sentencing" (1979) 7 Hofstra L.R. 11–28

Tyler, T.R., *Why People Obey the Law* (Princeton, NJ: Princeton University Press, 2006)

Tyler, T.R., "Procedural Justice, Legitimacy and the Effective Rule of Law" in M. Tonry (ed.), *Crime and Justice: A Review of Research,* Vol. 30 (Chicago: University of Chicago Press, 2003), pp.283–357

Urbinati, N, *Representative Democracy: Principles and Genealogy* (Chicago: University of Chicago Press, 2006)

Vass, A.A. and Weston, A., "Probation Day Centres as an Alternative to Custody" (1990) 30 Brit. J. Crim. 189–206

Vaughan, W.E., *Murder Trials in Ireland 1836-1914* (Dublin: Four Courts Press, 2009)

Vermeule, A., *Law and the Limits of Reason* (Oxford: Oxford University Press, 2009)

Vermeule, A., "Foreword: System Effects and the Constitution" (2009) 123 Harvard L.R. 4–72 von Hirsch, A., *Doing Justice: The Choice of Punishments: Report of the Committee for the Study of Incarceration* (New York: Hill and Wang, 1976)

von Hirsch, A., "Standards without Goals" (book review) (1979) 7 Hofstra L.R. 457–470

von Hirsch, A. and Ashworth, A., "Not Not Just Deserts: A Response to Braithwaite and Pettit" (1992) 12 Ox. J. Legal Stud. 83–98

von Hirsch, A., Bottoms, A.E., Burney, E. and Wikstrom, P-O, *Criminal Deterrence and Sentence Severity* (Oxford: Hart Publishing, 1999)

von Hirsch, A., and Jareborg, N., "Gauging Criminal Harm: A Living-Standard Analysis" (1991) 11 Oxford J. Legal Stud. 1–38

Waldron, J., "Is the Rule of Law an Essentially Contested Concept (in Florida)?" (2002) 21:2 *Law and Philosophy* 137–164

Walker, S., "Origins of the Contemporary Criminal Justice Paradigm: The American Bar Foundation Survey, 1953-1969" (1992) 9:1 *Justice Quarterly* 47–76

Walker, S., *Taming the System: The Control of Discretion in Criminal Justice 1950-1990* (Oxford: Oxford University Press, 1993)

Wallace, H.R., "Mandatory Minimums and the Betrayal of Sentencing Reform: A Legislative Dr. Jekyll and Mr Hyde" (1993) 57:3 *Federal Probation* 9–19

Walmsley, R., *World Prison Population List*, 8th edn (King's College London: International Centre for Prison Studies, 2009); *www.kcl.ac.uk/schools/law/research/icps* [Last accessed September 21, 2011]

Walsh, D., "Hospitalized Psychiatric Morbidity in the Republic of Ireland" (1968) 114 Brit. J. Psychiatry 11–14

Walsh, D. and Daly, A., *Mental Illness in Ireland 1750-2002: Reflections on the Rise and Fall of Institutional Care* (Dublin: Health Research Board, 2004)

Wandall, R.H., *Decisions to Imprison: Court Decision-Making Inside and Outside the Law* (Aldershot, Hampshire: Ashgate Publishing, 2008)

Ward, R. and Davies, O.M., *The Criminal Justice Act 2003: A Practitioner's Guide* (Bristol: Jordans, 2004)

Wasik, M., "Sentencing Guidelines: Past, Present, and Future" [2003] *Current Legal Problems* 239–264

Wasik, M., "What Guides Sentencing Decisions?" in Bottoms, Rex and Robinson, *Alternatives to Prison: Options for an Insecure Society* (Cullompton: Willan Publishing, 2004), pp.290–312

Wasik, M., "The Status and Authority of Sentencing Guidelines" (2007) 39 Bracton L.J. 9–18

Wasik, M., "Sentencing Guidelines in England and Wales – State of the Art?" [2008] Crim. L.R. 253–263

Wasik, M. and Taylor, R.D., *Blackstone's Guide to the Criminal Justice Act 1991* (London: Blackstone Press Ltd, 1991)

Watson, A., *Rome of the XII Tables: Persons and Property* (Princeton, NJ: Princeton Univ. Press, 1975)

Wechsler, H., "Toward Neutral Principles of Constitutional Law" (1959) 73 Harv. L.R. 1–35

Weigel, S.A., "Appellate Revision of Sentences: To Make the Punishment Fit the Crime" (1968) 20 Stanford L.R. 405–422

West, D.J. (ed.), *The Future of Parole* (London: Duckworth, 1972)

Whiteside, T.N., "The Reality of Federal Sentencing: Beyond the Criticism" (1977) 91 Northwestern Univ. L.R. 1574–1598

Wiggins, D., "Deliberation and Practical Reason" (1975–1976) 76 *Proceedings of the Aristotelian Society* 29–51

Wilcox, C., "Parole: Principles and Practice" (1929) 20 *Journal of the American Institute of Criminal Law and Criminology* 345–354

Wohlwend, R., "The Efforts of the Parliamentary Assembly of the Council of Europe" in Council of Europe, *The Death Penalty: Abolition in Europe* (Strasbourg: Council of Europe, 1999), p.55

Wolff, M.A., "Missouri's Information-Based Discretionary Sentencing System" (2006) 4 Ohio State J. Crim. Law. 95–120

Wood, P.B. and Dunaway, R.G., "Consequences of truth-in-sentencing" (2003) 5:2 *Punishment and Society* 139–154

Woodlee, J.G., "Congressional Manipulations of the Sentencing Guidelines for Child Pornography Possession: An Argument For or Against Deference?" (2011) 60 Duke L.J. 1015–1057

Wright, R.F., "Counting the Cost of Sentencing in North Carolina, 1980-2000" in Tonry (ed.), *Crime and Justice: A Review of Research* Vol. 29 (Chicago: University of Chicago Press, 2002), pp.39–112

Wright, R.F. "*Blakely* and the Centralizers in North Carolina" (2005) 18:1 Fed. Sent. Rep. 19–22

Yale Law School Project, "Parole Release Decisionmaking and the Sentencing Process" (1975) 84 Yale L.J. 810–902

Yellen, D., "Reforming the Federal Sentencing Guidelines' Misguided Approach to Real-Offence Sentencing" (2005) 58 Stanford L.R. 267–275

Young, E., "Rediscovering Conservatism: Burkean Political Theory and Constitutional Interpretation" (1994) 72 North Carolina L.R. 619–724

Young, W., "The Effects of Imprisonment on Offending: A Judge's Perspective" [2010] Crim L.R. 3–18

Young, W. and Browning, C., "New Zealand's Sentencing Council" [2008] Crim.L.R. 287–298

Young, W. and King, A., "Sentencing Practice and Guidance in New Zealand" (2010) 22 Fed. Sent. Rep. 254–261

Zalman, M., "The Rise and Fall of the Indeterminate Sentence" (1977) 24 Wayne L.R. 45-94 and 857–937

Zimmerman, J.F., *The New England Town Meeting: Democracy in Action* (Westport, CT: Praeger Publishers, 1999)

INDEX

Accountability *see* **Public accountability**
Alternatives to immediate imprisonment
community based sentences, 204
fines, 205
inappropriate and excessive use,
205–206
Appeals
assisted appellate review, 129–131
constructive use of discretion, 63
difficulties of regionalisation, 9
failure to disparity in summary
jurisdiction, 7
judicially developed principles,
111–115
part of a continuum, 52
Assisted appellate review, 129–131

Capital punishment
abolition, 78
continuing debate, 1–2
lessons of history, 67–71
Children and young persons
influence on crime statistics, 23–24
public response to young criminals, 25
Choice of penalty
alternatives to immediate imprisonment
community based sentences, 204
fines, 205
inappropriate and excessive use,
205–206
custody threshold
difficulties of definition, 192–194
gravity of offence, 194–197
importance, 190–191
mitigating factors, 197–198
problems of last-resort policies,
191–192
proportionality, 199–200
recidivism, 198–199
equivalence, 190
overview
community based sentences,
188–189

imprisonment, 186–188
relevant factors, 185–186
quantum of punishment, 209–210
recidivist offenders, 206–207
short prison sentences, 200–203
Commissions
federal guidelines, 145–150
history and development in US, 141–145
Community-based sentences
alternatives to immediate
imprisonment, 205
inappropriate and excessive use,
205–206
overview, 188–189
Computers *see* **Information systems**
Consistency *see* **Disparity in sentencing**
Constitutional dimensions
drugs and firearm offences, 101–105
justifications for reform, 9–13
mandatory penalties, 86–94
policy formulation, 245
statutory guidance, 109
Crime rates, 216
Crime reduction, 164–169
effectiveness, 80
reconciling penal purposes, 238
Crime statistics
cautions and informal warnings, 54
justifications for reform, 21–22
public overestimation, 25–26
US Department of Justice, 133
Criminal justice system
allocation of decision-making
competences, 241–245
distribution of discretion throughout
system, 54–57
impact of mandatory penalties, 84–86
influences upon discretion, 50–54
rediscovery of discretion throughout
process, 57–60
Custody threshold
difficulties of definition, 192–194
gravity of offence, 194–197

281

Custody threshold *(continued)*
  importance, 190–191
    mitigating factors, 197–198
  problems of last-resort policies, 191–192
  proportionality, 199–200
  recidivism, 198–199

Data *see* **Information systems**
Democracy *see* **Constitutional dimensions**
Desistance *see* **Recidivism**
Determinate sentencing
  Australian approach to murder, 99
  early release, 227
  exceptional circumstances, 101
  movement towards, 138–140
  remission, 214
Deterrence
  continuing debate, 1–2
  crime reduction, 36
  discretionary sentencing, 55–56
  mandatory penalties, 26, 77–78
  principled sentencing, 8, 14
  reconciling penal purposes, 238–239
  utilitarian goals, 28
Discharge of juries, 47–48
Discretionary sentencing
  constitutional interpretation, 34–37
  constructive use of discretion, 62–63
  continuing debates, 2–3
  disparity in sentencing, 7
  distribution of discretion throughout
      system, 54–57
  impact of mandatory penalties, 81–83
  influences upon which decisions are
      made, 60–62
  influences within criminal justice
      system, 50–54
  judicially developed principles, 112
  murder, 99–101
  nature of discretion, 45–48
  need for reform, 5–6
  need to counteract the limitations of
      formal rules, 42–45
  need to develop set of principles, 6
  proper exercise of discretion, 48–50
  rediscovery of discretion throughout
      criminal process, 57–60
  removal from mandatory penalties, 65

Disparity in sentencing
  impact of mandatory penalties, 83–84
  indeterminate sentencing, 139–140
  information systems, 164–165
  lessons from US experience, 150,
      152–154
  need for reform, 6–9
  overview, 4–5
  underlying principle, 236
  value of precedent, 159–160
Drug offences
  allocation of decision-making
      competences, 242
  constitutional and policy implications,
      101–105
  disparity in sentencing, 8, 84
  mandatory penalties, 4, 66, 72
  ratcheting up of sentences, 86

Early release
  alternative models, 226–230
  discretionary sentencing, 55–56
  guiding values, 221–226
  influence of public opinion, 27
  justifications for reform, 20
  overview, 211–212
  parole, 214–221
  proposals for reform, 230–235
  redistribution of discretion, 55–56
  remission, 212–214
Effectiveness
  allocation of decision-making
      competences, 244–245
  continuing debate, 1–2
  diversion of low-level offenders, 203
  information systems, 180–209
  Irish Parole Board, 231
  mandatory penalties, 65
  measurement of crime reduction, 80
  moral and empirical problems of
      crime reduction, 166–167
  policy formulation, 247–248
  problematic area, 36
  reconciliation with proportionality and
      fairness, 236–237
  short prison sentences, 201
  underlying principle, 236
Equivalence, 190

European Arrest Warrants (EAWs),
    17–19
Evidence-based sentencing, 165–167
Expert systems, 180–181

Fair trial
    instrumental value of procedural
        fairness, 13–15
    mandatory penalties, 94–97
Fairness
    federal Guidelines, 146
    legislative competence, 88
    overview, 4–5
    public confidence in, 49
    tailoring punishments, 81
    underlying principle, 236
    use of precedent, 156, 159
Fines
    alternatives to immediate
        imprisonment, 205–206
    remission, 213
Firearm offences
    allocation of decision-making
        competences, 242
    constitutional and policy implications,
        101–105
    mandatory penalties, 4, 66, 72
    ratcheting up of sentences, 86
Forfeiture theory, 10

General principles
    assisted appellate review, 129–131
    guideline judgments, 123–129
    judicially developed principles
        co-ordination constraints, 118–120
        history and development, 111–115
        opportunity constraints, 116–117
        transmission constraints, 120–123
    long history, 106
    statutory guidance
        constitutional competence, 109
        influence rather than
            determination, 109–111
        maximum penalties, 107–109
        scope, 106–107
Gravity of offence
    allocation of decision-making
        competences, 243
    custody threshold, 194–197

Guidelines *see also* **Precedent**
    commissions
        federal guidelines, 145–150
        history and development in US,
            141–145
    constructive use of discretion, 63
    continuing debates, 4
    development in US, 132–134
    judgments, 123–129
    lessons from US experience, 150–155
    movement towards determinate
        sentencing, 138–140
    retreat from indeterminate sentencing,
        134–138

Human rights
    detention, 226
    mandatory penalties
        constitutional dimensions, 88–89
        detention under Art.3, 96–97
        fair trial, 94–96

Imprisonment *see also* **Mandatory
    penalties**
    compatibility with Constitution, 10
    custody threshold
        difficulties of definition, 192–194
        gravity of offence, 194–197
        importance, 190–191
        mitigating factors, 197–198
        problems of last-resort policies,
            191–192
        proportionality, 199–200
        recidivism, 198–199
    deterrence, 8
    early release
        alternative models, 226–230
        guiding values, 221–226
        influence of public opinion, 27
        justifications for reform, 20
        overview, 211–212
        parole, 214–221
        proposals for reform, 230–235
        redistribution of discretion, 55–56
        remission, 212–214
    growth in its prison population, 20
    life sentences
        chances of release, 228

Imprisonment *(continued)*
    life sentences *(continued)*
        commutation or remission, 216
        constitutionality, 91–92
        dangerous offenders, 74
        departure from the prescribed
            minima, 73
        detention during the pleasure of the
            Crown, 25
        growth in guilty pleas for murder, 85
        guilty pleas to manslaughter, 244
        human rights, 96–97
        mandatory penalties, 64–65
        murder, 98–101
        no known date of release, 221
        non-parole period, 229
        recall, 232
        release on licence, 218
        tariff-setting, 233–234
        violation of separation of powers,
            88
    overview, 186–188
    short prison sentences, 200–203
Incapacitation
    discretionary sentencing, 56
    indeterminate sentencing, 138
    mandatory penalties, 77–80
    reconciling penal purposes, 238–239
Inconsistency *see* **Disparity in**
    sentencing
Indeterminate sentencing
    early release, 217
    erosion of faith, 139–140
    human rights, 97
    for public protection, 74
    retreat from, 134–138
Information systems
    aims, 164–165
    content, design and maintenance,
        175–177
    data processing, 177–178
    design and content, 165
    evidence-based sentencing, 165–167
    history and development, 169–174
    moral and empirical problems of
        crime reduction, 167–169
    role of precedent, 162–164
    usefulness and effectiveness, 180–209

Judgment, 46–47
Judicial reasoning
    arguments for deliberative democracy,
        38–41
    constitutional interpretation, 34
    democratic legitimacy, 33–34
    exercise of discretion, 34–37
    impact of public opinion, 37–38
    intuitive process, 28–29
    practical reasoning or prudence, 30–33
    "sentencing as a social practice", 29–30
    tension between formalism and
        intuition, 30
Judicial review
    judicially developed principles,
        114–115
    parole authority, 235
    prosecutors, 48, 83
    role of courts, 51
Judicially-developed principles
    co-ordination constraints, 118–120
    history and development, 111–115
    jurisdictional competence
        compatibility with judicial
            independence, 255–257
        District Court, 250–252
        overview, 248–250
        role of judiciary, 253–255
    opportunity constraints, 116–117
    quantum of punishment, 209–210
    transmission constraints, 120–123

Legality
    classic principles, 12
    Constitutional justice, 10
    detention, 226
    deterrent impact, 14
    justifications for reform, 9–13
    overview, 4–5
    parole, 219
    supervisory functions of courts, 51
    underlying principle, 236
Legislation
    constitutional dimensions, 88
    constructive use of discretion, 62–63
    contrast with deliberative democracy,
        40–41
    creation of commissions, 143

guidance on general principles
constitutional competence, 109
influence rather than
determination, 109–111
maximum penalties, 107–109
scope, 106–107
influences upon which decisions are
made, 61
mandatory penalties, 65
part of a continuum, 52
policy formulation, 246–247
role of precedent, 161–162
safety valve provisions, 93–94
scope, 2–3
Life sentences
chances of release, 228
commutation or remission, 216
constitutionality, 91–92
dangerous offenders, 74
departure from the prescribed minima,
73
detention during the pleasure of the
Crown, 25
growth in guilty pleas for murder, 85
guilty pleas to manslaughter, 244
human rights, 96–97
mandatory penalties, 64–65
murder, 98–101
no known date of release, 221
non-parole period, 229
recall, 232
release on licence, 218
tariff-setting, 233–234
violation of separation of powers, 88

Mandatory penalties
allocation of decision-making
competences, 242
changes over time, 65–67
comparative systems today, 71–78
constitutional dimensions, 86–94
continuing debates, 3–4
drug offences, 101–105
firearm offences, 101–105
human rights
constitutional dimensions, 88–89
detention under Art.3, 96–97
fair trial, 94–96
impact

conflict with fundamental
principles of justice, 80–81
criminal justice system, 84–86
deterrence, 77–78
disparity in sentencing, 83–84
displacement of discretion, 81–83
incapacitation, 77–80
influence of public opinion, 27
lessons of history, 67–71
meaning and scope, 64
murder, 98–101
public preference, 26
punitive impact, 64–65
redistribution of discretion, 55
removal of discretion, 65
safety valve provisions, 93–94
Maximum penalties
forfeiture theory, 10
legislative discretion, 52
mandatory penalties compared, 64
penal servitude for life, 34
presumptive sentences, 75
proportionality, 86
province of the legislature, 3
statutory guidance, 107–109
Mitigating factors
impact of mandatory penalties, 81
influences upon which decisions are
made, 61
mandatory penalties, 66
Murder
mandatory penalties, 3, 98–101
proportionality, 91
Mutual recognition, 17–19

Nulla poena sine lege, 12
Nullum crimen sine lege, 12

Parole
arbitrary and unsatisfactory system,
218–219
choice of penalty, 203
discretionary sentencing, 55–56
English system, 216–218
influence of public opinion, 27
influences within system, 51
justifications for reform, 20
legislative purpose, 215–216

Parole *(continued)*
  movement towards determinate
    sentencing, 140
  redistribution of discretion, 55–56
  right or privilege, 219–221
  scope, 214–215
  Sentence Review Group, 216
Plea bargaining
  arguments against mandatory
    penalties, 71
  police discretion, 58
Police
  discretionary powers, 50, 57–60
  influences upon which decisions are
    made, 61
  recorded indictable offences, 21
Policy formulation, 245–248
Poverty
  influence on crime statistics, 23
  relationship with crime, 2
Precedents *see also* **Guidelines**;
  Information systems
  deduction and identification, 159–160
  need for narrative precedents, 178
  organising legal principle, 158–159
  ratio decidendi, 156–158
  roles
    development of information
      systems, 162–164
    statutory interpretation, 161–162
Presumptive sentences *see* **Mandatory**
  penalties
Principled sentencing
  constructive use of discretion, 63
  continuing debates
    discretionary sentencing, 2–3
    effectiveness, 1–2
    guidelines, 4
    mandatory sentencing, 3–4
    relationship between crime and
      poverty, 2
  disparity in sentencing, 6–9
  judicially developed principles
    co-ordination constraints, 118–120
    history and development, 111–115
    opportunity constraints, 116–117
    quantum of punishment, 209–210
    transmission constraints, 120–123

  jurisdictional competence to develop
    principles
    compatibility with judicial
      independence, 255–257
    District Court, 250–252
    overview, 248–250
    role of judiciary, 253–255
  justifications for reform
    constitutional justice and rule of
      law, 9–13
    EU law, 16–19
    instrumental value of procedural
      fairness, 13–15
    prison populations, 19–24
    public accountability, 15–16
    public opinion, 24–27
  proper exercise of discretion, 48–50
  requirement for discretion, 5–6
  statutory guidance
    constitutional competence, 109
    influence rather than
      determination, 109–111
    maximum penalties, 107–109
    scope, 106–107
  value of precedent, 158–159
Prison population
  effect of short prison sentences,
    201–202
  grounds for temporary release, 19–24
  impact of mandatory penalties, 85
  justifications for reform, 19–24
Probation reports, 61
Procedural fairness
  early release, 222
  justifications for reform, 13–15
  preferred classification, 221
  principled discretion, 5
Proportionality principle
  conflict with incapacitation, 80
  constitutional dimensions, 90–93
  crime reduction, 165
  mandatory penalties, 81
  maximum penalties, 86
  need for narrative precedents, 178
  overarching sentencing norm, 56
  primary distributive principle, 18
  principled sentencing, 10
  quantum of punishment, 209–210

recidivism, 118
reconciliation with effectiveness, 236
reconciling penal purposes,
239–240
Prosecutors
discretionary powers, 50, 57
judicial review, 48, 83
Public accountability
discretionary powers, 56–57
early release, 232
justifications for reform, 15–16
redistribution of discretion, 56–57
value of information systems, 181
Public law rules, 50
Public opinion
impact on judiciary, 37–38
justifications for reform, 24–27

Ratio decidendi, 156–158
Recidivism
difficulties about prediction, 79–80
impact on choice of penalty,
206–207
information systems, 165
mandatory penalties, 84
proportionality, 118
public opinion, 26
Regulatory offences
mandatory penalties, 64–65
removal of discretion, 53–54
short prison sentences, 201
Rehabilitation
erosion of faith, 139
indeterminate sentencing, 138
parole, 215–216
principled sentencing, 8
reconciling penal purposes, 238–239
utilitarian goals, 28
Remission
alternative forms, 212–213
choice of penalty, 55–56

determinate sentences, 214
discretionary sentencing, 55–56
special cases, 213
Rule of law *see* **Legality**

Safety valve provisions, 93–94
Separation of powers, 86–88
Short prison sentences, 200–203
Social inquiry reports, 61
Statutory guidance
constitutional competence, 109
influence rather than determination,
109–111
maximum penalties, 107–109
scope, 106–107
Structured sentencing
allocation of decision-making
competences, 241–245
concerns about effectiveness,
236–237
four primary qualities, 236
jurisdictional competence to develop
principles
compatibility with judicial
independence, 255–257
District Court, 250–252
overview, 248–250
role of judiciary, 253–255
need for reform, 237–238
policy formulation, 245–248
reconciling penal purposes,
238–241
Summary offences
difficulties of regionalisation, 9
disparity in sentencing, 7
removal of discretion, 53–54

Victim impact reports, 61, 196

Young persons *see* **Children and young
persons**